INSIDE THE
AFRIKA KORPS

ALSO BY FRONTLINE BOOKS

THE ANVIL OF WAR
German Generalship in Defence on the Eastern Front

BATTLE OF THE BULGE: THE GERMAN VIEW
Perspectives from Hitler's High Command

FIGHTING IN NORMANDY
The German Army from D-Day to Villers-Bocage

FIGHTING THE INVASION
The German Army at D-Day

HITLER'S ARDENNES OFFENSIVE
The German View of the Battle of the Bulge

LUFTWAFFE FIGHTER FORCE
The View from the Cockpit

INSIDE THE
AFRIKA KORPS
The Crusader Battles, 1941–1942

Colonel Rainer Kriebel
and the
US Army Intelligence Service

Edited by
Bruce Gudmundsson

FRONTLINE BOOKS

Inside the Afrika Korps

A Greenhill Book

First published in 1999 by Greenhill Books, Lionel Leventhal Limited
www.greenhillbooks.com

This edition published in 2016 by

Frontline Books
an imprint of Pen & Sword Books Ltd,
47 Church Street, Barnsley, S. Yorkshire, S70 2AS
For more information on our books, please visit
www.frontline-books.com, email info@frontline-books.com
or write to us at the above address.

ISBN 978-1-84832-993-5

CIP data records for this title are available from the British Library

Printed and bound by CPI Group (UK) Ltd, Croydon, CR0 4YY

Contents

Editor's Introduction   11
    Sources   *12*
    Colonel Rainer Kriebel   *13*
    A Note on Terminology   *14*

Part One: History of the Campaign in North Africa   **17**

1 Political and Operational Conduct of the German and Italian
   High Command   19

2 Preparations for the Autumn Battle   28
   Organizational Activities   *30*
   Panzergruppe Afrika   *32*

3 The Defensive Battle on the Egyptian Frontier   34
   Construction of the Strongpoints   *34*
   The Enemy Situation   *37*
   Preparations for the Attack on Tobruk   *40*
   The Siege Front   *40*
   Arrival of German Artillery   *41*
   Ammunition Supplies   *42*
   The Plan for the Attack   *43*
   The Order for the Attack   *44*
   New Tactics for Armored Formations   *45*
   Cooperation of Weapons   *45*
   Command   *46*
   Reconnaissance   *47*
   Supplies   *48*
   The Situation in the Air   *48*

The Supply Position in Summer and Autumn 1941   *52*

4 Repulse of the First British Advance on Tobruk   57
     The Beginning of the British Attack (16–20 November)   *60*
     Events during 16/18 November   *61*
     The Beginning of the Battle on 19 November   *65*
     Decisions Taken on 19 November   *68*
     The Failure on 20 November   *69*
     21 November   *75*
     The Diversionary Attack of the Afrika Korps   *77*
     The Battle of the Cauldron of Sidi Rezegh   *81*
     The Battle on the "Bloody Sunday of the Dead"   *86*
     The Sollum Front, 18–23 November   *94*
     The Air Situation   *96*
     The Push to Egypt, 24–27 November   *102*
     Rommel's Instructions   *103*
     The Conduct of the Pursuit up to Arrival at the Sollum Position
       early on 25 November   *104*
     The Fighting around the Sollum Position   *107*
     Return of the Afrika Korps to the Tobruk Front on
       27 November   *114*
     Course of the Fighting on the Morning of 27 November   *115*
     The Fighting during the Afternoon of 27 November   *117*
     The Fighting before Tobruk, 24–27 November   *117*
     The Smashing of the 2nd New Zealand Division   *125*
     The Plan of Attack of the Afrika Korps   *126*
     The Course of 28 November   *127*
     Orders of the Africa Korps for 29 November   *128*
     The Battle for El Duda on 29 November   *129*
     Orders issued by the Afrika Korps during the Evening of
       29 November   *132*
     The Battle for Belhamed   *133*
     The Fighting for Sidi Rezegh on 30 November   *134*
     Plan for the Attack on 1 December   *135*
     The Morning Attack against Belhamed   *136*
     The Fighting during the Afternoon of 1 December   *137*
     Orders for 2 December   *138*
     Course of 2 December   *138*

Observations   *139*
The Last Fighting East of Tobruk, 2–4 December   *141*
The Fighting on 3 and 4 December   *143*
The Course of 4 December   *144*
Observations   *145*
The Situation in the Air   *146*
The Supply Situation   *148*

5 The Battle for the Gazala Position   152
The Attack on Bir el Gubi   *155*
Decision taken by the Afrika Korps   *155*
Events on 6 December   *156*
The Defensive Battle of 7 December   *158*
Evacuation of the Area East of Tobruk   *159*
The Withdrawal   *160*
Decision to Withdraw into the Gazala Position   *161*
The Withdrawal into the Gazala Position   *163*
The Withdrawal during 8–9 December   *164*
The Withdrawal on 10–11 December   *165*
The Battle in the Gazala Position, 12–16 December   *168*
The Beginning of the Battle on 11–12 December   *169*
The Crisis in the Battle, 13–14 December   *171*
Course of 14 December   *174*
The Fighting on 15 December   *174*
Conduct of Operations from 11 to 15 December   *176*
The Decision to Abandon Cyrenaica   *177*
First Orders for the Withdrawal   *180*
The Situation in the Air   *183*

6 The Withdrawal of *Panzergruppe Afrika* from Gazala to the Marsa
   el Bregha Position, 17 December 1941–12 January 1942   188
Breaking Away from the Gazala Position   *189*
The Withdrawal towards Benghazi, 19–21 December   *192*
The Warding off of British Pursuing Columns North of Agedabia,
   22–25 December   *194*
The Fighting around Agedabia, 25 December–5 January   *199*
The Counterattack on the South Wing of the Panzergruppe   *203*
The Fighting in the Morning on 28 December   *205*

Events on 29 December   *207*
Events on 30 December   *207*
Local Skirmishes in the Agedabia Area   *208*
The Withdrawal from Agedabia into the Marsa el Bregha
  Position, 6–12 January   *211*
The Actual Withdrawal   *213*
The Situation in the Air   *214*
The Supply Problem during the Withdrawal, 5 December–1 January   *217*

7 The German Counteroffensive for the Reconquest of
      Cyrenaica, January–February 1942   223
Planning and Preparations for the Attack   *225*
The Battle in the Area of Agedabia, 21–26 January   *226*
Appreciation of the Situation by the Panzerarmee   *228*
Events on 22 January   *228*
The Tank Battles in the Area of Saunnu, 23–24 January   *231*
Events on 24 January   *234*
The Advance of the Afrika Korps to Msus on 25 January   *235*
The Advance to Benghazi and Pursuit to the Gazala Position,
  26 January–6 February   *239*
The Coup de Main against Benghazi, 27–30 January   *242*
The Pursuit into Cyrenaica, 30 January–6 February   *243*
The Situation on the Ground   *245*
The Situation in the Air   *247*
The Supply Situation   *249*

8 Events on the British Side, 18 November 1941–
      17 February 1942   253
Conclusion   *257*

Part Two: Artillery in the Desert   **259**

Reconnaissance   *261*
Methods of Observation   *262*
Selection and Occupation of Positions   *263*
Terrain   *264*
Dispersion   *264*

Camouflage   *265*
Communications   *265*
Visual Signals   *266*
Wire   *266*
Radio   *267*
Codes   *267*
German Tactics   *268*
Effect of Terrain   *268*
Formations   *269*
Offensive Tactics   *269*
German Method of Forcing Gaps through Minefields   *272*
Defensive Tactics   *273*

British Tactics   274
The Approach   *274*
The Attack   *275*
The Defense   *275*
Withdrawal   *278*
Counterbattery   *279*
Naval Bombardment   *279*
Antitank Operations   *280*
Positions   *281*
German Tank Tactics   *282*
British Tactics   *282*
The Main Role: To Form a Secure Base   *285*
Effect of Artillery on Tanks   *288*
Smoke   *288*
Characteristics   *288*
Tactical Employment   *289*
Supply Methods   *290*

Part Three: German Defensive Tactics, 7 May–15 June 1941   293

Original Doctrine   *295*
The Plan Unfolds   *296*
The Theory Tested on the Frontier   *304*
The Action at Halfaya Pass   *306*

The Action at Point 208   *307*
The Action at Point 206   *308*
The Mobile Infantry Reserve   *308*
The Tank Striking Force   *309*
New Theory from Experience on the Frontier   *311*
    Neumann-Silkow   *311*
    Summermann   *312*
    Ravenstein   *312*
Rommel   *314*
The Action at Tobruk   *317*
The November Offensive   *320*
Comments and Lessons   *324*
Antimechanized Obstacles   *325*
Artillery   *325*
Reconnaissance   *325*
Morale   *326*

Bibliography   327

Index   329

Maps and Illustrations

1 The North African Theater of Operations, 1941   22
2 The Frontier Strongpoints, Summer and Fall 1941   36
3 The Sidi-Omar-Sollum Position, 1941   38
4 The British Crusader Offensive, 19 November 1941   64
5 The Retreat to the Gazala Position, 6 to 11 December 1941   162
6 The Retreat to Marsa el Bregha, December 1941–January 1942   212
7 The Reconquest of Cyrenaica, 1942   230
8 "Rommel Triangle", Squad Position   316
9 "Stützpunkt Cyrener", Company Posotopn   320

Editor's Introduction

In a world where the library shelves groan under the weight of books about Erwin Rommel and his campaigns in North Africa, the publication of yet another work on the subject requires some justification. Either the book must offer a new perspective on important events or it must present what is already known in a way that is particularly accessible to a broad readership. Put another way, if it is to be worth more than the paper it is printed on, a new version of this old story must either be controversial or handy.

The work that forms the heart of this volume, Colonel Rainer Kriebel's account of the German reaction to the British Crusader offensive of 1941, has the peculiar virtue of meeting both requirements. In contrast to the bulk of the literature on the subject, which was written from the perspective of one of Rommel's inner circle, Kriebel's point of view is that of the chief of staff of a *Panzer* division. He is thus close enough to the center of the action to see what is going on and yet distant enough from Rommel to avoid the kind of hero-worship that so often results from close contact with a such a dominant personality.

Just as the novelty of Kriebel's account is a function of his unique perspective, the accessibility is a result of his training as an officer of the German General Staff. Having made use of the long years of peace to study what we now call the operational art, Kriebel was well prepared to discuss the maneuvers of divisions, corps, and armies; the role played by logistics and organization; and the use of battles won and lost for the higher purposes of a military campaign. This training allowed Kriebel to step out of his own role in the Crusader battles and make sense of the campaign as a whole.

The story that emerged from this effort is somewhat different from the one told elsewhere. We discover, for example, that the "Desert Fox" was often in the dark about enemy dispositions and, as a result, was often surprised by British initiatives. We also find that Rommel was far more comfortable giving orders to individual battalions or battle groups than he

11

was making decisions about the potentially decisive employment of the *Afrika Korps* as a whole. In short, Kriebel paints a picture of Rommel as an extraordinary leader of men who was far better at fighting at the level of battalions and brigades than in knitting engagements into battles or battles into a successful campaign.

Because Kriebel's narrative, written just after the end of World War II as part of the US Army's Foreign Military Studies program, presumes a great deal of knowledge about weapons, organization, and tactics, I have attached two shorter documents, one dealing with the construction and defense of strongpoints in the period leading up to the Crusader battles and the other dealing with the combined-arms tactics of mobile formations, with special emphasis on the role of artillery. Many readers will profit from reading these after finishing Kriebel's first chapter but before jumping into the blow-by-blow descriptions of battles and engagements.

This book would not have been possible without the patient and painstaking work of Anita Erwin, who, after fighting her way through nearly illegible manuscript pages, fully qualifies as a combat veteran. Robin Cookson, Tim Nenninger, and the legendary John Taylor of the US National Archives and Records Administration at Archives II all went out of their way to help me find the documents that I needed. My fellow denizens of the Old Headquarters Building and brother Marines – John Murphy and John Sayen – gave generously of their time and considerable technical expertise.

Sources

The portion of this volume written by Colonel Rainer Kriebel is taken from the *History of the Campaign in North Africa*, a multivolume set of reports assembled under the direction of General Walther Nehring for the US Army Foreign Military Studies program. The English-language translation of this series, manuscript T-3 of the Foreign Military Studies series, can be found at Archives II in College Park, Maryland, a suburb of Washington, DC, USA.. The file on Colonel Kriebel from which I drew biographical information is also located at Archives II and is part of Record Group 338, Foreign Military Studies, Personnel Files of German Officers.

The document entitled "Artillery in the Desert" is taken from *Artillery in the Desert*, which was published by the US Army Military Intelligence Service during World War II and reprinted by the US Marine Corps (as *FMFRP 12-3*) on the eve of the Gulf War. "German Defensive Tactics" is an excerpt from *The Development of German Defensive Tactics in Cyrenaica – 1941*. This little book was likewise the work of the US Army Military Intelligence Service of World War II and was likewise reprinted (as *FMFRP 12-99*) by the Marine Corps in 1990.

Colonel Rainer Kriebel

Rainer Karl-Theodore Kriebel, a native of Bavaria, joined the 21st Infantry Regiment of the inter-war German Army on 4 January 1926. After four years of training, which included both time in the ranks and attendance at military schools, Kriebel was commissioned as a lieutenant in his regiment. Six years later, Kriebel, who had risen to command of a machine gun company, passed the *Wehrkreisprüfung* (district examination) that qualified young officers for general staff training.

At the outbreak of war in 1939, Captain Kriebel found himself in the Foreign Armies (West) section of the Army General Staff in Berlin and was one of the handful of German officers who kept an eye on the French while the majority of their colleagues focused their efforts on the conquest of Poland. During the 1940 campaign in France, Kriebel was the General Staff liaison officer at *Panzergruppe von Kleist* and, as such, had the opportunity to view, at first hand, the action and mutual support of several armored and motorized divisions. In October of 1940, Captain Kriebel became the senior general staff officer (Ia) of the *15th Panzer Division*. Promoted to Major in November of that year, Kriebel spent the winter of 1940–41 training his division, which had recently been converted from a muscle-powered infantry division, in the tactics of gasoline-powered warfare.

In the spring of 1941, Major Kriebel went to North Africa, where he continued to serve as Ia of the *15th Panzer Division* until March of 1942, when he was transferred to the Russian Front. After fifteen months as Ia of the *2nd Panzer Division*, Kriebel returned to Berlin to teach tactics at the *Kriegsakademie*. In May of 1944, Kriebel, who had since been promoted to lieutenant-colonel, returned to the Russian Front, where he served as chief of staff of various high level (corps, army, and army group) staffs. The end of the war found Kriebel in Bohemia, in what is now the Czech Republic, as a full colonel who managed to avoid surrender until 11 June 1945.

After the war, Colonel Kriebel settled in Munich and eased his transition to civilian life by writing, for pay, a number of studies for the US Foreign Military Studies program.

A Note on Terminology

In writing the *History of the Campaign in North Africa*, Colonel Kriebel used the standard German military terminology of the day, which he used to describe the organization and activities of German, Italian, and Commonwealth units. Kriebel's translators, on the other hand, used a mixture of British and American terms. The anonymous authors of the two intelligence studies used an American military vocabulary to make sense of British and German reports. The result was such confusing expressions as "the *7th British Panzer Division*." I have therefore attempted to impose a rational system of unit designation upon all three documents.

The first principle of this system is that unit designations should be rendered in a manner that most closely resembles their original form. Italian divisions are thus referred to by their name – *Infantry Division Savona* or *Armored Division Ariete*. German and Commonwealth divisions and brigades have a preceding ordinal number – *90th Light Division* or *4th Armored Brigade*. German regiments and independent battalions are designated by a postpositive cardinal number – *Antitank Battalion 33* or *Reconnissance Battalion 3*, while those battalions that are part of regiments are identified by a roman numeral and the name of the regiment – *I. / Schützen Regiment 115* or *II / . Panzer Regiment 8*. German independent companies are likewise designated by postpositive cardinal numbers – *Oasis Company 2* – while those that are part of a regiment are identified by arabic numbers and the name of the regiment – *2. / Schützen Regiment 104* . All unit names are in italics.

The second principle of this system is that special care must be taken when using the words "regiment," "brigade," "battalion," "troop," and "battery." A German brigade (of four to six maneuver battalions) was usually somewhat larger than a British brigade (with two to four maneuver battalions.) Most of the battalions of each German tank or infantry brigade, moreover, were organized into regiments (of two or three battalions).

A German infantry battalion (*Bataillon*) corresponded to a British infantry battalion. A unit of similar size belonging to a close-combat arm other than infantry – armor, reconnaissance troops, antitank troops – was called an *Abteilung*. While these units most closely resembled British regiments of their respective arms, calling them such would create such monstrosities as the "*I. Regiment* of *Panzer Regiment 8*." I have therefore chosen to follow the American practice and translate *Abteilung* as "battalion."

A German artillery "battery," usually of four pieces, corresponded most closely with a British "troop" of four to six pieces. A German artillery "battalion" of twelve pieces was the rough equivalent of a British "battery" of eight or twelve pieces. A German artillery "regiment" of twenty-four to thirty-six pieces was closest to the British "regiment" of twenty-four pieces.

Many German units underwent considerable reorganization in the course of a campaign, often without losing their functional titles. Thus, a machine gun company or battalion might be organized as motorized infantry and a motorcycle company might be mounted in trucks. Similarly, there was a strong tendency for German units to retain weapons in excess of their official allowances. These included captured enemy weapons and weapons (such as 37mm antitank guns) that units had conveniently forgotten to turn in when they were replaced by newer models. In short, there was little connection between a unit's official nomenclature and its actual organization.

The silver lining in this cloud of confused unit nomenclature is the insight that it offers about the character of many German units that fought in North Africa. Rather than letting themselves be defined by a narrow function, German units were constantly reinventing themselves, adding capabilities and shedding excess baggage as needs arose or opportunities presented themselves. This capacity for adaptation made it possible for the German forces in North Africa to deal with such difficulties as shortages of specific kinds of ammunition and the enemy superiority in both number and quality of tanks.

Paradoxically, the net effect of this liberation from official tables of organization and equipment was a tendency towards homogeneity. Thus, whether a unit was a battalion of combat engineers, antitank troops, motorcycle infantry, *Schützen* (motorized infantry of armored divisions), reconnaissance troops, or machine gun troops, the reader can safely assume that the chief motor vehicle was some sort of truck, that dual-purpose machine guns (usually the ubiquitous MG34) and obsolescent antitank guns (either German 37mm pieces or captured 2-pounders) were in plentiful supply, that a few 81mm mortars and/or 75mm infantry guns were handy, and that a handful of first-line antitank guns (28mm "squeeze bore" or 50mm) were in use. The proportion of these weapons would vary with the type of unit – an antitank unit would have more first-line antitank guns than other units. The basic arsenal, however, was the same.

The mutability of German units in North Africa was only exceeded by the degree to which German formations experienced metamorphosis. The shifting of battalions between brigades and divisions, as well as the formation of multi-battalion battle groups, was so frequent that it is impossible to speak of a standard organization for any of the three German divisions that fought in the Crusader battles. Indeed, the brief period when the *15th* and *21st Panzer Divisions* were organized in a manner resembling text-book *Panzer* divisions was, by far, the exception rather than the rule. The *Division zur besondere Verwendung Afrika*, which was later to become the *90th Light Division*, never enjoyed even the pretense of a standard organization. It was, from its beginnings until the summer of 1942, an organization custom-tailored to the task of besieging Tobruk.

During the Crusader battles, the *Afrika Korps* was the only corps-level headquarters available to the German leadership. Its principle purpose was to combine the two *Panzer* divisions into a single mobile formation, equally capable of serving as a powerful tactical reserve in the defense or the hard core of any offensive maneuver. Because the term *"Afrika Korps"* has long been used as a popular shorthand for all of the German troops in North Africa, care must be taken to distinguish between the *Afrika Korps* and *Panzergruppe Afrika*. The latter was the headquarters of General Erwin Rommel, the commander of all of the German ground forces in North Africa. (The term *Panzergruppe* was first used in the French campaign of 1940 to designate an echelon between army and corps.)

Bruce I. Gudmundsson
Quantico, VA, 1999

PART ONE

History of the Campaign in North Africa, 19 June 1941–6 February 1942

by
Colonel Rainer Kriebel

CHAPTER 1

Political and Operational Conduct of the German and Italian High Command

The successful spring campaigns in Africa and the Balkans, ending with the conquest of the island of Crete, gave birth to a number of long-range plans conceived by the Armed Forces High Command (*OKW*). These plans were not yet passed on to the subordinate military authorities in the shape of definite orders and instructions, but were mirrored in the *Führer* Directive date 30 June 1941, which for the time being was only for the used of *OKW* and which contained plans for the further conduct of the war, after victory had been won in the Eastern campaign. The contents of this directive are given in the following lines, as far as the war in North Africa is concerned.

> The campaign will take the form of a concentric attack on Egypt from Libya, from Bulgaria through Turkey, and, in certain circumstances, from the Caucasus area through Iran.
>
> With regard to North Africa, it will be important for Tobruk to be eliminated, to create the basis for the continuation of the German-Italian attack against the Suez Canal.
>
> The preparations for the attack will make it necessary to speed up transport by taking advantage of French North African ports and, if possible, by using the new sea route now available from southern Greece.

The attack on Tobruk was to be prepared in such a way that it could be launched by the end of September, and the operations against Egypt were to start by the end of November.

An order by the Navy High Command (*Seekriegsleitung*) dated 2 August 1941 and issued on the basis of the above-mentioned *Führer* Directive, shows that the beginning of the attack against Egypt was timed for not earlier than the New Year 1942. The reason for this postponement seems to have been the unexpectedly slow progress of the operations in the East. Regarding the attack on Tobruk, it was of the greatest importance to make the *Afrika Korps* as efficient and powerful as possible and let it have what supplies were needed on a generous scale. This also included the transformation of the *5th Light Division* into a fully armored division. Army artillery and infantry three

19

regiments strong were brought to Africa to be at Rommel's disposal. There was, however, no intention of transporting other large units to North Africa. During autumn 1941, Rommel established a *Division z.b.V.* [*zur besondere Verfügung*, "for special use"] "*Afrika*" from the means at his disposal in North Africa. This division later developed into the *90th Light Division*.[1]

In order to increase the tempo of supply, consideration was given to the use of the French harbors in Tunisia. Adequate German air force units and antiaircraft artillery were to be employed, when they became available and were no longer required in the East, to support our transports at sea and later to assist in the continuation of operations on land.

The *Comando Supremo* at the same time was hoping to continue the offensive to the Suez Canal after Tobruk had fallen. The *Comando Supremo* too was busy reorganizing, reinforcing, and strengthening its troops in Libya. Amongst others, the *Motorized Infantry Division "Trieste"* was brought to Africa.

The aims of the *Comando Supremo* were, however, not so ambitious as those of the *OKW*, one reason being that the last resistance in the Italian East African colonies was at the point of collapsing. On the other hand, the Fascist government intended to wrench Egypt from British influence and incorporate it into the Italian *Impero*.

In spite of the defensive victory of Sollum, by July 1941 the *Comando Supremo* anticipated that a large-scale British offensive from Egypt was imminent. However, it soon became evident that there were no grounds for this assumption.

By the end of July General [Ugo] Cavallero, Chief of Staff of the Italian *Comando Supremo*, paid a visit to Rommel at the latter's battle headquarters in Bardia. He agreed with General Rommel that a German-Italian offensive into Egypt was out of the question until Tobruk had been taken. For this reason Tobruk was to be the next operational objective. Cavallero issued relevant instructions to the Italian Commander-in-Chief in North Africa, General [Ettore] Bastico.

---

[1] During World War II Germans used the term "light division" (*Leichte Division*) to designate several very different types of formations. The term was first applied to the four motorized cavalry divisions that, reinforced with extra tanks and artillery, were used interchangeably with *Panzer* divisions during the invasion of Poland in September 1939. Starting in 1940, the term described a type of infantry division (later known as a *Jäger Division*) optimized for operations in wooded country and swamps. In North Africa, the term was used for three different formations. The *5th Light Division*, rich in antitank units and machine gun battalions, was originally designed to "stiffen" Italian units engaged in defensive operations. The *90th Light Division*, which evolved out of the forces assembled to besiege Tobruk, was originally a static formation with limited motor transport. The *164th Light "Afrika" Division* was custom-tailored for mobile operations in North Africa, with lots of half-tracks but very little field artillery. As the half-tracks never made it across the Mediterranean, the formation was, like the *90th Light Division*, a static one until enough British trucks could be found to motorize it.

For the time being, however, these plans of the High Command were frustrated by British successes at sea and in the air in the Mediterranean area.[1] During summer and autumn of 1941, the British waged a relentless war of ever-increasing intensity against the transport of troops and supplies from Italy to Libya. At first, German troops and supplies were transported on board German ships, but ship losses soon became so heavy that German troops and supplies had to use Italian ships on an increasing scale.

Malta proved to be a most important strongpoint and of the greatest advantage for British strategy. Submarines and torpedo-carrying aircraft based on Malta and at Alexandria launched their attacks on our convoys and ships with growing success. In order to lessen the casualties in men, troops were flown to Africa on an ever-increasing scale. It had become impossible to comply with the requirements regarding reinforcements and supplies for the German and Italian troops in North Africa. An additional drawback was the fact that harbor installations in Tripoli and Benghazi were limited and did not allow for the unloading of more than three or four ships at the same time. During September losses mounted to 18% of all supplies sent by sea, and during October losses were still increasing.

This was most unfortunate, the more so as the German and Italian High Command, according to the available intelligence, had to reckon with a large-scale British offensive during autumn, and the recapture of Tobruk became priority number one. If the capture of Tobruk was further delayed there was a danger that the British would launch their offensive before we could deliver our attack. *Panzergruppe Afrika* would then face a most dangerous situation.

In October 1941, *OKW* became convinced that the Italian Air Force would be unable to protect the transports to Africa and hold down Malta, after the German *X Fliegerkorps* had been transferred to southern Greece. *OKW*, with a heavy heart, decided to employ in the Mediterranean further German air forces transferred from the Eastern theatre of war.

On 24 October 1941, the German general attached to the headquarters of the Italian armed forces, General [Enno] von Rintalen, was instructed by Hitler at the *Führer*'s headquarters in East Prussia to suggest to Mussolini and the *Comando Supremo* the strengthening of the German Luftwaffe and the dispatch of further air corps to Sicily, Sardinia, and southern Italy. Von

---

[1] For German soldiers like Rainer Kriebel, the terms "command" (*Generalkommando*) and "high command" (*Oberkommando*) had very specific meanings. The former referred to command at the level of an army corps or *Gruppe* (an echelon between a corps and an army), the latter to command at the level of a field army or army group.

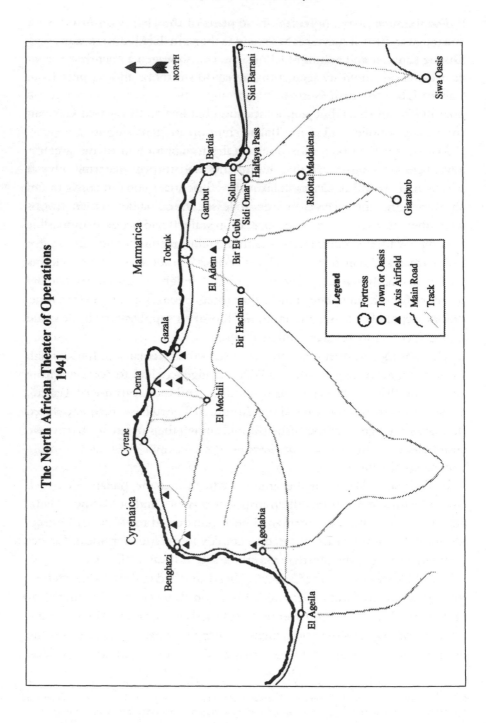

The North African Theater of Operations 1941

Rintalen was to offer the Italians Field Marshal [Albert] Kesselring, Commanding General of *Luftflotte 2*, as Commander-in-Chief South. It was to be Kesselring's task to organize the transports to Africa with the help of units of the Italian Air Force and Navy which were to be placed under his command for that purpose.

General von Rintalen had no difficulty in obtaining the approval of the *Duce* and of General Cavallero for the employment of one more air corps, as the *Comando Supremo* was convinced of the necessity to improve air escorts for the convoys. However, the *Comando Supremo* was not prepared to hand over to Kesselring full responsibility for the safety of transport at sea and in the air and the command over Italian air forces and naval units. The only thing that was agreed upon was a far-reaching and close cooperation between the Commander-in-Chief South, the general staff of the Italian Air Force and the Italian Admiralty. The *Comando Supremo* reserved to itself the final control.

Field Marshal Kesselring arrived in Rome in the middle of November and repeated his request to be given absolute control of all units of the Italian Navy and Air Force employed in convoy duties and in countering British supply through the Mediterranean. Colonel General Cavallero told the German general at the headquarters of the Italian Armed Forces with unmistakable clarity that Mussolini and the entire Italian Armed Forces regarded such arrangements as incompatible with their military honor. However, he, Cavallero, would see to it that an efficient and smooth cooperation should exist and that no friction need be feared. And that was that.

Cooperation between the Commander-in-Chief South and the General Staff of the Italian Air Force was assisted by the fact that the Chief of the General Staff, General Pricolo, had been replaced by General Fougier, who had fought under Kesselring in Belgium during autumn 1940. The personal charm of the Chief of the Admiralty Staff, Admiral [Arturo] Ricardi, and his desire to cooperate, also proved a great help.

During November *Luftflotte 2* suggested that *II Fliegerkorps* should be brought in for operations in Italy. The suggestion was accepted. However, before the formations of *II Fliegerkorps* arrived in southern Italy from the Eastern theater of war, and before any improvement in the transport situation could be effected by increased escort, the British, on 15 November 1941, launched their attack against Rommel's *Panzergruppe*.

It is true that the British had been compelled to limit and restrict their convoys sailing from Gibraltar across the Mediterranean to Alexandria, as the German and Italian aircraft and U-boats had been able to inflict very considerable losses on the British convoys, but the British would still sail around the Cape of Good Hope, which indeed meant a long voyage and much loss of time, but was not particularly dangerous and involved hardly any risk for troops and supplies sailing to Egypt. After the loss of the East African possessions the Italian Air Force had no opportunity of operating against enemy convoys through the Red Sea.

Thus it came about that, in autumn 1941, the British anticipated the German-Italian attack on Tobruk by a few days and were able to resume their offensive in North Africa.

In spite of all the difficulties encountered, the preparations on the German-Italian side for the attack on Tobruk had reached a stage by November which could be regarded as satisfactory in all spheres of the supply services. However, part of the heavy artillery which was regarded as indispensable for breaking through the fortifications was not yet available. In spite of this drawback, Mussolini tried to persuade Rommel, who paid him a visit in mid-November, to launch the attack at an early date, since he feared that the enemy offensive might anticipate our own. However, it was too late. What had been feared did actually happen. The British had won the race of supplies and convoys, and on 18 November they struck.

The *Comando Supremo* took a hand in the conduct of the war in Africa only as far as naval and air operations was concerned. At sea a few successes were achieved. On 13 November 1941, the [British aircraft carrier] *Ark Royal* was sunk by a torpedo and on 25 November 1941, the [British battleship] *Barham* was sunk near the Libyan coast from a torpedo hit. On 19 September 1941, six Italian one-man torpedoes had entered the harbor at Alexandria and had sunk the battleships *Valiant* and *Queen Elizabeth*.

In spite of these successes against the British Navy, transport by sea became increasingly difficult. By the end of November and at the beginning of December the losses became so shattering that the Italian Navy actually suggested the abandonment of the African war theater before the entire Italian merchant fleet found itself resting on the bottom of the Mediterranean. But that the *Comando Supremo* refused to contemplate. On 18 December 1941 and 5 January 1942, two convoys arrived in the Libyan harbors undamaged and without having encountered any enemy. These convoys had been escorted by battleships. Owing to the shortage of oil fuel, battleships requiring large quantities could only be made use of in exceptional circumstances. The oil reserves accumulated by the Italian Navy before Italy entered the war had been exhausted. In this case the employment of battleships as convoy escorts paid full dividends. Four German *Panzer* companies had been shipped to Africa in these two convoys and strengthened the fighting power of the*Afrika Korps* to such an extent that it was possible to launch the counteroffensive for the recapture of Cyrenaica.

Mussolini and the *Comando Supremo* fell back on the old line of demanding from the French the right to use the Tunisian ports. Hitler refused. Nevertheless, Mussolini, on 29 December 1941, wrote a personal letter to Hitler through the German general in which he said that an agreement must be reached with the French concerning the use of the ports of Tunis and Bizerte. If no agreement were arrived at he would take these ports by force. On 20 January 1942, Hitler replied that the French had asked so much in return for permission to use their ports that he had refused. Hitler rejected the idea of occupying those parts by force, as he was afraid of disagreeable repercussions and of the bad effect that such a step might have all over French North Africa.

During the entire summer the *OKW* had faithfully kept its part of the agreement with the Italian *Comando Supremo* and had been most careful not to interfere in the conduct of operations in North Africa. The Army High Command (*OKH*), under whose command *Panzergruppe Afrika* fell for all purposes except the tactical conduct of actual operations, had assisted and furthered the preparations for the attack on Tobruk by sending units, replacements, and supplies.

After the offensive had begun the *OKW* did not interfere with Rommel's conduct of operations but limited its activities to supporting Rommel in all other spheres. *OKW* regarded Rommel's position with grave concern, particularly after the great strength of the attacking forces had become evident. The fact that Tobruk was still in the hands of the enemy resulted in a division of the German-Italian forces which limited their freedom of action. Rommel would find it very difficult to carry on operations of any length so long as the difficulties of sea transport made the arrival of reinforcements for men and material a matter of uncertainty. The replenishment of fuel and ammunition supplies was another great question which remained unanswered.

Comando Supremo regarded the situation in North Africa as very serious from the moment the enemy launched his attack on 18 November. The main reason for this pessimistic attitude was the difficulty of the supply problem and another was the undeniable inferiority of our own air force. During the battles up to the end of November when we were sometimes successful and the result was generally in doubt and the situation fluctuated, the *Comando Supremo* was convinced of victory one day and full of pessimistic anxiety the next. During the early days of December it became quite clear that the British were able to fill the gaps in their formations at a rapid pace, whereas the German-Italian forces were not.

The Commander-in-Chief in North Africa [*Comando Superiore Africa Settentrionale*] was General Bastico, although the actual conduct of the defensive campaign was in the hands of the Commander-in-Chief of the *Panzergruppe*, General Rommel. General Bastico had reserved for himself the command of Italian *Motorized Corps*.[1] The actual corps commander was General [Gastone] Gambara, who was also Chief of Staff to General Bastico. It became evident that the Italian *Commando Superiore* in Libya had no means of interfering with the tactical conduct of operations. Urged by the German general accredited at the headquarters of the Italian Armed Forces, the Italian military authorities decreed on 23 November that the Italian *Motorized Corps* was also to be placed under the command of the *Panzergruppe*. This of course made it considerably easier from Rommel to conduct the campaign.

When, after weeks of fighting, Rommel was compelled to abandon the siege of Tobruk and also to evacuate Marmarica and to withdraw to the Gazala positions, the *Comando Supremo* and the *Italian Comando Superiore* in Libya demanded that Cyrenaica be defended. In a discussion at Berta in Cyrenaica (about 12 December 1941) Cavallero and Bastico tried to compel Rommel to defend Cyrenaica. Rommel, however, quite rightly pointed out that the high plateau of Cyrenaica between Derna and Benghazi could not possibly be held with the forces at his disposal, as it was an easy matter to cut it off.

In the end General Cavallero agreed that Cyrenaica should be evacuated. He insisted, however, most emphatically, that the withdrawal should be regulated so as to give the nonmotorized Italian infantry divisions enough time to carry out the withdrawal in an orderly fashion. This decision to withdraw from Cyrenaica brought about a certain tension between the Italian High Command and Rommel, which did not disappear until the successful counteroffensive in the second half of January 1942. There were times when the Italian government was afraid that Tripoli might be lost. That was the reason why the battleships were used to escort two important convoys to North Africa.

---

[1] The Italian *Motorized Corps* was also known as *XX Corps*.

When Rommel launched his counteroffensive, this move came as an extraordinary surprise not only to *OKW* but also to the *Comando Supremo*. Cavallero did not learn of Rommel's intention until the evening before the attack was actually launched, and it was Field Marshal [Albert] Kesselring who broke the news. Cavallero at once proceeded to the Libyan war theater and did his best to try and forbid Rommel to advance beyond the area of Agedabia and particularly to reoccupy Benghazi. Cavallero pointed out, just as Rommel had done in December, that Cyrenaica could not possibly be held. In the end he took away from Rommel the right to make use of the Italian infantry divisions, which were to remain in the Marsa el Bregha positions. Rommel, however, was not to be kept back. His surprising success did away with much of the doubt and anxiety prevailing.

On Rommel's arrival on the landing ground east of Benghazi at the head of an assault group, which he was leading personally against the enemy, he received a wireless message from Mussolini with his authority to recapture the town.

From 28 January to 4 February 1942, Göring was in Rome. He badgered Mussolini and Cavallero to issue orders to *Panzergruppe Afrika* for the immediate attack on Tobruk. Göring succeeded with Mussolini, who was impressed by the promise to fly over to Africa all the supplies the troops would need for the capture of Tobruk and afterwards. *Comando Supremo* however believed – and rightly so – that a continuation of the offensive was impossible, as the pursuit of the enemy had already exhausted "man and beast" or, rather, had already used up the last drop of fuel. According to the appreciation of the enemy situation available to the *Comando Supremo*, there were three British divisions to the west of Tobruk, whilst the fortress itself was held by the *70th Infantry Division*, with one or two divisions assembling to the east of Tobruk. For this reason Cavallero resisted the pressure exercised by Göring and Mussolini. This entailed a crisis between Mussolini and Cavallero which did not ease until *OKW* backed the opinion of the *Comando Supremo* fully in a telex, as suggested by the German general accredited to the *Comando Supremo*.

On 21 January 1942, the *Panzergruppe* had been renamed *Panzerarmee Afrika*. After the conclusion of the counteroffensive on 6 February 1942, it held positions with its mobile forces immediately west of the Ain el Gazala Line, which, as far back as the spring of 1941, had been suggested as the proper line of defense by [General Italo] Gariboldi and General [Friederich] Paulus.

CHAPTER 2

Preparations for the Autumn Battle, 19 June–12 November 1941

Before the campaign in North Africa began German and Italian authorities were of the opinion that during the summer months large-scale operations with European troops would be impossible for climactic reasons. *Comando Supremo* and the Italian Commander-in-Chief in North Africa, as well as the German Army High Command (*OKH*), thought it advisable to withdraw the German troops to Cyrenaica, where the climate in summer was more favorable than in the desert. This idea was not unlike the practice of earlier centuries when at the beginning of winter armies used to go into winter quarters.

With the siege of Tobruk continuing and in spite of the victorious defensive operations during June when the enemy offensive had been smashed, this policy of withdrawing to areas with more favorable climactic conditions could not be adopted. General Rommel had always been skeptical regarding this break in operations during the summer heat. Having gained much experience in the meantime, Rommel was now absolutely convinced that operations could be carried out in North Africa even during the summer, and that the enemy would certainly not shrink from an offensive for nothing more than climactic reasons.

The attitude of the enemy gave reason to doubt whether he had suffered a defeat crushing enough to force a longer spell of inactivity on him. As early as the beginning of July, enemy reconnaissance activity became quite intensive again. During the middle of July, quite large group movements were observed in the area of Sidi Barani and in the desert to the south thereof. It was difficult to see whether the enemy's aim was to discover any preparation for a possible German offensive, whether he wished to strengthen his own forces for the defensive, or whether he was even preparing a new offensive. The *15th Panzer Division*, which at the time was responsible for the Sollum front, regarded a British offensive as quite possible in the near future, as the enemy would have enough forces available after the conclusion of the campaign in Syria. Rommel himself did not think that the enemy would launch a new offensive in the next few months. He thought that this time the enemy would play safe and would not attack until thorough preparations had been made and forces very much stronger than those available in June should be at his disposal. Yet Rommel did not waste time, and at once began preparations to deal with an early attack. He made good use of his experience and the lessons he had learnt during the Sollum battle.

Rommel was guided by the following principles. The system of strongpoints had proved effective on the Sollum front. The system was therefore to be strengthened and gaps were to be closed. In order to compel the enemy to be far out into the desert and away from his supply route at the coast, the Sollum position was to be extended south of Sidi Omar, the whole line being more than 40 kilometers long. The German and the Italian armored and motorized units were not to be committed to a rigid defense but were to be assembled behind the front and on the one free wing in readiness for mobile operations. The positions themselves were to be held mainly by nonmotorized Italian forces, whose power of resistance was to be backed and strengthened by a few high-grade [German] infantry units and by antiaircraft units which were to serve in an antitank role.

As a matter of course, General Rommel was also considering new offensive plans whilst carrying on with these defensive preparations. It can be assumed that Rommel had not received the *Führer* Directives issued on 30 June.

After *Comando Supremo*[1] had decided in May on the continuation of the siege of Tobruk, as Rommel had suggested, it was quite clear that before an offensive against Egypt was considered, the recapture of Tobruk must be the first objective. For this reason Rommel urged the *OKH* to send the forces and supplies needed for this attack on Tobruk.

In the second half of July the Chief of the General Staff of the *Comando Supremo*, Colonel General Count Cavallero, accompanied by General von Rintalen, saw General Rommel in the latter's battle headquarters in Bardia. His main purpose was to convince Rommel that in no circumstances might an attack on Egypt take place until Tobruk had been taken. It soon became evident that the opinion of Cavallero did not differ in any way from the opinion of General Rommel. Cavallero promised energetic support for the attack on Tobruk. This support was not to be limited to assistance in the

---

[1] The original typescript reads "the Highest Command (*Oberste Führung*)." However, as there was no formal German organization by that name, and as decisions of that sort were normally made by *Comando Supremo* in Rome, I am convinced that "*Oberste Führung*" is merely a translation of "*Comando Supremo*."

German transport of troops and supplies but was to include a strengthening of Italian troops by sending the *Motorized Infantry Division Trieste* to Africa, by bringing *Armored Division Ariete* up to full strength, and by moving further Italian artillery into the battle area.

Organizational Activities

During June, the *5th Light Division* had been renamed *21st Panzer Division*. During July, the *15th Panzer Division*, which had been responsible for the Sollum front, was relieved by the *21st Panzer Division*. The *15th Panzer Division* moved its headquarters to Bardia, and the bulk of its troops were sent into a rest area near the front, west and south of Bardia, which would enable them to take immediate action in case of an enemy attack.

The *21st Panzer Division*, in charge of the Sollum front until the beginning of September, had the bulk of its troops assembled behind the western wing of the position, because in the meantime the troops of the Italian *Infantry Division Savona*[1] had arrived and taken up positions between Sidi Omar and the Halfaya Pass.

At the beginning of September, the *Infantry Division Savona* took charge of the Sollum front and also of the German troops in the position. The two German *Panzer* divisions were moved into rest areas at the coast, the *21st Panzer Division* to Marsa Luch, and the *15th Panzer Division* to Marsa Belafarid. As these areas were at the coast, the climactic conditions were more favorable for the troops than those in the desert high plateau to the south. Thus the German troops were given an opportunity for rest and replenishment, though on a limited scale. This was particularly necessary for the troops of the *15th Schützen Brigade* [the motorized infantry component of the *15th Panzer Division*], whose health had suffered considerably during the operations on the south-west front of Tobruk. Elements of the *15th Schützen Brigade* joined their divisions during July, but the bulk of the brigade did not arrive until September.

During the summer the two German *Panzer* divisions were completely reshaped with a two-fold aim in mind.

The *21st Panzer Division* (the former *5th Light Division*) was changed into a normal armored division with a view to giving the *Afrika Korps* the full striking power of a *Panzer* corps. For this purpose, certain units were exchanged with the *15th Panzer Division*. The *15th Panzer Division* transferred

---

[1] This was a nonmotorized infantry division.

Schützen Regiment 104 to the *21st Panzer Division* and received instead *Regimental headquarters z.b.V.* [*zur besondere Verfügung*, "for special use"] *200* and *Machine Gun Battalion 2*. Out of those, and by absorbing *Motorcycle Battalion 15*, the *15th Panzer Division* established *Regiment z.b.V. 200* as its second *Schützen* regiment.[1] To replace units lost at sea in transit, the division received from Germany the headquarters of *Motorized Artillery Regiment 33* and *Panzer Signal Battalion 33*.[2] The motorized artillery regiment, the *Panzer* engineer battalion, and the *Panzer* signal battalion of the *21st Panzer Division* were brought up to normal strength, and *Machine Gun Battalion 8* was reorganized. This reorganization of the two *Panzer* divisions was concluded by the beginning of September 1941. These two divisions now had the strength of two full *Panzer* divisions, with the sole exception that the *15th Panzer Division* had four *Schützen* battalions and the *21st Panzer Division* only three.

This, however, was not of great importance in mobile operations, as experience had shown that in desert warfare a rifleman does not play the important part he plays in European war theaters. It is true that the *Schützen* regiments, the motorized artillery regiments, and the motorized engineer battalions of both *Panzer* divisions had only a very few armored vehicles, and that the two reconnaissance battalions were unarmored with the exception of one armored reconnaissance company each.

In addition, *Panzergruppe Afrika* received further German troops in the course of the summer, which, however, were not meant for mobile operations but were to take part in the attack on Tobruk. Furthermore, five oasis companies with one battalion headquarters were received by *Panzergruppe Afrika* to operate on the Sollum front with the Italian troops of that sector.

The following troops were earmarked for the attack on Tobruk: the *Afrika Regiment* comprising three battalions, most of the rank and file being former legionnaires of the French Foreign Legion, and two more weak infantry regiments. All these units were given a temporary organization and placed under the command of *Division z.b.V. Afrika*. These units had been shipped to the North African theater partly by air and partly on board fast warships, whilst their vehicles and heavy weapons were shipped by ordinary convoys

---

[1] The machine gun and motorcycle battalions had earlier been transformed into mtorized infantry units that were *Schützen* battalions in all but name.

[2] This seems to be a mistake. *Panzer Signal Battalion 33*, the original signal battalion of the *15th Panzer Division*, was lost at sea on 16 April 1941. *Panzer Signal Battalion 78*, sent to replace it, reached North Africa on 19 July 1941.

and were taking a long time to arrive. For this reason, the troops were not fully operational until late in the autumn. They relieved [the battle group formed around] *Schützen Regiment 115* (three *Schützen* battalions and one artillery battalion, all from the *15th Panzer Division*) on the south-west front of Tobruk. The bulk of these units were assembled behind the east front of Tobruk.

During July, General Cavallero had promised to send Italian units to Africa. However, these troops were very slow in arriving. The Italian *Motorized Infantry Division Trieste* arrived during August and September, and together with the Italian *Armored Division Ariete* formed the Italian *Motorized Corps* with General Gambara as commanding general. For the time being, the corps was concentrated in the area around El Mecheli. On the other hand, the Italian infantry divisions, whose organization was unsatisfactory and antitank equipment poor, improved very slowly. *Ariete* was given 13 new tanks which, compared to the light tanks so far in use, were indeed an improvement, but even these new tanks were very inferior to the German and British in armor and the range of their guns.

Panzergruppe Afrika

Simultaneously with the above-mentioned changes, a reshuffle took place in the German command in North Africa. During June the staff of the German liaison officer attached to the Italian Commander-in-Chief in North Africa had been established in Germany. During July, this staff was re-formed into the staff of *Panzergruppe Afrika*. It took the Italian *Comando Supremo* until the end of July to approve its employment in North Africa. On 15 June 1941, this new staff took over the command of *Afrika Korps*, including army troops and also including the Italian *X* and *XXI Corps*. For the time being, the *Panzergruppe* established its battle headquarters at Beda-Littoria and soon afterwards in Ain el Gazala. An advance battle headquarters was established at Gambut between Bardia and Tobruk.

General Rommel assumed that the first aim of the British offensive which was supposed to be imminent could be the relief of Tobruk. Over and above that aim the British High Command would try to destroy the German-Italian troops in Libya. Even General Rommel watched with grave concern the supply position which was already precarious. In the opinion of the operations officer (Ia) of the *Panzergruppe* [Colonel Alfred Gause], Rommel did not, at that time, fully appreciate the limitations which the convoy situation imposed on the supply question. As was natural, he looked upon this problem more from the viewpoint of the person who makes the demands, and he believed that the possibilities of definite improvement were far from being exhausted.

It was General Rommel's intention to take Tobruk during September and to have all forces at his disposal to ward off the British large-scale offensive which was bound to come.

For the execution of his task he was anxious to be given command over all Italian forces in Marmarica, including the Italian *Motorized Corps*. However, it proved impossible to achieve this end and to get the Italian *Motorized Corps* under Rommel's command before the British offensive was launched in autumn, since General Bastico did not wish to lose his influence on operations and desired to maintain it by keeping the Italian *Motorized Corps* as a reserve in his own hands — an attitude which, after all, was quite natural.

CHAPTER 3

The Defensive Battle
on the Egyptian Frontier

After the victorious conclusion of the fighting in connection with the British June offensive, the *21st Panzer Division* issued instructions regarding the defense of the Sollum position. But on 27 June an order by General Rommel put the defense on the Egyptian frontier on an entirely new basis. He was not satisfied with giving instructions regarding the construction of a new position, laying down the general line the position was to take, but, making use of the experience which had been gained during the battles around Tobruk and during the Sollum battle, he took a hand in numerous practical details. With the great energy for which he was so well known, Rommel saw to it that the German and Italian units understood his ideas in the shortest possible time.

Unlike the Sollum position then existing, which protected no more than the area around Capuzzo and Bardia and showed a more or less local character, the new position was to be an operational one, which was to run uninterruptedly from the Halfaya Pass to Sidi Omar and the west, stretching into the desert for more than 40 kilometers. A continuous, broad minebelt was to protect the area in front of the line in its entire length. A few gaps were to be left open for our own armor, but were to be covered by fire from the positions.

Construction of the Strongpoints

The position proper was to consist of four large battalion strongpoints, which were to be set up at an interval of 10 kilometers between one another. The names of these strongpoints were: Sidi Omar, La Cova (Got el Adhidiba), Qabr el Qaha, and Halfaya Pass. Each of these battalion strongpoints was to be prepared for all-round defense. Each was to have an all-round barbed wire entanglement. The intervals between each of the defensive positions of a strongpoint were blocked by further minefields. The hard core of each battalion strongpoint was formed by an 88 mm antiaircraft battery which was to form the backbone of any defense against armor and which was to have an all-round field of fire. Each battalion strongpoint consisted of nine platoon strongpoints, each strengthened by antitank guns and wired in all round. Each platoon strongpoint was subdivided into several section strongpoints with antitank guns, which were an imitation of the posts to be found in the Tobruk defenses. Each section strongpoint had three open emplacements (for one antitank gun and two machine guns) interconnected by trenches and with bunkers for the crews. In addition, there were emplacements in each battalion strongpoint for several light or medium batteries. Two battalions together formed a *Section Command West* and a *Section Command East.*

The garrison of the strongpoint consisted of one reinforced Italian infantry battalion for each strongpoint with one Italian artillery detachment under command. Each infantry battalion was stiffened by a German oasis company. These oasis companies consisted of German volunteers. It is true they were not motorized, but they were given numerous heavy weapons and their own supply installations, which made them into independent battle groups. In addition, each of these Italian battalions had one German or Italian heavy antiaircraft battery under command.

At the beginning of July, General Rommel became convinced that the gaps between the strongpoints were too broad to allow an effective guarding of the minebelt. For this reason, a new battalion strongpoint called Frongia was erected between the strongpoints Sidi Omar and de Cova. In the eastern sector two new company strongpoints called Cirorer and Faltenbacher were set up. (These strongpoints were named after Italian and German officers killed in action who had distinguished themselves during the fighting in the spring.)

The construction of positions was entrusted to the troops which were to man them. The minebelt, however, was to be laid out by the engineer battalions of the German *Panzer* divisions. Its construction suffered much delay owing to supply difficulties, as it was very difficult to obtain the large number of German mines needed for the purpose. Instead of the German mines, which were unobtainable, the less suitable Italian mines were used and several fatal accidents occurred. The work was made extremely difficult by the fearful heat of the summer months. On the whole, the construction of the positions was completed by August. However, it proved necessary to work continuously to bring this system of positions to near perfection. Even as late as November the positions still lacked rearward mine protection.

From the end of June 1941, the positions were gradually taken over by the Italian *Infantry Division Savona.* Only in the Halfaya Pass, which was regarded

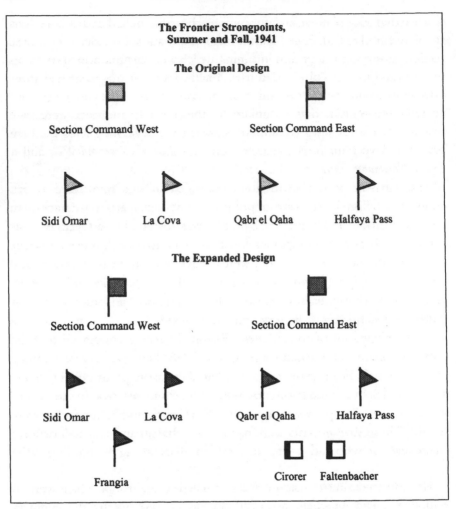

**The Frontier Strongpoints,
Summer and Fall, 1941**

The Original Design

Section Command West   Section Command East

Sidi Omar   La Cova   Qabr el Qaha   Halfaya Pass

The Expanded Design

Section Command West   Section Command East

Sidi Omar   La Cova   Qabr el Qaha   Halfaya Pass

Frangia   Cirorer   Faltenbacher

as particularly important, did a German infantry battalion remain. This was *I. / Schützen Regiment 104* under Major (Reserve) [Wilhelm] Bach, who had distinguished himself during the Sollum battle. In the middle of June the divisional staff of *Savona* was entrusted with the command of the western sector, and by the end of August it was made responsible for the entire system of defense.

The Sidi Omar–Sollum position was capable of comparatively large effect with a minimum of troops. Its strength rested chiefly in the excellent use which had been made of the terrain and in its well organized antitank defenses. It is true that these defenses could not, and were not expected to, hold out for a long period against a breakthrough attack carried out by strong, thoroughly equipped formations. For this purpose they were too thinly manned and stiffened with too few German troops. But even so the positions promised to keep considerable enemy forces busy for some time, thus blocking the coast road and affording the German armored formations time and opportunity for mobile operations.

After the Sollum battle, activity in front of our positions remained negligible for a long time. The two German reconnaissance units were the only units that remained actively operational, *Reconnaissance Battalion 33* [of the *15th Panzer Division*] reconnoitering in front of our positions, and *Reconnaissance Battalion 3* [of the *21st Panzer Division*] reconnoitering on our open flank. Stationary reconnaissance units were pushed forward to a distance of about 10 kilometers in front of our positions, forming a covering screen. Soon, however, it became evident that the enemy reconnaissance forces on our front and in particular to the south of our positions had been considerably strengthened. As early as July our two reconnaissance units began to find difficulty in breaking through the dense screen of enemy armored cars. It then became the main task of the two reconnaissance units to protect the units manning the positions, and with them the *Afrika Korps* and the *Panzergruppe*, against surprise.

At the end of August the *Panzergruppe* recalled the armored car reconnaissance patrols of the two reconnaissance units in order to avoid too many casualties. The *Panzergruppe* counted on air reconnaissance and on wireless intelligence to give a timely warning of a possible attack.

The Enemy Situation

Early in July it became evident that the enemy was receiving considerable reinforcements. The *4th Indian Division* was certainly still on our front, pushing infantry outposts up to 10 kilometers from our positions on the Halfaya Pass. It could also be taken as certain that the *7th Armored Division* was still somewhere near the front. In addition to these formations there were, moreover, indications that further forces were being concentrated in the area of Marsa Matruk. The German command suspected as far back as September that at least one South African and one New Zealand division were in that area. The enemy in Giarabub and Siwa had also been considerably strengthened. But it was not yet clear whether moderately strong fighting troops had not joined the reconnaissance detachments identified at these two oases. More formations were presumed to be in the Nile Delta. Of course, it was quite possible that they were meant for other

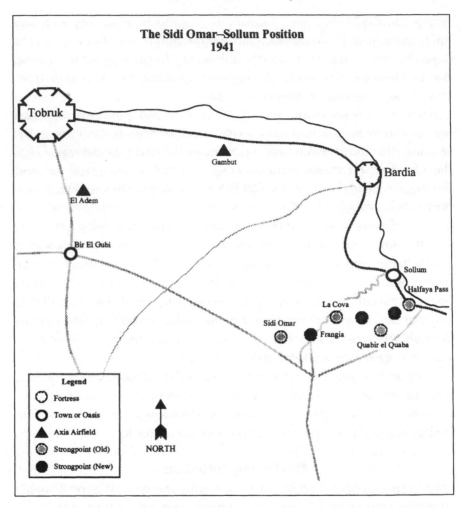

theaters, as Lower Egypt always served as the giant marshaling yard for the entire British Empire.

Since July, enemy motor traffic in the area Sidi Barani–Marsa Matruk and in the desert to the south had been steadily increasing. This led the German High Command to believe that the enemy was building up supplies for an imminent renewal of the offensive. In order to clarify the situation before the attack on Tobruk was launched, and in order to capture British orders which might give information on the enemy order of battle, General Rommel decided on a vigorous reconnaissance thrust during September in the area south of Sidi Barani. This operation was entrusted to the *21st Panzer Division*.

The operation, which had been given the code name "Midsummer Night's Dream" (*Sommernachtstraum*), began during the night of 13/14 September. The operation proved to be a failure because the leadership and fuel supply organization of the *21st Panzer Division* collapsed. The tanks of the *21st Panzer Division* remained immobilized on the battlefield for several hours, giving the enemy time and opportunity to move up reinforcements and to throw his air force repeatedly into the contest. The latter was responsible for the considerable losses suffered by the German forces. For the first time the German forces experienced carpet bombing of great density, frequently repeated. No British orders were captured which contained any intelligence.

Thus the German command remained in the dark, even after this reconnaissance, and nothing was known of enemy intentions, although it had become clear that the enemy air force had received considerable reinforcements. On the other hand, there was no evidence that the enemy was building up particularly strong supply depots in the frontier area. There was thus no reason to assume that the enemy would start his offensive for the next few weeks.

During October and the first half of November enemy reconnaissance became increasingly active. In the coastal area enemy infantry carried out reconnaissance operations, which were repulsed by the Halfaya Pass garrison. The main effort of enemy reconnaissance activity was made farther to the south in the area around Ridotta Maddalena and Giarabub. In the Maddalena area one or two South African reconnaissance units pushed far ahead. From there and from Giarabub enemy reconnaissance units penetrated into the area to the south and even west of Tobruk. (Wireless reconnaissance pointed to more units being moved into the area of Marsa Matruk.) Thereupon in October *Reconnaissance Battalion 3* was again entrusted with the covering of the south-west flank of our Sidi Omar–Sollum position. No reconnaissance operation in force was, however, arranged to clarify the situation in the Maddalena area. *Reconnaissance Battalion 3* alone would not have been strong enough for such an operation.

At the beginning of November it had to be assumed that the British offensive was indeed imminent. The continued strengthening of enemy forces and the ever-increasing enemy reconnaissance activity left no doubt. It seemed possible that the main thrust would not be made in the coastal region but farther to the south in the desert.

Preparations for the Attack on Tobruk

During the entire summer and during the autumn there was little fighting in front of Tobruk. The enemy made no more sorties. The *9th Australian Division* was gradually relieved by the *70th British Division*. In addition, the garrison of Tobruk had been reinforced by one army tank brigade (about 70 heavy tanks), by the Polish *Carpathian Rifle Brigade*, and by a Polish [motorized] cavalry detachment. During autumn the German command assumed that there were four and a half infantry regiments[1] in Tobruk, one of which was always in reserve. The original Italian fortress artillery, which had proved so great a nuisance to us during the spring, became silent, probably because there was no ammunition left for their guns. In autumn, about 70 guns of all calibers were supposed to be in the fortress. Probably this was an underestimate. Supplies for the garrison were moved in by convoys at night. The strengthening of the garrison made sorties at any time very likely. If an offensive were launched from Egypt, breakout attempts could be expected with great certainty.

For this reason the German command did all in its power to strengthen the positions of the besieging units by all available means. The fighting power of the Italian divisions was raised by refresher courses conducted by German officers. The movements of reserves behind the siege front was facilitated by the construction of the "Axis Road," which had been completed by the end of July and by-passed the fortress.

The Siege Front

General Rommel still regarded his main task as the capture of the fortress of Tobruk as soon as possible. He needed the troops operating against Tobruk as soon as possible to counter the British large-scale offensive which was expected late in autumn. Rommel was hoping to improve the difficult supply position of his troops by using the harbor of Tobruk, which was so near to the front, instead of the long land route from Tripoli and Benghazi. Rommel's most immediate care was the creation of the conditions which would make the early capture of Tobruk possible.

In order to make good use of the time before the arrival of the troops and supplies needed for the assault, local attacks were launched from the beginning of August which progressively tightened the ring around the fortress. This was particularly necessary on the south-eastern sector of the

---

[1] The author is using the German concept of a regiment, which was a tactical unit of two, three, or (rarely) four battalions.

fortress near Bir Asatein, where the British still held the advanced position in front of the line of fortifications, which they had taken during April. They were retaken by us during August and September, and isolated posts were captured in other sectors in well-prepared local attacks. These attacks were made by German troops, and the newly won territory was then taken over by the Italians, with German troops remaining in support for a few days. Some of these positions were lost by the Italians later after the German troops had been withdrawn. From September onwards the besieging forces worked their way nearer to the fortifications in all sectors.

The intention was to launch the attack against a spot on the south-east front of Tobruk south of the Via Balbia, because there the terrain was suitable for armored operations and because it was essential to open up the Via Balbia as early as possible.

During the summer and autumn troops were being relieved with a view to reorganizing the siege front for the attack. The infantry of the *Division z.b.V. Afrika* was now arriving. These troops relieved the reinforced *Schützen Regiment 115* of the *15th Panzer Division* on the south-west front of Tobruk. The bulk of the relieving troops was assembled in the rear of the west front of Tobruk. *Infantry Division Bologna* took over the sector of *Motorized Infantry Division Trento* on the east front. *Trento* took over the sector of *Infantry Division Pavia* to the west of El Aden and also the positions of the last elements of *Armored Division Ariete* on the south-west and west front of Tobruk. *Pavia* took over the positions formerly held by *Bologna* on the south-east front of Tobruk.

In Rommel's opinion the primary condition for the assault was the arrival of reinforcements of German infantry and artillery as well as the accumulation of the necessary supplies. This, however, was a slow process owing to the deterioration of the convoy position.

At the beginning of October the infantry of the *Division z.b.V. Afrika* had arrived at full strength, but their heavy weapons, transport vehicles and supply vehicles had not, as they were being shipped in ordinary convoys. Thus the division was not up to full fighting strength and its usefulness was limited.

Arrival of German Artillery[1]

In addition to the divisional artillery and Italian army artillery already on the spot, it was regarded as essential to have at least six more German heavy army

---

[1] This section was checked against the report of General Boettcher, "Artillerischtische Beiträge zur Belagerung von Tobruk, Teil I bis zur Herbst-Schlacht 1941, Oktober/November 1941," US National Archives, Foreign Military Studies, Document D045.

artillery battalions. Of these, the following elements had arrived at the beginning of October:

Headquarters of Artillery Command 104[2]
1 battalion of 10 cm guns
1 battalion of 21 cm howitzers (less one battery) [The missing battery had been lost at sea when the ship carrying it was torpedoed.]
2 army coast artillery battalions of 15 cm guns (French equipment of limited range) [Each battalion of three batteries.]

Not yet arrived:
1 observation battery
1 army coast artillery battalion
1 battery 17 cm guns
1 battery 21 cm howitzers
1 battalion French heavy field howitzers (15 cm)

These units, with the exception of the howitzer battery, arrived during the middle of November.

Artillery preparations for the attack were begun at an early stage. Artillery reconnaissance was started to identify the positions of the siege artillery. Gun emplacements were constructed with ammunition dumps ready and fire plans were worked out.

Ammunition Supplies

General Rommel regarded it as essential that not only the troops earmarked for the attack on Tobruk but the entire *Panzergruppe Afrika* be liberally provided with supplies. Being so near to the front the *Panzergruppe* had to have enough ammunition, fuel, and rations to be able to carry out the attack and immediately afterwards to turn and fight the enemy who was expected to launch an offensive with his main force. For this purpose seven ammunition units and five units of fire were regarded as the minimum requirement. However, at the beginning of October there were no more than one to one

---

[2] A German artillery command (*Arko*) was a floating headquarters that could control the fire of a large number of artillery battalions. On the eve of World War II, the German Army intended to put an artillery command in every division, giving that division the ability to control the fire of artillery units greatly in excess of the three or four organic artillery battalions. The rapid expansion of the German Army during the war, however, made this plan unworkable: there were simply not enough artillery officers qualified for this sort of work. As a result, each artillery command tended to serve as a sort of "flying circus" that moved from one part of the front to another. For details, see Bruce Gudmundsson, *On Artillery* (Westport, CT: Praeger, 1993).

and a half units of ammunition available. This was not nearly enough. During early November supplies of ammunition had risen to five units, which might have been just enough.

The slow arrival of reinforcements for German troops and supplies which were deemed essential for the success of the assault made it necessary to postpone the attack several times. Originally it had been planned for the end of September, then it was postponed until October, again until the beginning of November and later even until the beginning of December. After his visit to Rome in the middle of November, Rommel decided, however, to launch the attack on 21 November. And this decision was final.

The Plan for the Attack

Originally the attack was to be carried out by the entire *Afrika Korps* and the division *z.b.V. Afrika*. The fact that the attack had been postponed until November made it very timely that the enemy in Western Egypt would be able to conclude preparations for his offensive and that he would be in a position to open up his offensive immediately after we had launched our attack. Rommel decided to have the *21st Panzer Division* standing by north-east of Gambut to halt the first onslaught of the enemy if the offensive did occur. This meant that (apart from two Italian divisions) there were only the *15th Panzer Division* and *Division z.b.V. Afrika* available for the attack. Even the *15th Panzer Division* had to make its plans for the attack in a way that it could be withdrawn to support the *21st Panzer Division* in defensive operations.

Should the enemy start his offensive before we launched our attack against Tobruk, areas for the rapid assembly of the *Afrika Korps*, south-east and south-west of Gambut, were reconnoitered and preliminary orders were prepared. The Italian *Motorized Corps* was not under Rommel's command and was still back in the Mechili area. It was therefore not possible to move the corps up to assist in the operation. However, Rommel did succeed, with the greatest difficulty, in obtaining permission for the Italian *Motorized Corps* to move into the area of Bir El Gubi (*Armored Division Ariete*) and Bir Hacheim (*Motorized Infantry Division Trieste*), which meant that it would play its part covering the siege front against interference from the south.

In spite of all of these difficulties Rommel stuck to his decision to attack Tobruk. All units earmarked for the attack received intensive training and the commanders of the various formations and units were prepared for the task in several sand-table exercises.

The Order for the Attack

In contrast to the attempts made so far on Tobruk, this attack was to be launched by day. The plan of the attack provided for the breakthrough of the bunker line by the *Division z.b.V. Afrika*. The *15th Panzer Division* immediately afterwards was to proceed along the Via Balbia to Fort Solaro and from thence to the coast west of Tobruk, with a view to cutting off the town of Tobruk and the harbor from the other parts of the fortress. An unarmored battle group of the division, supported by artillery, was to advance to the harbor inlet south of Tobruk and to neutralize the harbor by artillery fire as soon as possible. *Division z.b.V. Afrika* was to cover the flank of the attack against interference from the north-east sector of the fortress and then to mop up this north-eastern sector.

Infantry Division Pavia and *Infantry Division Bologna* of the Italian *XXI Corps* were to attack on the left wing of the *Afrika Korps* with a view to broadening the breach. *XXI Corps* was then to advance in a north-westerly direction abreast of the *15th Panzer Division*, covering the latter's western flank, and cut off the remaining fortress area.

Artillery was to play a main role in the attack. *Artillery Command 104* had been made responsible for operations carried out by the army artillery battalions and the artillery of the attacking divisions in preparation for the attack. The artillery preparation proper was to last three hours. During this period the howitzer batteries were to shatter the fortifications in the sector of the attack proper. The remaining heavy batteries were to shell the fortress artillery and also to keep the command posts of the fortress under fire. The artillery of the assaulting division was to smash the infantry lines and installations.

After the attack had actually begun, the division artillery was again to be at the disposal of the various divisions, whilst army artillery was to protect the flanks with the mobile units of army artillery following the division into the fortress.

Luftwaffe formations of considerable strength were to support the attack with *Stukas* operating against the fortifications, enemy artillery, and command posts, and against the town and harbor of Tobruk.

Extensive deceptive measures were taken to keep the time and place of the attack a secret. The artillery was not allowed any ranging on the days before the attack. On the western and southern sectors of the fortress local attacks were to be launched with the support of *Stuka* attacks and rocket firing. These local attacks were to be continued before the main assault and even on the day of the attack.

New Tactics for Armored Formations

The operational lull during summer and autumn 1941 had been used by the German divisions for all sorts of preparations and for intensive training. The units in position around Tobruk were chiefly busy with the war against Tobruk, but the *Panzer* divisions were applying the lessons of the spring to bring up their training in mobile warfare to the desired standard. During summer and during the battle in autumn two divisions, but chiefly the *15th Panzer Division*, had developed battle tactics of a new kind. In order to understand the operations from November 1941 to February 1942 it is essential to understand these new tactics.

Unlike the European war theater, desert terrain almost everywhere allowed the use of vehicles of every imaginable kind. In the desert it was not necessary to have large formations moving in columns which, when time came, would have to adopt battle formation, with consequent delay. It was advisable to adopt a kind of formation whilst still on the move which allowed the full fighting strength of a division to be brought to bear immediately. Where there were no roads which justified a move in columns at the high speed obtainable on these roads, the divisions moved in *Flächenmarsch*, with the battle groups one behind the other. It must be understood that on such a move the depth of each battle group was no more than about four times its width.

Cooperation of Weapons

In desert warfare, operations against armored units were more frequent than operations against entrenched infantry. It was therefore advisable to have the most important arm of the division, i.e. the *Panzer* regiment, supported by all other units of the division, even if it was a question of operations against enemy armor. This kind of tactic, it is realized, was thus far customary only in operations against mixed formations of all weapons.

The most important support weapon was the heavy antiaircraft battery of 8.8 cm guns. This gun was able to pierce the armor of even heavy enemy tanks at a long range. The guns were therefore placed in the march column of the *Panzer* regiment, when the division was on the move. These 8.8 cm guns, together with elements of the *Panzer* regiment, fought the enemy armored formations, whilst the bulk of the *Panzer* regiment approached the enemy armor at top speed until they had reached the distance favorable to the armament they then carried.

Motorized artillery also proved a very valuable support weapon for armored operations. It was the task of motorized artillery to take over fire protection for their own armor as it attacked, to hold down enemy antitank artillery and armored artillery observers and also to lend flanking protection to attacking forces by fire. It became evident that enemy tanks were extremely vulnerable to concentrated artillery fire. It was frequently possible to disperse a concentration of enemy tanks which had been assembling for the attack or at least to delay the attack. For this purpose the artillery in question moved dispersed at intervals through the *Panzer* regiment. The armored artillery observation vehicles traveled with the leading tanks. The staffs of artillery units usually traveled with the commanders of the armored units. With the rear battle groups of the division on the move, there was usually only one artillery unit which was responsible for flank protection.

The artillery soon learned to take up positions and open fire so rapidly that the tank attack suffered practically no delay at all. It very soon became clear that enemy armored formations frequently avoided the attack of a well-led and powerful German *Panzer* division. Taking advantage of the higher speed of their tanks, they tried to bring their armor to bear against the unprotected flanks and rear of the *Panzer* division. For this reason the *Panzerjägerabteilung* (antitank battalion) was charged with covering the flank of the division most open to enemy attacks, and also with antitank operations in the vicinity of the soft-skinned parts of the division. There were, however, occasions when the antitank battalions were used in pursuit operations and also to strengthen and to broaden the attack of their own armor.

The *Schützen* of the division, organized in one or two battle groups, were kept as near to the armored battle groups as they could be, so that as far as possible they were covered against direct fire from enemy tanks. Thus they were rapidly available for the exploitation of any success achieved by the armor, to mop up or clean out infantry and artillery positions overrun by the armor, and to build up a front, thus freeing the armor for operations elsewhere.

The engineers usually traveled with the *Schützen*, but they had reconnaissance sections traveling with the armored regiments to be at hand for lifting mines or for laying mine obstacles at short notice.

Command

These new tactics offered great difficulties as far as the conduct of operations and the leaders responsible therefor were concerned. Even in a European war theater it is extremely difficult to issue orders in time for the swift changes to be expected in armored warfare. It is more difficult to give such orders from a headquarters well behind the actual fighting line. In desert warfare this is quite impossible. The uniform terrain and the particularly poor quality of the Italian maps were responsible for the fact that useful reports regarding locations and situations were hardly ever available at headquarters. Hence it became absolutely essential, not only for the divisional commanders, but also for the whole divisional tactical headquarters, to travel to the immediate vicinity of the armored formations, where they could see what was going on, and where they could direct the battle and give orders as the actual situation required. Inevitably this meant a terrific strain on the staff, as they were exposed not only to the moral but also to the physical effects of enemy fire. For this reason a division had to be led from armored vehicles.

The logical consequence was a simplification of the signal system. As had been tried out in other war theaters, the command vehicles of the divisional commander and of the operations officer (Ia) were equipped with ultra-short-wave sets which allowed them to listen in to the wireless traffic of the *Panzer* regiment.[1] This did away with the latter sending reports. The remaining battle groups of the division were contacted on the medium-wave network from the same vehicle. An armored signals vehicle traveling immediately behind the divisional command tank was responsible for wireless traffic with corps and also the reconnaissance units. Another advantage of this system was the fact that the officers commanding the *Panzer* regiment and the artillery regiment were usually very near and could be given verbal [i.e. face-to-face] orders. Conduct of operations was therefore most simple and orders could be given and were given over the air like simple commands.

Telephones were only used at night. On such occasions the headquarters of the various battle groups inside the hedgehog leaguer of a division were placed as near to each other as advisable.

Reconnaissance

The tactics of reconnaissance units hardly differed from those used in Europe. On the move in the vicinity of the enemy, it was usual to make use of the Mark II tank as mobile cover for front and flanks. This tank was still

---

[1] During World War II, the Ia (Eins A) was the senior staff officer of a German division, who combined the functions of the Chief of Staff and Assistant Chief of Staff G-3 (Operations) of a present-day NATO formation. The author, Colonel Rainer Kriebel, served as Ia of the *15th Panzer Division* from its formation in October 1940 until his transfer to the Russian Front in March 1942.

available at the end of 1941 and could not be used in battle. They usually traveled at the outer fringe of their ultra-short-wave wireless, that is, at a distance of about 10 kilometers.

Wireless reconnaissance played a most important part during operations. The inter-tank traffic of the enemy intercepted on the battlefield was immediately exploited and the results acted upon. This gave us the opportunity of countering actions and measures of the enemy which the latter had not even begun.

Supplies

In the desert war supply was rendered difficult, as the enemy had a vastly superior number of armored reconnaissance units, which harassed the supply routes of the divisions. For this reason supplies had often to be moved up under escort. The Ib (second general staff officer) of the division controlled supply from the rear, with a deputy attached to the tactical headquarters who was in contact with him by wireless.

During an armored operation it sometimes happens that the tanks were immobilized for quite long periods, which was tactically undesirable since the armored units had to bring up their supply vehicles for replenishing fuel and ammunition. In order to make such stops as short as possible, it was arranged that the *Panzer* regiment at least would be accompanied by its supply unit. Even in battle, but particularly during the pursuit, the supply units traveled in the immediate vicinity of the *Panzer* regiment. Later on, even divisional supply columns were sometimes ordered to accompany the division during operations. Such were the tactical principles. They were developed and improved during the first days of the British autumn offensive and proved very useful indeed. As from January 1942, they were made compulsory with all armored formations of the *Afrika Korps*.

The Situation in the Air

After the second Sollum battle there was a comparative lull in operations in the North African war theater as a result of the increasing heat and very frequent sandstorms. The main purpose of air reconnaissance, short-range or long-range, was the supervision of enemy ground forces. Sea traffic supplying Tobruk was watched with particular care. Apart from this limited activity, the air force developed its ground organization and antiaircraft defense, reorganizing the latter with the help of antiaircraft formations newly arrived from home.

Closer cooperation was established with that part of the *5th Italian Air Fleet* which operated in the eastern sector. The operations of the Italian and of the German air formations were already coordinated, which made them much more effective. German and Italian *Stuka* formations flew together, protected by Italian fighters. This cooperation strengthened the fighting power and raised the morale of the Italians to a remarkable degree.

In those days *Stuka* formations found it impossible to operate without strong fighter escort. For this reason attempts were made to take advantage of the African summer nights, which were never quite dark, for *Stuka* attacks. The pilots were trained for night operations and the training proved a great success. From then on, frequent night attacks were made against Tobruk and against the supply convoys arriving in Tobruk harbor by night. Destroyer aircraft (*Zerstörer*) with their greater range were also employed to harass supply columns which used to arrive with great regularity. On such occasions numerous dogfights took place.

On 15 July, four out of five transport ships were sunk by our air force in the Bardia area. One of the ships was a tanker. The fighters accompanying the *Stukas* succeeded in shooting down several enemy fighters of the ship's escort.

The rearward supply installations and supply traffic of the enemy were frequently attacked, particularly by Me 110 "destroyers." On 11 August 50 lorries were set alight. Bombers from Crete were also active. Of the attacks, which were spread over the entire summer and which were directed against supply bases and airfields, two operations deserve special mention: the bomber operations against the Fayum road near Cairo and a combined bomber and "destroyer" operation against the airfield of Giarabub, where twenty enemy aircraft were destroyed on the ground and much damage was caused to other equipment. In the latter operation surprise had been complete.

During the summer the organization of the air force in the Mediterranean area was considerably improved. Soon after the conquest of Greece and of Crete the staff of *X. Fliegerkorps* was transferred to Athens. *Fleigerführer Afrika* was under command of *X. Fliegerkorps*. This transfer meant that it was now once again the responsibility of the Italian Air Force to keep Malta down. The Italians were never sufficiently successful to allow the African convoys to sail to Tripoli or Benghazi with any degree of safety.

III./Jagdgeschwader 27, for the time being the only German fighter formation on the spot, was soon reinforced by *Fighter Squadron Muncheberg*, which had made a name for itself by its efficiency and dash and for the successes it had achieved over Malta.

The *Ergänzungsstaffel* [expansion flight] of *Lehrgeschwader 1* [training wing] was shifted to Benghazi-Benina during the summer. Its task was to escort convoys sailing to Benghazi and occasionally some small assignments in connection with ground operations were given to it in the framework of its training program.

The headquarters of *Stuka Geschwader 3* was given *I./Stuka 76*, which was still operating in Crete. The three *Stuka* groups changed their designations:[1]

I./Stuka 76 to *I./Stuka 3*
I./Stuka 1 to *II./Stuka 3*
II./Stuka 2 to *III./Stuka 3*

The strength of the German units was as follows:

Stuka Geschwader 3 (2 groups)	Approximately 70 Ju 87
III./Jagdgeschwader 27 and *1 Staffel*	Approximately 40 Me 109
9./Zerstörergeschwader 26	Approximately 10 Me 110
1./Fernaufklärungsgruppe 121 [long-range reconnaissance]	Approximately 10 Ju 88[2]
2. H/14 [short-range reconnaissance]	Approximately 10 Hs 126
	Total 140 aircraft

The Hs 126 was a single-engine army cooperation aircraft. Two-thirds of these 140 aircraft were ready for service. There were about 20 transport and other aircraft available. Altogether there were 160 aircraft available, of which 100 were ready for operations.

The Italian air units were also brought up to strength. However, their aircraft were all obsolete. There was, however, one Ju 87 *Stuka* group which

---

[1] The German system for designating aviation units was derived from that used for designating ground units. Just as a German infantry regiment consisted of twelve or so consecutively numbered companies grouped into two or three battalions, a German "wing" (*Geschwader*) was divided into twelve or so "echelons" (*Staffeln*) arranged into two or three "groups" (*Gruppen*). Battalions and groups were identified by a roman numeral, while regiments and wings, as well as companies and echelons, were marked by an arabic numeral. Thus, *I./Stuka 76* was the First Group (*Gruppe*) of Stuka Wing (*Geschwader*) 76, while *1./Stuka 76* was the First Echelon (*Staffel*) of Stuka Wing (*Geschwader*) 76.

[2] Independent groups and battalions were identified by arabic numerals.

achieved noteworthy success over Tobruk in cooperation with its German counterparts.

Their strength can be assumed as follows:

1 fighter *Geschwader*	Approximately 90 aircraft
1 *Schlachtflieger Geschwader* [Ground attack and antitank wing]	Approximately 90 aircraft
Reconnaissance aircraft	Approximately 20 aircraft
Bombers	Approximately 20 aircraft
	Total 220 aircraft

Two-thirds of these 220 aircraft were ready for operations. There were approximately 50 transport and other aircraft available. The total sum of the Italian aircraft was 270, of which 140 aircraft were ready for operations.

Cooperation with the Italian airmen was good. Working together with the German airmen gave them back their self-confidence.

The RAF continued to be very active. When convoys arrived in Tobruk a great many British fighters were sent up as escort and cover. The British knew very well that the German and Italian airmen would come up in strength to harass their convoys and the loading and offloading activities in the Tobruk harbor. It was only natural that during the summer many air fights took place over Tobruk; the German fighters scored many successes, shooting down a tidy number of their opponents. It was, however, impossible to stop convoys from bringing supplies to Tobruk; one of the reasons was that later on they sailed by night.

As from summer 1941, it became clear that the RAF in western Egypt had been considerably strengthened. This had become apparent for the first time during the German reconnaissance operations carried out in the middle of September and directed against Egypt. The full significance and volume of reinforcements was, however, not understood until a little time after the beginning of the British autumn offensive.

As mentioned above, it had been planned that our air force formation would take part in the attack on Tobruk. On the other hand, the possibility of a renewed enemy attack on the Sollum front could not be overlooked. Our forces were not strong enough to provide the necessary air formation for each of the two possible fronts. It was decided that the more important battle would be fought at Tobruk, and that it was on this front that the force would have to operate. It was, however ,arranged to have some air formations on the Sollum front, and airfields were laid out at the El Adem and Gambut for that purpose. The supply problem was just as difficult with the air force as it was with the army. However, ample use was made of air transport and of the continuous air traffic to Greece so that at least the food situation was adequate. Fuel and ammunition arrived in sufficient quantities to make good daily consumption, which was not much, in view of the minor operations carried out by our scanty forces; but it was quite impossible to build up a stock for operations or a larger scale. On 16 November Cyrenaica and Marmarica were soaked by pouring rain of unheard-of intensity. Bridges were carried away, roads became rivers and all the German and Italian airfields were under water, a quagmire and quite unusable; for days it was impossible for any aircraft to take off, and if there were exceptions they were few and far between.

Reconnaissance activity, of course was reduced to practically nothing. The consequences proved to be very grave, if not decisive. The enemy, on the other hand, was able to fly all the sorties because there was no rain in his area to wash out the airfields.

The Supply Position in Summer and Autumn 1941

When *Panzergruppe Afrika* took over all the German and most of the Italian troops in North Africa during August 1941, the entire supply organization was reorganized and put on a new basis. The staff of *Panzergruppe Afrika* was given a fully equipped Quartermaster-General's Branch, which was in a better position to tackle the complicated tasks connected with supplying troops in the North African war theater. This Quartermaster-General's Branch had under its command the staff of a commander rearward areas (*Korück*). This latter staff was responsible for the rearward army areas, and the field commandant Tripoli was placed under its jurisdiction.

The main task of the Quartermaster-General during summer and autumn 1941 was two-fold: providing the current supplies for the *Panzergruppe* and, secondly, stockpiling for the autumn offensive. As the first part of the second task, supplies had to be accumulated for the attack on Tobruk; the most important item was ammunition for the attacking troops and for army artillery taking part in the attack. Over and above this task, the *Panzergruppe* was intent on building up sufficient stocks, particularly of fuel, to allow for a campaign of longer duration, and if supply by sea became more difficult or stopped entirely. An important part of this task was the moving up of supplies to the strongpoints or the Sollum front, as these strongpoints had to be provided with enough ammunition, rations, and water to last them, even if they were cut off for a lengthy period from the supplies of the *Panzergruppe*.

The divisions of the *Afrika Korps* were the first to have their stocks of ammunition and fuel replenished. They built up their dumps on both sides of the Via Balbia in the area between Bardia and Tobruk. In addition, there were huge supply centers around the harbor of Benghazi and that of Tripoli, from which the army dumps were continuously replenished.

The supplying of the *Panzergruppe*, which should have been completed in September 1941, suffered more and more delays, because the ships bringing supplies from overseas suffered heavy losses; in October no supplies arrived at all. After 18 October no ships carrying German supply goods reached the African coast. Simultaneously ammunition and fuel dumps received more attention from the enemy air forces, and the attacks on these dumps became frequent. The main target of the attacks was the dumps to the west of Bardia; heavy damage was caused.

In spite of all these obstacles ammunition and fuel stocks, which were regarded as sufficient for the attack on Tobruk and for subsequent defense against the probable counteroffensive by British Eighth Army, had been accumulated in the front area by the beginning of November. Had that not been the case, it would have been impossible to last through the heavy fighting of the autumn with all overseas supplies cut off.

Regarding rations, difficulties had arisen during spring and the situation required precautions until August. By then it was possible to improve the food, particularly because of measures taken by the formations themselves: fresh meat was obtained by buying camels and by measures taken by the *Panzergruppe* on its own initiatives. It was, however, impossible to obtain fresh fruit and vegetables by air, which would have corrected the lack of certain vitamins in the existing ration scale.

The *Panzergruppe* was bent on improving the supply of drinking water, which was particularly bad in the area of Sollum and Bardia. German and Italian water construction units were working to reopen the wells of Bardia which had been destroyed by the enemy. By the end of October these water companies succeeded in providing suitable drinking water for the troops operating in that area and rendering them independent of the Derna water supplies.

Regarding health, gastric illnesses and intestinal diseases were sources of great anxiety to the persons responsible. Apart from amebic dysentery, infectious jaundice was spreading rapidly and caused many casualties amongst the troops. It was chiefly the commanding officers who fell victims to these diseases, and many charges in the command had to be affected. The reason for this unsatisfactory state of health of the troops was the fly pest and to some degree their inadequate diet. The elements of the *Panzer* division in positions at Tobruk were particularly affected.

The motor vehicle position deteriorated continuously during the summer; the motor vehicles were subjected to continuous wear and tear, as they were all constantly in operation, chiefly the supply vehicles of the *Panzergruppe* or the divisions; even the operational vehicles of the troop units had to be used on many occasions to secure the supplies necessary for the front lines. By the end of July the construction of the Axis Road had been completed, so that it was no longer necessary for the vehicles to travel on the very bad desert track south and east of Tobruk which had been responsible for very many breakdowns. The *Division z.b.v. Afrika,* which had been flown over and for which no motor transport was yet available, presented new transport problems which had to be overcome with the vehicles to hand. The engines of the tanks showed less wear and tear after the introduction of improved air filters. Tank maintenance installations were also improved.

The Italian formations of the *Panzergruppe* were similarly busy reorganizing and replenishing. A certain rivalry between the German and the Italian supply authorities and keen competition for available shipping space were inevitable. The inadequate equipment of the Italian troops in motor vehicles, which were, moreover, of poor quality, caused great anxiety.

This is how *Panzergruppe Afrika* made use of the lull in fighting during the summer. At the commencement of the enemy autumn offensive, *Panzergruppe* had all the reserves and supplies necessary to sustain battles of a longer duration.

During the summer and autumn of 1941, the German leadership in Africa had defined its task as the recapture of the fortress of Tobruk and the simultaneous creation of favorable conditions for the repulse of the expected large-scale British offensive. Naturally, General Rommel aimed at taking Tobruk before the British attack started. But, even in the most favorable circumstances, i.e. if Tobruk fell into our hands before the British offensive materialized, it was to be expected that the British would take very strong action to relieve the fortress as soon as our attack had started. For this reason the attack had to be planned in such a way that success would come soon, that is to say inside of two days, before the British counteroffensive could approach Tobruk. On the other hand, casualties as heavy as those incurred by our forces during the spring had to be avoided at all costs, as they would jeopardize the chance of repulsing the British offensive from Egypt.

The plan of attack was simple and to the point. This plan was followed in June 1942 with but slight local alterations and led to a brilliant success, although it must be mentioned that the forces engaged then were stronger than provided for the attack under discussion.

During spring both our attacks on Tobruk had failed because insufficient time was allotted to preparation and inadequate forces were allocated. It was quite understandable that this time Rommel did not want to rely on good luck and chance, but that he desired to start the attack only after enough German troops and ample supplies had arrived to make sure of success. Rommel could not possibly foresee that the arrival of troops and supplies would be as slow as they were owing to the extraordinary deterioration of the situation in the Mediterranean area which resulted in repeated postponements of D-Day.

It is easy to be wise after the event; it is a fact that during the first third of November the available artillery and supplies were the same as on 21 November, when Rommel intended to attack. Of course Rommel could not know beforehand that not a single ship with the promised supply goods aboard was to arrive before 21 November. On the other hand, Rommel realized the danger of postponement and delay. It is true that success might have been achieved if the attack had been launched at the beginning of November; but it would be unfair to blame Rommel for having postponed the attack until later.

Preparing for the countermeasures against the British autumn offensive, it was of utmost importance to avoid being surprised by the enemy, to delay his offensive, and, when it came, to force it into a direction which would afford the German and Italian mobile forces the opportunity of launching a promising counterattack against the enemy assault units.

The Sidi Omar–Sollum position was a defense line which as a whole and in detail proved to be a model of how small forces might achieve great results. The presence of this line compelled an advancing enemy to swing far out into the desert, which would involve lengthy preparations in comparison with those needed if an advance along the coast had been possible. There is no doubt that the Sidi Omar–Sollum position did delay the beginning of the enemy offensive quite considerably. The Sidi Omar–Sollum position also covered the supply installations of the *Panzergruppe*, and the ground installations of the *Luftwaffe* in the area between Tobruk and Bardia, against immediate attacks by the enemy; should the enemy decide on an attack against these positions, the German armored formations in this area would have enough time to deploy for approximating a counterstroke against the outer flank of the enemy. Should the enemy and his main forces go around the positions to advance on Tobruk it was reasonable to assume that considerable forces of the enemy troops would be employed in keeping the positions down; these forces would not then be available for the main attack. In such a case the German armored formations were in a favorable position to attack the inner flank of the advancing enemy.

One question needs careful consideration: whether everything possible had been done to prevent the enemy offensive from Egypt from coming as a surprise. No doubt it was difficult to obtain reliable information regarding enemy preparations, as the enemy forces were being assembled in the area of Marsa Matruk, which was well protected and far away from the front area. During September an offensive reconnaissance operation in force was made by us; but it failed because – apart from other reasons – the enemy preparations had not been advanced far enough to be recognizable and had not yet reached the area near the front. It might have been advisable after this reconnaissance operation to do more in the way of reconnaissance and particularly in the way of covering the area south and north-east of the frontier positions than actually was done; it is also an open question whether it would not have been better to wrench from the enemy the area of Ridotta Maddalena. Perhaps the German command relied too much on wireless intelligence, which had done so brilliantly before the British June offensive started.

CHAPTER 4

Repulse of the
First British Advance on Tobruk

The immediate result of the failure of the British June offensive was a change in the high command of the British forces in the Middle East. General Wavell was replaced by General Auchinleck. The first measure of reorganization carried out by the new commander-in-chief was the formation of the *Eighth Army* from British forces in western Egypt under the command of General Sir Alan Cunningham. The commander-in-chief of the air forces was Air Marshal Sir Arthur Tedder.

General Auchinleck started preparing a new offensive against Libya on the very day on which he took over his new command. After the start of the Russian campaign the British troops which had been kept standing by in case of a German move through Asia Minor were now available for the offensive against Libya. On the other hand, the gigantic initial successes of the German troops in Russia might result in the necessity of countering a German advance through the Caucasus in the direction of the Middle East. For this reason Auchinleck regarded it as indispensable first to conquer Libya and destroy the German and Italian forces in North Africa, in particular the very excellent German *Afrika Korps*.

General Auchinleck regarded it as essential to build up a strong superiority in men and equipment, and chiefly in supplies of all kinds; he also thought it absolutely necessary to have a liberal pool of reserves of every kind to feed the battles and replace losses. In addition he regarded a considerable strengthening of the British Air Force necessary in order to assure him of British air superiority great enough to prevent Axis air forces from taking any decisive part against Allied operations.

General Auchinleck had no doubt whatever as to the length of time all these preparations would take; the Mediterranean, after all, was closed to British supplies and the British ships had to be use the route around the Cape of Good Hope, involving an enormous waste of time. All these reasons caused Auchinleck to time the offensive, planned during the summer, for the middle of November.

During summer and autumn British operations were limited to covering the deployment of British forces in western Egypt. This task had been entrusted to the *4th Indian Division*, reinforced by a brigade of the British *7th Armored Division* and by an army tank detachment. The task of these troops was to fight delaying actions in case of a German attack and to withdraw step by step to Marsa Matruk in such a way as to give the *Eighth Army* ample time to assemble its forces. The garrisons of the oasis of Siwa were strengthened by considerable forces, mobile and cleverly adapted to desert warfare. Their task it was to reconnoiter in detail German-Italian positions and reserves.

During November General Auchinleck had the following forces under his command:

> *XXX Corps* under General Norrie, consisting of the *7th Armored Division* with a strength far beyond the usual – there were 450 tanks – and the *1st South African Division.*
>
> *XIII Corps*, consisting of the *4th Indian Division* and the *2nd New Zealand Division.*
>
> *2nd South African Division* (army reserve)

In addition, there were numerous army troops, in particular several light and heavy army tank units, army artillery and army antitank units. Moreover, Auchinleck could count on the cooperation of the *70th Division* (garrison of Tobruk) with four and a half regiments, 70 heavy tanks and strong army artillery. The mobile forces operating in and around the bases of Siwa and Giarabub were organized into the *29th Motorized Division*.[1]

The first step taken by Auchinleck to secure the supply position consisted of the establishment of a supply base in the Marsa Matruk area. As from October onwards, well camouflaged supply dumps were erected farther forward in the desert, as far as the frontier and even beyond the frontier of Libya. The railway line from Alexandria to Marsa Matruk was extended almost up to the frontier of Ridotta Maddalena. All these preparations were carried on without the slightest interference from our side, and the German-Italian commands had not the slightest idea of them. There had only been one reconnaissance attempt, namely the reconnaissance in force which had taken place during September.

The strengthening of the (British) Royal Air Force had been undertaken at an early date; thus it was able to smash the above-mentioned reconnais-

---

[1] The author mistakenly expanded the *29th Indian Brigade*, an independent brigade of motorized infantry, into a fully fledged division.

sance operation in the middle of September. In cooperation with the Royal Navy, the Royal Air Force from September onwards exercised pressure, with increasing success, on the supply line of the Axis forces running through the Mediterranean.

The intention of the *Eighth Army* took as its main object the destruction of the German-Italian armored forces which were assumed to be between Bardia and Tobruk. These armored forces were to be compelled to give battle by an attack on the siege positions of Tobruk. This task was entrusted to *XXX Corps*.

The existence of the Sollum position forced the advancing British troops to make a large detour through the desert. The line of advance for *XXX Corps* was planned to run on the desert high plateau. The frontier was to be crossed to the south of Bir Sheferzen; from there the advance would lead south of the Trigh Capuzzo in a general north-westerly direction towards Tobruk. The *1st South African Division* was to protect the left flank, and on the first day was to reach El Cuasc and on the second day Bir el Gubi.

XIII Corps was to launch the secondary attack on the Sollum positions, which must be taken because in the long run it would prove too serious a threat for the rear of the attacking troops, and a continuous danger to the supply lines. To make this attack a success the *4th Indian Division* was first to keep the garrison occupied and then to attack the position, with the main effort going in on the west wing. The *2nd New Zealand Division* on the fourth day of the attack was to go round the position and to cut it off from Tobruk. The garrison of Tobruk was to support the attack of the *Eighth Army* by a sortie on the south-eastern front. The command for this sortie was to be given by the commander of *XXX Corps*.

Originally Auchinleck had intended to advance with strong forces from Giarabub through the desert to Gialo, with a view to cutting off the line of withdrawal from Cyrenaica of the German-Italian forces. However, this plan had to be abandoned as impracticable. A flying column consisting chiefly of armored reconnaissance cars was sent in the direction of Gialo under command of the *29th Motorized Division* [sic], with the task of harassing Rommel's supply lines, and, if the operations developed favorably, they were supposed to take possession of the area south of Agedabia which would also have given them possession of the connecting links between Cyrenaica and Tripoli.

Extensive measures had been taken by the British to conceal their preparations for the attack and the beginning of the attack itself. For this purpose, the last moves of the development were to be carried out in full daylight on the coast road in order to create the impression that the attack was planned to come in along the coast. All the moves on the high level of the desert were carried out by night. In order to deceive our wireless reconnaissance, all the attacking formations had been instructed to end their wireless messages as if they had been sent by the forward elements of the *4th Indian Division.*

The British Air Force had been instructed to smother the German air reconnaissance as much as possible and to oppose any movement of German-Italian troops which threatened to endanger the British deployment. In addition, operations by parachute troops had been planned to take place in the area of Gazala and Taimi. A commando operation which was to eliminate Rommel and his operational staff had been planned to take place shortly before the actual beginning of the offensive.

The strength of the *Eighth Army* at the beginning of the attack amounted to 130,000 men and 755 tanks. This was a force considerably superior to Rommel's, assumed to be 83,000 men and a total of 440 tanks (actually no more than 250–300). Superiority of other British war material, particularly artillery, antitank weapons and armored reconnaissance cars, was even more staggering.

The beginning of the attack was finally timed for the night of 17/18 November. Before 17 November the attacking formations were being moved up, close to the frontier. During the night of 17/18 November the *Eighth Army* crossed the Libyan frontier: the attack had begun.

The Beginning of the British Attack (16–20 November)

The report on the enemy situation of 11 November 1941 by *Panzergruppe Afrika* gives a clear appreciation of the enemy as held by the *Panzergruppe.* According to this it would appear that the British preparations for the attack, the extension of the railway line to the border, and the establishment of supply dumps in the frontier area had escaped the attention of the Axis forces. The *Panzergruppe,* rather, regarded the enemy situation as unchanged since the middle of October. On the other hand, the enemy strength had been fairly accurately gauged. The *4th Indian Division,* a tank brigade, and further army troops had been identified in the frontier area; the intensified enemy reconnaissance activity in the Ridotta Maddalena area had been noted, and so had the presence of an enemy brigade with two reconnaissance units in the area of the cases. In the area of Marsa Matruk–El Daba the presence of the *7th Armored Division* had been suspected; two further motorized divisions were also assumed to be in that area.

Regarding the possibility of enemy operations, our report on the enemy situation had very little say about anything save the probable reaction of the British when the Germans and the Italians should attack Tobruk. The *Panzergruppe* assumed that the enemy would be unable to do anything against our attack with these forces in position on the Sollum front; he would not even be able to interfere by mounting a diversionary attack against the Sollum front. The *Panzergruppe* assumed that on the first day of our attack the British disposition of troops would still be unchanged; it also assumed that the British would take two days to bring their formations in position around and east of Marsa Matruk, forward to the frontier south of the Sollum front. Thus, according to the appreciation of the *Panzergruppe*, the British would not start their decisive offensive until the third day after our attack on Tobruk. Again according to the *Panzergruppe*, this enemy offensive would not be directed against the Sollum front but would go round it and would aim directly against Tobruk.

The possibility that the British would start a large-scale offensive, whether we attacked Tobruk or not, was only mentioned *en passant*, but at the same time it was stressed that this would not change anything.

Evidently the *Panzergruppe* assumed that air reconnaissance and wireless reconnaissance would give timely notice of the start of any offensive the British might launch.

Events during 16–18 November

During the days following, the *Panzergruppe* did not change its appreciation of the enemy situation. It is not quite clear whether the *Panzergruppe* knew that from 9 November onwards motor traffic with lights full on had been observed nightly south-west of Sidi Omar by the men occupying the strongpoints of the Sollum front.

During the evening of 15 November the German-Italian troops started deploying for the attack on Tobruk. Parts of the artillery of the *15th Panzer Division* took up their positions in the sector south-east of the fortress from which the attack was to be launched. Simultaneously, the *21st Panzer Division* left its rest area at the coast north-west of Bardia and moved into its assembly area around Gasr el Arid to the south of the Trigh Capuzzo. It received orders to attack enemy forces which might advance into the rear of the sector whence the Tobruk attack was to be launched, and to prevent these enemy troops from interfering with the Tobruk operation. *Reconnaissance Battalion 3* and *Reconnaissance Unit 33*, both until then under direct command of the *Panzergruppe*, passed under command of the *21st Panzer Division*. The latter formed them into *Reconnaissance Group Wechmar*, which was ordered to reconnoiter eastward across the border into Egypt, and southward across the Trigh el Abd, to determine whether enemy forces were advancing from there. *Reconnaissance Battalion 33* was sent into the area of Er Regham (30 kilometers east of Bir el Gubi), and *Reconnaissance Battalion 3* into the area of Bir Uesshet Refa (15 kilometers to the west of Sidi Omar).

As early as 16 November both reconnaissance units reported strong British reconnaissance forces crossing the frontier on both sides of Ridotta Maddalena and advancing westward. Our own armored reconnaissance cars at the border were forced to give way. On the very same day the men on the Sollum front observed repeated explosions of mines in the wire fence and to the south of Gasr el Arid. On the basis of this information the *21st Panzer Division* strengthened *Reconnaissance Group Wechmar* with one antitank (*Panzerjäger*) company. During the night of 15/16 November remarkably strong attacks took place in the area west of Bardia, evidently aiming at harassing the moves of the *21st Panzer Division*.

During 17 November strong British armored reconnaissance compelled the patrols of *Reconnaissance Group Wechmar* to pull back in a northerly direction towards Sidi Omar and across the Trigh el Abd. Enemy air reconnaissance covering the area of the *21st Panzer Division* and of the two reconnaissance battalions became conspicuously active.

During the evening a large-scale commando operation took place against the battle headquarters of the *Panzergruppe* at Beda Littoria; only the fact that General Rommel and his operational staff happened to be away saved them from destruction.

On 18 November the enemy situation changed radically. In the area forward of *Reconnaissance Battalion 33*, strong British armored forces advanced along the Trigh el Abd to Er Reghem about noon and thence to the north-west. During the afternoon *Reconnaissance Battalion 33* was attacked by enemy tanks and made a fighting withdrawal five kilometers to the north-east.

Also towards noon *Reconnaissance Battalion 3* was compelled to withdraw seven kilometers to the north to avoid envelopment by strong British reconnaissance forces supported by tanks and artillery. As from 1500 hours the detachment reported considerable British armored forces on its front.

Towards 1700 hours the detachment withdrew in the force of pressure exercised allegedly by 200 enemy vehicles with numerous tanks amongst them. This withdrawal brought the detachment a further 5 kilometers to the north-north-west. The reconnaissance patrols of the two reconnaissance units trying to push to the south and south-west were unable to penetrate a dense security screen which the enemy had thrown out along the Trigh el Abd.

From first light, British infantry in front of the west wing of the Sollum line moved up close to the German-Italian positions. Intensive reconnaissance of our positions and minefields to the south and west of Sidi Omar was carried out by the British. Enemy artillery started rangefinding on our positions. All these factors were now regarded as preparation for an attack. British reconnaissance activity also grew more intense on the east sector of the Sollum position, near the Halfaya Pass.

This news did not arrive at the *Afrika Korps* (battle headquarters Bardia) until 1750 hours. Simultaneously with this report the *21st Panzer Division* suggested pushing an armored battle group into the area north of Gabr Saleh with a view to making a flank attack against the enemy opposing *Reconnaissance Unit 33*; this flank attack could be launched on 19 November at first light.

The corps commander of the *Afrika Korps*, General Crüwell, had been repeatedly told by *Panzergruppe Afrika* that neither air reconnaissance nor wireless reconnaissance showed any indication of enemy deployment at the frontier for an attack. For this reason Crüwell regarded those enemy moves as a large-scale reconnaissance operation with the object of harassing the German-Italian preparations for the attack on Tobruk. He did, however, agree that this enemy advance might eventually lead to larger operations. He instructed the *15th Panzer Division*, which was disposed at the coast on both sides of Marsa Belafarid, to prepare to move, and he also approved of the proposal of *21st Panzer Division* to move *Panzer Regiment 5* into the area of Gabr Saleh.

At 1900 hours *Panzergruppe Afrika* was informed by telephone on the occurrences of the day and the intentions of the *Afrika Korps*. It would appear that neither air nor wireless reconnaissance achieved any noteworthy results on this day. Whether air and wireless reconnaissance were so directed to be able to clarify the disquieting reports from the frontier area on the previous days is, however, a question which is difficult to answer.

In a personal discussion with General Crüwell at 2000 hours, General Rommel voiced the opinion that the enemy's advance involved nothing

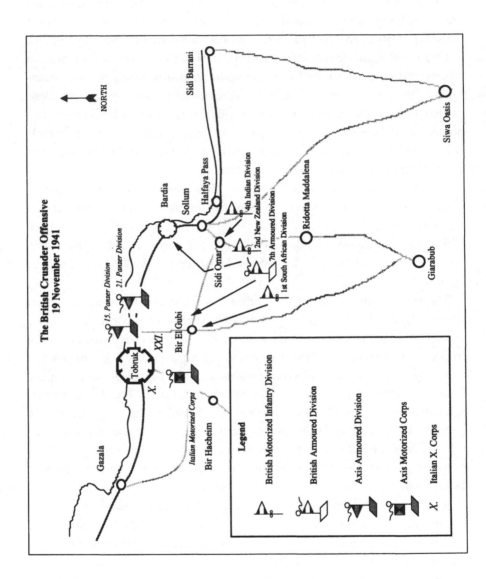

The British Crusader Offensive
19 November 1941

Legend

British Motorized Infantry Division

British Armoured Division

Axis Armoured Division

Axis Motorized Corps

X.   Italian X. Corps

more than negligible harassing operations. There was no need to lose one's nerve, and he forbade the movement of large portions of the *21st Panzer Division* forward into the Gabr Saleh area lest it should reveal our intentions to the enemy too soon.

As far as the then operations officer (Ia) of *Panzergruppe Afrika* remembers, the suggestion to move the entire *21st Panzer Division* to Gabr Saleh was not brought to the notice of the *Panzergruppe*. The version given above is based on the War Diary of the *Afrika Korps*. General Rommel also regarded it as unnecessary to alert the *15th Panzer Division*; the *Afrika Korps*, however, did not cancel their alert.

The Beginning of the Battle on 19 November

During the night of 18/19 November the depositions of a British prisoner of war revealed Auchinleck's complete offensive plan. This prisoner of war, who belonged to the *4th Indian Division* and had been captured in the sector of the *Italian Infantry Division Savona*, said that not only elements of the *4th Indian Division* but the entire *7th Armored Division* were already attacking west of the frontier, and that early in the morning of 19 November the artillery of the *4th Indian Division* would open fire on Sidi Omar. Two South African divisions were moving from Marsa Matruk across the frontier. The *Afrika Korps* received the prisoner's deposition towards 2300 hours and passed it on by telephone to the *Panzergruppe* without delay; the latter however, regarded it as incredible and stamped it as a deliberate attempt of the enemy to deceive. A further interrogation of this prisoner at the *Afrika Korps* on 19 November produced fresh information.

Simultaneously, on 19 November the situation developed very dangerously. Early in the morning *Reconnaissance Battalion 33* became involved in violent fighting with 20 enemy tanks; they made a fighting withdrawal to the north-west. Towards noon the unit reported that a reinforced British armored division was moving north-east against Tobruk, covering its flank against interference from the north-east.

The enemy in front of *Reconnaissance Battalion 3* was also pushing northward with about 100 vehicles, most of them light mobile tanks, self-propelled guns, and ground reconnaissance cars. The unit was compelled to pull out rapidly, and at noon it crossed the Trigh Capuzzo west of Sidi Azeiz on its way to the north. On the Sollum front the British forked their way from south and west to the strongpoints of Sidi Omar and Frongia, with their artillery laying down bursts of fire on the strongpoint of Sidi Omar.

With all these reports available, the *Afrika Korps* began to think that what the prisoner of war had said regarding the beginning of the British offensive might after all be true; but the *Afrika Korps* hesitated to send the *21st Panzer Division* forward to counterattack without Rommel's permission. The *Panzergruppe*, however, still stuck to its decision to attack Tobruk in spite of this development, and still believed that the enemy on this side of the frontier wanted nothing more than to harass our deployment.

At 1145 hours Rommel eventually gave permission to the *Afrika Korps* to alert the *15th Panzer Division* and to move it into its concentration area south of the Trigh Capuzzo and west of the *21st Panzer Division.* However, those parts of the divisional artillery which had already moved into the area of Tobruk where the attack was to be made were not returned to the division. The *21st Panzer Division* was now instructed to attack with its armored battle group towards Gabr Saleh in order to destroy the enemy group in front of *Reconnaissance Unit 3*. General Rommel, and his staff no less, still regarded what the prisoner had said as incorrect, or at least greatly exaggerated.

It was not until the afternoon of 19 November that the optimistic appreciation of the situation could no longer be maintained: towards 1700 hours an air report arrived at *Panzergruppe* headquarters to the effect that three long enemy motorized columns with armor – beginning and tail not visible – were moving north and between Giarabub and Bir el Gubi (these troops were the reinforced *1st South African Division* with a brigade of the *7th Armored Division* which had arrived at El Cuasc on the evening of 18 November and which on 19 November were moving from El Cuasc to the north towards Bir el Gubi). At virtually the same moment another message from another pilot arrived reporting several hundred armored reconnaissance cars advancing from Giarabub through the desert on Gialo.

It was probably only then that Rommel realized the extent of the enemy offensive. The idea of attending Tobruk was not abandoned, but the attack was postponed until the conclusion of the battle which was about to start. Rommel now realized that the British *Eighth Army* was seeking a decision. He assumed that the aim of the British offensive was the relief of Tobruk. However, this change in the appreciation of the situation was not expressed in new orders.

The afternoon of 19 November brought the first heavy fighting for the German-Italian troops. On the eastern and south-eastern sector of Tobruk the garrison launched reconnaissance sorties against the positions of the *Infantry Division Bologna* This division showed little power of resistance.

Several strongpoints were lost; in several places infantry and artillery streamed back in disorder. Local reserves finally succeeded in restoring the situation.

Armored Division Ariete of *XX Motorized Corps* had settled down in defensive positions around Bir el Gubi fronting south and east; the division was not under the command of the *Panzergruppe*. During the late afternoon, simultaneously with the arrival of the above-mentioned air message, the division was attacked by motorized infantry and approximately 60 tanks. As the positions of *Ariete* had been well prepared, all enemy attacks were repulsed during the afternoon and evening. From prisoners of war elements of the *1st South African Division* and *7th Armored Division* were identified as fighting against *Ariete*.

Reconnaissance Battalion 33 was again involved in heavy fighting with enemy armor during the afternoon and suffered heavy losses in vehicles. The unit again identified enemy armored columns moving along the Trigh el Abd in a north-westerly direction towards Tobruk.

The *21st Panzer Division* formed *Group Stephan* from *Panzer Regiment 5* with approximately 110 medium tanks, *II./Artillery Regiment 115* and *3./Flak Regiment 18*. This battle group began to advance southward from the divisional area at 1430 hours. It met British armor of about equal strength north of Gabr Saleh; gradually the heavier German tanks gained the upper hand and the enemy was pressed back across the Trigh el Abd to the south. Twenty-five enemy tanks were knocked out, but no decisive success was gained. When night fell the battle group took up a hedgehog position to the north-west of Gabr Saleh; the group was very short of ammunition. (The opponent which had fought *Group Stephan* was an armored brigade of the *7th Armored Division* which had been left at Gabr Saleh as guard to the flank.) The rest of the division, organized into *Group Knabe*, had remained in the concentration area south of the Trigh Capuzzo. During the evening lesser enemy formations were identified to the east of the division.

After nightfall the *21st Panzer Division* suggested to the *Afrika Korps* that *Group Stephan* be instructed to discontinue its attack as the enemy was far superior and the general situation was not clarified. The *21st Panzer Division* requested that the *15th Panzer Division* should be placed under its operational control.

During the afternoon *Reconnaissance Unit 3*, stating that it was hard pressed by the enemy, withdrew across the high ridge south of the Via Balbia and 20 kilometers to the west of Bardia and there took up hedgehog positions. The enemy pulled off in a south-easterly direction (the enemy apparently consisted of a reconnaissance unit reinforced by the light army tank unit of the *4th Indian Division*). Also during the afternoon the *15th Panzer Division* left its old area in four columns and advanced southward, crossing the Via Balbia into its new assembly area to the south of the Trigh Capuzzo; by 2100 hours the last units of the division had moved into the new area. During the move the troops were attacked by enemy bombers, but no noteworthy casualties were suffered. *Reconnaissance Battalion 33* reverted to command.

Decisions Taken on 19 November

During the evening of 19 November *Panzergruppe Afrika*, deeply impressed by the revolutionary change in the situation, was unable to come to a decision. Thus, for the time being, the initiative rested with the *Afrika Korps*. At that time the *Afrika Korps* was not yet quite clear whether the British had really started a large-scale offensive or whether this was only an attack launched with the intention of anticipating the German-Italian attack on Tobruk. The *Afrika Korps* believed that it had identified three further enemy groups apart from the one advancing on Bir el Gubi. They were:

(a) The enemy armor opposing *Reconnaissance Battalion 33* and moving on Tobruk.
(b) The enemy group against which *Group Stephan* was operating.
(c) The enemy group opposing *Reconnaissance Unit 3*.

General Crüwell, seeing that the enemy forces were considerably split up, and realizing their great strength as a whole, thought it advisable to attack the enemy groups in sequence and destroy them. This intention was submitted to the *Panzergruppe* for approval and it was requested that the *Afrika Korps* be allowed a free hand in the execution of this intention.

Late that evening the *Panzergruppe* wrestled through to the conclusion that it was very necessary first to beat the enemy who had penetrated into the area between Sidi Omar and Tobruk, before settling with the enemy advancing on Bir el Gubi. At 2150 hours they issued this instruction, which followed the wording of the *Afrika Korps*, for execution on 20 November:

> The *Afrika Korps* will attack and destroy the enemy who has broken into the area Bardia–Sidi Omar–Gabr Saleh–Gambut. Having done this, the *Afrika Korps* will stand by to attack south and south-west. *XX Motorized Corps* [the *Italian Motorized Corps*] will remain at Bir el Gubi and Bir Hacheim.

Thereupon the *Afrika Korps* decided to attack and defeat first the British group believed to be in front of *Reconnaissance Battalion 3*, because this group had penetrated farthest to the north and was therefore the most dangerous. The *Afrika Korps* issued the following orders:

The *21st Panzer Division* will advance to the east before first light, concentrate all forces in the direction of the area north of Sidi Omar, cut off the enemy's line of withdrawal to the south and destroy him.

The *15th Panzer Division* will advance at 0700 hours along the Trigh Capuzzo in the direction of Capuzzo.

Reconnaissance Battalion 33 will continue patrolling in the present area and reconnoitering as far as the Trigh el Abd.

Headquarters *Afrika Korps* will advance behind the *21st Panzer Division*.

General Rommel did not approve of this intention but in the end agreed after it had been urgently requested by the *Afrika Korps*.

The Failure on 20 November

In the morning of 20 November the *Afrika Korps* started its advance to the east. *Group Stephan* had spent the night at Gabr Saleh and had remained in contact with the enemy armor which had been pressed back the morning before, but remained immediately south and south-west of the group. At daybreak fighting flared up again. *Group Stephan* broke away from the enemy and moved off in an east-north-easterly direction towards the area of Sidi Omar. North-west of Sidi Omar minor enemy armored forces – probably the enemy encountered by *Reconnaissance Battalion 3* during 19 November – withdrew to the south after only light resistance. However, the enemy armor at Gabr Saleh did not follow suit.

During the morning the remainder of the *21st Panzer Division – Group Knabe* – identified some 30 enemy tanks in its area at Gabr Monfia. For this reason Knabe discontinued his attack and requested the *Afrika Korps* to instruct the *15th Panzer Division*, which was advancing to his north, to take a hand. The *Afrika Korps* issued the necessary orders. Shortly afterwards, however, General Crüwell personally ascertained that the enemy in front of *Group Knabe* consisted of minor reconnaissance forces with only a few tanks. Crüwell then got the attack going. The *21st Panzer Division* then concentrated in the area of Gabr Lachem. However, *Panzer Regiment 5* was still virtually without fuel and without ammunition; thus the division was practically immobilized. Fuel and tank ammunition were called for, to be sent in by air.

The *15th Panzer Division* moved at 0700 hours in plain formation, with the reinforced *Panzer Regiment 8* forward and two more battle groups behind, eastward along the Trigh Capuzzo. At 0930 hours Sidi Azeiz was reached in a steady advance. The few enemy armored reconnaissance cars which were met withdrew without delay. Apart from these nothing had been seen during the whole advance to Capuzzo, nor, incidentally, of *Reconnaissance Unit 3*. The latter, misinterpreting its orders, had spent the morning replenishing and remained on the Via Balbia west of Bardia without maintaining contact with the enemy. It was not until noon, on orders from the *21st Panzer Division*, that *Reconnaissance Battalion 3* resumed its advance to Sidi Azeiz.

With the enemy situation as it was and *Group Knabe* crying for help, the *15th Panzer Division* regarded its task – the advance to Capuzzo – as obsolete. At 1030 hours the *15th Panzer Division* turned off to the south-west in order to come to the assistance of the *21st Panzer Division* in the area of north of Sidi Omar. Contact was established between the two divisions at Gabr Lachem. Meanwhile, the enemy thus far in front of the *21st Panzer Division* had already withdrawn to the south before the threat of *Group Stephan*. At noon the *15th Panzer Division* settled down at Gabr Lachem for a rest, to refuel, and to replenish its ammunition.

The corps commander of the *Afrika Korps* realized before noon that the advance to the east behind the Sollum front should be discarded. In the meantime he had gained a clearer picture of the enemy: the *4th Indian Division* was obviously attacking the Sollum front at Sidi Omar. The main thrust of the enemy attack was clearly along the Trigh el Abd, where the bulk of British *7th Armored Division* was advancing on Tobruk. Reports from *Reconnaissance Battalion 33* indicated that further enemy forces were being moved in the same direction. There is still a strong group of enemy armor at Gabr Saleh, probably charged with covering the flank of the advance on Tobruk.

There was no time to be lost: it was imperative to attack the most dangerous of the enemy groups, which was now immediately threatening the rear of the line of investment of Tobruk. The *Afrika Korps* was in a favorable position for its compact force to thrust against this enemy from the east and destroy him. It had been too late to do this on 19 November as the *21st Panzer Division* was still immobilized on account of supply difficulties, and it was not yet possible to say when the division would again be ready for operations.

At 1430 hours General Crüwell decided to send the *15th Panzer Division* unsupported to Gabr Saleh with a view to defeating the enemy armored group in this area, blocking the Trigh el Abd to enemy supplies, and thus assuring a rapid result which might influence the battle for Tobruk.

The *15th Panzer Division* at 1500 hours moved off to attack to the south-east. As the advance would take it right into the middle of the enemy, the division adopted plain formation, echeloned far out to the right and left. *Panzer Regiment 5*, with the antiaircraft detachment and the bulk of the artillery, traveled in the van; the *15th Schützen Brigade* followed to the right and rear; *Regiment 200*, which had not yet come up, was to follow as the third battle group to the left and rear of the division.

At 1630 hours, ten kilometers north-east of Gabr Saleh, the division met strong enemy armored forces (about 80 tanks with artillery and much antitank equipment) evidently prepared for defence; violent fighting ensued and slowly the enemy was pressed back to the south-east. When night fell the foremost elements of the division had reached the Trigh el Abd. Very soon after, further enemy tank forces began operating against the west flank and a little later also against the south-east flank of the *15th Panzer Division*. However, the *15th Schützen Brigade* succeeded in warding off these enemy advances. After nightfall the enemy withdrew a few kilometers and settled down in a semi-circular position around the division. In the meantime it had become pitch dark and the *15th Panzer Division* could not continue to advance. Some 10 enemy tanks had been knocked out and a number of prisoners collected. On one of the tanks was captured an order with map attached which provided valuable information regarding the lines of advance and supply installations of the British *Eighth Army*.

On 20 November the nerves of the command of *Panzergruppe Afrika* had to undergo a severe strain. From very early morning it became clear that the investment of Tobruk was in immediate danger. Simultaneously, breakout attempts by the garrison of Tobruk were to be executed; on 19 November the garrison had already become much livelier.

Luckily two regiments of the *Division z.b.v. Afrika* had already been withdrawn from the front and were now standing by to take part in the assault on Tobruk. The greater part of the two regiments – *Infantry Regiment 361 (Afrika)* and *Infantry Regiment 155 (Regiment Mickl)* – were moved south-east to the escarpment on both sides of Sidi Rezegh the night of 19/20 November, to protect the line of investment. The important height of Belhamed was occupied by troops which were placed under command of General [Karl] Böttcher, the artillery commander of the *Panzergruppe*, who had his battle headquarters in this area and was put in charge of these defensive operations.

From early morning onward *Armored Division Ariete*, in the Bir el Gubi area, had been busy holding off further, though weaker, attacks of the *1st South African Division*. They held their positions but were unable to prevent the British from moving further units northward, to the east of them, past *Ariete*'s position in the wake of the *7th Armored Division*, which was moving on Tobruk.

During the morning of 20 November one armored and one rifle brigade of the *7th Armored Division* attacked the positions of the two infantry regiments on the southern high ridge. In spite of very stubborn resistance, the *Afrika Regiment*, which had very few heavy weapons, lost the escarpment at Sidi Rezegh. In order to counter an enemy enveloping movement from the east against the *Afrika Regiment*, the *Panzergruppe* brought *Reconnaissance Battalion 3* to Gambut as army reserve, and in the evening of 20 November ordered the unit to take up position on the left wing of the *Afrika Regiment*.

Faced by this situation, the *Panzergruppe* waited and hoped for news of the rapid success of the counterattack by the *Afrika Korps*, which alone could bring about a favorable change in the situation in front of Tobruk. But by midday nothing more was forthcoming than a message intercepted from the *21st Panzer Division* which reported that it had become immobilized by lack of fuel and ammunition and wished supplies to be flown in. The *Panzergruppe* had no transport planes; it assumed that the *Afrika Korps* had enough supplies to help the *21st Panzer Division*. For this reason it did not see its way clear to lend rapid assistance. Should, however, supply routes east of Tobruk be cut in the course of the battle, fuel and ammunition for the *Afrika Korps* was to be sent to Bardia by sea – a step which proved very useful indeed at a later stage. Later in the afternoon the *Panzergruppe* obtained a clearer picture of the situation at the *Afrika Korps* It became evident that the *Afrika Korps* had not been able to stage a coordinated attack, and that, whatever the reason, no decisive success had been gained.

During the afternoon General Rommel had decided to use the *Afrika Korps* on 21 November, to ease the Tobruk situation. At 1830 hours, therefore, he discussed and approved of General Crüwell's plans for the *Afrika Korps* for 21 November. Crüwell wished to attack with both divisions north-east towards Tobruk, to take the enemy in the rear and destroy him.

At 1845 hours the *Afrika Korps* issued the two divisions with the morning order for 21 November. At 2215 hours the *Afrika Korps* issued the following order by wireless:

The *15th Panzer Division* will break contact with the enemy during the night. At 0630 hours the *Afrika Korps* with the *21st Panzer Division* on the right and the *15th Panzer Division* on the left will cross the track Sidi Azeiz–Gabr Saleh and advance outside the line Maddalena–Belhamed to attack and destroy the enemy force which has advanced on Tobruk. The *15th Panzer Division* will leave behind a battle group with antitank equipment, engineers and artillery to act as rearguard. Headquarters *Afrika Korps* will move to Bir Bu Meliha at 0630 hours.

It must be stated as a fact that the British command succeeded in springing on Rommel not only an operational but also a tactical surprise. Fully 48 hours elapsed before Rommel realized the extent and aim of the enemy offensive. Valuable time was lost which could have been used for coordinated defensive preparation and employment of the reserves.

That the enemy had been able to surprise Rommel may be due to the fact that Rommel apparently relied blindly on air reconnaissance and wireless reconnaissance to provide once again an early warning of large-scale enemy movements. Indeed, it is surprising (and not very difficult to investigate how it was possible) that our air reconnaissance did not observe the extensive storing of cases of supplies for the offensive, the building up of huge supply dumps on the frontier and even on our side of the frontier, and the extension of the British supply railway line up to the very forward line. Even the large-scale enemy deployment seems to have remained completely unnoticed. The reason probably is that frequent sandstorms hampered air reconnaissance during the whole of November; and cloudbursts and torrential rains soaked all airfields on 17 November to such an extent that they remained useless for a number of days.

The German wireless reconnaissance evidently fell victim to the clever deceptive measures of the British signalers. Our ground reconnaissance may have failed in some cases or it may have brought in inaccurate information as, for instance, did *Reconnaissance Battalion 3*. On the other hand, there were so many informative messages available before the attack started, particularly the very explicit and perfectly correct reconnaissance results of *Reconnaissance Battalion 3*, that it should have been possible to see, not later than 18 November, that an enemy offensive was being prepared and was about to start.

One cannot avoid the impression that General Rommel was under the spell of a fixed idea. For months he had been preparing an attack on Tobruk. This was the time for this attack to get under way. Rommel was convinced that the enemy would not start an offensive until our air forces were occupied by the attack on Tobruk. But for precisely that reason it is difficult to understand why on 18 and 19 November Rommel was under the impression that the enemy advance aimed at harassing or preventing the attack on Tobruk. Surely, after months of preparation, the British were strong enough to strike when it pleased them, and there was no need, nor did they wish, to prevent the attack on Tobruk.

There is no known reason why, on 18 November, the *Panzergruppe* did not obtain certainty regarding the intentions of the enemy by a reconnaissance push in force made by strong units, for instance the *21st Panzer Division*. This would have been the only way to break through the enemy covering forces. Had a push like that been made, it would have been wrong to allot a definite task to the division, such as, for instance, the destruction of the enemy, because this would mean that the division might suffer a defeat at the hands of superior enemy forces. Rommel refused to consider such a reconnaissance push since he feared that it might disclose his troop dispositions to the enemy. Yet, it must be assumed that the enemy had learnt all he wanted to know regarding the disposition of the German forces from his most active air reconnaissance.

It is equally difficult to understand why the *15th Panzer Division* had not been moved into its concentration area by 18 November, for the *Afrika Korps* would then have been able to make a concentrated effort by 19 November. Had it then been found that the enemy operation was no more than an attempt to harass our operations, it would still have been possible for the *15th Panzer Division* to join in the attack on Tobruk without loss of time.

To have the armored battle group of the *21st Panzer Division* operating in the direction of Gabr Saleh during the afternoon of 19 November, under orders to fulfil certain tasks, was a dangerous gamble. The battle group did not possess the necessary means of protecting its flank and rear. It would have been better to have used the entire division for this operation. It was a lucky coincidence that the British had also split up their forces, with the result that *Group Stephan* encountered enemy forces of approximately equal strength.

Yet, in the evening of 19 November the situation was still favorable enough, and if the *Afrika Korps* had been ordered to operate on 20 November with all its available formations in the most effective direction, all would have been well. The *Afrika Korps* was actually placed on the flank of the enemy group advancing on Tobruk. It had only to smash the flank cover which the British had built up against it, cut the enemy communications, and then advance into his rear. It is true that it would have been of great importance to direct the *Afrika Korps* into the rear of the main forces of the enemy and to give the latter no chance to strike into the flank of the *Afrika Korps* in his turn.

Considering the great importance which must be attached to any operation of the *Afrika Korps* as the one and only really strong reserve of the *Panzergruppe*, it is surprising that Rommel on 20 November actually allowed the corps a free hand in choosing the enemy group against which it would like to turn. The *Afrika Korps* had no air reconnaissance of its own, so that it was not easy for General Crüwell to get a clear picture of the actual situation and to choose the point where an attack would be most offensive. As a matter of fact, the *Afrika Korps* was quite in the dark and its actions were guided by chance.

It is the opinion of the then operations officer (Ia) of *Panzergruppe* that during the early days of the British offensive the command of the *Panzergruppe* and the command of the *Afrika Korps* did not play sufficiently well into each other's hands. The command of the *Afrika Korps* was involved in a desert operation for the first time and had still to gather experience. Its decision on 20 November resulted in a thrust into thin air. It is understandable that the *Afrika Korps* should wish first to eliminate the enemy group opposing *Reconnaissance Battalion 3*, as it had no desire to be attacked in the rear later when advancing against Tobruk. It was just bad luck that the reconnaissance reports of *Reconnaissance Battalion 3* covering this area were either exaggerated or incorrect.

For these reasons the concentrated force of the *Afrika Korps* was not employed on 20 November, and that the situation on the Tobruk front was not eased, as the *Panzergruppe* had hoped. The advance of the *15th Panzer Division* during the evening brought no relief. The day was too far advanced and the division alone was too weak, because the enemy forces at Gabr Saleh had had grown to the strength of the armored brigades, which each equaled the strength of a German *Panzer* division.

During the fighting on the southern front of Tobruk, Rommel proved himself once again a master in the overcoming of crises. The fact that the regiments of *Division z.b.v. Afrika* had been sent to the high ground on either side of Sidi Rezegh and to Belhamed respectively prevented the collapse of the siege front during the night of 20/21 November; and this is the personal success of Rommel and of nobody else.

21 November

During the night of 20/21 November Rommel fully realized the seriousness of his position. In the course of the evening he had received the news of the loss of the oasis of Gialo. He reckoned that the lines of communication between Cyrenaica and Tripoli would be cut. Forces to stem this thrust there were none. He sent the few fighting units of the *Luftwaffe* which were serviceable against the enemy groups at Gialo. In addition, some Italian units were scraped together, the ground installations of the *Luftwaffe* were combed for men, and under the command of Major-General Osterkamp of *Luftgau Staff Afrika* an improvised defense position was erected at the Wadi el Faregh, 40 kilometers to the south of Agedabia. However, to the surprise of the German-Italian High Command, the British forces at Gialo contented themselves with reconnaissance thrusts along the track Gialo–Agedabia and patrols in the direction of the Via Balbia on both sides of El Agheila.

The German High Command saw itself faced by a large-scale British offensive, undertaken by superior forces and aiming at widely distributed objectives; on the German side, the forces were insufficient to counter this offensive effectively. The German Command was afraid that the available forces would not be enough to defeat the enemy in the field and at the same time to continue the investment of Tobruk.

The German Command realized that, without local German support, the Italian troops were in the long run no match for the enemy. The superiority of the British air force was such that *X. Fliegerkorps* found it impossible to carry on. In addition, the supply position caused serious anxiety, since not a single German supply ship had arrived in Africa after 18 October.

Rommel expected a further deterioration of the supply position as a consequence of the British advance to Gialo; he realized that it was of the utmost importance to inflict a rapid and crushing defeat on the British forces advancing on Tobruk, before grave strains appeared in the supply position. November 21 would be the decisive day. Hence the investment of Tobruk must be maintained until the diversionary attack of the *Afrika Korps* could become effective.

The situation became even more critical when, soon after first light, the garrison of Tobruk launched a large-scale breakout in the sector of the Italian *XXI Corps* on the south-east front. The enemy regiments, supported by 90 heavy tanks, attacked the Italian positions between Bir es Suesi and Bir bu Assatan and succeeded in penetrating the Italian positions in several places. The British broke through the Italian positions and advanced as far as El Duda.

A grave crisis developed, all the more serious since the artillery had suffered heavily during the fighting of 19 November. Rommel scraped together all the reserves of the *Division z.b.v. Afrika*, army artillery, antiaircraft artillery and all the signals people he could lay hands on and ordered *Reconnaissance Battalion 3* to move up by forced marches. At the head of these troops he halted the enemy by midday and finally, in bitter, costly fighting, threw the garrison of Tobruk back to its starting point. None of the British tanks broke through, and they were destroyed in the artillery positions on Belhamed.

The South African attacks on *Armored Division Ariete* around Bir el Gubi were weaker on 21 November. The British moved further forces thence towards Sidi Rezegh.

The Diversionary Attack of the *Afrika Korps*

On 21 November the *Afrika Korps* operated for the first time as an entity. The *21st Panzer Division* at length finished replenishing during the first half of the night, and by 0630 hours moved into the area abreast of the *15th Panzer Division*. Thence, with *Panzer Regiment 5* leading, the division advanced rapidly to the north-west. Towards 0900 hours, the division first encountered minor enemy armored forces to the south of Sciafsciuf, which were thrown back to the west after a short but fierce battle. The division continued to advance towards the high ground sloping towards the Trigh Capuzzo, bringing *Schützen Regiment 104* into action on the right of *Panzer Regiment 5*. By noon the high ground on both sides of Height 175 was in our hands.

The *15th Panzer Division*, which had been in continuous contact with the enemy on three sides throughout the night, found it no easy matter to get into position for an attack to the north-west. The enemy, who outnumbered it two to one, were deceived during the night by reconnaissance patrols, and the division was able to move unnoticed 9 kilometers to the north-east. Thus, at 0630 hours, the *15th Panzer Division* began its advance to the north-west, according to plan, *Panzer Regiment 8* leading in two columns with the bulk of the artillery and antiaircraft artillery. The *15th Schützen Brigade* followed as the second battle group and *Regiment 200* formed the rearguard which was to secure to advance of the division.

At first, the advance progressed rapidly. Only British reconnaissance forces followed the advance south of the divisional sector. At Abiar on Ebeidat the division encountered British motorized columns advancing northward from the south. (They were evidently part of the *1st South African Division* moving up from Bir el Gubi.) These columns were dispersed after a brief action. Advancing farther towards Sidi Rezegh, *Panzer Regiment 8* became involved in fighting with about 100 enemy tanks. The attack of *Panzer Regiment 8* did not go well in the beginning. After replenishing ammunition and fuel, *Panzer Regiment 8* resumed the attack and this time succeeded in throwing back the enemy armor. However, enemy infantry, well dug in on the high ground on both sides of Sidi Rezegh, offered stubborn resistance, which was broken in the early afternoon with the help of *Motorcycle Battalion 15*; several hundred prisoners were taken.

The disappearance of the *15th Panzer Division* did not long escape the notice of the enemy armored forces at Gabr Saleh. Soon they began to move northward and attacked the flanks of the *15th Schützen Brigade* and *Regiment 200*, which were the rear battle groups of the *15th Panzer Division*. During these battles enemy tanks penetrated far to the north into the sector of the *21st Panzer Division*. *Regiment 200*, which was the rearguard, was for some time in a very difficult position and lost motor vehicles. By the use of every antitank weapon, the attacks were in the end beaten off. During the action the heavy antiaircraft guns of corps headquarters (which followed behind the middle line of the advance) alone knocked out seven tanks. By noon all the battle groups of the *15th Panzer Division* had succeeded in fighting their way forward and had closed up on *Panzer Regiment 8*.

In the area south-east of Sidi Rezegh, a growing threat to the south flank could be detected towards noon. Very soon the *15th Schützen Brigade* with the bulk of *Antitank Battalion 33* had to be moved south on a broad front to cover the flank. Towards evening the weight of the enemy attack increased. All three armored brigades of the *7th Armored Division*, with well over 200 tanks, were now in action. The thrust of one armored brigade into the gap between *Motorcycle Battalion 15* and the *15th Schützen Brigade* could only be repelled by throwing in *Panzer Regiment 8*. Towards the evening an enemy armored brigade thrust unexpectedly from the south-east, from what had been the sector of the *21st Panzer Division*, into the rear of the division. An armored break-in could only be checked as it reached the headquarters of the *Afrika Korps*. By nightfall, however, a defensive line had been formed to the south-east through the intervention of *Engineer Battalion 33*.

The situation in front of Tobruk had become considerably easier towards noon, thanks to the attack of the *Afrika Korps* The enemy, advancing from the south towards Belhamed, had discontinued his attack, but was still holding positions on the southern and eastern slopes of the mountain. Thus, a truly peculiar situation had arisen. Not only did the German-Italian forces occupying the line of investment find themselves between two fires, but the

British forces on Belhamed were threatened by the *Afrika Korps* in the rear, while the *Afrika Korps* in its turn had also to hold off strong enemy attacks against its flank and rear.

Under the pressure of the very serious crisis of the morning, the command of *Panzergruppe Afrika* regarded as the most pressing task the restoration of the situation on the siege front and the recapture of Belhamed, the possession of which was absolutely necessary if the siege of Tobruk was to continue effectively. Ignorant of the strength of the enemy attacking the southern front of the *15th Panzer Division*, *Panzergruppe Afrika*, at 1530 hours, signaled the following instruction to the *Afrika Korps*:

> Attack to be continued as far as Axis Road so as to ease the position of *Infantry Regiment 155*. You will then go over to the defensive against the enemy attack from the south. Change of location towards the east into the area south of Gambut planned for the night.

The commanding general of the *Afrika Korps* believed, however, that it would be dangerous to strike down from the southern heights to the north. The enemy would then gain ground, whence he would dominate a wide area to the north with his artillery. Later on it would be very difficult to recapture this high ground once it had been abandoned. The only possibility for the German armor to overcome the British superiority lay in mobile operations. Abandonment of the high ground involved the danger that the *Afrika Korps* might lose its freedom of action and be encircled by the enemy. General Crüwell made up his mind to withdraw the formations of the *Afrika Korps* from the enemy envelopment eastward under cover of darkness, in order to regain his freedom of movement. He therefore launched the attack of the *21st Panzer Division* against Belhamed only as far as the Axis Road; the *15th Panzer Division* was ordered to hold off the attack of the enemy armor in its existing positions and to support the attack of the *21st Panzer Division* on Belhamed with its artillery. The division was at once to begin reconnaissance for the night march along the Trigh Capuzzo into the area around Gasr el Arid, whilst strong rearguard forces were to hold the existing positions of the division until 0300 hours on 22 November and to conceal the move.

The attack by the *21st Panzer Division* was begun late in the afternoon and reached the Axis Road by midnight without particular difficulty. Belhamed had been mopped up by *Infantry Regiment 155* previously. The enemy had withdrawn to the south-west on to the high ground south of the Trigh Capuzzo.

At 1930 hours the *Afrika Korps* issued the written order for the attack to both divisions which was to bring about the change of location into the area around Gasr el Arid.

The move of the *15th Panzer Division* was successfully carried out under cover of darkness and unnoticed by the enemy. The march through the pitch darkness over ground muddy and rain-sodden proved a most difficult operation; nor was it easy to find the descent from the high ground on the steep slopes down to the Trigh Capuzzo.

In view of a fresh instruction from *Panzergruppe Afrika* which placed *Infantry Regiment 155* and the *Afrika Regiment* under command of the *Afrika Korps*, the last abandoned its plan to move the *21st Panzer Division* to the east. The *Afrika Korps* instructed the *21st Panzer Division* after midnight to defend the high ground sloping to the south on both sides of Belhamed, using the two infantry regiments under command for this task, and also to cover the area as far as the escarpment south of the Trigh Capuzzo.

In the evening *Panzergruppe Afrika* appreciated the situation as having improved. At Gialo the enemy had advanced no further, and his first attempt to break through to Tobruk had been repulsed. However, the crisis had certainly not been overcome so long as strong enemy armored forces still lay in the rear of the *Afrika Korps*

November 21 had produced the first climax of the enemy autumn offensive and the first dangerous crisis for *Panzergruppe Afrika*. It was only by straining every nerve and making every possible effort that the British breakthrough to Tobruk had been prevented. The fact that the enemy had been denied success was due to the resolute leadership of Rommel, to the courageous resistance of the German-Italian troops investing Tobruk, in particular of *Division z.b.v. Afrika*, and to the powerful diversionary attacks of the *Afrika Korps*. In the evening the important high ground round Belhamed was once more in the possession of the *Panzergruppe*.

Even so, the situation was still tense. The enemy had succeeded in concentrating the bulk of his *XXX Corps*, and particularly of his superior armored forces, dangerously near at a point only 12 kilometers behind the siege line. The *Afrika Korps* was definitely threatened with encirclement, only a narrow corridor along the Via Balbia remaining open to communicate with the Sollum front.

The decision of the *Afrika Korps* to move the bulk of its forces during the night of 21/22 November eastward out of encirclement was undoubtedly happy. It created the possibility during the days that followed of taking the bulk of the enemy in flank and rear in their turn and achieving an early and complete success, which was so vitally necessary in view of the serious supply situation of the *Panzergruppe*.

The Battle of the Cauldron of Sidi Rezegh

The Fighting on 22 November. During the morning, the *21st Panzer Division* took up defensive positions facing south on both sides of Belhamed. *Infantry Regiment 155* was disposed on the right, and *Afrika Regiment* to the left of the division near Bir Sciuerat. On the east of the division *Reconnaissance Battalion 3* covered the ascent from Trigh Capuzzo south-west of Gambut. In the course of the morning the British launched only minor armored attacks against the center of the division, which were repulsed without difficulty.

The division commander soon realized that it would be impossible to send out covering formations on to the high ground south of the Trigh Capuzzo without serious fighting. From this high ground the enemy dominated the broad hollow of the Trigh Capuzzo for a considerable distance. The division commander decided to attack the high ground in order to hold the enemy forces and also to create favorable conditions for the flanking attack of the *15th Panzer Division*. For this purpose he sent *Panzer Regiment 5* on a wide sweep with a view to attacking the Sidi Rezegh landing ground from the west, whilst *Schützen Regiment 104* was allotted the frontal attack. *Panzer Regiment 5* succeeded in climbing the high ground from the west without having to fight. During the afternoon, however, superior enemy armor, strongly supported by artillery, was encountered on the landing ground of Sidi Rezegh, and towards evening the regiment had to be withdrawn to the edge of the high ground. Thanks to the enveloping advance of *Panzer Regiment 5*, *Schützen Regiment 104* succeeded in seizing the ground north of the landing ground and took up defensive positions. On their right *Infantry Regiment 155* also succeeded in reaching the same heights, whence the *Afrika Regiment* on their left could do no more than push lesser covering formations up to the northern slope of the escarpment at Height 175.

The *15th Panzer Division* had completed its concentration in the Gasr el Arid area at 0900 hours on 22 November. At no time did the enemy interfere. Apparently the British had not noticed the movement of the division. They did not reoccupy the high ground on both sides of Sidi Rezegh until the morning.

Late in the morning, enemy reconnaissance forces of considerable strength (40 light tanks and armored reconnaissance cars) felt their way forced from the south, towards the division. Towards 1200 hours, *Reconnaissance Battalion 33* reported strong enemy armor — about 280 vehicles — advancing from the south towards the positions of the *Afrika Regiment* near Sciafsciuf.

The division thereupon concluded that the opportunity had come to destroy much of this enemy force by a thrust in the flank. The division was aware that the ridge from Sciafsciuf westward was exceptionally steep and negotiable by tanks in very few places. Its plan envisaged swinging to the south-east to overthrow the enemy in a powerful thrust, pressing him against the precipitous slope, and annihilating him.

The division reported its intentions to the *Afrika Korps* by wireless and requested approval. The order of the *Afrika Korps* corresponding to the intention of the *15th Panzer Division* did not arrive until 1340 hours. The approach was to start at 1400 hours. As, however, the division commander was at the same time summoned to take part in a discussion at corps battle headquarters at Bir el Giaser, it was obvious that considerable delay would ensue. This was somewhat unfortunate because the time was now short and there was a risk that, if success were achieved, exploitation would be impossible before nightfall. The operations officer (Ia) of the division therefore ordered the advance to begin without awaiting the return of the division commander. The letter returned to the division at 1430 hours, when the advance to the south-west was already in progress. The corps commander and his chief of staff also accompanied the advance.

The division advanced in "plain" formation, the nonarmored battle group following immediately after *Panzer Regiment 8*, with the antitank unit echeloned out to the left as flank guard. About 10 kilometers south-east of Sciafsciuf, two large enemy tank formations were sighted south-west and north-west of the division. As the south-western group was approaching the division it was attacked forthwith. The group could not withstand the weight of our armored attack, supported by coordinated fire of our artillery and antiaircraft guns, and disengaged to the south-west with considerable losses in armor.

Thereupon the division suggested to the corps commander that it should not pursue the beaten enemy but turn to the north-west against the other enemy group. General Crüwell approved of this suggestion, and without delay the advance was continued in the new direction. The enemy did not accept battle but retired north and north-west. It was now 1700 hours and night began to fall. The division pursued the retreating enemy and in almost complete darkness reached Height 175, which projects to the north from the high ground.

It was here that *I./Panzer Regiment 8*, traveling at the head of the division, bumped a British armored brigade crowded together into a narrow space in front of the escarpment and evidently searching fruitlessly for a way down the precipice. The enemy, taken completely by surprise, was surrounded and compelled after a short fight to surrender. More than 50 tanks fell into the hands of the division, most of them undamaged. The officer commanding the British *4th Armored Brigade*, 19 officers and 250 other ranks were captured. The battlefield, lit up by burning British tanks, offered an unforgettable sight. The greater part of the British *4th Armored Brigade* had been destroyed.

The division immediately moved up the *15th Schützen Brigade*, and prepared defenses facing south to obviate being surprised in their own turn. In the course of the night British tanks indeed advanced against the defenses several times, but were repulsed. During the night contact was established with *Afrika Regiment*, which had abandoned the high ground late in the afternoon in face of a British armored attack. It now reoccupied Height 175.

In the course of 22 November a new danger was observed threatening *Panzergruppe Afrika* from the east. Two new enemy columns, each of regimental strength, were advancing to the west on the Via Balbia and on the Trigh Capuzzo respectively. The service troops and the depots of the *21st Panzer Division*, situated 20 kilometers west of Bardia on the north side of the Via Balbia, were attacked towards noon by motorized infantry in battalion strength and supported by a number of heavy tanks. The commander of *Antiaircraft Machine Gun Battalion 606*, with elements of his battalion and some troops scraped together from the service units, succeeded in halting the enemy until evening, when the bulk of the service troops had moved away to the west. Most of the supplies in these dumps were got away. The advance of the enemy approaching along the Trigh Capuzzo was delayed by elements of *Reconnaissance Unit 3*. By the evening the enemy had reached the area approximately 40 kilometers to the west of Bardia.

In front of Tobruk the enemy had remained inactive during the day. Towards evening a local push of the Tobruk garrison with tank support against the right wing of *Infantry Division Pavia* was repulsed after a short fight. *Armored Division Ariete*, at Bir el Gubi, was now opposed by no more than small enemy forces on the south and east. It was not attacked during 22 November.

Panzergruppe Afrika had already moved its tactical battle headquarters from the "Brown House" north of Gambut to El Adem during the evening of 21 November. Their appreciation of the enemy situation and intentions for the conduct of operations on 23 November may be gleaned from an order which the *Panzergruppe* sent to the *Afrika Korps* at 1530 hours by wireless, being still unaware of the fighting which had taken place during the afternoon:

Information on the General Situation:

(1) The Enemy: Approximately two armored brigades of the British *7th Armored Division* in front of the *Afrika Korps*, one of them somewhat knocked about. A third armored brigade assumed to be behind Sollum front. The *2nd New Zealand Division* in coordination with the *4th Indian Division* will attack those positions from the front and the rear on 23 November. The *1st South African Division* and *Group Giarabub* are in front of the Italian *Motorized Corps* which is holding positions in the line Bir Hacheim–Bir el Gubi; the British *7th Armored Division* is believed to be in supply difficulties. On 22 November no further break-out attempts from Tobruk. So far no further reinforcement from Egypt established.

(2) Intention for 23 November: Concentrated attack by the *Afrika Korps* and elements of *Armored Division Ariete* (one reinforced armored detachment) to destroy the British *7th Armored Division*. For this purpose the *Afrika Korps* concentrating its forces on the left wing (*Schwerpunkt*), will advance at 0700 hours in the general direction of Bir el Gubi. Central line of advance and thrust line will be made known in due course. At 0800 hours *Ariete* will advance towards Gambut. Recognition signals for German and Italian troops white Very lights.

This order shows that on the whole the *Panzergruppe* had assembled a correct picture regarding enemy dispositions. It would, however, appear that the strength of the enemy group south-east of Tobruk had been underestimated and that the intervention of the *2nd New Zealand Division* in the fighting east of Tobruk was unknown.

The plan to destroy the British *7th Armored Division* had been conceived about noon on 22 November after the situation had been consolidated somewhat when the high ground south-east of Tobruk had been recaptured. According to the plan the entire *Afrika Korps* was to attack from the north and elements of *Armored Division Ariete* from the south. As the Italian *Motorized Corps* had not yet been placed under command of the *Panzergruppe*, and as the Italian Commander-in-Chief in North Africa, General Bastico, had not yet shown himself at the battle headquarters of the *Panzergruppe*, General Gambara, the commanding general of the Italian *Motorized Corps*, was requested verbally to cooperate in the attack which had been planned. Gambara, however, seemed to have detailed only some elements of *Armored Division Ariete* to take part in the operation, whilst the Italian *Motorized Division Trieste* remained in the area south-west of El Adem.

The appreciation as held by the *Afrika Korps* differed from that of the *Panzergruppe* in essential points. General Crüwell believed that the success achieved on 22 November had favorably changed the underlying conditions for the attack which was planned to result in the destruction of the enemy. The hitting power of the British *7th Armored Division* had been considerably weakened. On the other hand, the *15th Panzer Division* was still in possession of its full fighting strength, though the *21st Panzer Division* had been considerably weakened.

In view of the favorable flanking position which the *15th Panzer Division* had taken up during the evening of 22 November, the *Afrika Korps* did not consider it advisable to attack the enemy from the north with both divisions and to throw him against *Armored Division Ariete*, which was not thought to be strong enough to carry out an attack from the south on its own or even merely to hold an enemy who had been driven south. General Crüwell decided therefore to reinforce the *15th Panzer Division* with *Panzer Regiment 5* from the *21st Panzer Division*, and direct them towards Bir el Gubi to meet *Ariete*, to attack northward in company, driving the enemy against the *21st Panzer Division*.

In conformity with this decision, and when, in spite of several requests, no further order arrived from the *Panzergruppe* before midnight, the following instructions were sent to the two divisions by wireless:

> The *15th Panzer Division* with *Panzer Regiment 5* will advance at 0700 hours on 23 November in the direction of Bir el Gubi. *Panzer Regiment 5* will arrive at a point 4 kilometers south of Bir Scianerut by 0600 hours, moving across the Trigh Capuzzo. The *21st Panzer Division* will hold positions attained. Further instructions from battle headquarters the *15th Panzer Division*.

At 0430 hours on 23 November there finally arrived at the *Afrika Korps* an order from the *Panzergruppe*, dispatched at 2230 hours by wireless, containing an appreciation of the general situation but, as concerning operations for 23 November as distinct from those of 22 November, making no alteration in the intention notified at midnight.

Afrika Korps made no further change in its arrangements for 23 November on the basis of this order from *Panzergruppe*.

The Battle on the "Bloody Sunday of the Dead"

There was a heavy morning mist at daybreak on 23 November, the day which was to see the fiercest battle of the entire campaign and which will remain unforgettably imprinted in the memory of all Africa warriors as the "Bloody Sunday of the Dead".

In the course of the night the *15th Panzer Division* had moved strong elements of the *15th Schützen Brigade* with artillery farther to the south with a view to covering the positions, as an enemy surprise counterattack appeared possible at any moment, in view of his local superiority. When, towards 0700 hours, the mist lifted, the enemy had withdrawn from our front. Fighting continued only with enemy riflemen on the extreme right wing. The division had disposed of its forces so that *Panzer Regiment 8*, in the van with *Panzer Regiment 5* in the second line, should advance to the south-south-west. The rest of the division would follow echeloned to the left under command of the *15th Panzer Brigade*.

Although at 0700 hours *Panzer Regiment 5* had not yet arrived, the advance began as planned. By 0730 hours several enemy batteries and numerous motionless motor vehicles were soon in the line of the advance, facing north-west and taken completely by surprise by the German advance. Simultaneously, some 20 tanks came into the action from the east – probably the remnants of a broken armored brigade – which seemed to attempt to divert the attack on themselves, but were easily kept off by our antitank weapons.

Panzer Regiment 8, in the van, turned west on its own initiative, and proceeded with the destruction of the enemy vehicles, which were in extraordinary depth. Thereupon the division brought the *15th Schützen Brigade* up on the right wing to mop up the vehicles captured by our tanks and collect prisoners. Towards 1000 hours the battle had been decided. Farther west, however, numerous batteries and supply units could be seen belonging to the British division which was in action facing north.

The Commander of the *15th Panzer Division*, Major-General Neumann-Silkow, in an appreciation of the situation, regarded the continued advance southward to Bir el Gubi as inexpedient. He believed that the division should wheel westward without delay, as the enemy had been completely surprised and would have no time to prepare to resist our attack. The General feared, further, that to continue to push to Bir el Gubi would waste much time, and the short November day could not allow the attack to be carried through to full success. It seemed necessary, however, that contact with the *21st Panzer Division* should be reestablished before the close of 23 November, to assure replenishment.

General Crüwell, however, rejected the suggestion of the division, but adhered to his decision first to gain contact with *Ariete* north of Bir el Gubi, to allow it to take a hand in the attack. The formations were then reorganized and supplied with ammunition, and at about 1130 hours the advance continued to the south-south-west. At 1230 hours the junction with *Armored Division Ariete* was effected, 8 kilometers north of Bir el Gubi. Meanwhile *Panzer Regiment 5* had arrived and moved to the left and rear of *Panzer Regiment 8*. It had held off several thrusts from the east by enemy armor, which had been reinforced in the mountains.

The *Afrika Korps* now issued orders to begin the northward advance at 1430 hours. *Armored Division Ariete*, which was not under command of the *Afrika Korps*, was invited to take part in the attack on the left of the *15th Panzer Division*. It would appear that no detailed coordination in the matter of objectives, boundary lines, mutual artillery support and signal service was arranged. The *21st Panzer Division*, on its side, received orders to cooperate in the destruction of the enemy by attacking to the south-east.

Reconnaissance patrols sent out by the *15th Panzer Division* to the north stated that in the meantime the enemy had prepared himself for attack from the south. The division was met by heavy artillery fire. The task allotted to the *15th Panzer Division* was difficult. The division had to break through a position which had a depth of more than 10 kilometers. The enemy had a manifold superiority in artillery and he dispensed moreover of numerous antitank weapons and more than 100 tanks. There was no more time left for thorough preparation if the enemy was to be destroyed before the end of 23 November and contact with *21st Panzer Division* was still to be established. But this was necessary, because otherwise the enemy would have eluded envelopment during the night or the division would have lain in the evening in the midst of the enemy without fuel and ammunition. Nor was it possible to concentrate the forces of the division for an attack on a narrow front. The attack had, rather, to be launched on a wide front in order to prevent the enemy from escaping.

The division organized its forces in successive lines. The first was formed by the two *Panzer* regiments, both under command of the commander of *Panzer Regiment 8*, with *Panzer Regiment 5* (40 tanks) on the right, where the enemy's strength had suffered during the fighting in the morning, and *Panzer Regiment 8* (110 tanks) on the left, where the strongest resistance was to be expected.

The second line was formed by the two infantry regiments under the commander of the *15th Schützen Brigade*. Of these two regiments, *Regiment 200* was on the right to cooperate with *Panzer Regiment 5*, whilst *Schützen Regiment 115* was to cooperate with *Panzer Regiment 8*. Both rifle regiments were to follow close on the heels of the *Panzer* regiments and, with the pressure of the *Panzer* thrust, should break into the enemy positions still seated in their vehicles. The division determined on this risky measure because the time required for an infantry attack through the deep enemy positions was certainly lacking.

The deployment of the division proved extremely difficult. From the first it was under heavy fire from over 100 enemy guns, which could not be kept down by our own weak artillery. To move the concentration area farther to the rear was impossible because an nonnegotiable swamp area lay to the south. *Panzer Regiment 5* could hardly disengage in time from the notice with enemy armor which was attacking from the east. Thus the attack could not begin before 1500 hours.

Heavy fighting broke out at once. A terrific fire front of well over 100 guns concentrated on the two attacking *Panzer* regiments and the two rifle regiments following close behind in their vehicles. A concentration of antitank weapons unusual in this theater of war and cleverly hidden away among the enemy vehicles which had been knocked out during the morning inflicted heavy losses on the two *Schützen* regiments. The flanking fire was particularly irksome, coming from the left, the sector of *Armored Division Ariete*, which had not yet embarked on the attack, and falling on *Panzer Regiment 8* and *Schützen Regiment 115*. The *15th Panzer Division*, on the opposite side, concentrated the fire of its artillery and the *Schwerpunkt* [main focus] of its tank attack on the left wing.

In spite of the unexpectedly stubborn resistance, *I./Panzer Regiment 8* soon broke into the enemy positions. The commander of *Schützen Regiment 115* immediately led his regiment into the breach regardless of personal danger. The riflemen broke into the enemy positions seated in their vehicles. In a short time over a thousand prisoners were taken and a large number of guns captured. At this juncture the enemy concentrated fire from a reoccupied British position and from the sector allotted to *Armored Division Ariete* on to the spot where the breach had been made. *Schützen Regiment 115* was compelled to debus. Most of its vehicles were blazing; heavy casualties were suffered. The commander of the regiment and the two battalion command-ers were either killed or gravely wounded. The regiment lay without any cover a few hundred yards in front of the enemy's second defense line. At this moment the enemy counterattacked with troops which had been kept back. 265 enemy tanks thrust into the flank from the sector of *Armored Division Ariete*. Oberleutnant Struckmann, the *Ordonnanz* officer of the regiment, hastily organized a defence.[1] A few yards in front of the position of the riflemen the British infantry attack broke down. The enemy armor was shot to pieces by our own tanks and antiaircraft artillery.

Meanwhile, *Panzer Regiment 8* pushed north in stiff fighting, broke the resistance of numerous enemy artillery and antitank positions and smashed strong enemy armored forces. But it took *I./Panzer Regiment 8* until 1700 hours to back its way through the deep enemy position and reach the north edge of the high ground where it sloped down to the Sidi Rezegh landing ground. Once our troops had reached this point, contact with *Schützen Regiment 104* of the *21st Panzer Division* was soon established. However, *Schützen Regiment 115*, to the south-west, was still under very strong enemy fire from the front and the flank. The division commander thereupon ordered *Panzer Regiment 8* at 1630 hours to get going once more the attack of the riflemen which had been pinned down.

Under most violent fire from enemy tanks and antitank weapons, the rear detachment of the *Panzer* regiment turned about and moved to meet *Schützen Regiment 115*. Taking advantage of the confusion created among the enemy by this and one move of our armor, Oberleutnant Struckmann set *Schützen Regiment 115* once more in motion. The depleted companies of the regiment broke into the second enemy position and thrust in the dusk as far as the escarpment between Point 178 and Point 175. Once more numerous prisoners were collected and a number of gun emplacements and battery positions were taken by storm.

Together with his operational staff, General Neumann-Silkow, the commander of the *15th Panzer Division*, had moved under heavy fire immediately behind the *Panzer Regiment*. He soon realized what danger threatened through the lagging behind of *Armored Division Ariete*. He repeatedly requested the *Afrika Korps* to urge on the Italians. But the *Afrika Korps* on its side had no contact with *Ariete*. Attempts were therefore made to establish contact by dispatch riders and liaison officers and induce the division to move more rapidly.

---

[1] During both world wars, the commander of a German regiment or brigade had a small staff consisting of an adjutant (usually a captain or a senior lieutenant) and one or two *Ordonnanz* officers (invariably lieutenants). The latter were used as "directed telescopes" or "empowered messengers" who sometimes took command of units in the heat of combat.

Owing to the destruction of several wireless links soon after the beginning of the attack, communications with the right wing had failed. *Panzer Regiment 5* and *Regiment 200* seemed to have strayed too much to the right. *Schützen Regiment 115*, on the other hand, had turned more to the north-north-east because of flanking fire from the area where *Armored Division Ariete* should have been, and threatened to split the attack of the division. The division therefore instructed the *15th Schützen Brigade* at 1640 hours to move *Engineer Battalion 33*, which had followed behind the right wing, to close the gap.

Before this order took effect, the beaten enemy with his last 20 tanks and riflemen on lorries made an attempt to escape to the south-east through this gap in the attacking front. As our *Panzer* regiments were much farther forward involved in fighting the enemy, the attempt was opposed by our staffs, who used machine guns and automatic rifles and carbines in driving the enemy back. One antitank company was brought up just in time to inflict heavy losses on the fleeing enemy. Only weak elements were able to get through to the south-east.

The fighting on the right wing of the attack developed on entirely different lines. In this sector *Regiment 200* attacked behind *Panzer Regiment 5*. Its advance also suffered under very strong enemy artillery fire. In spite of all the shelling, the attack was carried out by infantry in their lorries, until vicious enemy infantry fire compelled them to debus. Advancing with great dash, *Motorcycle Battalion 15* broke into the enemy positions, collected 600 prisoners and captured 20 guns. However, the attack broke down in front of another enemy position. The attack of *Regiment 200* was hampered from the beginning by some 20 enemy tanks which advanced from the east against its right flank. The regiment threw in against them a heavy *Flak* battery and a antitank company which effectively hindered the intervention of these tanks throughout the attack.

Meanwhile communications failed with *Panzer Regiment 5*, which has moved to the north-west and apparently joined on with the forward line of *Panzer Regiment 8*. The commander of *Regiment 200* then decided to get the attack moving again by placing *Machine Gun Battalion 2* on the right wing of *Motorcycle Battalion 15*. Here, too, both battalions did not succeed in breaking into the enemy positions until dark. The bulk of the enemy had escaped the last assault by flight, apparently to the east. However, numerous abandoned wounded were ample evidence of the severity of the fighting. During the first hours of the night contact was restored with the *Afrika Regiment*, which, in the course of the day, had lost the high ground south-west of Bir Scieuerat and now lay in the area north of the Trigh Capuzzo.

Fighting had continued far into the night. It had become pitch dark. Thus it was extremely difficult to disentangle the various units. The division instructed its regiments to reorganize their depleted formations during the night and to replace vehicle losses from their considerable booty. Contact was to be made with the *21st Panzer Division* all along the front. *Reconnaissance Battalion 33* was ordered to discover the whereabouts of the enemy units which had broken out to the south-east.

In the sector of the *21st Panzer Division* the enemy had launched minor attacks during the morning but discontinued them during the day. Only on the extreme eastern flank was the escarpment south of the Trigh Capuzzo lost to an enemy tank attack about noon. The *Afrika Regiment*, however, was able to establish itself on the south slope north of the Trigh Capuzzo. For reasons unknown the division did not carry out the attack to the south-east ordered by the *Afrika Korps* during the morning, in support of the operations of the *15th Panzer Division*.

The *Afrika Korps* did not interfere in the course of the attack. In spite of enemy efforts, it had been impossible to restore contact with *Armored Division Ariete*. What part it had taken in the attack is not perfectly clear. Apparently it moved away to the west in the face of strong enemy resistance.

During the evening the operational staff of the *Afrika Korps,* which lay behind the center line of the *15th Panzer Division*'s advance, was attacked by enemy tanks which had broken through. They were saved from their uncomfortable situation by elements of the *Flak* battery which were sent back.

During 23 November the situation east of Tobruk had grown more menacing. Early in the morning elements of the *2nd New Zealand Division* had attacked the Battle Headquarters of the *Afrika Korps* at Bir el Giaser and captured most of the operational staff. Enemy columns advancing westward along the Trigh Capuzzo were halted south of Cubbut by *Reconnaissance Unit 33*.

The enemy column advancing along the Via Balbia was pushed to the south 30 hours west of Bardia by the resistance of German covering units. It reached the Gambut airfield towards noon, where it was halted by elements of supply troops and services thrown together and led by the officer commanding *Antiaircraft Machine Gun Battalion 606*. The supply troops of the *15th Panzer Division* north-west of Gambut were not seriously endangered.

Early in the morning of 23 November Rommel left him Battle Headquarters at El Adem for the battlefield of Sidi Rezegh. He failed to arrive,
however, and did not intervene in the operations of either the *15th* or the
21st Panzer Divisions. It is probable that on his way to the *Afrika Korps* he
arrived at the *Afrika Regiment* south of Bir Sciuerat at a moment of crisis
and, as was his custom, took a personal hand in the defense. Thus it
appears that *Panzergruppe* was informed of the events of the day very late,
and even then insufficiently. Perhaps this was also the reason why the
German-Italian air forces did not operate against the penned-in enemy
formations, which, considering the dense concentration of enemy vehicles, would have had great effect. According to the then operations officer
(Ia), on 23 November the *Panzergruppe* do not seem to have realized the
importance of the advance of the *2nd New Zealand Division* along the Via
Balbia and the Trigh Capuzzo.

The plan of *Panzergruppe Afrika* to encircle and crush the British *7th
Armored Division* in the area south of Sidi Rezegh had fully succeeded by the
evening of 23 November. Even when the battle began on 22 November,
strong elements of the British *7th Armored Division* had been destroyed; on
23 November this division and half of the *1st South African Division* were
completely crushed. On 23 November alone the division lost more than
3,000 prisoners, two generals, 120 guns, numerous antitank weapons and 80
tanks. According to British sources, one brigade of the *1st South African
Division* was completely wiped out whilst the British *7th Armored Division* lost
almost all its guns, its antitank weapons, and most of its supply train, and had
only 40 battle-ready tanks on the evening of 23 November.

It is true that the *15th Panzer Division* had also suffered severe losses. *Panzer
Regiment 8* lost both its battalion commands, five of its six company
commanders and 44 tanks; the regiment had only 50 tanks left on the evening
of this day of hard fighting. *Schützen Regiment 115* had even heavier losses: all
senior officers were killed in battle or severely wounded, and the majority of
the troop carriers and other vehicles had been shot to pieces. *Regiment 200*
suffered losses heavily.

The victory of Sidi Rezegh was the fault of a series of happy decisions and
measures. The possibility had been created by the bold decision taken by the
Afrika Korps on the evening of 21 November. By the unexpected move of the
15th Panzer Division to the area of Gasr el Arid, it became possible to take
British *7th Armored Division* in the flank. The independent decisions taken by
the *15th Panzer Division* at noon on 22 November, approved by the *Afrika*

Korps, and resolutely and forcefully carried out, destroyed a considerable part of the British *7th Armored Division* and abolished its numerical superiority. This brought about a more favorable ratio of power and the conditions necessary for the fateful action on 23 November.

The decision of the *Panzergruppe* to fight the cauldron battle at Sidi Rezegh had been taken before the victorious conclusion of the fighting of 22 November. This was the crucial decision of the campaign. It is true that the method of execution favored by the *Panzergruppe* offered little prospect of the complete destruction of the enemy. Had the *Afrika Korps* attacked from the north, the enemy would have been thrown back on to his lines of communication to the south. The Italian *Armored Division Ariete*, which was to be thrown in from the south, would hardly be strong enough to prevent the enemy from withdrawing.

The plan of the *Afrika Korps* to march round the east flank of the enemy group and, in cooperation with *Armored Division Ariete*, to drive the enemy on to the *21st Panzer Division* offered a better prospect of destroying the enemy. It was, however, necessary in the first place that the full cooperation of *Armored Division Ariete* should be obtained. The *Afrika Korps* also had undertaken more than it could cope with on the short November day. Only if conditions were exceptionally favorable would the time have been sufficient to destroy the encircled enemy on 23 November.

When, during the morning of 23 November, it became apparent that the bulk of the enemy forces still faced north and were completely surprised by the appearance of the *15th Panzer Division* on their eastern flank, it might have been better to alter the plan and to send the *15th Panzer Division* into the attack from the east at once, without waiting for *Armored Division Ariete* to take a hand, which indeed had little effect during the afternoon. Had this been done, the enemy would have found no time to prepare for the defense against this attack. The attack would probably have led to complete success more rapidly and at lower cost. Only the outlet to the west would have been left open for the enemy, and it is more than doubtful whether numbers of any consequence would have been able to slip away, the more so if the *21st Panzer Division* had played its part and *Armored Division Ariete* had been brought to attack to the north-west.

The task allotted to the *15th Panzer Division* during the afternoon of 23 November – to attack an enemy in a position organized in depth and superior in every way, particularly in artillery, and to destroy this enemy in a few hours – was unusually difficult. In any case, the attack would have necessitated detailed reconnaissance, thorough preparation and a method applicable to an attack against prepared positions, namely narrow sectors, organization in depth, and an advance in bounds of the debussed infantry accompanied by tanks, through the deep zones of the enemy positions; particularly necessary would have been support by strong formations of the *Luftwaffe*, to paralyze the superior artillery and antitank defenses of the enemy. The shortness of the time available and the demand that the entire enemy force should be destroyed forbade the following of such a course of action.

It must be emphasized that the method of attack chosen by the *15th Panzer Division* was suited to the situation and the orders given. It made heavy demands on the courage and perseverance of the troops. There is no doubt that the attack of the *15th Panzer Division* was the most difficult which tanks and riflemen were called upon to carry out in the course of this campaign.

The arrangement of its forces in successive waves as adopted by the division did not prove a success. It would have been better if the division had been organized in two wings (*Flügelweise*), with battle groups formed of a *Panzer* battalion and a *Schützten* regiment apiece under a single command. This would have facilitated command by the division and the battle groups and avoided splitting up the attack.

Nonetheless, highest praise is due to the determination and the will to victory with which the command of the *15th Panzer Division* fought out the difficult battle, with its frequent crises, to a victorious conclusion; no less is recognition due to the courage and the unparalleled spirit of aggression manifested by all the troops of the division.

In any case the battle on the "Sunday of the Dead" remains an outstanding page of glory for the *15th Panzer Division*.

The Sollum Front, 18–23 November

The task Rommel had allotted to the Sollum front was to block the roads and tracks running along the coast, hold down strong enemy forces, protect the area between Bardia and Tobruk with its supply dumps and airfields and thus provide the opportunity of placing the *Afrika Korps* in a position from which it would be able to attack an enemy advancing on Tobruk in the flank.

The disposition of the forces on the Sollum front has already been dealt with. Behind them the fortress of Bardia had once more been prepared for defense, with an Italian garrison stiffened by local German supply troops when the British offensive started. The officer commanding the fortress of Bardia was Major-General Schmidt, originally officer commanding rear areas of *Panzergruppe Afrika*, while the defence of the Sollum front was entrusted to the Italian *Infantry Division Savona.*

As already mentioned, the men in the Sollum front saw and reported the approach of the enemy as early as 17 November. The enemy was nearing our positions in the coastal sector and particularly in the south-west wing near Sidi Omar; a very intensive reconnaissance activity developed, and enemy artillery began ranging the area at the strongpoints of Sidi Omar and Frongia. Around 19 November it became apparent that the enemy was preparing an attack against the west wing of the position. Enemy motorized infantry and armor went round our positions to the west and on 20 November occupied Bir Deheua. Interrogation of a number of prisoners established that the main body of the *4th Indian Division*, supported by an enemy tank detachment, was preparing an attack in this area. Before the center of the position, however, only enemy forces appeared, keeping at a respectful distance from our forward line. Nor were enemy preparations apparent in the coastal plain.

In the morning of 21 November strong enemy forces – which turned out afterwards to be the *2nd New Zealand Division* and an army tank formation – moved round to the west of our positions on Sidi Ameia, and towards evening reached the Via Balbia 20 kilometers west of Bardia. Elements of this enemy force moved eastward along the northern flank of the Sollum position during the evening of 21 November, and in the morning of 22 November captured the strongpoint of Capuzzo, which was garrisoned by a small Italian force.

Towards noon on 22 November began the long-expected attack of the *4th Indian Division* against the west wing of the Sollum position. The attack was launched from the northern side, which had not been so well protected by dense minefields as the southern. Towards 1300 hours infantry in brigade strength, supported by 70 heavy tanks, attacked the strongpoint of Frongia. The Italian garrison's morale was unable to stand up to the powerful artillery preparation and the heavy British Mark II tanks. At 1400 hours the strongpoint was overpowered.

At 1530 hours the strongpoint of Sidi Omar was attacked from the north-east. The Italian garrison had been stiffened by a German heavy *Flak* battery and a German oasis company. Thus the strongpoint offered a more stubborn resistance. But even here the enemy succeeded in breaking through the minebelt and entering the strongpoint with his armor. It was not until the enemy armor arrived in front of the positions of the German *Flak* and oasis company that the attack broke down. Seventeen heavy tanks were knocked out. When night fell enemy infantry was in the east part of the strongpoint a very short distance from the German defenders.

On 23 November the *4th Indian Division* attempted, in local attacks, to bring the strongpoint completely into its hands. Further positions held by Italian troops were lost; but the German nucleus of the strongpoint remained unshaken. It was under heavy fire from enemy artillery and mortars, and had to fight off numerous enemy air attacks. As during the first days of the battle, several enemy aircraft were shot down on 23 November.

Thus, six days after the beginning of the enemy offensive a considerable portion of the Sollum front had been broken up. Even so, considerable enemy forces were kept occupied by the courageous German garrison of Sidi Omar, valiantly supported by some Italian units. The enemy was denied passage through the western part of the position.

The Sollum position had fulfilled, during the first days of the battle, the task which General Rommel had allotted it. It was not expected that the strongpoint, denied of all outside support, would be able to resist a well-planned attack from strong British forces for any length of time.

The Air Situation

On 16 November 1941, an unaccustomed phenomenon was encountered. An unusually strong tropical storm raged in Marmarica and Cyrenaica, flooding out all airfields and rendering them unserviceable for several days. More particularly, the airfields of Ain el Gazala, where the German fighters were based, and Taini, on which lay one of the two German *Stuka* groups, were completely under water, so that all flying had to be suspended. Much material, which had been stored in depots in the deep wadis and also on the airfields, was lost. Rushing torrents poured down from the high ground and actually drowned a large number of men.

When, on 17 November, the British offensive began, the Axis air forces in North Africa were condemned to inactivity. On the other hand the RAF were able to take off from their still serviceable airfields in western Egypt and strike at the Axis formation without meeting opposition in the air. They inflicted further heavy damage and crippled the already outnumbered German-Italian air forces so seriously that the latter played no part whatever in the early days of the British offensive before 22 November.

The RAF showed unexpected strength and were continually in the air. Air superiority by day was all on their side. The situation in the air became more pronounced because most of our antiaircraft artillery was used in an antitank role and was thus not available for the air.

X. *Fliegerkorps* reinforced *Fliegerführer Afrika* by transferring *I./Stuka 3* from Crete to Martuba, and sent his bomber formations to contest the enemy offensive. The bombers, however, were still employed on ship convoy, and some days passed before they were available. Furthermore, bomber formations were unable to operate by day without fighter escort. The fighter formations, however, had been condemned to inactivity, unable to take off from the flooded airfields of Ain el Gazala. Hence the bomber formations operated only at night against the rear communications of the *Eighth Army* in Egypt, with an effect which was naturally slight. It took a long time to replace the losses which air formations suffered because the replacement parks of the *Luftwaffe* were at Wiener Neustadt [Austria] and Belgrade [Serbia] – a great distance. This is why, during the first days of the British offensive, the formations of the *Panzergruppe* remained practically without any support from the *Luftwaffe* in the heavy fighting.

The command of the *Panzergruppe* suffered particularly from the almost complete absence of air reconnaissance. It is an established fact that the British preparations for an offensive – the construction of the railway to the border, the building up of enemy supply dumps in the frontier area, the enemy approach march, and even the actual beginning of the attack – did not come to the knowledge of the tactical command. This is indeed difficult to explain, as the German long-range air reconnaissance (although often hindered by sandstorms) made daily flights during October and November, actually reconnoitering and also taking air photographs. In particular, there is no reason why the extension of the British supply railway to the border should not have appeared on the aerial photographs taken by our reconnaissance planes. It is now too late to try to discover whether it was owing to inefficient interpretation of aerial photographs by the operations officer (Ia) service of the army, or to the failure of the *Luftwaffe* to pass on the results of air reconnaissance to the army, that this knowledge escaped the authorities. Further, it cannot be excluded that the air reconnaissance had not been properly briefed.

After the beginning of the offensive, the complaints from the ground force about the lack of air reconnaissance increased. Until 25 November neither the *Afrika Korps* nor the two German *Panzer* divisions with which lay the *Schwerpunkt* of the defense had received any reports from the air. Consequently they were groping in the dark, as the ground reconnaissance, hampered by the vastly superior enemy reconnaissance formations, was seldom able to get through. The inaccurate placing of formations and time-wasting detours were the result. This is the more difficult to understand in that, even before the war, and still more during the early yeas of hostilities, the transmission of air intelligence to corps and divisions by air liaison officers and the dropping of reports had become a matter of routine.

With regard to the employment of bomber and *Stuka* formations, the liaison between the army and the *Luftwaffe* at the beginning of the enemy offensive was not nearly so strict as it was in other war theaters. Recognition of our own armored units from the air was regarded as very difficult in the beginning. For this reason the bomber and *Stuka* formations were made to operate far removed from the areas in which German armored divisions were employed. Ground troops were rarely informed as to where the *Luftwaffe* was operating. It may be that the general transport crisis was responsible for the fact that neither corps nor division had air liaison sections attached to their headquarters. Later on, when Field Marshal Kesselring took over command, it was shown that close liaison between ground and air forces was quite possible, and that it was feasible for the air force to take a direct hand in the ground operations of the army.

It would appear that *X. Fliegerkorps*, which was responsible not only for the North African war theater but also for operations in the eastern Mediterranean and for convoy escort to Africa, did not at this stage attach enough importance to its task in the North African theater. Between 18 and 20 November the newly appointed Commander-in-Chief South, Field Marshal Kesselring, arrived in Rome from Smolensk just after the British offensive had started. It was his task to regain air superiority in the Mediterranean, to make the escort of the convoys sailing to Tripoli and Benghazi more effective with the cooperation of the Italians, and for this purpose to hold down Malta. When Kesselring arrived, his whole staff comprised the two officers who had accompanied him, whilst the staff of *Luftlotte 2* had to remain on duty on the Eastern Front until 1 December 1941. *II. Fliegerkorps*, which had been detailed to reinforce the German *Luftwaffe* in the Mediterranean, could not be expected before the middle of December.

Faced with this difficult situation, the newly appointed Commander-in-Chief South, under whom came *X. Fliegerkorps*, threw himself into the direction with great energy. After the first discussions with the *Comando Supremo* in Rome, he proceeded at once to North Africa, and formed a clear idea of the difficult situation of *Panzergruppe Afrika*. He recognized that the whole business of supply must be stopped up and be better protected. Since the sea passage took us much time, and an interval must elapse before sea transport could be made secure, he called upon the Commander-in-Chief of the *Luftwaffe* to send air transport formations and bomber formations for transport by air. All transport aircraft on hand were assigned to supplying the operational front.

During the early days of the British offensive, *Panzergruppe Afrika* regarded the advance of enemy forces to Gialo as particularly dangerous. At first there were no forces available to counter this advance. Field Marshal Kesselring then ordered the concentration of *Luftwaffe* supply units, *Flak* batteries and surplus signals and ground personnel stationed on the airfields in the Benghazi area. With the approval of the *Panzergruppe*, he employed them under command of Major-General Osterkemp, Air Commander Benghazi, to protect the Agedabia area. Air formations from Greece and available Italian air formations operated against the enemy advance from the air.

Field Marshal Kesselring, still without a staff and without troops, and working merely with the forces he had found on the spot, directed his whole energy to restoring the striking power of the German-Italian air formations which had been so hard hit by the catastrophic weather and enemy attack. Liaison with the *Panzergruppe* was made much closer. The Field Marshal personally communicated the latest operational lessons to the formations on the air fields. *X. Fliegerkorps* and *Fliegerführer Afrika* were ordered to shift the main effort (*Schwerpunkt*) of their operations from escort duties, which up to then had been given first priority, to supporting the desperate battles of the *Panzergruppe*. That this conversion was rapidly successful is exclusively due to Field Marshal Kesselring's efforts.

The first operation of the bomber formation was still handicapped by the fact that the fighter formations were grounded on the Ain el Gazala airfields. A further drawback proved to be the rapid advance of the British forces, which reached the Gambut area by 23 November, thus putting out of action the forward landing ground. Hence air support of the Sollum front became a lengthy matter, and the early interception of enemy sorties by our fighters was made very difficult. As our air formations had first to learn to recognize friend from foe in the smoke and dust of a tank battle in the desert, the *Stuka* formations were at first used outside the battle area. During 21 and 22 November they attacked enemy motorized columns south of Bir el Gubi. Here the destroyer formations (Me 110) distinguished themselves by inflicting heavy losses on the motorized columns and British artillery in low-flying surprise attacks.

The fighter pilots also were gradually successful, in spite of British superiority, in holding off the enemy formations of 40–50 aircraft. On 22 November, while on escort duty and in dogfights, they shot down 10 multi-engined bombers and 14 Curtiss aircraft, and on 23 November 12 more enemy aircraft over the battlefield.

Flak artillery proved once more that it was the backbone of antitank defense in the frame of the German divisions. During the fighting for the strongpoints and in the armored battles in the Tobruk area, the 8.8 mm gun played a decisive part in the high figure of enemy tanks destroyed.

Although at the beginning of the British offensive the army did not enjoy the energetic support of the *Luftwaffe*, a fundamental change soon took place after Field Marshal Kesselring had assumed command. This change was not due to the arrival of new formations – which did not occur until December – but to the fact that he drove himself without mercy and demanded of all formations the utmost effort. Thus, he soon increased the activity of his numerically inferior formations and achieved the recovery of the command and men from the shock of the first days of the campaign.

On 23 November the first phase of the British autumn offensive closed with a defensive victory for the German-Italian command. The enemy had not succeeded in destroying the German-Italian armored forces, nor in relieving the garrison of Tobruk. The kernel of the British assaulting troops, the *7th Armored Division* and the *1st South African Division*, had suffered such heavy casualties that for days thereafter they were condemned to inactivity.

Auchinleck had started his offensive under the most favorable conditions. He had anticipated the German-Italian attack on Tobruk, and, thus, a large number of the German-Italian forces had been tied to the investment of the fortress and were not available to oppose the offensive. He had achieved complete operational and tactical surprise. For three days his advance on Tobruk went almost unopposed. Therefore, on 21 November he was very near his operational objective.

General Rommel, like many a strong-willed commander before him, long refused to allow the enemy to dictate his actions. He adhered to his plan to attack and stuck to his incorrect appreciation of the enemy situation until it was almost too late to take effective defensive measures. For this reason, the advance of the German armored formations from west of Bardia against the flank of the British attacking forces, as planned in the event of a British offensive, was not carried out. When, on 21 November, the *Afrika Korps* at long last had been concentrated for action, the crisis in the Tobruk area had grown so serious that the *Afrika Korps* was not employed as originally intended and the success therefore was unsatisfactory.

On 22 and 23 November *Panzergruppe Afrika* succeeded in moving the *Afrika Korps* against the inner flank and the rear of the enemy assault groups. The German command succeeded in compelling superior armored and motorized formations to form a front to the rear and then crushing them, a most difficult feat, particularly in the desert, with its almost unlimited freedom of movement.

During the first phase of this campaign Rommel had to cope with many obstacles and much friction. The German troop commanders, particularly those in the *Afrika Korps*, had first to play themselves in: it took a few days before their superiority over the British leadership took effect.

The absence of air reconnaissance blinded the German leaders and delayed and rendered difficult the exploitation of favorable opportunities. The superiority of the enemy air force and the absence of support by our own air force proved a great obstacle to our command.

The disadvantages of confederate operations became glaringly evident. General Rommel was well aware that the Italian formations under his command, with their lower fighting power and their lesser equipment, were no match for British attacks without German stiffening. Before 23 November Rommel was not able to dispose the two divisions of Italian *Motorized Corps*, which proved a great handicap in his operations. Finally, the fact that supply across the Mediterranean had been completely interdicted from the middle of October was a very great hindrance: the German command saw the time coming when the struggle would have to be discontinued because all supplies of ammunition and fuel would run out.

The fighting power of the German troops, their state of training, their aggressive spirit and their steadfastness did form a certain counterweight for all these difficulties. Tactics which had been practiced during the summer in hard training exercises proved their value in the mobile battles before 23 November and gave the German troops a sense of superiority, even in the face of British numbers. The numerical superiority of the British tank formations was to a certain extent offset by the fighting strength of the German tanks. It is true that the heavy fighting before 23 November left its mark on the German troops. Heavy, bloody losses had weakened their numbers. Equipment which had been lost could not be quickly replaced.

Thus, it was of first importance that the great success achieved on 23 November should be quickly exploited and followed up by the total destruction of the enemy.

The Push to Egypt, 24–27 November

On the morning of 24 November General Rommel was apparently under the impression that the British *7th Armored Division* and *1st South African Division* had been practically destroyed during the fighting on 23 November south of Sidi Rezegh. There are several contradictory reports regarding his appreciation of the situation and his intentions on the morning of 24 November. In a discussion with the operations officer (Ia) of the *Panzergruppe* at 0400 hours, before he left for the *Afrika Korps*, Rommel said that the task was now to complete the destruction of the remnants of the enemy and to cut their lines of withdrawal to Egypt. He would therefore put himself at the head of the *Afrika Korps*, with *Armored Division Ariete* under command, and begin the pursuit. He would probably be away from his battle headquarters until the evening of 24 November or until the morning of 25 November at the latest. In the meantime the operations officer (Ia) of the *Panzergruppe*, Lieutenant-Colonel (General Staff) [Siegfried] Westphal, would take over the command on the Tobruk front. It was of the greatest importance to continue the siege of the fortress, in any circumstances.

The operations officer (Ia) then submitted that it would be dangerous for the *Afrika Korps* to move too far away from Tobruk. There was a risk of further attempts by the garrison of Tobruk to break out, as new enemy forces were coming up again from the east.

At that time General Rommel had not yet realized that the *2nd New Zealand Division* was moving towards Tobruk, but assumed that the bulk of this division was still in the area north of the Sollum front. At first, therefore, he refused to accept the doubts of operations officer (Ia); but later he promised to consider whether he had not better at once attack the enemy forces east of Tobruk with the *Afrika Korps*. In the opinion of the operations officer (Ia), the Sollum front did not play a decisive role in Rommel's thoughts. The *Panzergruppe* at that time was of the opinion that the position on the Sollum front gave no cause whatever for anxiety. The enemy had indeed succeeded in making certain penetrations into the west wing. On the whole, however, the main positions still held firm. Further, the supply position of the troops garrisoning the Sollum front seemed assured.

On the other hand, Rommel described his intention to Major (General Staff) Weiz, at that time the *Qu. 1* of the *Panzergruppe*, deputizing for the quartermaster-general who was absent on sick leave, in different style.[1] He proposed to place himself with the *Afrika Korps* across the supply routes of the British *Eighth Army* and capture their supply dumps. This would mean that they would soon be compelled to give up the struggle. From this it was clear that neither Rommel nor the *Qu. 1* knew of a captured map which had fallen into the hands of the *15th Panzer Division* on 28 November and which showed the supply routes and supply dumps of the *Eighth Army*.

Towards 0600 hours Rommel arrived at the battle headquarters of the *21st Panzer Division*, where he met the commanding general of the *Afrika Korps*, General Crüwell, and the divisional commanders. General Crüwell reported on the success of 23 November. He proposed to pursue the remnants of the defeated enemy, to clear the area between Trigh Capuzzo and Trigh el Abd of the enemy, and to salvage the immense booty on the battlefield of Sidi Rezegh.

Rommel's Instructions

Rommel, who, according to the report of the Chief of Staff of the *Afrika Korps*, had had no information concerning the great success of Sidi Rezegh, did not approve of this suggestion. He preferred to order the *Afrika Korps*, with *Armored Division Ariete* under command, to advance to the south-east without delay, in order to liberate the encircled Sollum front. To this end they must push through to the Halfaya Pass that same day. The commander of the *Afrika Korps* pointed out that it would be necessary to supply and reorganize the divisions, particularly the *15th Panzer Division*, and their heavy equipment losses during the fighting should be made good from the spoils of Sidi Rezegh.

Thereupon General Rommel ordered the *Afrika Korps* to begin the move to the south-east at 1000 hours. The headquarters of *Panzergruppe Afrika*, under the operations officer (Ia) – since the chief of the general staff, with two liaison officers and a wireless link were accompanying the commander-in-chief – was not informed of this order of Rommel's and remained for days in ignorance of the direction of the advance and the mandate of the *Afrika Korps* There were moments when the operations officer (Ia) apprehended

---

[1] A German quartermaster general (*Oberquartiermeister*) was a senior officer responsible for the supply and administration of an army. The *Qu. 1* was a general staff officer serving as his principal assistant. For details, see US National Archives, Foreign Military Studies, MS #P-139, *Size and Composition of Divisional and Higher Staffs in the German Army*.

that the aim of the advance might be the occupation of the oases of Giarabub and Siwa.

The further messages sent by Rommel to his staff during the days following were unintelligible since he was notifying his location and the tactical situation according to thrust lines which were unknown to the staff of the *Panzergruppe*. Thus, on the morning of 24 November the unity of command between the Tobruk front and formations on the Sollum front was already almost completely disrupted.

The Conduct of the Pursuit up to
Arrival at the Sollum Position early on 25 November

Between 0800 hours and 0900 hours the commanding general of the *Afrika Korps* issued his orders to the divisions. In the meantime, reconnaissance had reported that an enemy battle group with several hundred vehicles, artillery and tanks had spent the night south of the Trigh Capuzzo near Sciafsciuf. The whereabouts of the enemy defeated the previous day could not yet be determined.

General Crüwell decided to dispose his divisions for the pursuit one behind the other. The *21st Panzer Division*, which had suffered less during the fighting on 23 November, was to take the lead, so as to give the *15th Panzer Division* the opportunity of making good its losses in equipment from the booty on the battlefield of Sidi Rezegh. The order to *Armored Division Ariete* seems to have been given by General Rommel direct. It was to follow echeloned to the right behind the *15th Panzer Division*. As the objective of the advance, which was to proceed in general along the Trigh el Abd, the area near Gasr el Arid was first laid down.

The *21st Panzer Division* left the airfield of Sidi Rezegh at 1000 hours for the pursuit. The divisional staff, with some tanks, formed the van, which was also joined by General Rommel, the Commander-in-Chief of *Panzergruppe Afrika*. *Panzer Regiment 5*, which after the fighting on the previous day now numbered about 35 tanks, followed immediately behind. *Group Knabe* – reinforced *Schützen Regiment 104*, with the bulk of the artillery and antitank troops – followed at some distance.

The advance proceeded at a rapid pace, constantly increased by General Rommel at the head. North-west of Gabr Saleh the vanguard bumped some 30 tanks with a few batteries, apparently the remnants of the enemy which had escaped from the battlefield of Sidi Rezegh. *Panzer Regiment 5* was thrown against them. In the face of its attack, the enemy tanks moved away to the east. The head of the *21st Panzer Division*, which had been joined by the staff of the *Afrika Korps*, continued the pursuit with an ever hotter pace to the south-east without waiting for *Panzer Regiment 5*. *Group Knabe* followed, overtaking in its turn *Panzer Regiment 5*, which was still in action. By 1600 hours the van had reached the frontier wire at Gasr el Arid. Rommel instructed it to continue without break to the north-east along the Sollum position and reach the high ground south-east of the Halfaya Pass before the end of 24 November.

At 1700 hours General Rommel gave a new order to the commanding general of the *Afrika Korps* which showed that in the meantime he had changed his decision. The destruction of the enemy forces south-east of Tobruk or the relief of the Sollum front were no longer the object of the pursuit, but the encirclement and destruction of the enemy forces north and south of the Sollum position.

General Rommel had formed an incorrect picture of the enemy situation on the Sollum front. On the one hand, he assumed that the enemy lay closer to the whole southern front of the position, particularly the strongpoint of Halfaya Pass in the south. On the other hand, he was of the opinion that the *2nd New Zealand Division* was still north of the Sollum position. His aim was now for the *Afrika Korps* to destroy the enemy east of the Sollum front, north of the Sollum front and at Bardia by encirclement. He therefore ordered that the elements of the *21st Panzer Division* which had been pushed forward to the high ground south-east of the Halfaya Pass should take the enemy in the rear, throw him back on the strongpoints of Cirorer and Faltenbacher, and force him to surrender. The *15th Panzer Division* was to go north on both sides of the border at Gasr el Arid, drive the enemy south of the strongpoint of Sidi Omar northward into the minefield and force him, too, to surrender. With its left wing, the *15th Panzer Division* should prevent the enemy on the Sollum from west of Sidi Omar from escaping to the west. To the north, the Italian *Armored Division Ariete* was to take up an extended position and cut off the area north of the Sollum front from the west; on the left, *Infantry Division Trieste* – with which there was no contact whatever – was to carry out the same task. *Reconnaissance Battalion 33* of the *15th Panzer Division*, reinforced by artillery and antitank weapons, was to move to Bir Habata without delay and block the ascent from the coast against enemy supply traffic.

The commanding general of the *Afrika Korps*, General Crüwell, on the other hand suggested first destroying the enemy north of the Sollum front by a coordinated attack by *21st Panzer Division* to the north-west through Capuzzo and by the *15th Panzer Division* through Sidi Omar to the north-east. This suggestion, which no less misinterpreted the tactical situation, was rejected by Rommel. General Crüwell then issued the necessary orders for the divisions.

Meanwhile, the *21st Panzer Division* had continued advancing in the direction ordered and arrived with the divisional headquarters, one company of antitank troops and one rifle company at the high ground east of the Halfaya Pass after dark. On its way the division only encountered supply troops of the *4th Indian Division*, which was in the area of Sidi Omar. Owing to the inordinately rapid advance, the *21st Panzer Division* found itself stretched out over a very wide area. The divisional staff did not know the location of the rest of the division. At that time *Group Knabe* was still fighting the rear elements of the *4th Indian Division* east of the frontier wire south of Sidi Omar, while *Panzer Regiment 5* was still engaged with enemy tanks 10 kilometers to the west of the frontier wire. Fuel had been almost exhausted in all the units of the division, and none could foretell when it could be replenished.

By 1200 hours, the *15th Panzer Division* had completed reorganization and was once more fully mobile with the help of captured British vehicles. The division soon entered upon the pursuit in the wake of the *21st Panzer Division*. Towards 1400 hours it came under artillery fire on the flank in the area of Sidi Buftah, from the enemy group near Sciafsiuf, but this did no damage. Towards 1600 hours, at Gabr Saleh, it had to beat off enemy tanks which had apparently withdrawn to the south before *Panzer Regiment 5*. The rear battle groups of the division – *Schützen Regiment 115* and *Regiment 200* – were hit by several air attacks.

When night fell the division had reached the area 25 kilometers west of the borders and was continuing its advance towards the objective for the day – Gasr el Arid. Soon, however, the division met enemy vehicle convoys with tanks, which were withdrawing at great speed from north to south. They were dispersed. In disposing of them the division came dangerously close to the rear elements of *Panzer Regiment 5* fighting in front; in order to avoid mutual shelling the *15th Panzer Division* discontinued its pursuit towards 2000 hours. At daybreak the division continued, and towards 0700 hours on 25 November reached the objective prescribed for 24 November. As *Reconnaissance Battalion 33* had very few reconnaissance cars left, and as there was not enough fuel, it had been impossible to dispatch the unit to Bir Habata as had been ordered.

The Italian *Armored Division Ariete* followed the *15th Panzer Division* at a slow pace. When night fell it had arrived in the area 10 kilometers north-west of Gabr Saleh, where skirmishes took place with some weak enemy armored forces.

The Fighting around the Sollum Position

In the course of the evening General Rommel had lost his accompanying wireless links, either by enemy air attacks or because he had sent them away to pass on messages and reports. He then joined the staff of the *Afrika Korps* and tried in their company to reach his tactical headquarters, which had been sent on to Gasr el Arid. Thereby he lost direction, and found himself in the course of the night in the midst of numerous enemy columns far to the south, north of Ridotta Maddalena. It was a miracle that he escaped capture. At 0700 hours on 25 November he arrived in the lines of the *15th Panzer Division* near Gasr el Arid.

At that time he had a clear picture neither of the enemy situation nor of the whereabouts of the *21st Panzer Division* and *Armored Division Ariete*. Why he did not try to contact the *Infantry Division Savona*, which, after all, was in charge of the Sollum position and would therefore have been able to give some information regarding the enemy situation, is incomprehensible. The probable reason is that neither Rommel nor Crüwell had a working staff with them. General Rommel had got rid of most of the staff and wireless links he had taken with him by sending them away on some mission, while the *Afrika Korps* had lost most of its operational staff during the fighting on 23 November. Above all, the absence of an Ic [intelligence officer] with either was disastrous. Thus General Rommel continued to work on appreciations of the enemy situation and his own troops which were in the sharpest contrast with the actual facts.

At that time he still believed that considerable enemy forces were behind the advanced elements of the *21st Panzer Division* and the Halfaya Pass. South and east of Sidi Omar, an enemy group of considerable strength with much artillery had been recognized, but it was erroneously assumed that the strongpoints of Sidi Omar and Frongia still held out. Why no attempt was made to contact the garrison of these strongpoints, which would have brought the actual situation to light, is likewise obscure. The *2nd New Zealand Division* was still assumed to be north of the Sollum position. South of Gasr el Arid, Rommel had met numerous enemy columns, probably enemy supply troops. An enemy group with armor of unknown strength appeared to be lying opposite *Armored Division Ariete* near Gabr Saleh.

On the other hand, our own forces were but weak and – particularly the *21st Panzer Division* – widely scattered. The supply position had become most critical. The headquarters of the *21st Panzer Division* reported that they were lying immobile for lack of fuel. Since the enemy still lay at Gabr Saleh, it was doubtful whether supplies could be moved up from the Tobruk area.

In this situation Rommel had the choice among several possible decisions:

(a) A thrust into the area south and south-east of Gasr el Arid, where numerous supply dumps of the *Eighth Army* were conjectured to be. It could be expected that the enemy would suffer heavy loss and thus lose the power to supply and reinforce his badly shaken formation south-east of Tobruk. At the same time it was possible to hope for fuel from captures which would improve the supply position.

(b) The crushing of the enemy groups south of the Sollum front. It was evident that the nearest, and probably the strongest, enemy group lay south and east of Sidi Omar. The *15th Panzer Division* and strong elements of the *21st Panzer Division* were in the immediate vicinity, ready to carry out this task. Thereafter, concentrated forces could have proceeded against another enemy group.

(c) An attack with concentrated forces, as proposed by the *Afrika Korps*, against the enemy who was supposed to be north of the Sollum position. This involved considerable movement. At least it offered the advantage that both divisions could have been supplied from the fortress of Bardia, where great stocks of fuel and munitions had been accumulated.

General Rommel, however, thought he was strong enough to pursue these aims simultaneously. At 0700 hours he issued the following orders to the commanding general of the *Afrika Korps*:

The *21st Panzer Division* would attack all the enemy groups south-east of the Sollum position and drive them into the minefield; that is, the enemy assumed to be to the east of the Halfaya Pass and also the enemy force at Sidi Omar.

The *15th Panzer Division* would destroy the enemy north of the Sollum position. To achieve this it would pass round Sidi Omar, then take up an extended position between Sidi Omar and Sidi Azeiz, and from thence drive the enemy eastward into the minefield.

The instruction for *Reconnaissance Battalion 33* to advance to Bir Habata was repeated, although the necessary forces and fuel were both lacking.

The *Afrika Korps* was further given the task of forming, under Lieutenant-Colonel Knabe, commander of *Schützen Regiment 104*, a strong mixed battle group of riflemen – if possible on armored troop carriers – antitank troops, antiaircraft artillery, motorized artillery and armored reconnaissance cars, and supplying it with fuel for a journey of 490 kilometers. They were to assemble at Gasr el Arid for the capture of the oasis of Giarabub. General Rommel would give the start order personally. What object he was pursuing with this commission and what advantage he hoped therefrom are difficult to discover. He may of course have assumed that Giarabub was the supply center for the British troops for the Tobruk area, which, in view of the great distances involved, was not particularly likely.

Thereupon the *Afrika Korps* issued its orders to the divisions. The *21st Panzer Division* was instructed to assemble its forces east of the Halfaya Pass; *Panzer Regiment 5*, which in the meantime had arrived south of Sidi Omar, was ordered to rejoin its division. The *15th Panzer Division* was to move off to the north without delay. In the case of the *15th Panzer Division*, it would be of great importance to "create as much dust as possible," in order to deceive the enemy concerning its scanty strength, and thus drive him into the minefield. The *Afrika Korps* wished to carry out the mandate for the formation of *Group Giarabub* by ordering the *21st Panzer Division* to detach the regimental headquarters of *Schützen Regiment 104*, one antitank company, and one antiaircraft battery, with adequate fuel; the *15th Panzer Division* was to detach one rifle battalion and one company of armored troop carriers, one light battery and two armored reconnaissance car platoons, and liberal ammunition and fuel.

As was only to be expected, Rommel's ambitious instructions were partly not carried out, and partly, owing to lack of manpower and supply difficulties, failed to secure the desired result.

From the *21st Panzer Division, Group Ravenstein* (division staff plus weak elements) arrived in the Halfaya Pass and Faltenbacher strongpoints without interference from the enemy. The enemy group assumed to be to the east of Halfaya Pass proved to be nonexistent. General Ravenstein reported his intention to continue the advance to the north-west to capture the enemy strongpoint of Capuzzo. This was forbidden by the *Afrika Korps. Group Knabe* (*Schützen Regiment 104*) finally joined the divisional staff at the Faltenbacher strongpoint at 1700 hours. In the end it too lacked fuel.

On the other hand, *Panzer Regiment 5*, which had been ordered by the *Afrika Korps* to join General Ravenstein, was unable to carry out this order.

General Rommel, without informing the *Afrika Korps*, now instructed it to attack the enemy group east of Sidi Omar. The attack, which had to be carried out without preliminary reconnaissance and without infantry and artillery support, failed in the face of resistance by an enemy superior in artillery and antitank weapons who had established himself in the positions and behind the minefields of the captured strongpoint of Frongia. The repetition of the attack during the afternoon against the enemy-occupied parts of Sidi Omar likewise achieved no result. In these attacks *Panzer Regiment 5* lost half of its strength, and by evening the regiment had little more than 17 tanks. Here, too, the fuel supply was exhausted.

In the morning, and before the beginning of the attack it had been ordered to carry out, the *15th Panzer Division* was struck by several heavy enemy air attacks and suffered losses. At 0830 hours it proceeded northward, passed round Sidi Omar on the west and thus came under the fire of several batteries in the strongpoint. Having replenished fuel and ammunition, the division continued its move to the north at 1300 hours and, fifteen kilometers north of Sidi Omar, collided with an enemy battle group with 20 heavy tanks. These were completely wiped out in a bitter tank battle.

In spite of grave doubts, the division strung itself out between Sidi Omar and Sidi Azeiz as ordered, though this kind of disposition seemed appropriate neither for an effective attack nor for repulsing a breakout attempt by strong enemy forces. The *15th Panzer Division* did not send away the detachments it had been ordered to contribute to *Group Giarabub* since all its formations were committed, and no fuel was available for the detachment. During the evening, the division reported its intention to attack in the morning of 26 November a smaller enemy group sighted near Sidi Azeiz and then to push through to Bardia, there to take in supplies of fuel and ammunition. Concerning the situation of *Armored Division Ariete*, no precise news was available. The division seemed to be engaged in fighting enemy armored forces, and to have reached Gabr Saleh during the evening.

The enemy situation south of the battle headquarters of the *Afrika Korps*, which had remained somewhat exposed near Gasr el Arid, was obscure. It seemed that a new enemy force was concentrating there, which towards evening shelled the battle headquarters of the *Afrika Korps*.

The only protective force available was *Reconnaissance Battalion 3*, which had suffered severe losses from five heavy enemy bombing attacks. For this reason Rommel refrained from sending it to Habata. Instead, the detachment, in extended positions on both sides of Gasr el Arid, was to block the roads from Tobruk leading to the south-east. During the evening the unit was pulled back once more by the *15th Panzer Division*, owing to a misunderstanding.

Reconnaissance Battalion 3 had been ordered by General Rommel at the beginning of the push to move south-eastward from its position near Gambut to join the *Afrika Korps* in the area of Gasr el Arid. During the night of 24/25 November the detachment succeeded in fighting its way with great difficulty through the *2nd New Zealand Division*, and during the afternoon of 25 November made contact with the *15th Panzer Division* north of Sidi Omar. The unit was regarded by the *Afrika Korps* as a welcome reinforcement for the weak forces south of Sidi Omar.

Throughout the whole day the troops of the *Afrika Korps* had been subjected to uninterrupted attacks from the air by strong enemy air formations. Serious casualties were suffered in many cases. The fighter support called for by wireless from the *Panzergruppe* could not be provided as the distance to the Sollum front was too great.

During 25 November the supply position of the *Afrika Korps* became increasingly critical. Not until the night of 25/26 November did a few supply columns of the *21st Panzer Division* arrive, which had been compelled to fight their way through several enemy groups. What they brought was not enough, however, to make the *21st Panzer Division* again fully mobile.

Throughout this period General Rommel learnt nothing of the development of the situation on the other battlefield of the North African war theater. He had no wireless links at his disposal and could not be reached by his operational staff, which was meanwhile conducting the battle around Tobruk. In the Tobruk area the situation was growing increasingly critical. The operations officer (Ia) of the *Panzergruppe*, Lieutenant-Colonel (General Staff) Westphal, kept sending more and more urgent wireless messages to Rommel in which he reported attacks by the *2nd New Zealand Division* growing in strength, breakout attempts by the Tobruk garrison, growing in violence, and the concentration of a new enemy group around Bir el Gubi. In language which became more and more urgent, Westphal begged for an attack by the *Afrika Korps* in the rear of the *2nd New Zealand Division*. This would be the last opportunity, never to return, of bringing the battle of Tobruk to a successful conclusion. As these messages did not reach General Rommel, he devoted himself from midday on 25 November to the *Afrika Korps* and to the two *Panzer* divisions. Finally, he tried to get situation maps to Rommel by air. Both aircraft dispatched for this purpose were, however, shot down. The wireless messages sent by Westphal did not come to the knowledge of General Rommel until 1000 hours on 26 November through the *Afrika Korps*. Westphal further realized that the supply position of the German troops in the Sollum area must automatically become most critical. He made every effort to have supply convoys taken through the enemy fighting formations south-east of Tobruk; only part of these convoys, however, arrived at their destination.

The *Afrika Korps*, which, as mentioned above, was without an adequate staff, had a most unreliable picture of the enemy situation on the evening of 25 November. An attempt was made to carry out the difficult tasks prescribed by Rommel to the best of its ability. It sought to carry out the order for the destruction of the southernmost of the enemy forces on the Sollum front by instructing the *21st Panzer Division* to send in all troops which could be spared north of the Sollum front against the enemy group south of Sidi Omar. However, the main body of the *21st Panzer Division* in the Faltenbacher strongpoint was still paralyzed by lack of fuel. Near Sidi Omar only the remainder of *Panzer Regiment 5* and *Reconnaissance Battalion 3* were available, in addition to those elements which the *21st Panzer Division* had earmarked for the Giarabub enterprise. The *Afrika Korps* continued preparations for the latter, although it was quite clear that the dwindling divisions could spare no more forces for it.

The task of destroying the enemy forces north of the Sollum front was left by the *Afrika Korps* to the *15th Panzer Division*. From its distant battle headquarters it certainly could not control the fighting in this area. It ordered the division to continue its attack on 26 November from Sidi Azeiz to Capuzzo and to ensure its replenishment from the fortress of Bardia. The *Afrika Korps* had no contact with *Armored Division Ariete*. On 25 November and on 26 November, the latter was left to its own devices.

At 1000 hours on 26 November, Rommel arrived at the battle headquarters of the *Afrika Korps*. There he received the wireless messages from his operations officer (Ia) on the situation at Tobruk. These, however, brought him to no new decision. On the contrary, he instructed the *Afrika Korps* first of all to destroy the enemy forces facing the Sollum front. The battle against these must be accelerated and brought to a conclusion. Further, the enemy was to be deceived regarding the meager strength of the German forces by the making of much dust. Rommel hoped he would thus be brought to the early abandonment of the battle. He even continued to persist in the Giarabub enterprise, with the proviso, however, that it should be begun only on his personal orders.

Withthe *21st Panzer Division* the day passed without any particular operational activity. The bulk of the division, less *Panzer Regiment 5*, was concentrated around the Halfaya Pass strongpoint. Through a mistaken interpretation of the order from the *Afrika Korps*, the division was preparing an attack northward in order to break through to Bardia to draw fuel and ammunition from its stocks. It began the advance, which was supported by the artillery of the Halfaya Pass strongpoint and that of Faltenbacher, at about 1700 hrs. After nightfall New Zealand positions at Musaid were overrun and a breakthrough to the north was achieved with some loss. To its surprise, the division met, east of Capuzzo, elements of the *15th Panzer Division*, which for its part had known nothing of the attack of the *21st Panzer Division*.

At Sidi Omar, *Reconnaissance Battalion 3* was sent into action, without the knowledge of the *Afrika Korps*, against the enemy group. The attack, which had to be carried out without armored or artillery support, failed once again.

During the afternoon, the *Afrika Korps* formed *Group Wechmar* out of *Reconnaissance Battalion 3* and the remainder of *Panzer Regiment 5* and ordered it to repeat the attack against the enemy at Sidi Omar after thorough reconnaissance. *Group Wechmar*, however, which had been given full discretion as to the timing of the advance, did not attack on 26 November.

Armored Division Ariete, before which the enemy armor had fallen back to the north, arrived at Sidi Omar on 26 November. It passed round to the north-west of the strongpoint and towards evening reached the area west of Bir Ghirba, where an enemy strongpoint was identified. Why the *Afrika Korps* had not brought up *Armored Division Ariete* to assist in the attack on Sidi Omar has not been explained.

South of the *Afrika Korps* battle headquarters at Gasr el Arid, the enemy continued to grow in strength during 26 November. Towards noon an enemy battle group launched a surprise attack from three sides against corps battle headquarters. Corps headquarters fell back to the north, suffering casualties, and into the arms of *Group Knabe*, which was standing by for the Giarabub undertaking.

The *15th Panzer Division* had been listening in to the increasingly urgent wireless messages of the operations officer (Ia) of the *Panzergruppe* during 25 November and in the morning of 26 November. It considered a plan to push to the south-west on 26 November, join up with *Ariete*, which was assumed to be still at Gabr Saleh, and order its supply columns into this area, from which it would advance on Tobruk together with *Ariete*. This seemed attractive, the more so as it was uncertain whether there would be enough fuel and ammunition available in Bardia.

In the early morning, before a decision was taken, the division was attacked by weak enemy armored forces. These were thrown back to Sidi Azeiz by a counterattack. Towards 0730 hours the division decided to push on to Bardia after all. Enemy forces of lesser strength, which were encountered in the north-east, withdrew. Towards 1130 hours the fortress area of Bardia was reached. Replenishment of the division was immediately set in train, but through lack of preparation in the fortress wasted much time.

In order to carry out the orders of the *Afrika Korps*, the *15th Panzer Division*, during the afternoon, ordered *Schützen Regiment 115*, supported by the bulk of the artillery, to advance from the north to the firmly held strongpoint of Capuzzo. By nightfall the left wing of the attack had driven into Sollum, while the right wing had worked its way to within assaulting distance of Capuzzo. At that moment General Rommel made a personal appearance on the battlefield. He had intended to attack on a broad front against the entire northern side of the Sollum position between Sidi Omar and Capuzzo, which, naturally, had little tactical chance of success. He ordered the immediate cessation of the attack and the withdrawal of the attacking forces to their start lines. Before the order could be carried out, however, the forward elements of the *21st Panzer Division* approached from the south, along the Via Balbia. This, too, was not at all what General Rommel desired, but no more changes could be made. Thus, the *21st Panzer Division* reached the fortress of Bardia during the night and replenished its fuel and ammunition.

In the course of 26 November the wireless messages of the operations officer (Ia) of the *Panzergruppe* on the Tobruk situation became increasingly urgent. Lieutenant-Colonel (General Staff) Westphal reported that the enemy attacking from the east with 30 tanks had reached Belhamed immediately south of *Group Böttcher*. Its south wing was now being attacked by tanks. He called for an immediate attack by the *Afrika Korps* into the rear of the *2nd New Zealand Division*. These wireless messages, too, failed to reach General Rommel until the evening of 26 November in Bardia.

Return of the *Afrika Korps*
to the Tobruk Front on 27 November

General Rommel's Orders for 27 November. General Rommel issued his orders to the two divisions for 27 November between 0100 hours and 0200 hours on the same day. He appreciated that the situation around Tobruk was serious. The destruction of the enemy forces on the Sollum front had therefore to be carried through to its end without delay, so that all available forces could thereupon move to the assistance of the Tobruk front. *Group Wechmar* must therefore bring the attack on Sidi Omar to a close in the early morning. At dawn the *15th Panzer Division* must attack from the line Azeiz–Bardia on a broad front against the line Sidi Omar–Capuzzo.

Against this, the commander of the *15th Panzer Division* objected that such an attack would take up much time. An advance on Tobruk would then hardly be feasible on the same day. Moreover, he was of the opinion that an attack, launched with forces thus dispersed, would have little chance of success against an enemy well prepared for the defense and would involve heavy casualties. For this reason he would suggest that a large enemy supply dump – at Sidi Azeiz – reported by *Reconnaissance Battalion 33* during the previous night should be attacked; and thus a preliminary condition for the return trip to Tobruk would be assured. General Rommel dismissed these objections and insisted on the attack.

The *21st Panzer Division*, whose fighting power was very low and whose *Panzer* regiment was still at Sidi Omar, was ordered to proceed towards Tobruk without delay in two columns, on the Via Balbia and on the edge of the high ground to the south thereof.

Course of the Fighting on the Morning of 27 November

Knowing what the position around Tobruk was like, the commander of the *15th Panzer Division* expected that Rommel would soon have to give up the plan of attacking Capuzzo. To gain time, he ordered the bulk of his forces, with *Panzer Regiment 8* and the bulk of the artillery in the van, to move towards Sidi Azeiz. Closely behind followed *Regiment 200* with *Engineer Battalion 33*; *Rifle Regiment 115* and an artillery battalion followed two hours later. On the way out of Bardia, there was a difficult route crossing with the *21st Panzer Division*, which was moving northward along the same road.

Towards 0700 hours the divisional reconnaissance patrols reported a strong enemy force with a very large number of vehicles, ten tanks and several batteries. *Panzer Regiment 8*, supported by the bulk of the artillery and followed closely by *Regiment 200*, at once attacked this enemy. After a short and bitter fight, it broke into the enemy positions. A huge supply dump, all the baggage of the *2nd New Zealand Division*, six guns and 800 prisoners, including a brigadier-general, fell into our hands.

At this moment, towards 0900 hours, General Rommel appeared on the battlefield. In the meantime he had changed his mind. He instructed the division to proceed along the Trigh Capuzzo towards Tobruk at top speed, in order to relieve the closely pressed *Group Böttcher*. At the same time he held back the reinforced *Schützen Regiment 115*, which was first to carry through the attack on Capuzzo. *Engineer Battalion 33* was to remain at Sidi Azeiz as its reserve.

Owing to the further development of the situation before Tobruk, General Rommel sent *Schützen Regiment 115* during the afternoon after the *15th Panzer Division*, which it caught up with towards evening. On the other hand, he personally threw *Engineer Battalion 33* into an attack on Capuzzo, in their vehicles and without artillery support. This attack was, as was only to be expected, a complete failure. In it the battalion lost half of its fighting strength and more of its vehicles.

The *21st Panzer Division* bumped with its two columns a well constructed enemy strongpoint 15 kilometers west of Bardia, on the ridge south of the Via Balbia, which was stubbornly defended by a reinforced enemy battalion. The advance of the *21st Panzer Division* came to a halt in front of this strongpoint.

On the morning of 27 November the commanding general of the *Afrika Korps* was in no available position. He had no news of the bulk of his divisions. General Rommel continually interfered in his command sphere, without informing him of his interventions. The attack he had been ordered to launch on Sidi Omar he regarded, in view of the meager forces remaining at his disposal, as offering few prospects. He regarded himself, however, as bound nevertheless to carry out his instructions. Lieutenant-Colonel Westphal's wireless messages had long convinced him that it was high time to move the *Afrika Korps* back to Tobruk. And so he decided, on the morning of 27 November, to go back himself to his divisions after instructing *Reconnaissance Battalion 3 (Group Wechmar)* to carry through the attack against the enemy at Sidi Omar with all speed and energy. He decided to proceed to Sidi Azeiz and thence to make contact with his divisions. On his way he met *Armored Division Ariete*, which was exchanging fire with the strongpoint of Bir Ghirba. On his own responsibility, he ordered it to break off the attack and follow the *15th Panzer Division* south of Trigh Capuzzo towards Tobruk.

East of Gasr el Arid, at about 1230 hours, he met the *15th Panzer Division*, which had been advancing west from Sidi Azeiz since 1030 hours. He was informed concerning the situation of the division and, with the Corps headquarters, followed its advance.

The Fighting during the Afternoon of 27 November

Shortly afterwards, at about 1330 hours, the *15th Panzer Division* was involved in heavy fighting east of Sciafsciuf. The division bumped a strongly manned enemy position which blocked the Trigh Capuzzo west of Sciafsciuf and was soon attacked from the south by very superior enemy armored forces supported by strong artillery. The division decided to attack and take the ridge south of the Trigh Capuzzo in order to drive off the enemy artillery which was keeping the entire valley under direct observation and effective direct fire. The attack proved to be very difficult indeed as the enemy was greatly superior in armor. For a short while the division was in a serious position, as fresh enemy armor descended from the south-east, advancing against the soft-skinned part of the division down in the bottom of the valley. The supply services of the division withdrew to the north.

At that moment 15 tanks arrived in timely fashion from the repair shops of the division in Gambut. They were immediately thrown into a counter-attack. The attacking enemy armor was thus halted just in front of our battery positions. A great number of enemy tanks were thus destroyed. The division urgently requested the *Panzergruppe* to allow the units which had been kept back at Sidi Azeiz to be brought forward at once. Towards 1730 hours, when the reinforced *Schützen Regiment 115* arrived, the danger to the rear had passed.

Towards evening, the advance of the division finally gained ground. The southern ridge was taken; the enemy armor withdrew to the south, in spite of their superior numbers. After nightfall the division moved 10 kilometers to the west along the southern ridge in order to break the enemy encirclement and gain more favorable positions, and to reach the area south of Sciafsciuf.

The *21st Panzer Division* had not succeeded by evening in taking the enemy strongpoint 15 kilometers to the west of Bardia, so it wheeled to the south in the evening in order to place itself behind the *15th Panzer Division* on the Trigh Capuzzo.

Towards evening, *Armored Division Ariete* was also approaching from the east. Its action may have contributed to the easing of the situation for the *15th Panzer Division* during the evening of 27 November.

The Fighting before Tobruk, 24–27 November

On the morning of 24 November, the operations officer (Ia) of *Panzergruppe* was faced with a difficult task. He had to shoulder the responsibility for the entire Tobruk front, and had to assert his authority over the Italian Corps commanders, who were far senior to him both in service and in years. It must be said that these accepted his authority without friction, and carried out his orders without a murmur. In particular, General Navarini, who as com-mander of *XXI Corps* was in charge of the east sector of Tobruk and who carried the main burden of the fighting, supported 'him in the most comradely way. Some minor difficulty arose with General Gambara, who was in command of the Italian *Motorized Corps* and simultaneously Chief of Staff to the Italian Commander-in-Chief in North Africa, General Bastico. He considered that in this capacity he was justified in many ways in altering orders issued by the *Panzergruppe* to Italian divisions without reporting the alterations – which would naturally lead to friction.

The situation east of Tobruk had become difficult in the course of 24 November. In the morning of that day it had been established beyond dispute that the main body of the *2nd New Zealand Division* was in the area and advancing to the west. It is true that the battle group of *Antiaircraft Machine Gun Battalion 606* succeeded in defending the area around Gambut and the supply installations of the *15th Panzer Division* to the north-west. In spite of having been outflanked on both sides, *Reconnaissance Battalion 3* also held its ground, where the track goes up between Gambut and the Trigh Capuzzo, until the evening of 24 November. Neither of these units, however, was able to prevent strong enemy forces with 30 tanks from advancing between the Via Balbia and the Trigh Capuzzo farther to the west. On the evening of 24 November the positions of *Group Böttcher*, which had been entrusted with the task of defense against the east, had already been attacked east of Belhamed. On the morning of 25 November the New Zealanders succeeded in making a penetration, which was ironed out in a counter-attack towards noon. The enemy, however, steadily increased his strength in this area until nightfall.

During the evening of 24 November the garrison of Tobruk resumed its breakout attempts. The main effort of its attacks was directed against Height El Duda with the apparent object of stretching out a hand to the New Zealand division, which was coming up from the east. Early on 25 Novem-ber the Tobruk garrison succeeded in making a number of lesser penetrations in the sector of the *Infantry Division Bologna* which were, with some difficulty, contained by reserves from *Division z.b.v. Afrika*.

During 25 November the breakout attempts became more violent and included the southern front of Tobruk. The resistance of the Italian troops became less energetic under heavy enemy artillery fire and attacks by heavy British tanks. The siege front had to be moved back in several places. A gap which appeared on the southern Tobruk front between the *Pavia* and *Trento* divisions could barely be closed by throwing in a regiment of *Motorized Division Trieste*. Permission for its use had to be wrung from General Gambara with the greatest difficulty.

During the evening of 25 November the enemy, who had been defeated in the area of Bir el Gubi, began to stir again. A report from the air indicated that considerable enemy armored and motorized forces were concentrating in that area. Enemy armored reconnaissance felt forward towards the southern wing of *Group Böttcher*.

On the morning of 25 November, Lieutenant-Colonel Westphal regarded the situation in front of Tobruk as most disturbing. He was certain that, in view of the decline in the Italian powers of resistance, he would not be able to hold the line of investment, threatened as it was from the rear, with his own forces. Unless support came soon its early collapse was inevitable. On the other hand, he realised that an attack by the *Afrika Korps* from the east into the rear of the *2nd New Zealand Division* would offer a unique opportunity of destroying that division, before the British *7th Armored Division* again became fit for action. The latter might happen very soon, and with it the position of the entire *Panzergruppe* would become most dangerous. As already mentioned, he begged General Rommel in numerous wireless messages of ever increasing urgency from the morning of 25 November onward to intervene speedily with the *Afrika Korps* in the rear of the *2nd New Zealand Division*.

November 25 was the critical day in the battle for Tobruk. All day long bitter fighting raged for the possession of Belhamed and El Duda. The gallantly fighting troops of *General Böttcher*, and with them a Bersaglieri regiment from *Infantry Division Trieste*, suffered heavy and bloody casualties and lost many prisoners. During the evening of 25 November, the *2nd New Zealand Division* attacked and captured the German positions on Belhamed. Simultaneously a particularly strong breakout attempt of the Tobruk garrison resulted in the final loss of the important height of El Duda. This meant that at this spot the siege front had burst open and the *2nd New Zealand Division* and the Tobruk garrison had joined hands.

The situation on the south of wing of *Group Böttcher* also became more grave. An attack by the British *7th Armored Division* against the southern flank at Bir Bu Creimisa could be repulsed only with the greatest difficulty.

Under the stress of this situation, Lieutenant-Colonel Westphal decided to withdraw *Group Böttcher* during the night of 25/26 November to the line

Bir Salem–Bir Bu Creimisa–El Adem and to strengthen the defensive flank between Bir Bu Creimisa and El Adem with the remainder of *Infantry Division Trieste*. The *Division z.b.v. Afrika*, with elements of *Infantry Division Bologna*, which was holding the sector to the north of the enemy penetration, were to form a defensive flank facing south, on the north of Belhamed, and to maintain contact with Gambut. On this day, too, all wireless messages asking Rommel to dispatch the *Afrika Korps* to Tobruk remained without result.

On 26 November the situation on the siege front and on the defensive positions of *Group Böttcher* became more stable. The enemy was unable to achieve further penetration; the corridor between the Tobruk garrison and the *2nd New Zealand Division* was only narrow. The British *7th Armored Division* did not intervene in the fighting on this day, perhaps under the impression that the *Afrika Korps* was approaching.

On 27 November a reconnaissance push by *Group Böttcher* established that the British had meanwhile occupied Belhamed and El Duda with considerable forces, including artillery and heavy tanks.

Rommel's advance to the Sollum front appears in retrospect as a bad dream. It was indeed the turning point of the whole campaign. On 24 November the victorious conclusion of the great defensive battle seemed to be within grasp. The ring around Tobruk stood unshaken. The British *XXX Corps* had been heavily defeated. Its remnants seemed hardly capable of mounting a new attack. The *2nd New Zealand Division* stood isolated and in a dangerous position east of Tobruk. It would indeed be fortunate if it were able to escape destruction by a rapid withdrawal. On the other side, the *Afrika Korps*, although weakened by losses, was still fully battleworthy. It seemed that all that remained was to complete the victory already begun.

However, during the four days between 24 and 27 November, the situation of the *Panzergruppe Afrika* took a turn as surprising as it was unfortunate. On 27 November the situation in front of Tobruk had become critical. The ring encircling Tobruk had been broken open; the German and the Italian investing forces had suffered heavy losses and were at the end of their tether. The British leadership had succeeded in filling the gaps in the shattered *XXX Corps*. Once again this corps stood menacingly south-east of Tobruk. The supply position began to be critical. After unlucky operations, and with its striking power reduced, the *Afrika Korps* had returned to the Tobruk area. It had become doubtful whether it was still possible to restore the situation before Tobruk and keep off the superior forces of the enemy.

Rommel's decisions taken during his push to the Sollum front and the manner of their execution are not understandable unless one takes into consideration the technical condition under which the German command functioned during these days. General Rommel intended, when he left his headquarters on 24 November, to return in the evening of the same day. For this reason he had taken with him no staff to deal with enemy intelligence or with supplies. The signalers who he had with him were quite inadequate. They fell away, moreover, after a few hours through being sent off or by enemy action, which made the correct handling of operation quite impossible. Rommel therefore acted during the whole thrust with no knowledge of the general situation, and merely on his personal impressions based on local conditions. Unfortunately the *Afrika Korps* labored under the same disabilities since, with few exceptions, its own staff and the corps signals detachment had fallen into enemy hands during 23 November.

Early on 24 November, General Rommel evidently assumed that after the defeat of 23 November the British leadership had no alternative but to withdraw to Egypt. Apparently he had not yet realized that the *2nd New Zealand Division* was advancing from the east towards Tobruk. Thus he decided to annihilate the enemy which had been shattered on 23 November by means of an energetic pursuit to the south-east, instead of turning against the enemy group east of Tobruk.

This decision was not without a certain justification. Had it been possible to capture the battle headquarters and supply installations of the enemy in the frontier area in the course of this advance, it would have been practically impossible for the British to resume their offensive. Then there would still have been time to fall on the enemy groups east of Tobruk from the south-east – a particularly effective direction – and annihilate them. It is a fact that the commander of the British *Eighth Army*, General Cunningham, under the influence of this thrust, had decided to withdraw to Egypt – a decision which was not carried out, for the sole reason that General Auchinleck replaced General Cunningham with General Ritchie. Since, for the rest, General Rommel was not in possession of the available information regarding the location of British supply installations, the battle headquarters and the supply dumps of British *Eighth Army* remained unmolested, unless they happened to be in the line of Rommel's advance. Thus the British leadership was able to continue supplying its formations in the Tobruk area and in the course of a few days to provide fresh war equipment.

In the course of 24 November General Rommel changed his intentions. He now regarded the relief of the encircled Sollum front as the objective of his thrust, although its position was in no way precarious; very soon, however, it was the destruction of the enemy forces opposite the Sollum front. This new decision was undoubtedly questionable. It meant the displacement of the immediate and most important task, namely the destruction of the enemy in the Tobruk area, in favor of a remote and time-consuming objective, to attain which would cost much time. The second stop would thus be completed before the first. For days on end the Tobruk front was left to its own devices, which, considering its insufficient forces and means, involved a considerable danger. The enemy to the south-east of Tobruk was allowed time to make his beaten and scattered forces once more fit for battle. Further, so long as the enemy groups to the east and south-east of Tobruk had not been finally eliminated, the supply of the the *Afrika Korps* in its operations on the Sollum front would prove extremely difficult.

In no circumstances was it justifiable for General Rommel to stay so long away from his battle headquarters without an adequate staff, without signal facilities and without appointing a responsible commander for the Tobruk front: the reins of the whole African theater were left dragging along the ground. For three days Rommel remained without information regarding the development of the situation on the Tobruk front. The results of air reconnaissance, inadequate in any case, did not come to his knowledge, the German-Italian air force cold not be called upon to support the *Afrika Korps* in its operations, and Rommel's decisions were not adjusted to the general situation. On the other hand, the staff of the *Panzergruppe* before Tobruk were unaware of the development of the situation with the *Afrika Korps*, and on their side had not enough information on which to base their decisions.

Rommel's conduct of operations during his thrust in the Sollum area appears confused and purposeless. Even when the inadequate staff machinery at his disposal is taken into consideration, it is impossible to escape the conclusion that, during the period of the thrust, he was not on the accustomed level of his ability.

If Rommel's decision be accepted, then the proposed destruction of the enemy on the Sollum front must be quickly and easily completed in order then to be free for other tasks. Here clarity must be achieved as quickly as possible as to where the enemy actually was. Since the results of air reconnaissance could not be secured, and *Reconnaissance Battalion 33*, which was all that was at his disposal, was very weak, it would have seemed natural to make immediate contact with *Infantry Division Savona* and the German strongpoints holding out in Sidi Omar, which in any case must certainly know the strength and disposition of the enemy forces. Most surprisingly, contact was not made with *Infantry Division Savona* at all; and with the garrison of Sidi Omar not until 27 November, after several offensive operations had ended in failure and caused much loss. Instead, Rommel made his decisions on the basis of arbitrary and most inaccurate appreciations of the enemy's situation.

Rommel's orders disregarded the weakness of the available troops and the difficulties of their supply problem. Reliance was placed on forces which in reality did not exist; tasks were allotted which were beyond the power of the formations, because these were doomed to immobility through shortage of fuel and ammunition.

The conduct of operations also suffered because Rommel had not clearly defined the sphere of command of the *Afrika Korps*, and often interfered personally in the command of particular units, without informing the division in question or the *Afrika Korps*. A number of mutually contradictory orders was the result. In the end, the divisions took matters into their own hands simply by acting on their own initiative without reference to orders, as the situation required.

Frequently the orders given by Rommel on the spot contradicted every tactical principle and resulted in expensive failure. For instance, tanks were repeatedly sent in to attack well-mined field fortifications with no support from other weapons. On 25 and 26 November, the *15th Panzer Division* was given the task of attacking a line of enemy infantry stretching over 25 kilometers. Particularly glaring examples of such tasks were the orders to *Engineer Battalion 33* to attack an enemy regiment in the strongpoint of Capuzzo in their vehicles and to *Reconnaissance Battalion 33* to advance against the whole of the *4th Indian Division* at Sidi Omar.

In the morning of 25 November it would still have been possible to achieve a rapid success. For that, Rommel would have certainly had to keep together the dwindling forces of the *Afrika Korps* with a firm hand. The conditions therefore were favorable enough. At that time, the *21st Panzer Division* was indeed rather split up and some of its units were immobile, but the *15th Panzer Division* and essential parts of the *21st Panzer Division* stood ready for use south of Sidi Omar, and, further, the Italian *Ariete Division* could have been brought up.

With these forces Rommel could either have attempted a blow against the British supply services in the area south-east of Gasr el Arid, or have concentrated them for an attack on the rear of the *4th Indian Division* south and east of Sidi Omar. This attack would have offered a good chance of speedily annihilating this, the strongest of the enemy groups on the Sollum front. Thereafter, it would have been possible, as the situation developed, to deal with the various enemy groups to the north of the Sollum front or to move off to Tobruk, to destroy the *2nd New Zealand Division.*

Rommel, however, decided to tackle those various tasks simultaneously. The *21st Panzer Division* should hold down the enemy to the south of Sollum and the *15th Panzer Division* those to the north of Sollum on a broad front. *Reconnaissance Battalion 33* should thrust to Bir Habata to cut the enemy supply line. Altogether fantastic was the raid on Giarabub, which took no note of the force available and the fuel position. Although in the end it did not materialize, it did withdraw considerable forces of the *21st Panzer Division* from other tasks for days on end.

It is not surprising that the forces of the *Afrika Korps* were insufficient for the simultaneous solution of all these tasks, and that, in spite of all their efforts and losses, no success was achieved worth mentioning.

The question remains why Rommel did not make up his mind to return to the Tobruk front until 27 November. Had he taken this decision and carried it out on 25 November, the *2nd New Zealand Division* would most probably have been rapidly destroyed: the breach in the investment of Tobruk could have been prevented. On 26 November it was still possible to attack the rear of the New Zealanders before the British *7th Armored Division* was in a position to intervene in the fight. The return of the *Afrika Korps* to the Tobruk front on 27 November happened, literally, at the very last moment for the prevention of the complete collapse of the front.

Rommel learned of the precarious situation before Tobruk only on 26 November, and even then maintained with great stubbornness his intention to destroy the enemy facing the Sollum front. The return to the Tobruk front would not have taken place even on 27 November but for the decision of the *21st Panzer Division* to advance from Halfaya Pass to Bardia on its own initiative, of the *15th Panzer Division* to advance towards Sidi Azeiz, and of the *Afrika Korps* to abandon the attack on Sidi Omar. Thus it was possible, by the evening of 27 November, at least to concentrate the forces of the *Afrika Korps* on the Trigh Capuzzo west of Sidi Azeiz, although not without heavy fighting.

The responsibility which the operations officer (Ia) of *Panzergruppe Afrika* had to shoulder during the advance to the Sollum front was extraordinarily heavy. He not only had to look after the interests of the *Panzergruppe* in dealings with the German and Italian supreme commands, he was also responsible for the conduct of all the operations on the entire Tobruk front. The fact that there was practically no friction is a credit to his skill and tact, and a testimony also to the loyalty of the commanders of the three Italian corps. It must be mentioned that in this case the difficulties of coalition warfare (*Bündniskrieg*) were solved in exemplary fashion. It is true that, in the long run, he did not succeed in preventing the breach of the investing line. For that the superiority of the British forces attacking from the east and also from within the fortress was too great, and he had nothing comparable to throw against their many heavy tanks. Nonetheless, he succeeded in delaying the collapse of the investing front by agile and versatile leadership and in limiting the breakthrough to so narrow an area that the conditions for a successful counterattack by the *Afrika Korps* already existed. It must be stressed that, during the fighting around Tobruk, not only German, but Italian troops as well, fought with great courage and persistence.

The Smashing of the 2nd New Zealand Division

On the evening of 27 November General Rommel was able, for the first time since the morning of 24 November, to make mutual contact from Gambut with his battle headquarters in El Adem. There the situation before Tobruk was regarded as extremely critical. It is true that on 27 November the British had not continued their attack, probably under the influence of the return of the *Afrika Korps*. But the power of resistance of the Italian formations began to decrease to an alarming degree. On the morning of 27 November the operations officer (Ia) of the *Panzergruppe* had only with great difficulty prevented the Italian corps commanders of the *Motorized Corps* and *XXI Corps* from withdrawing their battle headquarters from El Adem to the rear, which in the opinion of operations officer (Ia) would certainly have resulted in the disintegration of the siege front.

The orders group during the night of 27/28 November, with the commanding general of the *Afrika Korps* and the commanders or the operations officers (Ia) of the *15th* and *21st Panzer Divisions* and *Ariete*, was held by General Rommel under the impact of a most serious appraisal of the situation. It served not only to clarify previous misunderstandings but principally to lay down the plan for the destruction of the *2nd New Zealand Division*. Therein a fundamental difference of opinion became apparent between General Rommel and the commanding general of the *Afrika Korps*, General Crüwell, regarding the conduct of the attack.

General Rommel was of the opinion that the *Afrika Korps* should be moved northward into the area of *Division z.b.v. Afrika* near the junction of the Axis Road with the Via Balbia east of Tobruk, and from there conduct the attack to the south-west to close the gap in the siege front and cut off the *2nd New Zealand Division* from its contact with Tobruk. Only thus could the intervention of enemy armored forces south-east of Tobruk be prevented: otherwise, to hold them off would demand too great a force. On the other hand, General Crüwell held that the attack should be launched against the line Belhamed–El Duda by both divisions of the *Afrika Korps* from the south-east, astride the Trigh Capuzzo, to drive the *2nd New Zealand Division* into Tobruk. Crüwell regarded the abandonment of the southern escarpment south of Trigh Capuzzo as dangerous, since the enemy held favorable artillery positions there from which he would dominate the breach in the siege front. Later it would be very difficult to drive him off these heights. If the *Afrika Korps* attacked from the south-east, *Armored Division Ariete* could easily be used to cover the southern flank.

This order group did not result in a final decision; nor did another discussion held by General Rommel and General Crüwell at 0800 hours on 28 November. General Rommel ordered the *Afrika Korps* to work its way further west during 28 November, so as to reach a start line for the attack on 29 November, but to avoid any serious engagement. For the rest, reconnaissance patrols should explore possibilities of attack, particularly from the area of *Division z.b.v. Afrika*, so as to provide the necessary information for a final decision. *Armored Division Ariete* was placed under command of the *Afrika Korps*.

On 28 November, immediately after this discussion, Rommel flew back to his battle headquarters at El Adem, which he had left early on 24 November.

The Plan of Attack of the *Afrika Korps*

The result of his investigation in the sector of *Division z.b.v. Afrika* convinced General Crüwell that conditions for an attack by the *Afrika Korps* from the north-east were unfavorable. Ground reconnaissance and reconnaissance results forwarded by the staff of *Panzergruppe Afrika* indicated that the bulk of the *2nd New Zealand Division* was still to the north of the Trigh Capuzzo in the area Zaafran–Belhamed–El Duda. Two to three British armored brigades lay on the southern flank of the *Afrika Korps* to the south and south-west of Gasr el Arid, whilst a new group seemed to be in the process of formation around Bir el Gubi.

At 1445 hours, therefore, the *Afrika Korps* wirelessed to *Panzergruppe Afrika* the following suggestion for an attack on 29 November:

Attack by the *Afrika Korps* on the line Belhamed *(21st Panzer Division)*–El Duda *(15th Panzer Division)* against the line Point 145–Bir Bu Assaten with the object of driving the enemy into Tobruk and of regaining the old siege front. *Armored Division Ariete* to act as rear cover against enemy forces south of the Trigh Capuzzo.

At about the same time *Panzergruppe Afrika* wirelessed that the old order would remain in force. No answer to the suggestion made by the *Afrika Korps* had been received by evening.

The Course of 28 November

November 28 passed without heavy fighting for the troops of the *Afrika Korps*. During the night of 27/28 November the *21st Panzer Division* broke off its attack against the British strongpoint on the Via Balbia west of Bardia and placed itself on the Trigh Capuzzo behind the *15th Panzer Division*. Going round Sidi Azeiz, which in the meantime had been reoccupied by the enemy, it reached Gasr el Arid by noon on 28 November, and by evening the track Gambut–El Giaser, without enemy interference, being covered by *Armored Division Ariete* which was advancing further to the south.

The *15th Panzer Division* reaped the benefit from its night march on the southern escarpment to the west as far as the area south-west of Bir Sciafsciuf. In its new positions it repulsed without much difficulty the advance of considerable British armored forces coming from the south and south-east in the course of the morning. At 1430 hours it advanced to the west and asked the *Afrika Korps* that *Armored Division Ariete* should follow the attack, echeloned on the left, and protect its flanks and rear against enemy interference. The advance met little opposition at first and moved rapidly to the west. Soon, however, enemy armored attacks against the southern flank made it necessary to employ artillery and antitank troops on the left. This was most inconvenient as reconnaissance on the right flank had observed in the low ground to the west of Bir Sciuerat great numbers of enemy vehicle columns which would have offered an excellent artillery target.

Towards 1530 hours the advance to the west was halted 5 kilometers west of Abiar en Nboidat by violent British artillery fire. Elements of *Regiment 200* were moved off to the north and succeeded before nightfall in capturing at Rugbet en Wbeidat a large British tented camp with more than 800 German prisoners; 150 British prisoners were taken, and during the day's fighting 20 enemy tanks were knocked out. During the evening *Armored Division Ariete*, which had followed without serious fighting, joined up in the south-east with the *15th Panzer Division*.

On the front of *Group Böttcher*, north, east and south of Bir Bu Creimisa on the Tobruk front, and with *Division z.b.v. Afrika,* the enemy did not continue his attacks. *Divisioin z.b v. Afrika* reconnoitered towards the area of the penetration. During the afternoon *Group Böttcher* launched an attack with a battalion reinforced by artillery and antiaircraft guns and 10 tanks against Sidi Rezegh. Towards 1700 hours the escarpment of Sidi Rezegh was reached after a combat with British tanks and infantry. After nightfall, however, Rommel for some reason unknown ordered the withdrawal of the attacking troops to Bir Bu Creimisa.

Orders of the *Afrika Korps* for 29 November

During the evening the *Afrika Korps* decided, since no new order had arrived from *Panzergruppe Afrika*, to adhere to its plan of attack and drive the *2nd New Zealand Division* into the fortress of Tobruk on 29 November. For this purpose the *21st Panzer Division* was to advance on the central escarpment by way of Zaafran and was to take Belhamed as its first objective; the *15th Panzer Division* would attack the height of El Duda as its first objective along the southern escarpment by way of Sidi Rezegh. *Armored Division Ariete* would gain the area around Sidi Huftah and prevent the British *7th Armored Division* from interfering with the attack. The relevant orders were issued at 2030 hours, fixing 1000 hours on 29 November for the beginning of the attack. *Division z.b.V. Afrika* was asked to support the attack of the *21st Panzer Division* against Belhamed with artillery fire. This intention was reported to *Panzergruppe Afrika* by wireless, with the simultaneous request that the attack by the *15th Panzer Division* on El Duda should be supported by the artillery of *Group Böttcher*.

At 2120 hours the answer to the suggestion made by the *Afrika Korps* for the attack at last arrived in the shape of the following wireless message from *Panzergruppe Afrika*:

> On 29 November the *Afrika Korps* will destroy the enemy around Belhamed and to the south in an attack from the east, the south, and south-east thereof. It will prevent the enemy from escaping into Tobruk. Be ready for defense against an enemy from the south. The area west of Sidi Muftah will be harassed by artillery and reconnaissance troops during the night to prevent the enemy from moving off into Tobruk. *Group Böttcher* will be prepared for defense against the south. The *Afrika Korps* will report troop dispositions and start of attack.

This order was, clearly, opposed to the plan for the attack submitted by the *Afrika Korps* and insisted unmistakably that the New Zealanders must be cut off from the fortress instead of being driven into the fortress. For this purpose the left wing of the attack was to advance from the south and from the south-west, that is, from the area of *Group Böttcher.*

Most surprisingly, the *Afrika Korps* did not carry out this order, apparently because it regarded the envelopment of the *2nd New Zealand Division* from the south as impossible. In verbal orders issued at 0800 hours on 29 November General Crüwell reiterated his original order for the attack. He merely added an instruction to *Armored Division Ariete* not only to be prepared for defensive action towards the south, but also to hold itself in readiness to intervene on the left of the *15th Panzer Division.*

The Battle for El Duda on 29 November

The *15th Panzer Division* began advancing to the west at 0950 hours. The enemy in front had retired to the south during the night. Ground was rapidly gained to the west. Soon, however, strong artillery fire from the high ground at and to the east of Sidi Rezegh made itself felt on the right flank. From earlier actions the division knew of the steepness of the escarpment at Sidi Rezegh. The divisional commander therefore decided to pass south of Sidi Rezegh, to make the descent further to the west, north-west of Bir Bu Creimisa, and then to attack El Duda from the west along the ridge. This seemed to accord with instructions issued by the *Panzergruppe* which had been intercepted by the division. *Machine Gun Battalion 2* was turned off to the north, with the order to keep the enemy on both sides of Sidi Rezegh occupied on a broad front and to prevent him thrusting to the south.

At Bir Bu Creimisa the division passed through the positions of *Group Böttcher*, turned to the north and, in spite of heavy artillery fire, crossed the low ground south of Bir Salem from the north without serious loss. At Bir Salem contact was established with the artillery support for the attack against El Duda as arranged.

Towards 1200 hours, the division turned away to the east at Bir Salem and, under artillery cover, advanced along the ridge towards the height of El Duda with *Panzer Regiment 8* leading and *Schützen Regiment 115* following.

The *21st Panzer Division* ascertained during the morning that it was actually farther to the east than had been assumed, owing to inaccurate calculations. It reported, therefore, that it would be unable to attack until 1030 hours. Whilst still in the forming-up area, it was struck by enemy armor from the west, which further delayed the beginning of the attack. Soon, much enemy armor was observed advancing against the southern flank and the rear of the *21st Panzer Division*, which inflicted heavy casualties by artillery fire from the high ridge south of Trigh Capuzzo and paralyzed all movement. The *21st Panzer Division* was compelled to withdraw considerable forces from the front where the attack was to take place, and employ them to cover the southern flank on the southern edge of the escarpment, without, however, eliminating the enemy artillery fire.

Towards noon *Reconnaissance Battalion 3*, which up to then at Bir el Giaser had covered the rear of the division, was moved up westward to Hagfet esc Sciomar, where it had to hold off several attacks by enemy armor from the south-east. And so there remained for the westerly attack of the division no more than one weak battalion, in addition to the few battleworthy tanks of *Panzer Regiment 5*; little progress, therefore, could be made.

Armored Division Ariete, which had followed the *15th Panzer Division* in the advance from the area south-east of Sidi Muftah towards Hareifet en Nbeidat, was also frequently attacked by enemy tanks from the south. It was compelled to turn the greater part of its forces against them.

Towards 1000 hours, soon after the beginning of the attack, the *Afrika Korps* received a wireless message from *Panzergruppe Afrika* with the information that strong motorized forces with artillery and armor were advancing from El Duda to the south-east towards Sidi Rezegh. The *Afrika Korps* interpreted this move as an attempt by the New Zealanders to break out to the south-east and join up with the armor coming from this direction. At about the same time it became clear to the commanding general of the *Afrika Korps* that, owing to the lagging behind of the *21st Panzer Division*, the attack made by his corps was threatening to disintegrate. He therefore ordered the *15th Panzer Division* at 1030 hours to halt its attack south of Sidi Rezegh and to open up the local descent northward from the escarpment. This order, however, was not carried out, as it arrived at the *15th Panzer Division* too late, and at a time when the division was already advancing on Bir Salem. *Armored Division Ariete* was ordered to advance along the ridge east of Sidi Rezegh , there to prevent a breakthrough of the enemy to the south-east – an order which was difficult to carry out in view of the enemy threat in the south.

Towards 1130 hours the battle headquarters of the *Afrika Korps* was moved to Bir Bu Creimisa. Soon afterwards Rommel, accompanied by several Italian commanding officers, appeared at the headquarters of the

Afrika Korps. He emphatically repeated his order to press the *2nd New Zealand Division* away from Tobruk and surround it in the area Belhamed–Zaafran–Bir Sciuerat–Sidi Rezegh.

At this juncture the *Afrika Korps* abandoned its intention to drive the New Zealanders into Tobruk. It endeavored through rapid orders to comply with Rommel's instruction. The *21st Panzer Division* was urged to drive against Zaafran in a more rapid advance from the east: *Armored Division Ariete* was given the task of blocking the ridge east of Sidi Rezegh against the north. The time had come for the wheel of the *15th Panzer Division* to the west, and its attack on El Duda from the west, to bear fruit. General Crüwell went in person to this division and ordered it not to continue the attack towards Tobruk after the capture of El Duda, but to move east towards the northern slope of Belhamed.

The attack of the *15th Panzer Division* on El Duda proved really difficult. The British had moved strong artillery from the fortress of Tobruk to the south-east, and fought the attack with numerous batteries from the north and the north-east: which could not be kept down by the artillery of *Group Böttcher*. Further, the British had occupied El Duda with strong elements from the fortress garrison, including 20 heavy tanks. In spite of all this opposition, *Panzer Regiment 8* had penetrated the enemy positions on the height by 1400 hours, made 150 prisoners, collected numerous weapons, and knocked out six tanks. *Schützen Regiment 115*, however, was not able to reach the top of the high ground until 1600 hours in the face of heavy artillery fire. Meanwhile, *Panzer Regiment 8* advanced to the descent of the Axis Road, on the north-eastern slope of El Duda. It was not possible, however, to effect a junction with the troops of *Division z.b.v. Afrika*. The riflemen of *Schützen Regiment 115* lay pinned down on El Duda by heavy artillery fire. Towards evening the British artillery fire increased to even greater violence. At 2000 hours enemy forces from the fortress launched strong counterattacks, supported by tanks, which could be repulsed only with great difficulty. The division organized itself on El Duda for defense and called on the *Afrika Korps* for early relief by infantry and antitank weapons, in order to have a free hand to continue the attack on 30 November.

About 2200 hours, however, when *Panzer Regiment 8* had been withdrawn into the hollow south-east of Bir Salem to replenish fuel and ammunition, fresh enemy forces launched another counterattack from the fortress and again dislodged *Schützen Regiment 115* from the height. The regiment suffered considerable loss, particularly in stragglers.

The plan to recapture El Duda came to naught because towards 0030 hours the division received a wireless message from *Panzergruppe Afrika* which was interpreted by the commander as placing the division under direct command of the *Panzergruppe* and ordering it to move to El Adem forthwith. The commander of the division traveling ahead cleared up the mistake at *Panzergruppe* headquarters at 0300 hours. (The order had been meant for *Reconnaissance Unit 33*, but *Panzergruppe Afrika* had erroneously used the call-sign of the *15th Panzer Division*.) The division was able to halt at Bir Salem and took up defensive positions facing east.

During the afternoon of 29 November *Group Böttcher* supported the attack of the *15th Panzer Division* with its artillery. On its south wing, south-west of Bir Bu Creimisa, it was attacked, as was *Reconnaissance Battalion 33* to its east, by enemy armor and artillery. *Armored Division Ariete*, north of Sidi Muftah, had also to hold off the attack of an enemy armored brigade. It held its own in heavy fighting and towards evening small parties reached the high ground six kilometres east of Sidi Rezegh , in accordance with orders from the *Afrika Korps*.

Major-General von Ravenstein, commanding the *21st Panzer Division*, did not return in the morning from an order group at the *Afrika Korps*. As was discovered later, he had lost his way and had fallen into the hands of the British. In his place the division was taken over by the commander of *Schützen Regiment 104*, Lieutenant-Colonel Knabe, and as from noon on 30 November by Major-General Böttcher, the artillery commander of the *Panzergruppe*. Enemy pressure against the southern flank increased still more during the afternoon. The division suffered heavily under the crossfire of enemy artillery. Their advance to the west, kept up by no more than weak forces,came to a halt during the evening north-east of Bir Sciuerat.

Orders Issued by
the *Afrika Korps* during the Evening of 29 November

During the afternoon the *Afrika Korps* realized how difficult the attack of the *15th Panzer Division* on El Duda had been. It realized that a continuation of the attack on Belhamed on 29 November could no longer be expected. It therefore ordered the *15th Panzer Division* to hold on to El Duda during the night and reestablish contact with *Division z.b.v. Afrika* by means of reconnaissance patrols. Nothing was done, however, to comply with the request of the division to be relieved in its positions on El Duda.

During the late afternoon the corps commander of the *Afrika Korps* realized that the junction of the *15th Panzer Division* with *Division z.b.v. Afrika* and the consequent complete encirclement of the New Zealand division had not been achieved. Nor was the encirclement complete in the south-east and south; in particular, a great gap still yawned between *Armored Division Ariete* and the *21st Panzer Division*. Moreover, it was not at all certain whether it would be possible to ward off all the diversionary British attacks from the south-east and the south, where the entire British *7th Armored Division* had been identified, with a further group of enemy forces evidently being assembled in the Bir el Gubi area.

Unaware of the setback on El Duda, the *Afrika Korps* ordered for 30 November the continuation of the attacks which had been prescribed for 29 November, although it remained open whether the *15th Panzer Division* would still have the strength to defend El Duda against the attacks of the Tobruk garrison and simultaneously to advance towards Belhamed.

The Battle for Belhamed

The *Afrika Korps* did not learn that El Duda had again been lost and that the *15th Panzer Division* had moved off to the west until after 0300 hours on 30 November. With this, its plan for the continuation of the attack on 30 November broke down. Once again, the New Zealanders had a safe link-up with the fortress of Tobruk and, further, had pushed strong forces to the southern ridge at Sidi Rezegh , only a few kilometers away from the British *7th Armored Division*, which was attacking from the south. In view of the diminishing fighting strength of the formations and the increasing threat to the rear, it now seemed doubtful whether the destruction of the *2nd New Zealand Division* was still possible. The situation eased somewhat when it became known by 0600 hours that the *15th Panzer Division* was near Bir Salem, ready for defensive operations facing east. It received orders to move to Bir Bu Creimisa without delay.

At 0830 hours, General Rommel appeared at the battle headquarters of the *Afrika Korps*. With his customary stubbornness he stuck to his intention to destroy the *2nd New Zealand Division* and placed under command of the *Afrika Korps*, in addition to *Division z.b.v. Afrika*, *Group Mickl* – formerly *Group Böttcher*, whose commander had been given the *21st Panzer Division*. Rommel ordered that the advance on Sidi Rezegh be renewed from the south, with *Group Mickl* and *Armored Division Ariete*. It should be supported by the heavy artillery of the *Panzergruppe*.

When *Group Mickl* was given its orders at 1200 hours, it became clear that it would take a considerable time to disengage its forces from their positions, and that by the evening hardly more than two battalions would be available for the attack. Yet, Colonel Mickl was ordered to prepare for the attack against Sidi Rezegh with all available forces. The time would be laid down by the *Afrika Korps* later. After the objective had been reached, *Group Mickl* was to go over to the defense, facing north and south.

On 30 November *Armored Division Ariete* was again attacked by enemy armored forces from the south and was therefore thoroughly engaged. When, towards 1215 hours, the *15th Panzer Division* arrived with its forward elements at Bir Bu Creimisa, the divisional commander received the order to place his division in such a position that it would be able, as from 1500 hours, either to advance from the area north of Bir Bu Creimisa to support the attack of *Group Mickl* to the north-east, or to take the enemy in the flank in front of *Armored Division Ariete* to the south-east.

At 1330 hours, General Rommel again appeared at the battle headquarters of the *Afrika Korps*. This time General Crüwell suggested placing the *15th Panzer Division* on the left flank of *Group Mickl* for the attack on the saddle west of Belhamed, and postponing the attack until the evening so as to give *Group Mickl* time to assemble stronger forces for the attack. General Rommel agreed, and ordered further that *Division z.b.v. Afrika* should attack Belhamed simultaneously from the north. He refused, however, to allow the postponement of the attack.

Thereupon, at 1400 hours, the *Afrika Korps* ordered the *15th Panzer Division* and *Group Mickl* to attack. The beginning of the attack was fixed for 1500 hours; the edge of the escarpment of both sides of Sidi Rezegh was given as the first objective.

The Fighting for Sidi Rezegh on 30 November

During the morning the *15th Panzer Division* had moved its formation via Sidi Veimum into the dip north-west of Bir Bu Creimisa, making use of smooth depressions. *Schützen Regiment 115* was left south of Bir Salem to organize its units. Forming up for the attack proved difficult, owing to the need to avoid a minefield in the sector of the assault. A violent air attack at 1445 hours on the division and corps battle headquarters caused further delay. Thus, it took until 1540 hours for the *15th Panzer Division* to the left of and next to *Group Mickl* to get ready and attack after a really unsatisfactory preparation by the army artillery. It attacked in its usual order – *Panzer Regiment 8* (50 tanks) with antiaircraft artillery and the bulk of artillery forward, and *Machine Gun Battalion 2*, *Motorcycle Battalion 15* and *Antitank Battalion 33* behind – drawn up in depth, echeloned to the north-east. In order to broaden the attack, it was decided to push forward the attack of *Group Mickl* with its tanks and artillery.

A heavy barrage by two artillery battalions was rapidly traversed. At 1630 hours the foremost elements broke into well-constructed New Zealand positions on the ridge. The first wave of *Panzer Regiment 8* advanced as far as the lower ground on the Trigh Capuzzo, while the main body rolled up the enemy positions in the sector of *Group Mickl* towards the east. The British – one reinforced regiment of the *2nd New Zealand Division* – offered stubborn resistance. It was not possible to clear the ridge completely of the enemy until darkness fell. Six hundred prisoners, 12 guns and numerous antitank weapons were captured. The remainder of the enemy withdrew to the north on to Belhamed, where enemy tanks stood ready for a counterattack to the south, but did not cross the Trigh Capuzzo. In the sector of *Armored Division Ariete*, 30 November brought uninterrupted attacks by British armor from the south supported by strong artillery. The division held its positions.

The *21st Panzer Division* also suffered considerably on 30 November under strong enemy pressure from the south and south-east. The reinforced *Reconnaissance Battalion 3*, facing south-east at Hagfet esc Sciomar, was sorely pressed. The attack by elements of *Schützen Regiment 104* west and in the direction of Zaafran made no progress. The division regarded its situation as precarious quite early in the morning, and requested urgently that *Armored Division Ariete* be charged to attack eastward to relieve them.

At 1700 hours, it radioed to the *Afrika Korps* and *Panzergruppe Afrika* that neither the attack to the west nor the defense against enemy attacks in its flank and rear promised any further success. The division intended to fight its way through westward towards Bir Bu Creimisa after dark. The *Afrika Korps* rejected most decidedly the intention of *21st Panzer Division* and issued a categorical order that it should hold its position and prevent the *2nd New Zealand Division* from breaking out to the south.

Plan for the Attack on 1 December

The successful attack by the *15th Panzer Division* could be watched from *Afrika Korps* battle headquarters. Before the end of the evening, General Crüwell, at the battle headquarters of the *15th Panzer Division*, gave the order to continue the attack through the night until Belhamed had fallen. The commander of the *15th Panzer Division*, Major-General Neumann-Silkow, asked him, however, to assist, as Belhamed was strongly occupied and could only be captured by a well-organized attack with all weapons well coordinated. In the end, General Crüwell dropped his demand but required that the attack should be so conducted that the descent of the Axis Road on the north-west slope of Belhamed should be reached before daybreak. To ensure that the attack would be safely covered against any threat from the south, *Afrika Korps* assigned to *Group Mickl* the task of using all its forces on the defensive against the south. *Armored Division Ariete* was again given its task – defense to the south and closing of the ring east of Sidi Rezegh with its front to the north.

There was still a gap, however, between *Armored Division Ariete* and the *21st Panzer Division*, not only in the ring around the bag but also in the defense to the south, the more so because the *21st Panzer Division* had occupied a hedgehog position east of Bir Sciuerat in order to keep off attacks from the south and south-east.

The Morning Attack against Belhamed

On 1 December the *15th Panzer Division* was assigned the last attack which was to bring about the decision in the battle of annihilation against the *2nd New Zealand Division*. Its task was not easy. The *2nd New Zealand Division* had indeed suffered losses, but was still unshaken in its fighting strength. Reconnaissance patrols had ascertained that Belhamed and the saddle to the east were strongly held by infantry and liberally dotted with artillery and antitank weapons. Moreover, the position of the New Zealanders was very strong. Belhamed slopes to the south in a regular gradient like a glacis and dominates the broad valley of the Trigh Capuzzo which lies before it. On the north the slopes are steep. Deeply channeled wadis offer cover for reserves and artillery.

The *15th Panzer Division* therefore decided to traverse the broad low levels of the Trigh Capuzzo by night; by morning, *Regiment 200, Motorcycle Battalion 15* and *Machine Gun Battalion 2* had worked their way to the southern slopes of Belhamed. There it was to allow the armor to pass through, and then, together with *Panzer Regiment 8*, it would break into the enemy position. The bulk of the artillery, including the army artillery under command, would support the attack from emplacements south of the Trigh Capuzzo; the antiaircraft artillery and two batteries would accompany the attack of the armor in their vehicles.

The armored attack began at dawn. It had been possible to traverse the low ground south of Belhamed in the morning mist, without interference. While climbing the height, however, the division was met by very heavy fire from all weapons. Then, when the mist lifted, large concentrations of transport were seen, particularly in front of the right wing, and on the saddle east of Belhamed. The enemy was evidently on the point of moving off to the south-east. While the forward wave of *Panzer Regiment 8* had broken the enemy resistance by 0830 hours and penetrated to the north slope of the mountain, the rearward elements had to be diverted against an outflanking threat in the east. In stubborn fighting, several batteries and numerous antitank weapons were captured. At the same time, the forward wave was diverted to the west in order to roll up the positions on the saddle west of Belhamed.

At this moment, towards 1000 hours, an attack by 80 enemy tanks made itself felt, which evidently had broken through the gap between *Armored Division Ariete* and the *21st Panzer Division* from the south-east. The artillery of the *15th Panzer Division* was rapidly turned against them. The attack soon came to a halt before their fire. *Panzer Regiment 8* was concentrated with utmost haste. Before its counterattack the enemy tanks fell back to the south-east.

A serious shortage of ammunition in *Panzer Regiment 8* enforced a long lull in the fighting on the east slope of Belhamed. Offensive reconnaissance patrols advanced further to the east and captured two more batteries.

The *21st Panzer Division* took no part in the morning's assault. The bulk of the division was still engaged in repelling enemy attacks against its southern flank. Neither did the attack which *Division z.b.v. Afrika* had been ordered to make against the north slope of Belhamed materialize during the morning, for reasons unknown. *Group Briel*, consisting of supply troops and elements of *Antiaircraft Machine Gun Battalion 606* in the Gambut area, was attacked several times from the east by motorized rifle units and artillery on 30 November and 1 December. The enemy involved were evidently forces which were blocking Bardia from the west and were advancing merely to relieve the *2nd New Zealand Division*.

The Fighting during the Afternoon of 1 December

On 1 December General Rommel and the *Afrika Korps* were occupied in efforts to bring the destruction of the *2nd New Zealand Division* to a rapid conclusion. Rommel was chiefly induced to do so by the news from the Sollum front, where supply difficulties were steadily increasing. He therefore planned a diversionary attack against Bardia and ordered the *Afrika Korps* to complete the mopping up of the "bag" that same day.

Thereupon the *Afrika Korps* ordered the *15th Panzer Division* at noon to continue the attack to the east as soon as possible and capture Zaafran. The

21st Panzer Division was ordered to attack westward towards the *15th Panzer Division* during the afternoon with all its force regardless of the southern flank. *Division z.b.v. Afrika* was to occupy the northern slopes of Belhamed, and *Armored Division Ariete* would close the "bag" south of Zaafran.

The attack of the *15th Panzer Division* was pushed on to the east with all its force at 1500 hours. Two more batteries were captured; enemy resistance decreased rapidly. After Height 143 south-east of Zaafran had been reached, the attack was discontinued as a wireless message from the *Afrika Korps*, meant for *21st Panzer Division* but wrongly directed to the *15th Panzer Division*, had ordered the immediate cessation of the pursuit. The booty of the day consisted of more than 1,000 prisoners, 26 guns, numerous antitank weapons and many motor vehicles.

The advance of the *21st Panzer Division* did not begin until the late afternoon. It was directed westward from Bir Sciuerat and met no further resistance. It was evident that strong elements of the *2nd New Zealand Division* had succeeded in fighting their way out to the south-east between the *15th* and *21st Panzer Divisions*. The attack of *Division z.b.v. Afrika* against Belhamed did not materialize on 11 December.

Orders for 2 December

Panzergruppe Afrika ordered the *Afrika Korps* to mop up the "bag" on and south-east of Zaafran on 2 December. For the rest, the day was to be used for reorganization. Reconnaissance towards Bardia was to be undertaken by patrols along the Via Balbia and Trigh Capuzzo. "Advance detachments", each one a reinforced battalion strong, were to be pushed towards Bir el Giaser and Gambut respectively.

At dawn *Division z.b.v. Afrika* was to attack south-west in cooperation with *XXI Italian Corps*, which was to advance northward from the Bir Salem area to regain the old line of investment along the line Height 146-145–Bir Bu Assaten. For this purpose, General Navarini's *XXI Corps* was to be reinforced by 15 tanks from the *Afrika Korps*. *Armored Division Ariete* was to revert to the Italian *Motorized Corps* as from 2 December, *Infantry Division Trieste* of this corps having been pulled out from the front of *XXI Corps*.

Course of 2 December

On 2 December the mopping up of the "bag" as ordered continued without further fighting. The enemy on Zaafran had disappeared. The *15th Panzer Division* occupied Belhamed, which has been temporarily left vacant, without opposition and left a battalion there as a security garrison. In accordance with instructions from the *Panzergruppe*, the advance detachment of the *21st Panzer Division* had reached Bir el Giaser by evening, where contact was established with *Armored Division Ariete*. The advance detachment of the *15th Panzer Division* reached Gambut without opposition, where *Group Briel* had arrived.

The attack by *XXI Corps* to recover the old line of investment began in the early morning. It failed, principally because it was under cross-fire from both sides by the Tobruk fortress artillery, particularly from El Duda, which was not being attacked. The attack by *Division z.b.v. Afrika* to the south-west had also become stuck. The attacking troops had to be withdrawn to their start line during the morning, therein suffering heavy losses in men and material.

Observations

December 2 brought the conclusion of the fighting against the *2nd New Zealand Division*. After five days of severe and fluctuating struggle, *Panzergruppe Afrika* had succeeded in smashing this particularly strong and powerful division, so that during the rest of the campaign only one brigade of the division was in action. Apart from heavy and bloody casualties, the division lost 2,500 prisoners, 45 guns and a large amount of its equipment. Only parts of the division were able to fight their way into Tobruk or out to the south-east. At the same time, it had been possible to close the ring around the fortress of Tobruk once more, though it had not been possible to restore the old siege front in the south-east. During 27 and 28 November, the British command did not shrink from any sacrifice to block the way of the *Afrika Korps* into the rear of the *2nd New Zealand Division*. It threw against it the restored *7th Armored Division*, which in armored strength outnumbered the *Afrika Korps* three times. It became evident, however, that the striking power of the *15th Panzer Division* was still sufficient to enable it to fight its way to the west in stubborn battle.

Thus, on 28 November the necessary conditions had been created for the attack on the New Zealanders and for the closing of the gap in the siege front. General Rommel's original plan was to take the *Afrika Korps* into the area of *Division z.b.v. Afrika* on the Via Balbia and attack thence to the south-west, to reestablish the siege front and cut off the New Zealanders from Tobruk. Against this, the *Afrika Korps* thought it inadvisable to give up the important high ground south of Trigh Capuzzo. Actually, the plan of the *Panzergruppe* would probably have resulted in the junction of the New Zealanders with the

British *XXX Armored Corps*. In that event the situation south-east of Tobruk might well have become untenable. To drive the *2nd New Zealand Division* into the fortress of Tobruk, as was the aim of the *Afrika Korps*, was certainly the simplest solution. But, even if this were achieved, the garrison of Tobruk would be so much strengthened thereby that it would hardly be possible thereafter to hold the siege front.

Rommel did not conceive the plan for the concentric attack against the New Zealanders until his return to the battle headquarters at El Adem. Since the *Afrika Korps* adhered to its own solution, the plan would not have been carried out if the *15th Panzer Division* had not, by turning off to the south-west of its own accord, acted in harmony with the concept of the *Panzergruppe*. Without doubt, Rommel's plan was very difficult to carry out. It was in fact beyond the strength of the available forces to form an unbroken ring around the New Zealanders and at the same time to set up a second front against the British *XXX Corps* and hold off the latter's diversionary attacks, which threatened to burst open the encircling ring. Thus, it is not surprising that the *Afrika Korps* had to overcome a number of crises in the course of the battles. After the setback on 29 November on El Duda, it would hardly have remained possible to cut off the *2nd New Zealand Division* from Tobruk. But the British command had apparently ordered it to break out to the south-east and join hands with *XXX Corps*. Thus, Rommel still had another opportunity of launching his concentric attack.

This time Rommel had learnt the lesson from his dash to Egypt, and not only put aside all secondary tasks but also created a unified command on the field of battle. On 29 November *Armored Division Ariete* and *Division z.b.v. Afrika*, and on 30 November *Group Böttcher* (Mickl) as well, were placed under command of the *Afrika Korps*. This undoubtedly bore fruit.

Nonetheless, the course of the struggle between 29 November and 1 December shows how difficult it is to bring dispersed formations to a unified, concentrated cooperation. In this connection, the depletion of the *Afrika Korps*' operational staff may have played a part. The failure to reinforce and relieve the *15th Panzer Division* on El Duda with *Group Böttcher* on 29 November certainly contributed to the setback experienced on the evening of that day. The success on 30 November, and particularly that on 1 December, would have been more complete if the time and direction of the advance of *Division z.b.v. Afrika* from the north, and of the *21st Panzer Division* from the east, had been coordinated with the attack of the *15th Panzer Division*.

In the defense to the south-east there were also very critical moments. On 29 and 30 November the *21st Panzer Division* evidently took an exaggerated view of the difficulties of its situation. It was, indeed, thanks only to the rapid and energetic interference of the *Afrika Korps* that the crisis there was overcome. On the other hand, *Ariete Division* was able to carry out its defensive task with success. It demonstrated that, under efficient leadership, even Italian units were able to do well, in spite of their inadequate armament and equipment.

The smashing of the *2nd New Zealand Division* proved that, after his unlucky dash to Egypt, General Rommel had regained the customary high level of his leadership. The *Panzergruppe* and the *Afrika Korps* were entitled to be proud of the victorious battle, and so were the brave troops, particularly the *15th Panzer Division*, which had had to shoulder the main burden of the battle.

The Last Fighting East of Tobruk, 2–4 December

While the struggle against the *2nd New Zealand Division* was still in progress, General Rommel busied himself with plans for the continuation of operations after the conclusion of the battle, and on 1 December he gave his first orders. From the messages which he received during these days, he seems to have gained the impression that the British were encircling the Sollum front, and the Bardia fortress in particular, with comparatively weak forces. On the other hand, the supply position, particularly in Bardia, seemed to have become so critical that the resistance of the fortress of Bardia and of the Sollum front was of the greatest importance as essential forces of the British were kept occupied there and the blocking of the coast road greatly aggravated their supply problem. At times Rommel seems also to have hoped that the destruction of the *2nd New Zealand Division* and the renewed investment of Tobruk might, after all, persuade the British to abandon their offensive and to withdraw to Egypt. An air reconnaissance report of 1 December on large convoy movements on the coast road to Sidi Barrani eastward pointed to the existence of such intentions.

An early advance to the Sollum front seemed necessary to Rommel in order to reestablish contact at least with Bardia, even if only temporarily, and to get through a sizable quantity of supplies by land, and, on the other hand, to conceal our weakness from the enemy and to provide perhaps the last impulse needed for his withdrawal. It is characteristic of General Rommel that at times he also played with the idea of encircling and destroying the weak enemy forces north of the Sollum front.

However, the situation of the *Panzergruppe* was by no means satisfactory, even after the successful battle for Belhamed. The two *Panzer* divisions of the *Afrika Korps* were badly exhausted. Before further operations could be undertaken, they urgently needed a few days' rest for the restoration and technical overhaul of their *Panzer* regiments, in order to restore the number of their tanks. Only the soft-skinned parts of the division were quickly ready for operations again. That the *Italian Motorized Corps* was available with its two divisions provided a certain, though by no means decisive, compensation.

The ring around the fortress of Tobruk had indeed closed once more. But the Tobruk garrison still held the important height of El Duda, thus blocking the Axis Road, and was able to harass traffic on the Trigh Capuzzo by artillery fire. In addition, the siege front was lengthened by 10 kilometers, which, in view of the lowered fighting strength of the Italian division, consituted a considerable burden. Particularly dangerous was the fact that strong British armored forces still lay south-east of Tobruk at a short distance from El Duda.

The next step should have been to attack these armored forces with all available force, especially the *Afrika Korps*, and to destroy them. For the time being, however, this was out of the question, as the tanks of the *Afrika Korps*, essential for this task, were not available for some days.

General Rommel also realized the necessity of restoring bearable conditions in front of Tobruk and, for this, to recapture El Duda and the old investment front. But, once again, he believed that he would be able to carry out this task with a fraction of his whole force. Thus, he decided to advance along the Trigh Capuzzo and Via Balbia to Bardia on 3 December with weak elements of the *Afrika Korps*, in order to reestablish communications with the fortress and enable it to be supplied. The Italian *Motorized Corps* would be responsible for protection against the enemy south-east of Tobruk and later would advance to Sidi Omar to create a diversion for the Sollum front. On the Tobruk front, *Group Mickl*, reinforced by elements of the *Afrika Korps*, was to recapture El Duda on 3 December and afterwards to continue the attack in cooperation with *XXI Corps* and *Division z.b.v. Afrika* until the original siege line had been restored.

At noon on 2 December, General Rommel ordered the *Afrika Korps* to carry out the attack on Bardia with two advanced detachments of all weapons, battalion strength. These advanced detachments would be sufficient for this task as the enemy was encircling Bardia with no more than one brigade. The *Afrika Korps* regarded the forces assigned to this task as much too weak, and at 1700 hours suggested that the advance be carried out by the whole *Afrika Korps* less the two *Panzer* regiments. General Rommel, however, rejected this suggestion.

The Fighting on 3 and 4 December

During the night of 2/3 December the *Afrika Korps* charged the commander of the *15th Panzer Division* with the command of the two advanced detachments and placed *Reconnaissance Battalion 3* under his command as an additional unit. General Neumann-Silkow in his turn objected to the weakness of the forces employed, with no more success. He ordered the two advanced detachments to reconnoiter thoroughly and not to allow themselves to be involved in action with superior enemy forces. He himself traveled with *Reconnaissance Battalion 3* behind the two advanced detachments, in the area between the Trigh Capuzzo and Via Balbia.

The advanced detachment of the *21st Panzer Division*, under the command of Lieutenant-Colonel Knabe, proceeded by way of Gasr el Arid and, after clashes with enemy patrols, arrived at Sidi Azeiz at 1000 hours, where it was engaged by superior enemy infantry, mingled with artillery and tanks, which attempted to pass round the detachment.

The advanced detachment of the *15th Panzer Division* – the reinforced *Motorcycle Battalion 15* under Lieutenant-Colonel Geissler – advanced rapidly along the Via Balbia towards Bardia. At about 1200 hours the detachment ran into an ambush 20 kilometers west of the fortress owing to inadequate reconnaissance, suffered heavy losses, and was almost destroyed by a counterattack. An attempt by the *15th Panzer Division* to assist by sending *Detachment Knabe* from Sidi Azeiz failed because Knabe himself had been involved in an action. *Reconnaissance Unit 3*, delayed by an enemy armored thrust from the south, had only reached the Gambut airfield. Thereupon the *15th Panzer Division* withdrew *Detachment Knabe* to Gasr el Arid and the remnants of *Detachment Geissler* to Gambut.

On 3 December the Italian *Motorized Corps* advanced with *Armored Division Ariete* against slight opposition as far as Gasr el Arid, where it took *Detachment Knabe* under its wing. *Infantry Division Trieste* followed in the west.

Before Tobruk the bulk of the *Afrika Korps* was busy with the reorganization of the formations and the repair of tanks. In the course of the morning *Group Mickl* advanced to the attack against El Duda. The attack was struck by strong enemy artillery fire in the front and on the left flank and pinned down half way. In the evening the men were withdrawn to their start line.

The Course of 4 December

In spite of the failure on 3 December, General Rommel decided to try once more, this time in greater strength, on 4 December and to force the relief of Bardia and the restoration of the siege front. He instructed the *Afrika Korps* to thrust with the *15th Panzer Division* along the Trigh Capuzzo to Bardia, and to take El Duda with the *21st Panzer Division* and *Group Mickl.* The Italian *Motorized Corps* was given the task of thrusting from Gasr el Arid to Sidi Omar. The *Afrika Korps* directed the *15th Panzer Division* – less one battalion of *Panzer Regiment 8, Engineer Battalion 33,* which remained as a security garrison on Belhamed and less *Group Geissler,* which was covering near Gambut – on Sidi Azeiz.

At 0800 hours the *15th Panzer Division* advanced from Bir el Giaser, driving enemy armored reconnaissance off the Trigh Capuzzo, and towards 1000 hours joined up with *Armored Division Ariete* and *Detachment Knabe* at Gasr el Arid. Thence it thrust on Sidi Azeiz, where a small enemy battle group, supported by tanks and artillery, was thrown back to the east, suffering losses. It was just about to advance northward from there towards the enemy strongpoint on the Via Balbia west of Bardia when, at 1345 hours, the *Afrika Korps* ordered by wireless that the advance be discontinued and the division return into the old assembly area. While the division was refueling for the return march, the *Afrika Korps* ordered at 1500 hours that the movement should be begun without delay. The divisional commander was ordered to corps battle headquarters forthwith. Thereupon the division began the return journey; and at 2000 hours the foremost elements arrived at corps battle headquarters at Bir el Giaser. The attack of the Italian *Motorized Corps* from Gasr el Arid towards Sidi Omar did not materialize, for reasons unknown. At 1300 hours the corps was ordered back to El Adem.

During the night 3/4 December, *21st Panzer Division* took up positions for the attack on El Duda. The attack was to be carried out by *Machine Gun Battalion 8* from the south-east, the engineer battalion from the south and *Group Mickl* (under command) from the west. The divisional artillery and the heavy artillery of the *Panzergruppe* were to provide an artillery preparation on El Duda from 0645 hours to 0735 hours.

At first the attack went well. The machine gun battalion occupied the saddle between Belhamed and El Duda in the morning, but was then caught by crossfire from machine guns and artillery on its north flank. The rest of the division reached the highest point of El Duda by noon. During the afternoon, however, the attack broke down under the heavy fire of the fortress artillery, and at 1700 hours had to be completely abandoned.

Towards noon weak enemy armored forces, supported by artillery, attacked the batteries of the *21st Panzer Division* from the south and necessitated the use of *Panzer Regiment 5* to clear the southern height of the enemy.

Observations

During 2 December there was still some hope of a successful conclusion to the fighting east of Tobruk, but on 4 December the situation had become untenable. Rommel's plans for the continuation of the fighting had failed. Early on 2 December, General Rommel faced the unavoidable necessity of giving his exhausted formations, especially the *Panzer* regiments, a rest and allowing them the time to increase the number of their tanks by carrying out technical repairs. This precluded an immediate attack against the *7th Armored Division* and the enemy group around Bir el Gubi. It is arguable whether the decision to advance on Barbia and the way in which this advance was carried out was justified, or whether it would have been better first to restore the situation on the south-east front of Tobruk by recovering the old siege front.

General Rommel believed that the thrust to Bardia should first be carried out, because otherwise the resistance of the fortress and of the entire Sollum front would break down through lack of supplies. The actual course of events shows that this appreciation was wrong, since it proved impossible to supply Bardia by land, yet the fortress held out for another four weeks and the Sollum front actually another seven weeks. This demonstrates that Rommel, in taking his decision, was the victim of obviously exaggerated appeals for help from the fortress of Bardia.

On the other hand, it was clear that it would not be possible to maintain the investment of the fortress of Tobruk by the German-Italian troops, who had been weakened by many casualties, if the enemy remained in possession of the dominating heights of El Duda and the south-eastern outlying area of the fortress. Thus, the recapture of El Duda and the original position on the south-east front of Tobruk was the indispensable condition for the continuation of the battle and the most pressing task before the *Panzergruppe*. That this would mean very heavy fighting had become absolutely clear after the heavy fighting for El Duda on 29 November. It is not easy to understand, therefore, why General Rommel did not make use of all his available forces, including the the *Afrika Korps*, and why he believed that part of his forces would be sufficient to do the work.

One cannot but feel that the *Afrika Korps* and the *15th Panzer Division* were right when, on 2 and 3 December, they objected to sending weak forces to Bardia, which were even split up into two separate "advance detachments." Failure was bound to result. Even if it was assumed that the enemy west of Bardia was not strong, he was at least so powerful that the *21st Panzer Division* had been unable to break his resistance on 27 November. Had the entire *Afrika Korps*, less the two panzer regiments, been thrown in, as General Crüwell had suggested, the desired success would probably have been gained, and the enemy would have got the impression which Rommel hoped to achieve by sending off his "advance detachment."

The Situation in the Air

Between 24 November and 4 December the *Luftwaffe* was confronted by the marked superiority, if not air supremacy, of the RAF. The British formations intervened in the ground fighting with strong forces almost without a break. They inflicted heavy losses on the *Afrika Korps* during the push to the Sollum front between 24 and 27 November, and contributed much to the failure of the advance. At the same time, they were supporting with strong forces the breakout attempts from Tobruk and the attack of the *2nd New Zealand Division* against the rear of our siege line. Their complete mastery of the air during these operations had a marked effect on the morale of the Italian troops. The supply traffic of the German-Italian troops was harassed in continuous low-level attacks. Movement by day was already impossible on the Via Balbia. Sea traffic in the Mediterranean was attacked from Nulta and Egypt so fiercely during this period that virtually no further Axis convoys reached the North African coast.

On the German side, Field Marshal Kesselring took a hand in the conduct of air operations during this period. The means at his disposal, however, were very limited. The headquarters staff of *Luftflotte 2* and the formations of *II. Fliegerkorps* had not yet arrived. The gross numerical inferiority of the German-Italian air forces in North Africa provided the greatest obstacle. In any case, Kesselring was intent on raising the fighting spirit of the formations and stepping up their operations, but even he was unable to do without the formations of *X Fliegerkorps* in the air war above the Mediterranean.

Thus, the practical support of *Panzergruppe Afrika* by the *Luftwaffe* remained most inadequate. The thrust of the *Afrika Korps* to the Sollum front between 24 and 27 November was virtually unsupported. At that time the *Fliegerführer Afrika* had nothing more under his control than a single fighter group much depleted by casualties. This could no longer reach the Sollum front after the loss of the landing grounds at Gambut. Thus the employment of *Stuka* and bomber formations in this area fell away. British air supremacy in this area was so great that the staff of the *Panzergruppe* were not even able to reach General Rommel with courier aircraft. Two attempts in this direction resulted each time in the shooting down of the courier aircraft involved.

In the struggle against the *2nd New Zealand Division* between 28 November and 2 December. conditions for the employment of the German *Luftwaffe* were somewhat more favorable; but even here British air superiority was so great that the German pilots were able to take a hand in the ground fighting for short periods only. On the other hand, the German formations were not yet trained in close cooperation with the armor, and numerous blunders were perpetrated. Thus, the German attacks were chiefly directed against the British units in the area south-east of Tobruk and around Bir el Gubi. They may have contributed to the weakening of British offensive activity thereby. In addition, bomber formations were used for night attacks on British supply traffic from Egypt. Naturally, the success of these attacks could be no more than slight.

The enemy battle group in the Gialo area was further watched and attacked from time to time. Formations made up from ground personnel and from men of *Luftwaffe* antiaircraft formations, under command of General Osterkamp, covered at this time the area south of Agedabia against this enemy group.

Air reconnaissance, hampered by many difficulties, particularly by the absence of fighter protection, did not work to the satisfaction of the army during this period. Indications of an improvement in cooperation with the army command were, however, noticeable. On occasion the latter were informed of important reconnaissance results by the dropping of messages. In order to bring about a thorough change in this sphere of operations, Field Marshal Kesselring at the beginning of December established the post of "*Koluft Lybia*" ("Air Commander Libya") on the staff of the *Panzergruppe* and filled it by the appointment of Lieutenant-Colonel (General Staff) Heymer, an efficient officer having Africa experience.

Field Marshal Kesselring also tried to increase the fighting strength and achievement of the Italian Air forces in North Africa. In this he was helped by a friendly relations he had established with the newly appointed commander-in-chief of the Italian Air Force, General Fougier, who had been under his command during the air offensive against England in autumn 1940. Here too, much time had to pass before a fundamental improvement in the situation could be achieved.

Field Marshal Kesselring regarded the revival of the German-Italian supply traffic by sea as his chief responsibility. Here, also, the measures which he took could not bear fruit until much later. In order to meet the most crying needs, he arranged for the transfer of German air transport units, which flew across to North Africa such supplies as were most urgently needed – ammunition and spare parts. Simultaneously, steps were taken to supply the German-Italian units on the Sollum front and in Bardia by air – which, however, proved very costly from the outset.

The Supply Situation

The supply position at the beginning of the British autumn offensive was overshadowed by the complete stoppage of supplies by sea. It was impossible to foresee when this supply route would be reopened. *Panzergruppe Afrika* was thereupon entirely dependent on its supplies in the North African war theater. How long these supplies, in particular the fuel, would last depended principally on the course of operations, especially on the scale of movement of the armored formations. The peculiar character of operations in North Africa, which sometimes compelled armored formations to operate in the midst of the enemy for a considerable length of time regardless of rearward communications, presented the quartermaster-general of the *Panzergruppe* with extraordinarily difficult tasks.

At the beginning of operations the two *Panzer* divisions of the *Afrika Korps* had been generously supplied and had established their supply depots east of Tobruk, in their immediate rear. Their supply was considerably facilitated thereby. Nonetheless, the *21st Panzer Division* experienced considerable supply difficulties on 19 and 20 November, which proved to have serious consequences for the course of the opposition. The difficulties were, however, not due to the supply position but to frictions inside the supply organization of this division. In any case, this crisis led to the establishment of a supply base in Bardia by *Panzergruppe Afrika*, a step which later on proved to be of the greatest advantage.

The fact that the division had been supplied on a very generous scale bore fruit when the *Afrika Korps* was cut off from supply by the *Panzergruppe* during the blocking of the Axis Road between 20 and 22 November. This was the reason that no supply crisis came about.

Rommel's dash to the Sollum front sprang from the whim of the moment and so no preparations were made for supply. From 25 November the supply route to the Sollum front was not only seriously endangered but at times was completely blocked by the enemy forces south-east of Tobruk. Only a few convoys could be smuggled through the enemy by night. The steady air attacks on replenishment traffic aggravated supply difficulties to the utmost.

Thus, the formations of the *Afrika Korps* experienced the gravest shortage of fuel and ammunition during this advance, the more so as they were at the same time also cut off from their divisional supply depots. This crisis was overcome only by drawing on the supplies deposited in Bardia.

On 22 November, the advance of the *2nd New Zealand Division* west of Bardia had already necessitated the evacuation of the supply depots of the *21st Panzer Division* north-west of Gambut, which could be held only with the greatest difficulty. This was of the greatest significance in the carrying out of the attack against the *2nd New Zealand Division* from 28 to 30 November, as the Axis Road was once again blocked by the loss of El Duda.

On 4 December the supply position had deteriorated a great deal in comparison with that at the beginning of the enemy offensive. Fuel stocks had dwindled considerably. It is true that large-scale movements of the *Panzergruppe* were still possible; but in planning operations it had become necessary to take the probable fuel consumption into serious consideration. As for ammunition, an extreme shortage of certain kinds had come about, particularly of 2 cm antiaircraft ammunition, and heavy antitank rifle and mortar ammunition. Tank-gun and artillery ammunition had also become very tight. Regarding rations, no difficulties had yet been experienced, particularly since much food had been captured in the many successful battles. Water supplies caused no difficulty.

On the other hand, the mechanical condition of the motor transport, and particularly of the *Panzers*, gave cause for grave anxiety. The life of a tank engine is much shorter in the African theater of war than in Europe. By this time the mechanical condition of the engines had deteriorated to such an extent that the majority of the tanks were in urgent need of engine replacement. In the event of continued operations, the steady falling out of a great number of tanks for mechanical reasons must be reckoned with. The situation was aggravated by the evacuation of the area east of Tobruk, which necessitated the transfer of the repair shop company of the *15th Panzer Division* from the Gambut area to the west. During the withdrawal, the majority of damaged tanks and of those which had failed for mechanical reasons were abandoned to the enemy for lack of transport facilities. Whereas it had been possible in the past to keep up the tank strength of the *15th Panzer Division* – which represented the chief fighting force of the *Afrika Korps* – by prompt repair, a rapid decline in tank strength must now be anticipated.

The decrease in soft-skinned vehicles was also very marked, particularly as a result of enemy air attack. Fortunately, the most serious gaps could be filled by the capture of British vehicles. By the beginning of December, numerous German units already bore the external appearance of British motorized troops.

The supply difficulties of the Sollum front, which had been provisioned for a fortnight's encirclement, now began to cause serious anxiety within the High Command. At an early stage, the quartermaster-general urged the establishment of an air supply service for the Sollum front, which in the beginning created considerable difficulties owing to the lack of air supply formations. He strove to control the pressing shortage of supplies in the fortress of Bardia by dispatching supplies in submarines.

On the whole, the supply position of the *Panzergruppe* had actually given cause for anxiety from the beginning of December. A speedy reopening of the sea routes across the Mediterranean was therefore the most urgent demand, not only of the quartermaster, but also of the tactical command of the *Panzergruppe*.

With Rommel's push to the Sollum front on 24 November, the British autumn offensive ceased to be a battle of decision and became a battle of attrition. In the latter, the British superiority in men and material and their plentiful supplies were bound to tell. Moreover, whatever successes Rommel might achieve on the battlefield each day of fighting brought new losses in German soldiers, weapons and vehicles which could not be replaced, while the British command was able to replace rapidly its much greater losses. With every day of fighting the stock of supplies so laboriously collected during the summer months melted away, and there was no possibility of bringing further ships to North Africa with German supplies. The day was in sight when the German-Italian troops, as a result of their drastic bloodletting, would come to the end of their resources.

Up to 23 November, Rommel's conduct of operations had taken account of these circumstances, and aimed at a rapid decision against the most dangerous British assault group. On 23 November he stood on the threshold of victory and had not only made good his inferiority against an enemy who outnumbered him two to one, but had changed it into superiority. After 24 November he succumbed more and more to the temptation to run after distant successes of secondary importance. Auchinleck, on the other hand, in an apparently hopeless situation, adhered with great tenacity to his original plan of forcing the German-Italian troops to give battle by thrusting against the south-east front of Tobruk, and to wear them down. The main reason for the failure of Rommel's dash to the Sollum front was the fact that he had underestimated the tenacity of the British command and mistakenly assumed that Auchinleck would be compelled to withdraw to Egypt after the failures of the first week of the campaign.

When, on 27 November, the *Afrika Korps* returned from its dash, the balance of forces had again been lost and the scale of the fortunes of war dipped against Rommel. The commander-in-chief of *Panzergruppe Afrika*, however, did not acknowledge defeat even in this difficult situation, but concentrated all his forces against the most dangerous enemy group – the *2nd New Zealand Division*. It is to the credit of his powerful and unruffled leadership as much as to the hitting power of his troops that he again succeeded with his diminished forces in smashing the *2nd New Zealand Division* and once more closed the ring around Tobruk. As soon, indeed, as he turned to new secondary tasks instead of following up his victory, it became apparent that his forces had become too weak to hold what he had gained.

Thus, his decision of 4 December to raise the siege of Tobruk took the actual ratio of forces into account. Only in this way could he hope to regain the freedom of movement which was necessary to meet the growing menace of the British forces on his south flank and, at the same time, prevent the threatening disintegration of the Italian divisions before Tobruk.

This decision was certainly not easy for him. After all, it meant renouncing the capture of Tobruk, to which he had adhered for eight months with exemplary persistence. It also meant a final resignation to the abandonment of the Sollum front, which was very dear to Rommel's heart. The German-Italian troops shut up there must now, sooner or later, fall victim to British superiority. Most importantly of all, the abandonment of the siege was the first obvious success of the British autumn offensive – and it would certainly be exploited by the British propaganda services.

CHAPTER 5

The Battle for the Gazala Position

As early as 28 November 1941, doubts had arisen at the headquarters of *Panzergruppe Afrika* whether it would be possible in the long run to keep up the investment of Tobruk. The victorious conclusion of the fighting against the *2nd New Zealand Division* had once again revived the hope for a happy outcome of the campaign. In an order of the day issued on 2 December and read to all troops, Rommel spoke of the successful conclusion of the first phase of the campaign.

On 4 December, however, the situation had again considerably deteriorated. The vain attacks on El Duda and the advance with insufficient forces on Bardia had brought new and irreplaceable losses in men and material, and had further weakened the fighting power of the German troops. Now there was hardly hope of regaining the old and shorter line of investment. As the fighting power of the Italian formations kept on decreasing, the chances of containing new breakout attempts by the Tobruk garrison were dwindling.

The issue was decided by the news which was forthcoming about the enemy south of Tobruk. As from the last days of November, it had become increasingly difficult for ground reconnaissance to get an insight into the area south of Trigh Capuzzo. The enemy had superior reconnaissance formations at his disposal, and had built up a dense screen of armored reconnaissance troops reinforced by artillery and armored cars. This screen stretched from the west, south of Trigh Capuzzo, to the area east of Gasr el Arid; from there it turned to the north-east, joining the strongpoints of the New Zealanders south-west and west of Bardia. The few armored patrols of *Reconnaissance Battalion 33* and *Reconnaissance Battalion 3* were able to pierce this screen only in exceptional cases. The few reports which become available from air reconnaissance not only showed that the *7th Armored Division* was being further replenished in the Sidi Muftah area, but that a new group of forces was in the process of formation around Bir el Gubi. Whilst this latter group had remained inactive up to 1 December, on that day, for the first time, an enemy column of 50 tanks and armored reconnaissance cars was sighted advancing from Bir el Gubi to Bir Hacheim. On the same day, another strong enemy column was moving from Er Reghem to Bir el Gubi. On 3 December, and still more on 4 December, increased enemy reconnaissance activity in the direction of El Adem and Bir Hacheim made itself felt. On 4 December the battle headquarters of *Panzergruppe Afrika* was attacked for the first time by enemy armored reconnaissance cars and artillery from the south.

On 4 December, air reconnaissance sighted several strong motorized columns with artillery advancing from the Sidi Omar area towards Bir el Gubi. Their forward elements were further advancing from there to the north and north-west, towards El Adem and Acroma. The *Panzergruppe* drew the conclusion that the British were moving up another large formation from the Sollum front – probably the *4th Indian Division*. It was to be expected that they would advance with these forces and with the *7th Armored Division* into the area south and south-west of Tobruk, in order to attack the rearward communications of the main body of the *Panzergruppe* fighting east of Tobruk. Thereby it not only became impossible for the *Panzergruppe* to continue its attacks east of Tobruk, but it would be an extremely dangerous maneuver to withdraw the forces fighting east of Tobruk.

Thus, in the long run, there was little hope of keeping up the investment of Tobruk and at the same time warding off this enemy group. The decisive factor, however, was the irretrievable dwindling of our fighting strength, whilst on the other hand the enemy forces were continuously increasing.

Hence, on 4 December, in the morning, Rommel decided to give up the area east of Tobruk and to take his troops back into a position west and south-west of Tobruk, to make use of the western front of the investment ring between Acroma and the sea. This evacuation was bound to be difficult, as in the area east of Tobruk there were spread out not only the *Division z.b.v. Afrika* and the rest of the *Infantry Division Bologna*, but also innumerable immobile baggage trains, supply installations, tank repair shops and supply dumps which had been set up in the area. The withdrawal of all these forces required time, which had to be gained by a correspondingly longer resistance by the fighting troops. Of greatest importance, however, was that the move had to be protected against attack by enemy formations from the area south-east and south of Tobruk.

The *Panzergruppe*, therefore, decided on 4 December at noon to move the *Afrika Korps* and the Italian *Motorized Corps* into the area south-west of Tobruk without delay, to clarify on 5 December the situation south of Tobruk by advancing from the south-west to the south-east against the west flank of the new enemy group, to defeat the enemy around Bir el Gubi, and to get some elbow room for the withdrawal of the troops from the area east of Tobruk. Towards 1400 hours the two corps received the order to move off immediately into the area west and south-west of El Adem, there to stand by, either to ward off enemy attacks from the south-west or themselves to attack to the south-east.

The rapid execution of this order met with considerable difficulties. The Italian *Motorized Corps* stood far in the east near Gasr el Arid, ready to advance on Sidi Omar. The *Afrika Korps* was involved in a battle. Whilst the *21st Panzer Division* was busy attacking towards El Duda, the *15th Panzer Division*, the stronger of the two, was still far to the east near Sidi Azeiz, involved in the attack on Bardia. Other elements of the *15th Panzer Division* were widely dispersed in their rest area east of Tobruk. In this area there was also the bulk of their supply troops, and the nonmobile baggage troops of the units, with a great number of sick personnel; most of these troops could not be contacted by signals, as they were widely dispersed in the wadis around Marsa Belafarid. Thus, it was more than doubtful whether the two corps could be assembled south-west of Tobruk early enough to start the attack on 5 December as had been planned.

The *21st Panzer Division* could not break away from the action on El Duda until after nightfall. In a night march it reached the area south-east of Scentaf according to plan.

The headquarters of the *15th Panzer Division*, traveling in advance of the division, reached the former position of the *Afrika Korps* battle headquarters east of Sidi Rezegh on the Trigh Capuzzo towards 2000 hours. The corps headquarters had already moved. The corps order for the regrouping did not arrive until 0300 hours on 5 December owing to a breakdown in wireless communication. However, an officer who had been left behind by the *Afrika Korps* informed the commander of the division in broad terms of the intentions of the *Afrika Korps*, and also of the fact that the Trigh Capuzzo south of El Duda was under enemy fire. Thereupon the troops east of Tobruk were withdrawn and supplied for their further move. Owing to lack of time it had been impossible to place the supply troops at the head of the troops when withdrawing. They were ordered to follow into the area of Acroma.

In spite of all these difficulties, the *Afrika Korps* was assembled by 0900 hours on 5 December with the *15th Panzer Division* south-west and with the *21st Panzer Division* south-east of Bir Scentaf. The divisions were posted 10 kilometers to the south on the escarpment edge in such a way that they were able either to ward off an enemy attack or themselves to attack to the south-east. During 5 December, the Italian *Motorized Corps* was moved 20 kilometers southward into an area on the Trigh Capuzzo around Bir el Harmat.

The Attack on Bir el Gubi

On 5 December, towards 1200 hours, *Panzergruppe Africa* gave orders to the *Afrika Korps* to attack from its concentration area south-west of El Adem to the south-east, to defeat the enemy group at Bir el Gubi and to throw it back towards Gabr Saleh.

At 1300 hours, the *Afrika Korps* issued the divisions with the order for the attack. At the same time, *Reconnaissance Battalion 3,* under command of the *Afrika Korps,* moved off to reconnoiter on the front and south-west flank of the *Afrika Korps*. The more powerful *15th Panzer Division* was to attack on the right, that is, on the outer wing, and the *21st Panzer Division* on the left. The divisions were to have their riflemen and their artillery moving in front and their armored regiments behind. Their attention was drawn to the possibility of Italian strongpoints still being in the area of Bir el Gubi. (However, there were none.)

The attack began at 1430 hours. In the sector of the *15th Panzer Division,* enemy covering units with armored cars and artillery gave way rapidly to the south-east. As the attack progressed, weaker enemy armored forces advanced against the west flank of the attack. *Panzer Regiment 8* was quickly thrown against them and drove them back to the south-west. By 1630 hours the division had advanced to 10 kilometers from the track-fork north of Bir el Gubi, when *Reconnaissance Battalion 33* to the south of the right wing of the attack discovered a large British tented camp with armor, riflemen and artillery. On its own initiative, the division turned off to the south and attacked the new enemy with all it had. When night was falling, *Panzer Regiment 8* broke into the enemy camp. The enemy hurriedly moved off to the south. One hundred and fifty prisoners of the *4th Indian Division* were collected. Because of the complete darkness, the attack was not continued. The division took up a hedgehog position and rested.

The *21st Panzer Division,* too, had met only weaker opposition in the beginning, but later in the evening met stronger resistance, and at nightfall while in contact with the enemy went over to rest.

Decision Taken by the *Afrika Korps*

In the evening of 5 December the situation had become far clearer. It was now confirmed that the enemy group at Bir el Gubi had received considerable reinforcements and that the *4th Indian Division* had arrived from the Sollum front. From depositions of prisoners of war, it was elicited that it was already advancing against the line El Adem–Bir Bellefaa. The participation of the *7th Armored Division* in the attack had also to be reckoned with. The attack by the *Afrika Korps* had not hit the west flank of the enemy, but had pushed right into the his centre. If the advance were continued in the same direction, strong enemy forces would remain in the west flank of the *Afrika Korps* and would become a danger for its rearward communications. For such an operation in the middle of the enemy, the forces of the *Afrika Korps* had become too weak, as the two divisions together had only 55 tanks left.

The *Afrika Korps* decided, therefore, to get once more on the flank of the enemy, and for this purpose and under cover of the night to move across the various enemy groups to the south-west and to gain the area 20 kilometers west of Bir el Gubi on the track to Bir Hacheim. The corps commander submitted to *Panzergruppe* that the Italian *Motorized Corps* should on 6 December advance along the Trigh Capuzzo in a south-south-easterly direction in support of the *Afrika Korps*. For this purpose the divisions were to concentrate in such a way that the *21st Panzer Division* would first move to the west and join up with the *15th Panzer Division*, and then the *Afrika Korps* would carry out the dangerous maneuver moving in one column.

Events on 6 December

The concentration of the corps led to considerable friction. The *21st Panzer Division* missed the area of the *15th Panzer Division* and was placed by the *Afrika Korps* at the head of the column. The *15th Panzer Division* was to follow behind. *Reconnaissance Battalion 3*, which had spent the night near Bir Berud, was to advance to Gburet esc Scieb and to reconnoiter to the south and the east.

During the night move to the south-west, the *Afrika Korps* bumped enemy vehicles on several occasions. When dawn broke on 6 December, it was still about 8 kilometers north of the Bir Hacheim–Bir el Gubi track in the midst of enemy columns, which hurriedly gave way in all directions. This situation, however, could not be exploited as both the divisions of the *Afrika Korps* had got themselves completely mixed up and first had to be disentangled and made ready for operation. The *15th Panzer Division* was concentrated further south on the Bir Hacheim–Bir el Gubi track and the *21st Panzer Division* to the north thereof, both to get ready for the defense to the east.

Whilst these moves were proceeding, the divisions received artillery fire from a strong enemy column in the east which had followed a parallel course to the south and now was moving further away to the south-east, protected by the fire of several light and heavy batteries. In the south there was also a weaker enemy group with artillery, and in the south-west enemy baggage columns were in flight to the south.

On 6 December, the *Afrika Korps* appreciated the situation in the morning, stating that the enemy had also moved to the south during the night and for this reason it had been impossible to get into his flank. A further swing to the south, however, would have brought the *Afrika Korps* too far away from Tobruk. The *Afrika Korps* commander therefore decided, in spite of enemy superiority, to attack to the east, relying on the superior fighting qualities of the *15th Panzer Division*.

Information was received from *Panzergruppe Afrika* that the Italian *Motorized Corps* had in the morning moved from Bir El Hamat along the Trigh el Abd, and was now on its way to Bir el Gubi. The *Afrika Korps* was to be supported by the *Luftwaffe* and was to cooperate with the same. Towards noon, there were actually *Stuka* attacks observed in the east. The direct cooperation, however, did not materialize.

Towards noon, the *15th Panzer Division* had warded off the enemy artillery by a tank attack to east. At 1300 hours, the *Afrika Korps* gave the order for the attack. Accordingly, the *15th Panzer Division* was to attack in front with the *21st Panzer Division* echeloned to the left, as the enemy had also been sighted in the left flank. *Reconnaissance Battalion 3* was to reconnoiter further to the south and protect the right flank. The first objectives of the attack were to be the heights 10 kilometers west of Bir el Gubi. There an attack by German *Stuka* formations which had been requested was to be awaited.

The attack by the *15th Panzer Division* started at 1330 hours. It was met by strong artillery fire. The enemy batteries soon gave way to the east. In the southern flank, too, considerable enemy artillery was identified. At 1515 hours, after the first objective had been reached, the attack was halted. Soon the enemy settled down again, and by concentrated artillery fire from several light and heavy batteries inflicted serious losses on the division. At this stage, the brave commander of the division was fatally wounded. The commander of *Reconnaissance Battalion 33* dropped out, having received a slight wound.

The *21st Panzer Division* had not yet joined up with the division. Nor had the expected *Stuka* attack materialized. The *15th Panzer Division* therefore asked for permission from the *Afrika Korps* to continue its attack. At 1645 hours, the division resumed the advance and, disregarding the enemy in the south flank, pushed rapidly on to the east. In almost complete darkness, strong forces of enemy infantry and artillery were driven off the heights around Bir el Gubi and the track crossing of Bir el Gubi was reached. In the line which had been reached, *Schützen Regiment 115* and *Regiment 200*, the former fronting east and the latter south, took up defensive positions as far as this was possible in the prevailing darkness. *Reconnaissance Battalion 33* was brought into position west of Bir el Gubi, and *Panzer Regiment 8*, under the protection of the two *Schützen* regiments, was withdrawn behind the front.

The *21st Panzer Division* had greatly delayed the beginning of its attack, and towards 1500 hours had followed up behind the *15th Panzer Division* without fighting. When night fell, it was halted 10 kilometers west of Bir el Gubi.

Reconnaissance Battalion 3 had advanced towards Gburet in the morning, but immediately to the north of Gburet had encountered several enemy columns with artillery. It sent out covering patrols 5 kilometers north of the objective of its attack and reconnoitered further to the south and south-east.

The Italian *Motorized Corps* did not advance until noon on 6 December, moving along the Trigh el Abd, and towards evening pressed back lesser enemy forces to the south-east. During the night it rested 15 kilometers north-west of Bir el Gubi.

The Defensive Battle of 7 December

During the evening an order from *Panzergruppe Afrika* arrived at the *Afrika Korps* with the instruction to discontinue a further attack to the south-east and to go over to the defensive in the line reached so far. The *Panzergruppe* would intend to withdraw the corps (all of them) to the Gazala position. The *Afrika Korps* was also to be ready to withdraw to the north-west as early as 7 December.

Thereupon the *Afrika Korps* decided to place the *15th Panzer Division* in defensive positions on the heights south and east of Bir el Gubi, and the *21st Panzer Division* to the north thereof. The protection of the southern flank on Heights 181 and 180 south of the Bir Hacheim–Bir el Gubi track was entrusted to the two reconnaissance units. The division received an order to move their baggage trains to the north-west during the night and to start reconnoitering the route for the withdrawal. On receipt of this order, the *15th Panzer Division* took up positions in depth and prepared for the counterthrust to be made by *Panzer Regiment 8* on both wings of the defensive front.

The enemy on the front had received considerable reinforcements during the night. At dawn the division faced a strong enemy line on the heights east and south-east of Bir el Gubi. Enemy artillery fire increased during the day and soon reached great intensity. Strong armored forces appeared on the front. Already, at 0830 hours, a thrust made by 80 tanks from the east and north-east had to be warded off by *Panzer Regiment 8*, which knocked out 10 tanks.

The junction with the *21st Panzer Division* on the north wing did not come off. Later on it appeared that the division, owing to faulty navigation, had taken up defensive positions 8 kilometers to the west of the *15th Panzer Division*. Thereby the north wing of the *15th Panzer Division* became exposed to envelopment. At 1000 hours, an enveloping attack made by 30 tanks had to be halted by the fire of *Artillery Regiment 33*. Soon, however, the arrival of *Armored Division Ariete* of the Italian *Motorized Corps* brought relief. This division had resumed its advance at dawn along the Trigh Capuzzo, chasing weaker enemy columns ahead of its front. Now this enemy was withdrawing to the south on the front of the *15th Panzer Division*, and enabled it to take them under effective artillery fire. The operation of *Armored Division Ariete* caused the enemy armor to break off the attack against the north wing of the *15th Panzer Division*.

However, the threat to the southern flank of the division was much more serious, as, during the early morning, enemy enveloping moves made themselves felt there. Towards noon Height 208 was attacked from the south and *Reconnaissance Battalion 33* in the west was hard pressed. The *15th Panzer Division* had to take out more and more forces from its far-flung east front to lengthen its south-west wing with them. During the afternoon the *Afrika Korps* decided to throw in its corps reserve (elements of the *21st Panzer Division*) on the west of the *15th Panzer Division* to ward off the enemy. Towards evening, enemy pressure on the east and south front of the *Afrika Korps* increased. The concentrated fire of the very superior enemy artillery caused losses, mainly of transport. Nevertheless, the *Afrika Korps* was able to hold all its positions.

Thus, the *Afrika Korps* had successfully stood its ground on 7 December against the attack of the entire *XXX Armored Corps* (*7th Armored Division*, *4th Indian Division*, *1st Guards Brigade* and the replenished *1st South African Division*).

Evacuation of the Area East of Tobruk

The order to evacuate the area east of Tobruk put *Division z.b.v. Afrika* and *Group Mickl* in a very difficult position. After the *21st Panzer Division* had been drawn out, *Group Mickl* was unable to hold on to the parts of El Duda which had been captured, and had also to be taken back to its position of departure.

This brought the Axis Road further into the hands of the enemy, and the troops east of Tobruk had to rely on the detour east of Belhamed in their withdrawal from the area. All troops had to be sluiced through the narrow pass south of El Duda, which on 4 December had been under fire from both sides.

Division z.b.v. Afrika and elements of *Infantry Division Bologna* were still in their positions on the former investment front east of Tobruk between the coast and the Via Balbia. Eastward thereof, as far back as the area of Gambut, the supply troops, the baggage troops and the repair workshops of the *15th Panzer Division* were dispersed all over. They and the heavy artillery had to be moved back to the west, and at the same time mobile enemy forces had to be prevented from interfering from the south-east and the south with the evacuation.

The only formation available for this task, *Group Mickl*, was weakened by losses and mobile only in parts, and was hardly sufficient for it. Thus, the move could only succeed if the *7th Armored Division* were engaged by a push by the *Afrika Korps* into the Bir el Gubi area, and thus prevented from interfering in the evacuation.

The plan of the *Panzergruppe* provided for the withdrawal during the night of 4/5 December and during the whole of 5 December of the heavy artillery, baggage troops and supply troops into the area west of Tobruk and for the beginning of the evacuation by *Division z.b.v. Afrika* of the positions on the Via Balbia and the coast. The Italian *XXI Corps* and elements of *Group Mickl* were to cover the move against El Duda, whilst the bulk of *Group Mickl* was to cover off towards the south.

During the night of 5/6 December all fighting troops were to be withdrawn as far as the Bir Bu Creimisa–Bir Salem investment front south of Bir Assaten, then during the night of 6/7 December a line of resistance was to be reached south of the Bir el Garaa–Bir el Adem investment front south of Tobruk.

During the night of 4/5 December the headquarters of the *Panzergruppe* had been subjected to a very heavy air attack which lasted more than eight hours. On 5 December it was moved into the area north of Acroma and on 6 December to Giovanni Berta, behind the Gazala line.

The Withdrawal

Against all expectations, the interference of the British with our withdrawal remained on a small scale. By the evening of 5 December, the bulk of the baggage troops and of the supply units had been successfully withdrawn into the area west of Tobruk. Enemy artillery fire south of El Duda caused but light losses. But it had been impossible to salvage numerous immobilized tanks and other vehicles from the repair shops which had been operating in that area. It had also been impossible to contact some baggage units and numerous sick personnel; they fell into the hands of the British in the course of the following days.

The main danger had passed when, in the morning on 6 December, the fighting troops of *Division z.b.v. Afrika* arrived in the line of resistance as ordered and were ready for defense. The dreaded push of mobile British forces had been warded off by the attack of the *Afrika Korps* on Bir el Gubi. During the succeeding days, the withdrawal of *Division z.b.v. Afrika* and of the Italian *XXI Corps* also proceeded according to plan, covered as they were by German rearguard troops of *Division z.b.v. Afrika.* During the night of 7/8 December the Italian *XXI Corps*, with *Division z.b.v. Afrika* under its command, occupied the line south of Bellefaa on the Trigh Capuzzo escarpment east of Acroma. There it joined the Italian *X Corps*, which had remained in its old positions opposite the west front of Tobruk. The losses suffered during the withdrawal were slight: only the Italian troops of *XXI Corps* lost prisoners on the south front of Tobruk in sorties made by the Tobruk garrison.

Decision to Withdraw into the Gazala Position

On 4 December, General Rommel had the intention of holding the area west of Tobruk as long as possible, and, to this end, to place the German-Italian troops of *XXI Corps*, which had been in position on the east and south fronts of Tobruk, into a defensive line south of Acroma. At that time, he was still hoping that the Italian *X* and *XXI Corps*, in their shortened positions and narrower sectors, would be able to continue their defensive fighting successfully. He intended to hold at bay the British *XXX Armored Corps* to the south of this position with the *Afrika Korps* and the Italian *Motorized Corps* employing mobile tactics, and to prevent envelopment of this position from the south. In the course of the succeeding days, however, he realized to what level the fighting strength of the Italian divisions had sunk, and that their morale had suffered very severely.

Thus, General Rommel gained the impression and the conviction that, in particular, *XXI Italian Corps*, which until then used to carry the brunt of the burden in the fighting around Tobruk, would not be able in its positions south-west of Tobruk to withstand a strong breakthrough attempt by the

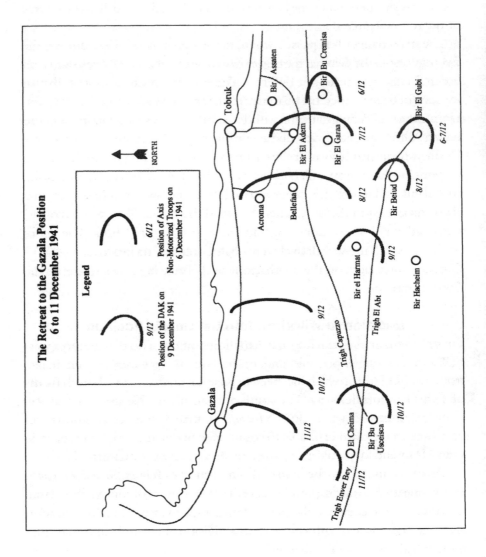

The Retreat to the Gazala Position
6 to 11 December 1941

Legend

6/12
Position of Axis
Non-Motorized Troops on
6 December 1941

9/12
Position of the DAK on
9 December 1941

British. He therefore regarded it as necessary to withdraw the Italian corps into a well-constructed position to which it could cling. The only position of that kind was the Gazala position.

The further strengthening of the British armored and motorized forces on the southern wing, which had been apparent in the fighting at Bir el Gubi may also have contributed to Rommel's decision to abandon the defense of the area west of Tobruk. The reason for his discontinuing the push to Bir el Gubi may have been the fact that the object which he wanted to achieve, *viz.* to gain room for the withdrawal east of Tobruk, had actually been achieved by the evening of 6 December. In these circumstances, it would have been senseless to continue the advance beyond Bir el Gubi to the east, though it had been successful at the beginning. It would have entailed further considerable losses, which the German troops could ill afford.

Thus, on 6 December General Rommel decided to evacuate the area west of Tobruk and to go back, section-wise following a preconceived plan, into the Gazala position.

The Withdrawal into the Gazala Position

The withdrawal into the Gazala position was a difficult one. The enemy, with his fully motorized divisions, was far superior in mobility to the formations of the Italian *X* and *XXI Corps*. Thus, it would be very difficult to gain a good start before the enemy in this withdrawal. The manifold superiority of the enemy armor might have a particularly unfavorable effect.

Rommel's chief worry was the enemy in the Bir el Gubi area. He feared that these enemy forces would try and overtake him and would outflank the *Panzergruppe* during its withdrawal and when in the Gazala position. He decided, therefore, to have the *Afrika Korps* following the withdrawal in formation echeloned to the south-east, with the instruction to prevent an overtaking enemy pursuit if need be by means of a counterattack.

This was also the reason why Rommel had ordered the *Afrika Korps*, together with the Italian *Motorized Corps*, to hold their positions at Bir el Gubi even during 7 December. On 8 December they were to cover only a short distance and move north-westward to Bir Beiud, and on 9 December they were to halt the British pursuit in the area of the track-crossing south of Bir el Harmat. The north wing of the *Panzergruppe* – the Italian *XXI* and *X Corps* – was to withdraw to the Gazala position as early as during the night of 8/ 9 December, and to reach the position in three night marches. The Italian *Motorized Corps* had been allotted the task of maintaining communication between the *Afrika Korps* and the south wing of *XXI Corps* and of preventing an enemy advance against the southern flank.

General Rommel also feared that mobile forces of the enemy, swinging far to the south and traveling through the desert, might outflank the *Panzergruppe* during its withdrawal or after its arrival in the Gazala position, and advance to Agedabia, join forces with the troops at Giala and cut off its rearward communications. He decided, therefore, to move *Division z.b.v. Afrika* into this area as soon as the withdrawal of the Italian *XXI Corps* had been set in motion as planned. This intention was objected to by the Italian commander-in-chief in North Africa, General Bastico. He was against the sending of a German division, but would consent to the sending of a mixed German-Italian formation. General Rommel, however, insisted that the choice of the means with which to carry out his operational aims to be left exclusively to him.

The Withdrawal during 8–9 December

Against expectations, the breaking away of the the *Afrika Korps* passed off according to plan and without undue interference from the enemy. The *Afrika Korps* disguised its withdrawal from the positions east and south of Bir el Gubi by demonstrations of its armor and by artillery shoots during the evening hours of 7 December. With rearguard troops left behind in the positions, the corps assembled its troops for the withdrawal by midnight and on 8 December, at 0300 hours, moving in one column, marched off to the new line of resistance on both sides of Bir Beiud, reaching it at dawn.

The enemy did not interfere. During the morning he followed the *Afrika Korps* only with reconnaissance forces, and only in the afternoon did enemy armor and artillery feel forward against its front and the south-west flank.

The withdrawal during the night of 8/9 December into the second position of resistance along the line Point 186–Bir el Harmat, on the track leading from Bir Hacheim to the north and to Acroma, also passed off according to plan. The enemy followed hesitantly with reconnaissance forces, and not until noon 9 December did he force the reinforced *Motorcycle Battalion 15*, which had been left behind as rearguard near Carmus el Baar, to fall back to the line of resistance. Before the counterattack of *Panzer Regiment 8*, however, the enemy armor withdrew to the east without showing fight.

The withdrawal of the Italian *Motorized Corps* during the night of 7/8 December from the area Bir el Gubi to Bir Bu Maafes passed off without fighting of any importance. During the night of 8/9 December the corps, with *Armored Division Ariete* on the right and *Motorized Division Trieste* on the left, withdrew from the area west of Bir Bellefaa, moving along the Trigh Capuzzo. In this area, however, stronger enemy motorized forces advanced during 9 December along the Trigh Capuzzo to the west. In order to keep contact with *XXI Corps*, the motorized corps withdrew further to the west as far as the area of Sidi Muftah, but was unable to prevent the enemy pursuing column from infiltrating into the gap separating it from the *Afrika Korps* echeloned forward and south-eastward, and from penetrating between *Ariete* and *Trieste*.

On the north wing, in the area of *XXI* and *X Corps*, heavy artillery and baggage trains had been moved behind the Gazala line as from 7 December onwards. Here, the withdrawal to the next line of resistance 10 kilometers west of Eluet Et Tamara–Sidi Mgherreb–Sidi Daud was carried out successfully during the night of 8/9 December, apparently unnoticed by the enemy. Strong rearguard troops – in the sector of *XXI Corps* provided by the German *Division z.b.v. Afrika* – remained in the old positions south of Acroma and on the waterfront of Tobruk until the next morning. But in the morning of 9 December strong enemy motorized forces and heavy tanks pressed forward, particularly in the sector of *XXI Corps*, and forced the rearguard troops of *Division z.b.v. Afrika* towards midday to give way and move into the new line of resistance.

Nevertheless, on 9 December, in the evening, General Rommel took the bulk of *Division z.b.v. Afrika* out of the front and sent it to the rear, traveling along the Via Balbia on army supply columns. The commander of the division received the instruction to protect the area of Agedabia against the attack of mobile forces from the desert to the east. Besides this,he was also to cover locally [on the escarpment 50 kilometers east of the Via Balbia, between Benghazi and Agedabia] the descents of the tracks leading from the desert to Antelat and Scheleidimia. The motor convey of the division was heavily attacked by the RAF. Losses in men and motor transport occurred. On this occasion the commander of the division, Major-General Sümmermann, was also killed. But by 13 December the division had reached the area of Agedabia and had set up the covering system as ordered. On 15 December, the division was renamed the *90th Light Division* without a change in its organization or equipment, at least for the time being.

The Withdrawal on 10–11 December

Even after 9 December the withdrawal of the *Afrika Korps* remained almost entirely unmolested by the enemy. During the night of 9/10 December the divisions took up positions on both sides of the Trigh el Abd astride the track-fork north of Bir Bu Usceisca, and during the morning of 11 December withdrew to the high ground north of the Trigh Enver Bei north of El Cheima. The rearguards which had remained on the track-fork were not withdrawn to El Cheima until the evening.

The pressure of the enemy pursuit was directed against the two central corps of the *Panzergruppe*. The enemy followed close on the heels of the Italian *Motorized Corps*, particularly on the north wing, and on 11 December, simultaneously with the corps, reached the area south-west of the Gazala position, west of Gabr el Abid. He started infiltrating into the gap between *Ariete* and *Trieste* and enveloping the corps also from the south. In order to counter this danger, the *Afrika Korps*, in the afternoon of 11 December, moved 6 kilometers to the north and joined up with the south wing of *Armored Division Ariete*.

Some embarrassing moments were also experienced in the sector of *XXI Corps* adjoining in the north. During the evening of 9 December, enemy armor and artillery smashed into the withdrawing corps. Two infantry battalions and one artillery battalion fell into the hands of the enemy. The *Panzergruppe* had great difficulty in closing the gap thus opened and in keeping the front intact.

Pursuit columns of the enemy also followed close on the heels of *X Corps* withdrawing along the Via Balbia. During the night of 9/10 December, both corps, in a long night march, were taken back to the second line of resistance, which ran from Bir Aluse to the airfield of Ain el Gazala only 8 kilometers east of the Gazala position. Strong elements were sent in advance to occupy the Gazala position. It was possible to hold the above-mentioned line of resistance until 10 December, and on 11 December to occupy the Gazala position. On the other hand, the enemy stood also in front of the Gazala position on the evening of 11 December, ready for the attack.

On 4 December, the *Panzergruppe* found itself in an extremely dangerous situation. The British *XXX Corps*, reinforced by the the *4th Indian Division*, had advanced from Bir el Gubi to attack to the north-west. It threatened to cut the rearward communications of the *Panzergruppe* to the west of El Adem and to cause the investment front south-west of Tobruk to collapse. The withdrawal of the German-Italian divisions would then only be possible with very serious losses, if at all.

On 4 December, the decision to evacuate the area east of Tobruk was, therefore, no longer to be deferred. It was carried out resolutely and skillfully. By sending the *Afrika Korps* and the Italian *Motorized Corps* into the area south-west of El Adem and by having them advance to the south-east, Rommel had made the only countermove which promised success. Though the task allotted to the *Afrika Korps* – crushing the enemy forces at Bir el Gubi and advancing to Gabr Saleh – had hardly any chance of success in the face of the superiority of the enemy, he was after all dealt a blow, and the forces east of Tobruk were given time to carry their withdrawal.

The leadership displayed by the *Afrika Korps* during this advance was bold and vigorous. The enemy was evidently taken by surprise by the advance of the *Afrika Korps* on 5 December. The following move to the south-west right through the enemy during the night of 5/6 December constituted a very daring move. Had it been successful, a favorable opportunity would have offered itself to get into the enemy's flank and to inflict on him a heavy defeat after all.

But the difficulties of this move had been too great. On 6 December, in the morning, the surprise sprung on the enemy could not be exploited, because the corps had first to be reassembled. When eventually, during the afternoon of 6 December, the attack on Bir el Gubi got going, the day had advanced too far to complete the success which had begun to take shape.

It is difficult to decide whether Rommel did right in halting the attack of the *Afrika Korps* in the evening of 6 December. All the mobile forces of the *Panzergruppe* – the *Afrika Korps* and the Italian *Motorized Corps* – were concentrated to give battle in the evening of 6 December, and a nice initial success had been achieved. But during the night of 6/7 December, the enemy had time to reorganize his forces and to build up his defenses. The course the fighting took during 7 December demonstrated his vast superiority, particularly in artillery. Thus, a continuation of the attack on 7 December, even if it had been successful eventually, would have cost us serious losses which would have been hard to bear seeing how much the fighting force of the *Afrika Korps* had dwindled. Moreover, even a victory at Bir el Gubi would not have brought about a decisive turn in the situation, because, owing to the state the Italian troops were in, the withdrawal to the Gazala position was in any case inevitable.

Even though the battle at Bir el Gubi had not been fought to the end, Rommel was entitled to book it as a success insofar as it was due to this battle that the mobile forces of the British were kept engaged, and the time necessary for the evacuation of the area east of Tobruk was gained.

The rapid and smooth evacuation of the area east of Tobruk doubtless constitutes a fine achievement by the command. As, after all, there was the possibility even before 4 December of an evacuation of this area, it might have been more to the point to remove the baggage trains, supply troops, and depots east of Tobruk and not needed for the battles at an earlier date. Thereby much loss of material might have been avoided.

One is inclined to ask whether Rommel was really compelled to withdraw from his position west of Tobruk to the Gazala position. In the African theater of war, the evacuation of a 70 kilometer deep stretch of desert does not mean much. But, after al, the positions west of Tobruk were further away from Cyrenaica and not exposed to the danger of envelopment to the same degree as the Gazala position. Any withdrawal with Italian troops is a dangerous enterprise, as their morale easily collapses in a difficult position. Thus, the withdrawal was a risky matter in the face of the enemy's superiority in mobility.

On the other hand, Rommel's hope that the Italians would gain new confidence in the Gazala position was quite understandable. In the Gazala position his rearward communications would be shorter and those of the enemy longer. Time would be gained to bring about a more favorable ratio of forces by reestablishing the supply route across the sea.

In reality, the withdrawal turned out to be more difficult than Rommel had expected. It is true the British did not, as Rommel had feared, go forward to overtake him in pursuit. But the rapidity with which the enemy followed up, as well as the fact that he exercised his main pressure in the center, came as a surprise to the *Panzergruppe*.

The *Panzergruppe* was indeed successfully withdrawn to the Gazala position, but the withdrawal entailed losses and did not gain the time Rommel had hoped it would. For the fighting in the Gazala position, it was a great handicap that the troops thus did not find sufficient time to install themselves in their positions.

The Battle in the Gazala Position, 12–16 December

In the western part of Marmarica, around El Gazala, the prevailing ground conditions are different from those in the Tobruk area. The steep coast of the Marmarica becomes lower towards the west until, on the peninsula of Ain el Gazala, it is no more than a flat coastal strip. The plain on both sides of the Via Balbia descends to the west to nearly sea level and at the same time grows narrower. To the south of the bight cutting inland west of Ain el Gazala, it is no more than a strip of plain four kilometers broad and constitutes a veritable bottleneck. The escarpment south of the Via Balbia becomes steeper and more rugged towards the west. It reaches a height of 100–150 meters, and is in a few places negotiable by vehicles. The most important ascents are south of the bottleneck of Ain el Gazala and 10 kilometers north-west thereof. Deeply eroded wadis 2 to 4 kilometers in length extend from the escarpment to the south into the desert plateau.

The desert south of the escarpment is almost everywhere negotiable for any vehicle, but more undulating than further in the east. From Sidi Mgherreb to Sidi Alluso and Sidi Bregisc, another escarpment runs from east to west, which on the whole falls away to the north at a height of no more than 20 meters, but in many places is so steep and rugged that it forms a veritable obstacle. It has several elevations which provide excellent possibilities for all-round observation and, therefore, played an important part during the fighting. This applies particularly to Height 208, Alem Hamza, which forms the south-west pivot of the Gazala position, and to Height 204. Twenty kilometers further to the south, along the Trigh Enver Bey between El Cheima and Segnali, there is another chain of hills, which affords good observation particularly to the north, although it does not constitute an obstacle for movement.

The construction of the Gazala position had been ordered by Rommel in May 1941, and had been completed by the end of June 1941. The position was to serve as a support in case of a setback on the Tobruk front. It consisted of two lines:

(a) A *forward line* running from Sidi Mgherreb to Sidi Resciasc on top of the high ground, then swinging back to the west and reaching Gasr el Ascar, and then the coast to the east of the airfields of Ain el Gazala.

(b) The *main line* takes advantage of the bottleneck of Ain el Gazala, where the entire coastal plain can be dominated by fire from the escarpment. The line swings forward on the escarpment to the east as far as to the ascent of the track coming from the desert, then runs on the desert plateau in an arch along Heights 181–187 to the south-west until it ends on the second escarpment at Height 208–Alem el Hamza.

The fortifications of the Gazala position were similar to those of the Sollum position. They consist of various strongpoints, which are composed of antitank gun and machine gun nests. The minefields in front of the Gazala position were not so dense as those in front of the Sollum position.

The Beginning of the Battle on 11–12 December

General Rommel had decided to accept the enemy attack in the Gazala position and there to bring the enemy offensive to a final halt. In this he used the eastern forward line as the last line of resistance in the withdrawal, and chose as his main line of resistance the main line running south of the bottleneck of Ain el Gazala. In the Gazala position proper, between the coast and Alem el Hamza, Rommel placed the Italian infantry divisions, *X Corps* in the coastal plain and on the escarpment, and *XXI Corps* between Height 181 and Height 208. South-west thereof the Italian *Motorized Corps* was to cover the south-west wing of the position. The *Afrika Korps* was to remain in the area of Cheima, echeloned to the south, and was to cover the flank of the *Panzergruppe* against envelopment.

The *Afrika Korps* organized its forces for the defense in a new manner. It formed, with the two armored regiments, motorized rifle units, one motorized artillery battalion, antitank troops, engineers and antiaircraft artillery, an assault group under the staff of the *15th Panzer Division* which was to be kept in readiness for a counterattack behind the front. The remainder of the *15th Panzer Division* – the *15th Schützen Brigade* – was put in position on the *Afrika Korps'* south wing, which was leaning against the high ground south of Trigh Enver Bey. To the north thereof, the *21st Panzer Division* had its defensive positions fronting as far as the area north of El Cheima. The front of the two divisions was organized in strongpoints, and the artillery was so placed that it could be brought to bear on the front and the open south flank. Antitank troops and *Flak* artillery were also kept back for the protection of the southern flank. *Reconnaissance Battalion 3* was put in an echelon position on to the heights east of Segnali, with the instruction to reconnoiter to the south and south-east and to cover the deep flank of the *Afrika Korps*.

On 11 December the enemy had advanced against the north wing of the *Afrika Korps* and into the gap to the Italian *Motorized Corps*. This gap, however, was closed during the evening of 11 December by extending the north wing with *Group Schuette*, without fighting.

On 12 December stronger enemy forces, with infantry and artillery, advanced against the entire front of the *Afrika Korps*. They were repulsed and dug in two kilometers from the front line. During the afternoon strong armored forces advanced from the east against the southern strongpoint of the *15th Schützen Brigade*. Before the counterattack of the assault, however, the enemy withdrew to the east. Owing to the poor material condition of the tanks, unnecessary moves had to be avoided, and as a result the assault troop did not pursue the enemy, but went into its lines of departure.

At the Italian *Motorized Corps*, the pursuing enemy arrived on 11 December in the area south-west of the Gazala position simultaneously with *Armored*

Division Ariete and *Motorized Infantry Division Trieste*. Thus, it was no longer possible to occupy the allotted positions. Whilst *Motorized Infantry Division Trieste* was to occupy Height 204, *Ariete* held up the advance of the enemy to the west on a front west of 204. Owing to a mistake in navigation, *Trieste* did not reach the allotted position at 204. Thus, from the beginning a gap resulted in the west wing of *XXI Corps* on 208. This could lead to a serious crisis, if enemy forces pushed through this gap to the north-west towards Bir el Temrad.

XXI Corps placed *Infantry Division Pavia* on the right wing and the remainder of *Infantry Division Bologna*, and *Infantry Division Trento*, on the left wing. Enemy motorized infantry advanced on 12 December against the position of the corps. As the divisions during the withdrawal had suffered considerable losses and their moral had been shaken by the impression of the fighting and the continuous enemy air attacks, it seemed doubtful whether they would stand firm against a strong breakthrough by the British.

At *X Corps,* similar conditions prevailed, but here there was hope that the particularly strong position on the narrows might be held.

The Crisis in the Battle, 13–14 December

The commanding general of the *Afrika Korps*, on the morning of 13 December, was faced with a difficult decision. The enemy stood along the entire front ready to attack the positions of the corps. On the south wing, superior armor forces had been sighted which at any time might go round the position in the south, although at that time there were no reconnaissance results available as to that. Since the morning of 13 December, a serious crisis had developed with the northern neighbor. There the enemy, with motorized and armored troops, pressed forward into the gap between *Ariete* and *Trieste* to the north-west in the direction of Bir el Temrad. *Trieste* seemed to have lost Height 204. Where the division was at that moment was unclear. General Gambara was of opinion that the enemy had directed the main effort of his attack against the front of his corps, and that he intended there to break through to the north-west into the rear of the Gazala position.

In this situation, General Crüwell decided, in spite of the threat to his south flank, to assist the Italian *Motorized Corps* with strong armored forces, and to close the gap west of 204 by means of a counterattack by his assault-group, and to move the Italian divisions into the positions allotted to them.

For this purpose he and the commander of the *15th Panzer Division* proceeded to the battle headquarters of the Italian *Motorized Corps*, 6 kilometers north-west of El Cheima, in the morning of 13 December. General Gambara informed them of his intentions to have *Ariete* attacking to the east at 1200 hours in order to reestablish communications with *Trieste*. He requested that the assault group of the *Afrika Korps* attack to the right. They agreed upon *Ariete* delaying its attack until the arrival of the assault group of the *Afrika Korps*. The commanding general of the *15th Panzer Division* regarded the attack planned by General Gambara as difficult and likely to entail heavy losses, as it would pass along the position of the enemy opposite the *Afrika Korps*. He suggested instead that the assault group attack from the front of the *Afrika Korps* in a north-easterly direction and with the support of the entire artillery, in order to roll up the enemy in front of the Italian *Motorized Corps*.

General Crüwell decided, however, in favor of the plan of General Gambara, as he wished to bring him help quickly and also hoped at the same time to encourage the Italians by this assault to greater efforts. He ordered, therefore, the assault group to move to the battle headquarters of Gambara forthwith and to get ready for the attack to the east, so as to take Height 204 together with *Armored Division Ariete*, and afterwards either to return to its lines of departure or to turn northward against the rear of a group of forces alleged to have advanced to Bir el Temrad, as the situation may require.

At 1330 hours, the assault group arrived at the concentration area for the attack to the east. According to information from the Italian *Motorized Corps*, at that time *Armored Division Ariete* was already in the process of attacking to the east. Therefore, there was no time left to reconnoiter the enemy and terrain of the sector concerned as actually should have been done. The concentration was protected by *Group Schuette* of the *21st Panzer Division* on the height, 8 kilometers south-west of 204. At 1415 hours, the assault group launched its attack with reinforced *Panzer Regiment 8* (40 tanks) forward in two waves, the bulk of the artillery immediately behind and, echeloned to the left, *Machine Gun Battalion 2* following in their transport.

The position of *Group Schuette* was quickly gone through. Then a violent barrage from some six batteries came down from the east and south-east. Nevertheless, the attack was rapidly carried forward. An embussed enemy rifle battalion and ten tanks refused to accept battle and quickly moved off to the south-east. In the further course of the attack south-west of 204, the assault group encountered 20 heavy tanks, 12 of which were knocked out.

The flanking fire of several batteries from the hollow to the right of the sector of attack, and more so from the heights to the south thereof, caused losses and compelled the assault to turn away to the south. *Panzer Regiment 8* attacked two batteries in the hollow in an enveloping move, capturing them after stiff resistance. However, it was not possible to carry the attack forward to the heights to the south thereof, as resistance was too strong, causing considerable losses in tanks.

The assault group, therefore, assembled, and at 1600 hours, it continued the attack on the old objective to the east in order to carry forward *Armored Division Ariete* to Height 204. Of *Motorized Infantry Division Trieste*, however, there was not a trace to be found. During dusk the assault group returned to the start line, as it had become too late for a further advance towards Bir el Temrad.

After his return to the Italian *Motorized Corps*, the division commander suggested to the *Afrika Korps* that it allow *Group Schuette* of the *21st Panzer Division* to move into the captured terrain four kilometers to the east of its present positions, so as to render the contact with *Ariete* on Height 204 firmer. The *Afrika Korps* approved of the suggestion and placed *Group Schuette* under command of the assault group (the *15th Panzer Division*). The latter moved the battle group into its new positions during the night. As, however, the enemy was very strong in artillery, it placed its entire artillery (*I./A.R.33*) behind the battle group to support it with its fire.

During the night, the division met strong elements of *Motorized Infantry Division Trieste*, north of battle headquarters Gambara, moving to the northeast. Thus, the puzzle where this division had been had solved itself. It had evidently withdrawn far to the west; it was now to be hoped that the division would be ordered by the Italian *Motorized Corps* to take up positions in the gap.

A serious gap had also developed in the south wing. Whilst the east front of the *Afrika Korps* was only under enemy artillery fire, 60 enemy tanks, apparently the bulk of the British *7th Armored Division*, went around the southern strongpoint of the defensive front and, taking the troops unawares, pushed from the south into the flank of the *Afrika Korps* under the personal leadership of the Chief of the General Staff of the *Afrika Korps*, Colonel (General Staff) Bayerlein. All elements of artillery, *Flak* artillery and tank destroyers of the *15th Panzer Division* which were within reach were scraped together and thrown against the attacking enemy. When the enemy tanks were at the level of corps, they were successfully held and driven back to the south. Eighteen enemy tanks were knocked out.

Panzergruppe Afrika had noted the enemy advance into the gap at the Italian *Motorized Corps* as early as 12 December, and strove to block the gap; for this purpose, elements of *Infantry Division Pavia* were dispatched to the west of Height 208, and a mixed detachment of *X Corps* to the north of the gap. This decision was hard to take for the *Panzergruppe*, as the enemy was also taking up position for an attack on the northern part of our position; on 13 December, he actually made local attacks against *XXI* and *X Corps*. Some local penetrations occurred which were blocked; but they showed once more that the fighting power of the Italians had decreased alarmingly.

Course of 14 December

On 13 December, the *Afrika Korps* received the order not only to take over the protection of the south flank of the *Panzergruppe*, but also to prevent the enemy from piercing the front of the Italian *Motorized Corps*. In spite of the threat to its southern flank, the *Afrika Korps* left the assault group in the rear of the Italian *Motorized Corps*, as early as 14 December, sizable enemy forces had again been sighted on Heights 190 and 189 east of Bir el Temtad.

During the day the east front of the *Afrika Korps* was attacked repeatedly by lesser enemy forces. The southern flank remained quiet. However, the corps had the impression that British armor was concentrating to south of the Der Herrier ridge.

In the sector of the Italian *Motorized Corps*, *Group Schuette* held its new positions in spite of heavy enemy artillery fire. It held loose communication with *Armored Division Ariete* on Height 204, 2.6 kilometers to the north-east. Towards noon, the Italian *Motorized Corps* sent word that *Ariete* had again lost Height 204. Thereupon, the assault group was once more made ready for an attack – which did not take place, however, as *Ariete* had allegedly retaken the positions itself.

On the north wing of the *Panzergruppe*, the local enemy attacks continued throughout the day.

The Fighting on 15 December

During 15 December the crisis in the gap near the Italian *Motorized Corps* developed. Height 204 was again lost. The enemy group east of Bir el Temrad became visibly stronger.

Thereupon, the *Afrika Korps* gave instructions to the assault group in the morning to settle the trouble in the gap for good and all. For this purpose, a further artillery detachment, a regimental headquarters and a rifle battalion would be attached to the assault group. The assault group was to proceed to the area around Bir el Temrad, to destroy the enemy forces which had broken in, and then turn in to the south and regain the ridge at 204.

The assault group reached Bir el Temrad towards 1000 hours. As the situation in the gap was utterly confused, the division commander thought a detailed reconnaissance before the attack absolutely necessary. Patrols of all arms (*Reconnaissance Unit 33* had only one reconnaissance troop left) established contact with all the Italian troops engaged in blocking the gap north and east, and with the armored regiment of *Ariete* 5 kilometers south-east of Bir el Temrad. This regiment was requested to take part in the attack. The enemy which had effected the breach – two or three infantry battalions, two artillery detachments and 10 heavy tanks – was found in positions on Heights 190 and 189 (8 kilometers east of Bir Temrad).

The plan of attack of the *15th Panzer Division* provided that *Machine Gun Battalion 2*, under the protection of artillery fire, would be sent forward against the enemy positions, the men in their vehicles. If considerable resistance was encountered, the unit was to debus and *Panzer Regiment 8* was to advance to the attack passing through their lines (*Panzer Regiment 8* had 20 tanks left). The bulk of the artillery was to supervise from its positions the attack, and one battery together with the *Flak* artillery, both traveling on their transport, were to accompany it. The armored regiment of *Ariete* was to attack on the right wing of the division. The reinforcements as promised by the *Afrika Korps* had not arrived by that time.

After a thorough preparation, the attack led to a full success which, moreover, cost but few casualties. Under the protection of a sandstorm, *Machine Gun Battalion 2* advanced to a point 2 kilometers from the enemy positions on Height 190, debussed in a hollow not overlooked by the enemy, and continued the attack on foot. The fire of the enemy guns which had taken up positions in the open ground was rapidly brought under control by the well-aimed shooting of our own artillery.

At 1600 hours, *Panzer Regiment 8*, simultaneously with the right wing of *Machin Gun Battalion 2*, broke into the enemy positions on Height 190. On the left wing of *Machine Gun Battalion 2*, the enemy was continuing to resist, but was also overwhelmed after *Panzer Regiment* had wheeled in. Only weak forces of the enemy escaped to the south-east. Eight hundred prisoners, among them a brigade commander, numerous antitank weapons and 26 guns were the booty of the day. Six enemy tanks had been knocked out.

During the attack one battalion of *Schützen Regiment 115* arrived at the division, but not in time in the forward line to help exploit the success.

Together with the armored regiment of *Ariete*, the battalion was wheeled to the south in order to regain the high ground near Height 204; in doing so the troops did not encounter opposition.

Panzer Regiment 8, together with *Machine Gun Battalion 2*, continued the attack to the east, without meeting any resistance there, and then established contact with those elements of *Infantry Division Pavia* which held positions there.

With this success, the enemy penetration into the front of the Italian *Motorized Corps* was fully eliminated. Now the entire the *Afrika Korps* was available for the protection of the southern flank. On 15 December, the enemy did not attack on the south wing, but it was impossible for own reconnaissance to the south to go beyond the high ground of Der Herier.

The *Afrika Korps* had the impression that there the enemy was slowly moving further to the west. But it felt that it could cope with the situation, particularly since, on 16 December, the entire assault group would be available once more. The corps, as well as the two divisions, felt that, as far as fighting qualities were concerned, they were superior to the enemy; they had the impression that the fighting power of the enemy had suffered considerably through the long period of fighting.

Thus, on the evening of 15 December the *Afrika Korps* regarded the crisis as having passed.

Conduct of Operations from 11 to 15 December

It had been General Rommel's intention to bring the enemy to a final halt in the Gazala position. But from the very beginning he entertained strong doubts as to whether he would be successful in carrying out this intention. The attitude the enemy would adopt would be a decisive factor.

If he allowed the *Panzergruppe* time to reorganize in the new position, then the Italian troops would gain some new confidence, and the fighting power of the German troops would be raised. If that were the case, the defense could be continued with a chance of success. Moreover, it was of importance to find out whether the enemy was going round the position in the south and advancing towards Agedabia. If that happened, a most serious situation would arise for the *Panzergruppe*.

As early as 12 December, General Rommel understood that the German-Italian troops would not have the time to consolidate their position for the defense, but that the battle for the Gazala position would start at once. It had turned out that the withdrawal into the Gazala position had not afforded the

Italian troops any relief, but had resulted in further losses and in a decrease in their morale. *Division z.b.v. Afrika* was now no longer standing behind them as an operational reserve.

General Rommel realized that he would have to go through with this battle without the supply route across the sea having been reopened. The danger that, with the continuation of the battle, German fighting power and the last supplies available would be exhausted was a very real one.

General Rommel watched the situation on the southern wing with anxiety. Here the enemy had evidently concentrated his force of armor. At any time he might send them round south of the position, and cause the line to collapse by an advance to the north via El Mechili or by a push towards Agedabia against the rearward lines of communication.

All this made Rommel look upon the crisis, which arose on 12 December caused by the enemy breaking into the line of the Italian *Motorized Corps*, with increased misgivings. It meant that there was a danger that the enemy might advance over Bir el Temrad into the rear of the Gazala position proper, thus separating *XXI* and *X Corps* from the mobile forces of the *Panzergruppe*. Therefore, all efforts had to be concentrated on warding off such a breakthrough, and the entire force of the *Panzergruppe* had to be employed for this purpose. At noon on 15 December, the position in the breach had not yet been restored and the southern wing was still exposed.

On the north wing, the rapid deterioration of the Italian fighting power also caused increasing anxiety. It was uncertain how long it would be possible to hold the front without committing German reserves.

For Rommel the issue was decided when he received a message from the air that strong enemy armored forces south of the Der Herier ridge were moving via Segnali to Mechili in a westerly direction. He saw no possibility of meeting this advance as the assault group of the *Afrika Korps* was still involved in operations at the breach in the lines of the Italian *Motorized Corps*. Moreover, the fuel supplies were no longer sufficient for a mobile operation on the south wing. General Rommel knew that his pessimistic appreciation of the situation of the south wing was not shared by the *Afrika Korps*, which viewed the situation much more confidently. Nonetheless, he decided, after due consideration, to give up the Gazala position and with it the whole of Cyrenaica.

The Decision to Abandon Cyrenaica

On 15 December the Chief of the Italian *Comando Supremo*, Colonel-General Cavallero, and the Italian Commander-in-Chief in North Africa, General

Bastico, arrived at the battle headquarters of the *Panzergruppe* for a discussion with General Rommel on the situation in North Africa. With them was the newly appointed Commander-in-Chief South who, although not Rommel's superior, held a very influential position as the Commander-in-Chief of the German air force, and as the senior German officer in the Mediterranean area.

General Rommel submitted to them his appreciation of the situation. He described the increasing deterioration of the fighting power of the German and Italian troops for whom there was no chance of replenishment; he described the mounting supply difficulties due to the failure to reopen the sea route and the persistent inferiority of the German-Italian air forces. As the point carrying most weight, he submitted that, from the information available, he had gained the impression that the enemy intended to outflank the position in the south with strong armored forces and to advance to Agedabia. The geographical situation, with Cyrenaica protruding far to the north, allowed the enemy a far shorter route to Agedabia than the *Panzergruppe* holding the Gazala line. Therefore, he regarded the withdrawal of the *Panzergruppe Afrika* from Cyrenaica into the Marsa el Brega position as necessary, as it was only there that the enemy could be prevented with certainty from outflanking the *Panzergruppe*. He saw no alternative for meeting this danger, as mobile operations with the *Afrika Korps* and the Italian *Motorized Corps* promised little success in the face of the superiority the enemy enjoyed, and since the precarious fuel position made the employment of mobile tactics impossible. He intended, therefore, to start the withdrawal of the *Panzergruppe* on 16 December.

The effect this suggestion had on the Italian General was like that of a bombshell. A certain suspicion had been aroused in General Bastico when *Division z.b.v. Afrika* had been sent to Agedabia, lest one day Rommel might extract himself from a tight corner by rapidly withdrawing the mobile forces of the *Panzergruppe* away from the enemy, sacrificing the nonmobile divisions of *X* and *XXI Corps*. The withdrawal of the nonmotorized German division to Agedabia had revived this suspicion. Careless remarks from the staff of the *Panzergruppe* which had reached the ears of the Italians had strengthened their mistrust. Moreover, during the past weeks some criticism had been voiced by the Italian leadership regarding measures taken by the *Panzergruppe*; faith in Rommel had been shaken.

Thus, hot-tempered counterarguments came from the Italian generals, particularly from General Bastico, who in an excited manner emphasized that if Cyrenaica were again lost, and, above all, if the Italian Africa army were sacrificed, the effect on the Italian people's determination to see the war through would be incalculable. He, as the Commander-in-Chief, therefore, forbade the evacuation of the Gazala position.

Thereupon, General Rommel pointed out that he knew of no other way to counter the enemy advance to Agedabia, and he asked to be given instructions as to how otherwise to meet the advance. General Bastico avoided answering this question by pointing out that his task as the Commander-in-Chief was only to give decisions and general lines of directions, and that he would have to leave the choice of the means to General Rommel.

At this juncture, Field Marshal von Kesselring intervened in order to blunt the increasing sharpness of the arguments. He associated himself with the view expressed by the Italian generals. He pointed out that, after all, there were indications that on the British side the fighting power was also beginning to diminish. He emphasized that the measures taken by him were beginning to take effect, which would soon cause supplies to roll in, thus lifting the fighting power of the *Panzergruppe*. He also announced that the *Luftwaffe* would soon receive reinforcements, so that enemy air superiority would be seriously diminished if not entirely eliminated. He was of the opinion that the situation was not yet quite so hopeless as to justify resorting to the last step, *viz.* that of withdrawing.

General Rommel repeated that all this assistance was now too late, as the enemy had pushed forward in the Agedabia direction. The deciding factor was, after all, that the danger of envelopment could be eliminated by nothing other than a withdrawal.

Thereupon, Field Marshal Kesselring suggested, as a compromise, that, if there had to be a withdrawal, the corps should be given one day more to get ready so as to ensure an orderly execution of the movement. The speed of the withdrawal was to be adapted to the march capacity of the Italian divisions, which must in no circumstances be sacrificed. He would guarantee personally that the formations of the *Luftwaffe*, particularly those of the *Flak* artillery, would support the operations of the Italian rearguard, regardless of possible loss of equipment. General Rommel himself gave the assurance that, whatever happened, the withdrawal would be carried out on these lines. Nonetheless, the Italian generals reserved their final decision. Approval for the withdrawal to start on the evening of 15 December was not given until Rommel, on the evening of 15 December, was able to submit a new report from the air which indisputably seemed to point to the beginning of an advance of enemy armored forces in the direction of Mechili.

Thus, the decision was in favor of Rommel. However, discord remained between the allies, which made itself felt for some time.

First Orders for the Withdrawal

During the night of 15/16 December, the *Panzergruppe* issued the warning order for the withdrawal on the evening of 16 December. During 16 December all the positions were to be held; reconnoitering of the withdrawal routes was to start at once, and so was the withdrawal of the supply troops, the baggage trains, and the heavy artillery.

The Italian *Motorized Corps* was allotted the northern branch of the Via Balbia and *XXI Corps* the southern branch as a line of withdrawal. Strong rearguards were to delay the enemy following up, which surely would easily be possible in the mountainous area of Cyrenaica. The *Afrika Korps*, with the Italian *Motorized Corps* behind, were put on the Trigh Enver Bey to move via Mechili towards El Abiar.

On 16 December, the *Afrika Korps* would have the task of preventing an advance of enemy armored forces towards Mechili. The German-Italian air force was to concentrate its efforts in operations against the enemy armored forces on the southern wing.

X and *XXI Corps*, during 16 December, succeeded in holding their positions. Enemy offensive activity decreased. On the front of the Italian *Motorized Corps*, the enemy remained inactive, possibly as the effect of his setback suffered at Bir el Temrad.

On the *Afrika Korps'* front, however, increasing pressure by the enemy against the southern flank made itself felt from early in the morning. Strong enemy armored reconnaissance forces pushed deep into the rear of the corps into the area of Bir el Temrad, endangering supply operations. Fresh reports from the air confirmed the advance of an enemy group consisting of armor to west as far as Segnali. It was not clear whether this enemy would continue towards Mechili or whether it would turn northward into the rear of the *Afrika Korps*, which latter move seemed to be indicated by the move of enemy reconnaissance forces.

The *Afrika Korps* thereupon strengthened *Reconnaissance Unit 33*, which stood in the deep flank with elements of the *21st Panzer Division*. During the morning the *Afrika Korps* dispatched the assault group (of the *15th Panzer Division*) to the west in order to ward off the advance of the enemy, if need be by means of a counterattack and in order to keep the road open for the withdrawal of the *Afrika Korps* to Mechili. For the time being, the assault group was to reach Bu Sciara, where high ground seemed to offer favorable opportunities for a halting position.

The assault group started its move towards 1000 hours. First it turned to the north-west in order to effect the junction with its supply columns, which were being pressed west of Cherima by enemy armored reconnaissance forces. In this advance, the enemy armored reconnaissance forces were dispersed and withdrew in all directions, losing 6 armored reconnaissance cars. During the afternoon, Der Bu Sciara was reached, which proved to be a swampy depression. The halting position for the withdrawal of the *Afrika Korps* was occupied as ordered. No enemy armored forces were encountered.

On the front of *Reconnaissance Unit 3*, an enemy column with 30 tanks had advanced during the morning at Gueiret el Abd to the north. The units, being in favorable positions, were able to bring the enemy advance to a halt. During the afternoon, the enemy repeated the attack with 60 tanks and artillery. Meanwhile, the reinforcements of the *21st Panzer Division* arrived. Thus, this new attack was also repulsed. Towards the evening, enemy offensive activity decreased because of effective German *Stuka* attacks.

The battle for the Gazala position began for the *Panzergruppe Afrika* under very unfavorable conditions. Its corps had hardly occupied their positions when they were involved in heavy fighting with the enemy pressing on. Thus, crisis arose on all parts of the front. By 15 December, however, the *Panzergruppe* had overcome all these crisis, had held most of the positions on the north wing, had changed the break-in of the enemy in the Bir el Temrad sector into a sharp setback for the British, and had also frustrated a decisive British success on the south wing.

The German Command broke off the battle on its own accord for fear of an outflanking enemy operation, and also because of the unfavorable supply position. Thus, the question arises whether these reasons were really sound ones. There is much which speaks against them. The course of the battle had shown that the offensive power of the enemy had diminished during the long and costly fighting. It was indeed possible that now the British would discontinue their attack after they had failed to destroy the *Panzergruppe* during the pursuit. A further withdrawal might just have been that last cause for an outflanking move by the enemy towards Agedabia.

The withdrawal from Tobruk had already shown how difficult and dangerous it is to withdraw nonmotorized troops from an enemy who enjoys superiority in mobility, and who has strong armored forces at his disposal. Particularly in the case of the Italians, any withdrawal usually brings about a dwindling of morale. This time it was to be feared that the long withdrawal would bring about signs of disintegration in the Italian divisions. With regard to the German troops, the poor condition of their equipment spoke against a continuation of the withdrawal. It was more than doubtful whether the last 30 tanks, which had been left to the *Afrika Korps*, would survive the long journey back. The guns of the artillery also started to fall out in increasing numbers owing to broken axles.

In any case, many valuable supplies would be lost in an evacuation of Cyrenaica at such short notice, as a complete clearing of the supply dumps, mainly around Benghazi, was certainly not possible within time with the transport available.

Finally, the unfavorable political consequences of the decision had to be reckoned with, as it meant a great disappointment for the Italian people, and as it certainly would be hailed and exploited as a victory by the enemy.

On the other hand, one had to admit that Rommel was right when he was of opinion that there was, factually, hardly any other way to meet an enemy outflanking attempt, particularly since the fuel position and the state of the equipment of the *Afrika Korps* no longer allowed large-scale operations in the south of Cyrenaica. It is not at all certain, and it cannot be clarified from the sources available, whether the enemy did actually consider such an opera-tion. The small size of the enemy tank formations with their limited hitting power, as it became evident during the withdrawal, allows the conclusion that the enemy would not have dared to risk his armor in so far-flung an operation separated from the rest of his army.

However, there were still other reasons which spoke in favor of Rommel's decision. The British *Eighth Army* had further formations in Marmarica and in western Egypt at its disposal, which could have been moved up without much loss of time if the first onslaught on the Gazala line had decisively failed. The *Panzergruppe* would hardly have been able to cope with such a new attack, particularly since until then neither supplies nor reinforcements would have arrived.

Every withdrawal shortens one's own lines of communication and lengthens those of the enemy, who, in addition, would have to protect his rearward communications in the air and on the ground, thus weakening his forces considerably. Thus, the withdrawal brought about a certain leveling off of the strength ratio and made a later counterattack possible.

Rommel can in no way be blamed if by reason of the available information he regarded the withdrawal as necessary. The skill with which it would be carried out would prove whether it was justified or not.

The battle around the Gazala position was conducted by the German-Italian leadership with a sure hand and resourcefully. The strength of nerve and the daring of the *Afrika Korps* deserve particular mention. It was certainly no easy decision to throw in all reserves in order to wipe out the breach made by the enemy in the sector of the Italian *Motorized Corps* regardless of the danger in the southern flank.

In spite of everything, the German troops, dwindling in number and equipment, proved unbroken in their aggressive spirit and hitting power. More than ever, they felt superior to the British, and never understood the necessity of a further withdrawal.

The Situation in the Air

On 4 December, when the *Panzergruppe* decided on the evacuation of the area east of Tobruk and on the attack on Bir el Gubi, the German-Italian air forces was numerically still very weak. The main task allotted to *Fliegerführer Afrika* by the *Panzergruppe* was the support of the *Afrika Korps*, and of the Italian *Motorized Corps* in the battle for Bir el Gubi. It had been arranged that the *Luftwaffe* would operate according to the requirements of the *Afrika Korps*. At that time, liaison between the *Luftwaffe* and the ground troops was not yet running smoothly, so that a direct support of the armored divisions did not materialize. Even so, the *Stuka* attacks against enemy formations in the Bir el Gubi area did much to relieve the situation of the *Afrika Korps*, if only indirectly.

During the withdrawal, operations against British armored formations advancing along the south wing had formed the main task of the German-Italian air forces. It carried out attacks in the area of Bir el Gubi and Bir Hacheim, and thus may have delayed the advance of the British formations. On account of its numerical weakness, the *Luftwaffe* was, however, not able to delay to a great extent the moves of the British pursuit columns on the remaining front and to afford the *Panzergruppe* time to settle down in the Gazala position.

With the withdrawal to the Gazala position, the situation in the air began to improve. It is true that the RAF was now also in possession of the airfield of Tobruk. On the other hand, the British formations stationed in Egypt had to be moved forward. This weakened the British air force, so that the withdrawing formations of *Panzergruppe Afrika* were no longer attacked from the air to the same degree as during the preceding operation. The autumn weather, with sandstorms and violent downpours, limited air activity more frequently than hitherto. For these reasons, it was no longer possible to speak of British domination of the air; the British air superiority decreased, although the German-Italian air formations had still not yet been reinforced.

The German-Italian air forces had been compelled on 8 December to evacuate their landing ground in Gazala and Tmimi, and to concentrate around Derna and Matuba after the withdrawal to the Gazala position. The latter landing grounds were situated at a favorable range regarding the new front. From there, the supply columns and installations of the enemy were attacked more often now, and considerable success was achieved. The result was increasing difficulties experienced by enemy formations in bringing up their supplies for the battle for the Gazala position.

The main task allotted to the fighters during the withdrawal was the cover of the rearward moves of the *Panzergruppe*. On 12 December, 23 British aircraft had been shot down.

During the battle for the Gazala position, the German-Italian air forces were again employed in attacks against enemy armored forces on the south wing. The critical situation on the north wing and in the center of the position, however, made it necessary to employ the air forces on these sectors on several occasions.

Summing up, it can be said that, from the beginning of December, the activity of the German-Italian air forces was coordinated with the operations of the *Panzergruppe* for the first time during the British offensive, and that the *Luftwaffe* exercised a noteworthy influence on the course of the operation.

Meantime, the Commander-in-Chief South had seen to it that supplies from Europe came in more frequently by air and by sea. All measures had been taken to protect supply routes from Italy to North Africa more effectively. In this connection, it was of particular importance to eliminate the island fortress of Malta, which was the main strongpoint for light British naval forces and for the torpedo-carrying aircraft of the enemy.

During the first half of December, when the first bomber formations of the *Luftwaffe* arrived in Sicily, they began to attack Malta without delay in spite of unfavorable weather conditions and insufficient ground organizations.

The post of *Fliegerführer Sicily* was held by Colonel Roth, commodore of a bomber *Geschwader* with special experience gathered in naval warfare. The operations of the Italian air force were coordinated with those of the

German formations in the enterprise against Malta. All preparations were made for *II. Fliegerkorps* to operate after it had arrived by the middle of September from the Eastern war theater. Landing grounds had to be enlarged. Signals installations had to be created and ammunition and fuel dumps laid on. This took much time, as south of Naples there were only single-track railways and as the carrying capacity of the ferry system across the Straits of Messina was limited.

The fortress of Bardia and the Sollum front were supplied by more numerous transport formations. However, the losses increased because British antiaircraft artillery and night fighters were employed in increasing numbers. It was difficult to drop the supplies into the narrow space into which the Axis formations had been pressed together, the more so since the British, using deceptive light signals, often caused the aircraft to drop their supplies on wrong spots. Here, as in other war theaters, it became evident that this was not a way to provide sufficient supplies, and that this method entailed more losses than the operational purpose justified.

Whilst the exhaustion on both sides and, with it ,the supply problem generally had played an important role even during the fighting prior to 4 December, these things now began to be of decisive importance.

Even now the German troops of the *Panzergruppe* and, in particular, of the *Afrika Korps* achieved many a brilliant success on the battlefield. But this no longer altered the general situation. Each victory was bought with the loss of irreplaceable troops and diminished the number of the valuable tanks; each move brought about the loss of equipment through technical breakdowns, and caused the reserves of fuel to decrease.

Thus, the decisive problem in the war in North Africa was the struggle for the reopening of the supply routes. The appointment of Field Marshal Kesselring to the post of Commander-in-Chief South and the fact that he was entrusted to conduct the struggle for sea communications in the Mediterranean area was of special significance in this connection. He understood at once that this struggle was no longer to be conducted defensively as it had been up to now, but that it was to be an offensive operation directed against the enemy naval and air bases, and particularly against Malta. Much time passed before the necessary air forces were concentrated, and before the attack on Malta bore fruit and became effective enough to improve the situation in the Mediterranean area. Everything depended on the question whether the bloodletting and the lack of supplies of every description would have brought about the complete collapse of the

Panzergruppe, as it was impossible to deal a decisive blow to the supply organization of the British Eighth Army and as the strength ratio changed more and more to the disadvantage of Rommel.

In order to hold out until supplies across the sea started to arrive smoothly, a further withdrawal to the west remained the only way out of the dilemma. The enemy would move away from his supply resources, his equipment would be subjected to wear and tear during his advance, and his reinforcements, as well as his superior air force, would be weakened owing to the necessity of protecting his long rearward communications.

The struggle during this period of the campaign was characterized by the struggle for the open southern flank of the desert. This struggle was conducted skillfully and successfully by the *Afrika Korps*, and by the Italian *Motorized Corps* in the battle of Bir el Gubi during the withdrawal on the Gazala position, and also during the battle around this position. The enemy tanks were frequently thrown back in spite of their superiority; the tempo of their advance was dictated to them, and they were denied any noteworthy success.

The nonmotorized Italian corps were less successful in their operations during the withdrawal. It is natural, of course, that troops moving on foot find themselves during a withdrawal from a mobile enemy in a precarious situation, and that it is extremely difficult for them to get a sufficient start on the pursuing enemy. Another reason was the peculiarity of the Italian troops. During the battle for Tobruk, on the occasion of British breakout attempts and relieving attacks from the outside, it frequently happened that Italian units of platoon and company strength were captured. After 4 December, and when the withdrawal began, losses of this kind occurred at an alarming rate. When enemy armored thrusts took place, entire battalions and artillery detachments were now lost. The rapid dwindling of the fighting power of the Italian divisions placed Rommel in a difficult position, because without the Italian divisions it would not be possible to cover the vast spaces of the war theater and to occupy the positions.

The German troops in North Africa frequently grumbled about their Italian allies. In most cases, the Italian failure was blamed for setbacks which occurred. These reproaches did not do full justice to the efforts of the Italian troops. It must be stated that the leadership of the Italian corps and the Italian divisions during the fighting around Tobruk and the following withdrawal and its battles fully understood the importance of holding out, and that they did their utmost to fulfill the tasks Rommel had allotted to them.

The Italian soldier was enthusiastic, moderate in his demands and of a persevering nature. His Mediterranean temperament, however, meant that he easily panicked when the situation became critical. He was more easily impressed and depressed by setbacks than his German comrade-in-arms. In most cases, his training left much to be desired, which resulted in correspondingly higher losses. For years the Italian soldiers had not been relieved nor given leave; they were insufficiently fed and they were underpaid; and thus their physical and psychological power of resistance naturally weakened in the course of the campaign. They felt very bitter about their very inferior equipment and armament. In this connection, the small range and the obsolete system of laying their guns deserves particular mention. On many occasions, Italian guns were shot to pieces by British batteries at long range before they could even open fire. The caliber of the Italian antitank guns was insufficient; the Italian tanks were insufficiently armored and armed; and the Italian antiaircraft artillery was obsolete.

It is, therefore, not surprising that the troops felt that they were inferior to the British. Nonetheless, individual Italian units have achieved good results, and some of them fought to the bitter end. Such individual cases do, however, not change the general picture.

Rommel's decision to withdraw from Cyrenaica led to the most serious crisis which the relationship between the two allies ever had to overcome until then. Field Marshal Kesselring was instrumental in the avoidance of an open rupture.

CHAPTER 6

The Withdrawal of *Panzergruppe Afrika* from Gazala to the Marsa el Bregha Position, 17 December 1941–12 January 1942

The decisive reason for General Rommel's withdrawal from Cyrenaica was indeed the dwindling of German-Italian fighting power and their supply problem in general. But the immediate cause for the decision to withdraw into the Marsa el Bregha position was the desire not to expose the German-Italian formations to the danger of an envelopment from the south by the superior enemy and to avoid the cutting off of the rearward communications. The geography of Cyrenaica is such that, during the withdrawal, the *Panzergruppe* was even more exposed to such danger than when in the Gazala position. The formations would not enjoy a certain measure of safety until they had reached the area around Agedabia, where they could come under the protection of the *90th Light Division*, which had been sent in advance.

To reach this area meant an enormous effort, particularly for the nonmotorized Italian infantry division. Moving on the Via Balbia from the Gazala position, they had to cover about 550 kilometers to reach Agedabia. Even if this journey was speeded up by a leapfrog-like employment of motor transport columns, it would at least take eight days, i.e., if the withdrawal was to start on 17 December, the Agedabia area could not be reached until 24 December. The motorized formations of the *Panzergruppe*, which had to travel on the El Mechili–El Abiar–Benghazi route, had to cover a stretch of 450 kilometers. The British armored formations, on the other hand, traveling on the south wing, could use the route across the desert south of Cyrenaica, running on the line Bir Tengeder–Msus to Sceleidima or Antelat, covering no more than 250–300 kilometers. It is true that this desert journey offered some difficulties. They were, however, by no means insuperable, as the experience gained during Wavell's winter offensive of 1940/41 and Rommel's push during April 1941 had shown.

For this reason, the chief anxiety of General Rommel was that the enemy armored formation might reach the coastal plain between Benghazi and Agedabia before the *Panzergruppe* did and might there cut the latter's withdrawal. It was, therefore, Rommel's main purpose to reach this area with the *Afrika Korps* and the Italian *Motorized Corps* as early as possible and, together with the *90th Light Division*, to keep the Via Balbia open for the Italian divisions and to delay the advance of the pursuing British long enough to allow the entire *Panzergruppe* to reach the Agedabia area.

For this purpose, it seemed to be of great importance that the south wing – the *Afrika Korps* and Italian *Motorized Corps* – take possession of the important road junction of El Mechili without delay, so as to secure the use of the route to El Abiar–Benghazi for the purpose of the withdrawal and to prevent enemy forces from advancing via Mechili to the north against the route of withdrawal of the north wing at Derna and Berta.

The immediate task of the north wing – the Italian *XXI* and *X Corps* – was to withdraw in forced marches and covered by rearguard troops into the area south-west and west of Derna and to reach the two branches of the Via Balbia before the enemy did. Once the mountain area of Cyrenaica had been reached, even lesser rearguard troops would find many an opportunity to delay the pressing enemy and to win for the two corps the necessary time for an unhampered continuation of their withdrawal.

It was the task of the German-Italian air forces to operate against enemy motorized and armored formations on the south wing, and to delay them in their attempt to overtake our ground troops. In addition, they had to deny the enemy a rapid advance along the Via Balbia.

On these lines, orders for the withdrawal were issued during the night of 15/16 December. December 16 was to be reserved for reconnoitering the withdrawal routes and for the dispatch of supply troops and baggage trains. During the night of 16/17 December the withdrawal proper was to start under the cover of rearguards.

Breaking Away from the Gazala Position

During the night 16/17 December, leaving its positions east and south of El Cheima, the *Afrika Korps* withdrew to the west and in the morning joined the assault group which covered the area of Bu Sciarah; then, it continued moving back to El Mechili with the *15th Panzer Division* leading and the *21st Panzer Division* following behind. This location was reached before noon on 17 December. Rearguard troops remained in the old positions until 17 December. The enemy did not follow up in this section.

On 17 December, the *Afrika Korps* took up a covering position south of El Mechili, whilst the Italian *Motorized Corps*, which during the afternoon approached from the east and the area of Bir el Temrad, marching via Bir Halegh el Eleiba, was placed in a semi-circular position, east of El Mechili.

During these moves *Reconnaissance Battalion 3* had been entrusted with the protection of the south flank; during the morning on 17 December it drove back enemy reconnaissance forces at Guerat el Mogharreb and in the afternoon the unit was moved into the area 10 kilometers south-east of El Mechili. During the afternoon enemy reconnaissance approaching from the south felt forward towards the area of El Mechili.

Panzergruppe Afrika watched with anxiety the moves of the enemy armored forces on the south wing and tried to find out in which direction they would advance. Air reconnaissance, which concentrated its main effort in the area south of Mechili, reported, in the afternoon of 17 December, that at least 300 vehicles, including 60 tanks, were advancing to Bir Tengeder. Thus, General Rommel's fears seemed to be confirmed, i.e. that the enemy would advance through the desert towards the area north of Agedabia in an attempt to overtake the withdrawing troops. He therefore ordered the *Afrika Korps* by wireless to withdraw immediately and at top speed all its forces to El Abiar.

The *Afrika Korps* during the afternoon on 17 December had reorganized its formations around Mechili and had once again joined the assault group with the *15th Schützen Brigade* under the command of the *15th Panzer Division*. The movements necessary, therefore, were still being carried out when the march order arrived from the *Panzergruppe*. Orders for the immediate continuation of the withdrawal were issued without delay. The *Afrika Korps* was to move off in the one column to El Abiar at 2200 hours, with the *15th Panzer Division* leading and the *21st Panzer Division* and then the Italian *Motorized Corps* following. *Reconnaissance Battalion 3* and *Reconnaissance Battalion 33* were to accompany the move in its southern flank and, at a distance of 20 kilometers to the south, cover it against enemy interference. Their reconnaissance patrols were to check up on the whereabouts of the armored forces of the enemy.

At 2200 hours on 17 December, the *15th Panzer Division* departed for El Abiar, but after a few hours it had to halt as several sandy wadis proved very difficult to negotiate by night and caused long interruptions to the move. The journey was not resumed until after dawn, and with improved going progressed more smoothly in a westerly direction with much terrain being gained. As it was possible to travel in extended formation, enemy air attacks did not cause much damage.

Nor was the breaking away of the north wing from the Gazala position during the night of 16/17 December much harassed by the enemy. By the morning the bulk of the troops had been moved behind the narrow stretch of Tmimi. The German *Luftwaffe* formations still were in possession of the airfields at Martuba and Derna, and on several occasions they assisted the rearguards of the two Italian corps. During 17 December British motorized columns pressed forward along the Via Balbia, but in the evening of 17 December they were driven away from the narrow stretch of Tmimi by Italian rearguard troops supported by German *Stuka* formations.

The main threat to the withdrawal of the north wing came from the area of Bir el Temrad. There the Italian *Motorized Corps* had withdrawn during the night of 16/17 December westward towards Mechili, thus opening the way for the *4th Indian Division* to the north into the rear of *XXI Corps*. On 17 December, in spite of supply difficulties and heavy going, the *4th Indian Division* advanced to the north far beyond Bir es Sferi and, taking advantage of the night, reached the southern branch of the Via Balbia at Gasr el Carmusa by noon on 18 December. Thus, the rearguards of *XXI Corps* which were to follow their corps on the southern road found the route to the west cut. From Carmusa the British did not advance along the Via Balbia to the west towards Bu Halfaya, but turned off to the east towards Martuba. As early as the evening of 18 December, British motorized infantry and artillery reached the large airfield in this area, overwhelmed the airfield guards of the German *Luftwaffe* and attacked the rearguards of *X* and *XXI Corps* withdrawing to the north-west. Some of the rearguards were cut off, and a number of aircraft and antiaircraft batteries and several hundred prisoners were lost to the enemy. On their further advance to Derna, the British met with tough resistance from Italian rearguards and were unable to reach the town until the evening on 19 December.

Another pursuing column of the *4th Indian Division* advanced from Martuba to Berta, aiming at cutting off the Italian troops retreating from Derna. This advance was halted by Italian rearguards on the high ground 10 kilometers south of Berta, and the enemy advancing from Derna were stopped in the evening of 19 December, and on 20 December on the serpentine road ten kilometers west to Derna.

On 20 December, *X* and *XXI Corps* had succeeded in shaking off the British columns pursuing them, thanks to the tough resistance of their rearguards. Both the corps now continued their withdrawal to the west at top speed. On several occasions they were attacked by British planes in high and low level attacks and suffered losses.

The Withdrawal towards Benghazi, 19–21 December

The withdrawal of the *Afrika Korps* and of the Italian *Motorized Corps* from Mechili to the west was carried out without contact with the enemy. But numerous attacks by the British air force caused considerable casualties in all the divisions, particularly since, in the mountainous terrain of south-western Cyrenaica, the troops had again to move in columns and the vehicles were hardly able to get off the road. The *15th Panzer Division*, which moved at the head, reached Gabr Bu Taghielen (30 kilometers south of Maraua) as early as the evening of 18 December, and in the evening of 19 December it reached Ain Gbara (15 kilometers east of El Abiar). The division succeeded in moving its supply columns from the Via Balbia at Maraua to Bir Tecasis, thus enabling it to continue its move to Benghazi. Negotiating the steep southern spurs of the mountainous country of Cyrenaica east of El Abiar proved difficult. Nonetheless, El Abiar was passed through early in the morning on 20 December, and during the afternoon the airfield of Benina, east of Benghazi, was reached. The division traveled around Benghazi to the south-east thereof as the place itself was jammed full with Italian columns, and at nightfall it reached the area north of Giardina, having traveled on the track leading to Solluch.

The arrival of the *15th Panzer Division* in the area south of Benghazi in the evening of 20 December was a great relief to *Panzergruppe Afrika*. Whatever may happen, there was now one formation available in the coastal plain ready for operations, and able to ward off enemy pursuing columns should they advance towards the Via Balbia north of Agedabia. On 21 December, the division was moved further to the south by General Rommel, and by the evening had reached Sidi Saleh (25 kilometers west of Antelat), having traveled via Solluch–Beda Fomm.

Contact with the *90th Light Division* in Agedabia was resumed through *Reconnaissance Battalion 33*, which had accompanied the move of the division through Cyrenaica in the south without meeting the enemy and which had again been moved forward. By order of the *Panzergruppe*, the reinforced *Motorcycle Battalion 15* – strength one reinforced company – was placed at Sceleidima to block the track leading from the desert in the east at and north of this location; the covering patrols of the *90th Light Division* at this place were put under its command. The reinforced *Reconnaissance Battalion 33* was dispatched to Antelat with a similar task.

Whilst the move of the *15th Panzer Division* had progressed smoothly, the moves of the *21st Panzer Division* and of the Italian *Motorized Corps* were considerably delayed owing to the supply difficulties. On 20 December, the *21st Panzer Division* was immobilized north of Charruba through lack of fuel, and was unable to continue until early on 21 December, after it had been possible to send fuel columns from El Abiar to meet the division. On 21 December, before noon, it passed through El Abiar and in an uninterrupted move reached Beda Fomm early on 22 December.

The Italian *Motorized Corps* traveled behind the *21st Panzer Division* from El Mechili towards Abiar. On 18 December, it was subjected to an attack by a German *Stuka* group on both sides of Mechili, which had been meant for the enemy pursuing columns and which resulted in considerable losses, mainly of transport vehicles. The two divisions of the corps reached El Abiar on 21 December. *Motorized Infantry Division Trieste* was ordered to defend the steep heights 10 kilometers east of the town, with a view to preventing the British from pressing on along the track leading from El Mechili. *Armored Division Ariete* was moved into the area south-east of Benghazi.

Panzergruppe Afrika endeavored to hasten the withdrawal of *XXI* and *X Corps* on the Via Balbia as much as possible. Army supply columns, as far as they were not needed for the clearing of the dumps around Benghazi, stood by, together with Italian columns, to assist the two corps. Thanks to them and thanks to the forced marches of the Italian infantry divisions, the first fighting troops of *XXI Corps*, moving ahead, reached Benghazi as early as 21 December. They kept on moving to the south towards Agedabia, where they were to occupy prepared positions north and east of the town with a view to strengthening the *90th Light Division.*

The order for the evacuation of the supply center of Benghazi had been issued by *Panzergruppe Afrika* simultaneously with the order to the corps for withdrawal during the night of 15/16 December. To evacuate all supplies would have taken three weeks. The Quartermaster-General was not able to evacuate more than the most valuable supplies during the few days and with the limited loading space he had at his disposal. The evacuation of the wounded and the destruction of all supplies which had to be left behind was started without delay. The operation was considerably hampered by the mutinous attitude of the native population, which soon started looting. For this reason, the Quartermaster-General asked General Rommel for German protecting troops and was given *Reconnaissance Battalion 3* on 21 December.

The Warding Off of British Pursuing
Columns North of Agedabia, 22–25 December

In the evening of 21 December, the greatest menace threatening the withdrawal of the *Panzergruppe* into the area round Agedabia had been removed with the arrival of the *Afrika Korps* in the area Antelat–Sidi Saleh–Beda Fomm, and of the Italian *Motorized Corps* at and south of El Abiar. What remained to be done was to protect the Via Balbia between Benghazi and Agedabia against flanking attacks by enemy columns from the east long enough to allow the nonmotorized Italian infantry divisions of *XXI* and *X Corps* to march through to Agedabia. Considering the forced marches, it would be possible for these formations to carry out this by the evening of 24 December. Already it was evident that enemy pressure had decreased, and that the enemy had allowed the opportunity to pass by to cut off the retreat south of Benghazi whilst this area was still unprotected.

Not until 21 December did *Panzergruppe* receive the first reports of the enemy approaching from the east and nearing the steep descent to the coastal plain between El Abiar and Antelat. Air reconnaissance reported an enemy column with tanks advancing from Msus to Sceleidima and another from the north-east to Antelat. The *Afrika Korps*, which in the evening of 21 December had moved its battle headquarters from Benina to the Via Balbia west of Beda Fomm, ordered the *15th Panzer Division* early on 22 December to reinforce *Motorcycle Battalion 15* at Sceleidima with a antitank company and a light battery. In the morning of 22 December, *Motorized Infantry Division Trieste* reported that the enemy was advancing in some strength from the east towards El Abiar. However, reconnaissance patrols which were sent out sighted no more than weak reconnaissance forces in the area around Charuba el Abiar.

At noon on 22 December, the situation became more tense. The reinforced *Motorcycle Battalion 15* was attacked during the afternoon by enemy armor, and during the evening it was thrown back to Solluch. On the tracks north of Sceleidima leading down into the coastal plain at Wadi Jusef and Sidi Brahim, covering posts of the *90th Light Division* were also forced to withdraw to the south-west by the advancing enemy.

The reinforced *Reconnaissance Battalion 33* at Antelat was attacked by 10 enemy tanks. supported by several batteries. towards noon. During the afternoon it withdrew 10 kilometers to the south-west.

Towards 1230 hours, the *Afrika Korps* received a message from the air giving a summary of the enemy situation in the desert east of the coastal plain.

An enemy column with 25 tanks, its head at Antelat, was advancing to the south-west; another column with 30 tanks and several batteries had descended on to the coastal plain north of Antelat at Abiar el Charez and was advancing on Beda Fomm. Further enemy columns with tanks and artillery were moving westward at and north of Sceleidima.

Thus, it appeared that the enemy had organized his pursuit on a broad front on the line Sceleidima–Antelat to move westward and south-westward to the Via Balbia with a view to catching the Italian infantry divisions moving south in their flank, and to preventing them from withdrawing southward. The British formation involved was probably the *7th Armored Division*. Thus, a total of 120 tanks would have to be reckoned with.

As the *21st Panzer Division* was very weak, and as the remnants of its *Panzer Regiment 5* — eight tanks only – were under command of the *15th Panzer Division*, the *Afrika Korps* ordered the *15th Panzer Division* at 1400 hours to prevent the British columns advancing between Antelat and Sceleidima from approaching Via Balbia.

This was a most difficult task to perform. The enemy columns were advancing on a front 100 kilometers broad and were no more than 40–60 kilometers away from the Via Balbia. Defensive tactics and a splitting up of forces in order to stop all the columns promised no success. On the other hand, it was quite clear that resistance of the weak forces in position at Antelat and Sceleidima could not last long. Therefore, the *15th Panzer Division* ordered *Reconnaissance Battalion 33* and *Motorcycle Battalion 15* to withdraw step by step before the pressure of the enemy. The division decided to adopt offensive tactics to carry out the *Afrika Korps'* order, and to hurl the bulk of its forces against the central column of the enemy which had come nearest to the Via Balbia and was already approaching the area south of Beda Fomm. For this purpose, the division intended to advance to Beda Fomm without delay, to defeat the column and then to turn either against the northern or the southern enemy column, according to the development of the situation. Fortunately, a fresh *Panzer* company had joined *Panzer Regiment 8* which had been off-loaded from the first convoy that arrived in Africa on 17 December in Benghazi. Thus, the tank state of the division again showed over 40 tanks, in spite of the casualties suffered during the withdrawal.

When the division reached the area south of Beda Fomm, it began to grow dark as the winter days were short. From wireless reconnaissance, it was learnt that the enemy was in the immediate neighborhood east of Beda Fomm. The division decided to halt in order to be able to fall upon the enemy at first light on 23 December, and to throw him on to the *21st Panzer Division* to the north. Every step was taken to hide the presence of the division from the enemy. The *21st Panzer Division* was requested to take part in the attack but declined, pointing to its weakness.

The attack at dawn on 23 December was highly successful. The enemy was completely taken by surprise. After a short tussle, 30 enemy tanks withdrew to the east, having suffered considerable losses. Two enemy batteries had been overrun without having found time to fire a single round. Prisoners of war disclosed that they belonged to the British *4th Armored Brigade*, which had opposed the *15th Panzer Division* on many previous occasions.

Further to the north, 23 December was to become a critical day. It is true that the bulk of *XXI Corps* had occupied the positions at Agedabia in the morning on 23 December. *X Corps*, however, was still moving through Benghazi and its rearmost elements would not be able to arrive in Agedabia until noon on 24 December.

At Sceleidima the situation became particularly precarious. The enemy column approaching from Sidi Brahim advanced to Sollum during the night of 22/23 December, and entered the town at the same time as the withdrawing *Motorcycle Battalion 15*. The *Panzergruppe* therefore recalled *Reconnaissance Battalion 3* from Benghazi, placed *Motorcycle Battalion 15* under its command and instructed it to halt the enemy column at Solluch. General Rommel soon abandoned the plan which he had conceived for a short while, namely to retake the town with *Reconnaissance Battalion 3* and the Italian *Infantry Division Brescia*, which latter had just reached the height of Sollum on the Via Balbia. Covering patrols of *Reconnaissance Battalion 3* west of the town repulsed lesser enemy pushes. Only enemy armored reconnaissance groups harassed traffic on the Via Balbia west and south-west of Solluch during 23 December.

After the success south-east of Beda Fomm, Major-General von Baerst, the Commander of the *15th Panzer Division*, had to decide whether to pursue the beaten enemy eastward as far as the escarpment, or whether he should turn against the nearest column. In a wireless message, the *Afrika Korps* warned against an advance towards the escarpment at Abiar el Charez as it was strongly occupied by the enemy. Nonetheless, the *15th Panzer Division* continued pursuing the enemy to the escarpment, occupying it without encountering resistance. From there it intended to advance into the rear of the enemy at Antelat. This plan did not come off as the enemy had already begun withdrawing to the north-east as a consequence of the defeat suffered by the *4th Armored Brigade. Reconnaissance Battalion 33* followed up and reoccupied Antelat.

Influenced by the situation around Solluch, the *Afrika Korps* ordered the *15th Panzer Division* at 1400 hours to return to Sidi Saleh immediately. At 1430 hours the division started its return march, leaving a rearguard on the escarpment. At 1500 hours it unexpectedly encountered two strong enemy columns at Sidi Greibil which were advancing from Sceleidima to the south, probably in answer to calls for help from the *4th Armored Brigade*. The more western of the two enemy columns was smashed in an immediate attack. The attack by the eastern enemy column was brought to a halt by the rearguard, which arrived just in time. After this skirmish the division continued its march back as far as the area south of Sidi Saleh. Reconnaissance patrols found that the enemy had remained in the area north of Sidi Greibil. Thus, the division had engaged all three enemy columns advancing from the desert and prevented them from pushing to the Via Balbia. As during the night of 23/24 December, *Infantry Division Brescia*, as the last division of *X Corps*, had reached the Agedabia area, the task of the *Afrika Korps* had been successfully carried out.

On 24 December the Italian *Motorized Corps*, moving behind the rearmost elements of *X Corps* from the area south-west of Benghazi, withdrew on the Via Balbia. It drove enemy armored reconnaissance forces off the road and towards noon reached the area west of Sidi Saleh. During these operations it was joined by *Reconnaissance Battalion 3* and *Motorcycle Battalion 15*, which had covered the area south-west of Solluch.

On 24 December the *Afrika Korps* had no encounters with the enemy. The enemy which had been beaten the day before had indeed driven *Reconnaissance Battalion 33* out of Antelat, but did not cross the line Antelat–Sidi Greibil to the south-west. The *Afrika Korps* concentrated around Sidi Saleh towards noon. Greatly relieved, *Panzergruppe Afrika* was able to state as early as noon on 24 December that, generally speaking, the withdrawal of its various corps into the area of Agedabia had been successfully achieved. The position north and east of Agedabia had been occupied by the *90th Light Division* and the bulk of *XXI Corps. X Corps* was busy moving into the position. In the case of the Italian infantry divisions, the withdrawal had also gone off in tolerable order. Naturally, the fighting strength of the units had considerably decreased. It would take a certain time before all the stragglers would have found their way back to their units. In wise anticipation, the *Panzergruppe* had instructed the Commandant of Tripoli to set up a straggler-collecting point on the Via Balbia west of El Agheila, where all the stragglers of the Italian and the German divisions would be collected and sent back to their units.

On 24 December, at 1100 hours, orders were issued to the *Afrika Korps* and the Italian *Motorized Corps* to start withdrawing on the Via Balbia behind the Agedabia position. The *Afrika Korps* was to join in behind the Italian *Motorized Corps* west of Sidi Saleh. The Italian *Motorized Corps* was to reach the area 20 kilometers south of Agedabia and the *Afrika Korps* the area 40 kilometers south of Agedabia, there to take up the cover of the southern flank of the Agedabia position. As the first target of the move, the *Afrika Korps* was given the area on the Via Balbia 30 kilometers south-west of Agedabia.

The move during the night of 24/25 December did not progress at all smoothly. Strong enemy reconnaissance troops, supported by artillery, stabbed into the moving Italian *Motorized Corps* from the east after nightfall and at times blocked the road at Zuetina. It became necessary to throw in the forward elements of the *15th Panzer Division* to drive the enemy off and to get *Motorized Infantry Division Trieste*, which was in front, moving again. Difficult going delayed the Italian *Motorized Corps* when it left the Via Balbia south-west of Agedabia and caused long halts for the *Afrika Korps*. Nonetheless, by 0900 hours on 25 December the *15th Panzer Division* had reached the area 40 kilometers south-west of Agedabia, and the *21st Panzer Division* the area on the road 30 kilometers south-west of Agedabia.

This withdrawal of *Panzergruppe Afrika* from the Gazala position to Agedabia constituted a difficult and dangerous operation. On the whole, it may be regarded as a complete success. It is true that some losses were incurred when the north wing broke away from the enemy and through attacks of the RAF during the march. The *Panzergruppe* also lost some equipment which could not be salvaged in the rapid evacuation of Cyrenaica. On the other hand, all the divisions arrived in the Agedabia position in full fighting strength. The British had not succeeded in changing the German-Italian withdrawal into a defeat.

The difficult breaking away from the Gazala position proceeded according to plan for the time being even on the north wing. On 18 December, however, the rapid advance of the *4th Indian Division* via Bir el Temrad to Carmusa led to a dangerous crisis and brought about a considerable loss. Undoubtedly, it had been very risky to withdraw the Italian *Motorized Corps* from Bir el Temrad to El Mechili before the Italian *X* and *XXI Corps* had reached the mountain area of Cyrenaica in their withdrawal. It would have been more advisable to leave at least *Motorized Infantry Division Trieste* in the area of Bir el Temrad until the rearguards of the north wing had passed through Martuba and Derna. After having carried out its instructions to act as covering unit, *Division Trieste* would still have had time enough to follow in the withdrawal of the south wing and move to El Mechili. The courageous resistance offered by the Italian rearguards during 18 and 19 December deserves full recognition. Thanks to them alone, it had been possible to shake off the enemy pursuit on the north wing as early as the evening of 19 December, and to continue the withdrawal without noteworthy interference from the enemy. The distances covered by the Italian infantry divisions were extraordinary. They were supported by the skillful organization of the moves by *Panzergruppe Afrika*.

General Rommel had appreciated the intention of the British correctly. He had been right in regarding measures against the overtaking pursuit of the enemy through the desert to Agedabia as of first-rate importance. In reality, the British pursuit progressed more slowly and was carried out with weaker forces than Rommel had feared. Not until 22 December did the leading elements of the British *7th Armored Division* appear in the neighborhood of the Via Balbia between Benghazi and Agedabia, when the move of the *Panzergruppe* was nearly completed. The British armored forces had been split up in various pursuing columns which were separated from one another by large intervals. This enabled the *15th Panzer Division* to shake off the British by means of powerful attacks, in spite of their superior overall strength, and to prevent them from reaching the Via Balbia.

Thus, the *Afrika Korps* had carried out its mandate to cover the retreat and had protected the withdrawal against interference even through the last stage.

On the whole, the withdrawal from the Gazala position into the area of Agedabia was a successful operation, of the planning and the execution of which *Panzergruppe Afrika* could justly be proud.

The Fighting around Agedabia, 25 December–5 January

Whilst the terrain north of Agedabia differs but little from the desert plain on the southern edge of Cyrenaica and is negotiable almost everywhere, the area south of Agedabia is of special character. In the south it is bordered by the Wadi el Faregh a broad dry valley which runs from west to east for several hundred kilometers, and is negotiable for all vehicles in very few places owing to the deep sandy ground and the high and often steep banks. The passages where a crossing is possible played an important role in the fighting, particularly El Haseiat on the Agedabia–Gialo track. The terrain south of the Wadi el Faregh is difficult to negotiate owing to boulders and numerous sand fields. The area to the north thereof is characterized by high dunes 10 to 15 kilometers long running a general north–south direction, between which there are broad depressions, in most cases with a clayey ground. These dunes, as for instance the Tual el Naam east of Gtafi, offer opportunities for excellent positions and good possibilities for long-range observation. Outside this area of high ground, the movements of wheeled vehicles are hampered by the peculiarity of the ground. To the west of this area on both sides of the Via Balbia, sandy stretches, difficult to negotiate, and salt swamps, partly impassable, predominate. Further eastward, north of El Haseiat, drift sand fields appear which form of obstacle even for tracked vehicles.

The operational plan of *Panzergruppe Afrika* after 24 December envisaged bringing the pursuit of the enemy along the Via Balbia to a halt in a position stretching east and north of Agedabia in a semi-circle. Here, the *90th Light Division*, which had been preparing this position since 13 December, took the infantry divisions of *X* and *XXI Corps* into the prepared positions. There was reason for hope that the two Italian corps, in close disposition and stiffened by the *90th Light Division*, which had been spread over the whole front, would once again gain stability. For later, it was intended to withdraw the two Italian corps gradually into the Marsa el Bregha position under the protection of the *90th Light Division* halting in the Agedabia area and of the mobile forces of the *Panzergruppe*; there, they were to be given some time to settle down in these positions to regain their old fighting power before new defensive operations began.

General Rommel expected the British *7th Armored Division*, after, in the course of the pursuit, it had bumped the Agedabia position, to attempt once again a swing to the south, with a view to bringing about the collapse of this position by means of the same tactics which had been observed in all the fighting since the battle of Bir el Gubi. For this reason he placed the *Afrika Korps* to the east and north-east of Gtafi (40 kilometers south of Agedabia) and the Italian *Motorized Corps* at Rugbet Hagina (25 kilometers south of Agedabia), with the instruction to prevent an envelopment of the Agedabia position by enemy armored forces, if need be by means of an attack.

The divisions of the two corps, after their night march, had assembled on the morning of 26 December in rest areas along the Via Balbia south-west of Agedabia. During the afternoon on 25 December, they started for the positions allotted to them by the *Panzergruppe*. First they had to drive out two British reconnaissance detachments supported by artillery, which had at times reached the Via Balbia with strong armored reconnaissance patrols approaching from Bir el Aamria and from Bir el Gelulia.

On the right wing, the *15th Panzer Division* prepared defensive positions on the dominating Alem el Turch–El Haseiat height, because this position seemed more favorable than the position indicated by the *Afrika Korps* six kilometers further east. On the left thereof, the *21st Panzer Division* took up position on the heights north-east of Bir el Aamria. The corps battle headquarters of the *Afrika Korps* was set up behind the center of the front south of Bir el Aamria. To the north thereof the Italian *Motorized Corps* occupied positions west and north-west of Bir Gelulia.

On 25 December no reconnaissance results were available at the *Panzergruppe* which could confirm the appreciation that enemy armored formations were advancing towards the area south of Agedabia. On the other hand, the *Panzergruppe* feared that the mobile enemy desert formations around Gialo, there since 20 November, would take a hand in the operation. It instructed the *Afrika Korps*, therefore, to dispatch a mixed formation in battalion strength to El Haseiat, with a view to cover the Gialo–Agedabia track where it crosses the Wadi el Faregh. At noon on 15 December, the *Afrika Korps* passed this order to the *15th Panzer Division*. The latter objected, though vainly, because in its opinion the forces meant for it were too weak to defend themselves 40 kilometers away from the front, with nobody to rely on but themselves, in case enemy armored forces were to advance from the north-east into this area. *Motorcycle Battalion 15*, reinforced by one light battery, one tank destroyer company and one engineer company, under command of Lieutenant-Colonel Ballerstedt, was dispatched to El Haseiat on the same day, 25 December. The detachment reported its arrival at El Haseiat as early as 1900 hours.

During the morning of 25 December it was found out, however, that in reality they were still 18 kilometers away from their objective. As the terrain was extremely difficult, and particularly because of large stretches of deep drift sand, the forward elements did not arrive in El Haseiat until 1530 hours. While they were still busy setting up a strongpoint, they were attacked from the north and north-west by 30 British tanks at 1645 hours. They penetrated into the western part of the strongpoint, overran the positions of the artillery and tank destroyers, but withdrew from the strongpoint during the evening.

The *15th Panzer Division*, whose reconnaissance meanwhile had noted during the afternoon on 26 December that enemy armored forces were advancing 30 kilometers east of the positions, came to the conclusion that it would be purposeless, and that it would mean a useless sacrifice of *Group Ballerstedt*, if it were left in el Haseiat. It therefore sent a wireless instruction to the division to withdraw under cover of the night. The important factor would be that it joined up with the division before first light, as otherwise its movements would be exposed to extreme danger. For reasons unknown, Lieutenant-Colonel Ballerstedt did not start on his way back until after midnight, and at first light on 27 December was still 20 kilometers to the east of Tual el Naam.

As early as 26 December, a message from the air reached *Panzergruppe Afrika* that a British column with armor en route from the north-east had reached Giof el Matar and Bir el Fenscia. Strong armored reconnaissance appeared along the entire south wing. On 27 December, a strong enemy group, with 500 motor vehicles and 60 tanks coming from the north-east, advanced as far as Chor es Sufan. Thus, an attack against the north wing and the center of the *Afrika Korps* seemed to be imminent.

Thereupon the *Afrika Korps* decided, early on 27 December, to concentrate its forces in the north in order to ward off the enemy attack and to throw back the enemy in a counterattack. For this purpose, it adopted the same disposition of forces which had been employed successfully during the Gazala battle. The *15th Schützen Brigade* was to come under direct command of the corps, move to the north and occupy a position in the northern sector of Height Tual el Naam and on the heights south-east of Bir el Aamtia. The assault group (the *15th Panzer Division*), with *Panzer Regiment 8*, two rifle battalions and two artillery detachments as well as *Antitank Battalion 33* (less one company), was to move behind the center of the front into the area south of Bir el Tombia, there to be at the disposal of the corps.

The *15th Panzer Division* appreciated the position differently. In its sector, strong enemy armored reconnaissance had also become active on its front and in the southern flank on 24 December. *Reconnaissance Battalion 33* reported 60 tanks with artillery and several hundred motor vehicles advancing from the north-east towards the position of the *15th Panzer Division*. *Group Ballerstedt*, which at 0800 hours was 10 kilometers to the east of the division, was thus in greatest danger. The division intended to cover Ballerstedt's approach with a counterthrust by elements of *Panzer Regiment 8*.

In accordance with the instruction, the division dispatched the *15th Schützen Brigade*, but reported to the *Afrika Korps* that the attack of superior enemy armor was imminent on the very same day, 27 December. The division regarded it as impossible to withdraw the assault group from its very strong positions astride the very important El Haseiat–Gtafi track in the prevailing circumstances. Moreover, the return of *Group Ballerstedt* was first to be waited for. The *Afrika Korps* concurred with the suggestion of the *15th Panzer Division* and left the assault group in its position.

At 0900 hours, whilst still seven kilometers east of the division, *Group Ballerstedt* was attacked from the north-east by enemy armor. Thereupon, one panzer company was dispatched on a counterattack to relieve *Ballerstedt's* situation. The counterattack had the desired result. At 1100 hours, the battle group arrived at the positions of the division, and was placed on the south-west wing, extending the line.

Sixty enemy tanks followed on the heels of the *Panzer* company which was withdrawing in accordance with orders, and at 1130 hours they attacked the position of the *15th Panzer Division* but were easily driven off. During the afternoon the enemy resumed the attack, supported by the fire of several light and heavy batteries which had been brought into position behind Height Alem Derbua opposite the division. Elements of the enemy force tried to envelop the position from the south. Once more all the attacks were repulsed. The enemy left several tanks disabled on the front.

In the evening of 27 December, the *15th Panzer Division* expected the main British effort on its own front. For 28 December a continuation of the British attack with stronger forces was anticipated.

The Counterattack on the South Wing of the *Panzergruppe*

In the evening of 27 December, General Rommel appreciated the situation as follows:

The enemy had advanced against the north and east front of the Agedabia position with no more than weak motorized infantry and artillery and a few tanks, and had not attacked. Nor was there any indication that an attack was imminent there. Considerable enemy forces, possibly the *4th Indian Division*, were assumed to be in the Benghazi area.

On the other hand, the British seemed to be about to go round the Agedabia position in the south with considerable forces, and to cut off and destroy the forces in the position by a push from Chor es Sufan to the Via Balbia.

The enemy group on the front of the *15th Panzer Division* was assumed to be of lesser strength. Probably it was no more than a group echeloned out in order to protect the flank. The strongest group of the enemy (800 vehicles and 60 tanks) had been sighted at Chor es Sufan on the center of the *Afrika Korps*. Further enemy forces, mainly motor transport, seemed to be moving into the area around Gief el Matar. *Panzergruppe* supposed that the *1st South African Division* was at that locality. A number of the British formations were evidently still in the Tobruk area and in the area of the Gazala position. The activities of the British air force had been remarkably restrained so far.

On the other side, the *Panzergruppe* had increased its fighting power owing to a few restful days. The tank state of the *Afrika Korps* was higher. The *21st Panzer Division* now had 20 tanks; the *15th Panzer Division*, which had received a fresh *panzer* company, had 50 tanks. A further *Panzer* company also meant for the *15th Panzer Division* could be expected to arrive on 28 or 29 December from Tripoli.

For these reasons, the *Panzergruppe* thought the opportunity had come to fall on the enemy so near to the front with concentrated forces and to defeat him. General Rommel decided to attack him with the *Afrika Korps* and the Italian *Motorized Corps* in a general south-easterly direction, to cut him off from his rear communications and to throw him back to the Wadi el Faregh. The main effort of this attack was to be on the left wing, and all the forces taking part in the attack, including the Italian *Motorized Corps*, were to be under the command of the *Afrika Korps*.

By reason of the changed situation on the front of the *15th Panzer Division*, the *Afrika Korps* altered the original plan. Now the *21st Panzer Division* was to attack in the sector of the main effort together with the Italian *Motorized Corps* from the Sidi Hameida area over Rugbet Hagina–Bu Ain towards Beda Fomm on the Wadi Faregh. It was particularly important that this group advance rapidly in order to hit the rearward communications of the enemy at the earliest possible time. On the right, the *15th Schützen Brigade (Group Geissler)*, which had no armor, was to engage the enemy at Chor es Sufan in a frontal attack, and to press him back towards the Height Alem Derbua. Originally, the assault group of the *15th Panzer Division* should have attacked to the east simultaneously with the other attacking groups. However, General Crüwell had allowed himself to be convinced that this attack across a ten-kilometer broad depression against strong positions on the Alem Derbua would be particularly difficult. Moreover, there was the danger that if the attack were successful, the enemy might be able to avoid the push by the *21st Panzer Division* by withdrawing to the east in time. Therefore, he gave the *15th Panzer Division* a fresh order early on 28 December, instructing it to repulse the enemy attack expected early on 28 December, and only to counterattack to the east after the attack by the group had become effective.

The Fighting in the Morning of 28 December

The *21st Panzer Division* began its attack at 0730 hours. It had to proceed with great care as it had very few tanks and as the enemy was vastly superior in armor, and also because the attack of the Italian *Motorized Corps*, advancing on the right, was lagging behind from the very start. Enemy covering troops tried to delay the attack, but were soon pressed back to the south. Towards 1200 hours, the advance had not progressed further than Rugbet el Hagina. The *Afrika Korps* was unable to make the Italian *Motorized Corps* move faster. The latter evidently regarded its task more as a demonstration.

Group Geissler had the strongest of the enemy groups – over 60 tanks – close to its front. As it had no tanks, it took tank destroyers and antiaircraft artillery forward when attacking, and advanced in bounds under the fire protection of the artillery. Naturally, its attack gained ground very slowly.

Everything depended on the course the fighting would take on the front of the assault group of the *15th Panzer Division*. At 0900 hours, after strong artillery preparation, the enemy launched the expected attack with 60 tanks. At this time he tried to go round the position also to the north, but was quickly driven back by a counterpush of *Panzer Regiment 8*. In the south flank, he extended his enveloping move further to the west. Strong reconnaissance forces felt forward towards Gtafi. *Reconnaissance Battalion 33* was dispatched to extend the west wing. The positions were held.

Meanwhile, the division had made all preparations for the counterattack. For the first time in the course of the autumn battle, liaison officers of *Fliegerführer Afrika* functioned at the division in order to discuss the support of the attack with *Stuka* operations. Reconnaissance troops watched over the advance of *Group Geissler*.

At 1100 hours, the effect of the advance of the other attacking troops had not yet made itself felt. But at that time British vehicles were seen moving on the Height Alem Derbua, indicating changes taking place with the enemy. Thereupon, the division commander decided to start his attack in order to prevent the enemy from moving forces against the *21st Panzer Division*. As anticipated by the division, the attack turned out to be very difficult. The enemy tanks found cover behind Height Alem Derbua, and were supported by strong artillery which dominated the depression in front of the position. Thus, the attack of the *15th Panzer Division* reached the enemy positions only on the left wing. On the right wing the advance had to be halted towards 1200 hours because of flanking gunfire, and because of an attack by enemy armor into the right flank. Shortly afterwards, the movements of vehicles behind the enemy front increased. Apparently the attack of the other assault groups became effective. The positions of the enemy were attacked twice by German *Stuka* formations.

Thereupon, the division commander reorganized his forces, this time placing the main effort on the right wing, and at 1400 hours he resumed the attack. The enemy defended himself desperately. After bitter armored fighting and after 25 enemy tanks had been knocked out, enemy resistance collapsed. It had evidently been his intention to cover the withdrawal of his forces coming from the north.

Major-General von Vaerst, the division commander, immediately advanced to the pursuit, and, disregarding the enemy forces in the southern flank, he pushed on to the east with all the forces of the division. Wherever British armor tried to make a stand, it was overrun. The fresh *Panzer* company which was just arriving from Tripoli did not halt at all, but at once took part in the pursuit. At 1645 hours, the deeply cut-in and sandy Wadi el Faregh had been reached at El Gelulia. At this strong sector the enemy tried to bring the pursuit to a halt. However, he was soon hit by a strong *Stuka* attack. While the last bombs were still exploding, *Panzer Regiment 8* crossed the Wadi el Faregh and broke the enemy resistance on its southern flank. The division advanced a further 10 kilometers to the east, and did not break off the pursuit until complete darkness prevailed. Fifty-five enemy tanks, numerous motor vehicles and four batteries had been left behind by the enemy in the area of the pursuit. The crossing of the Wadi el Faregh had proved particularly costly for him, and he had lost numerous vehicles.

The advance of the remaining assault group had brought less success. The enemy had been able to halt the attack of *Group Geissler* with a few tanks. The *21st Panzer Division* encountered very difficult terrain and did not reach the Wadi el Faregh north-east of El Gelulia until late in the evening. By that time, the bulk of the enemy had succeeded in escaping to the east, suffering heavy losses.

The attempt by the *Afrika Korps* to cut the enemy off from his rearward communications and to throw him back to the south had not fully succeeded; nonetheless, the British *7th Armored Division* had suffered a heavy defeat. Moreover, thanks to the attack by the *15th Panzer Division*, strong elements had been driven into the area south of the Wadi el Faregh. The

Afrika Korps assumed that on 29 December the enemy would try to move these forces back to the north-east by way of El Haseiat. For this reason, the corps intended to exploit its victory on 29 December by means of an energetic pursuit to the east. It is true that lack of fuel did not allow the crossing of the El Haseiat–Agedabia track and a move further east.

The *Afrika Korps* therefore ordered *Group Geissler* to advance along the Wadi el Faregh as far as the area north-west of El Haseiat, and the *21st Panzer Division* to the north-east thereof. The assault group of the *15th Panzer Division* was not to continue the pursuit south of the Wadi el Faregh, but to return to the north bank, where it would be moved up, behind the *Afrika Korps*, into the area north-west of Bu Ain.

Events on 29 December

On 29 December, the battlefield was cleaned up and more tanks and motor vehicles which had got stuck were brought in as booty. The advance of the *Afrika Korps* to the east turned out to be a very laborious affair owing to the extensive stretches of drift sand on both sides of Bu Ain. All wheeled vehicles had to be towed through the sand fields by the few tractors available. Thus, in the evening, the right wing of the *Afrika Korps* had gone no further than 8 kilometers north-west of El Haseiat and the left wing 10 kilometers west of the El Haseiat–Agedabia track. The assault group had reached the area 5 kilometers north-east of Bu Ain. The Italian *Motorized Corps* reported its location as 15 kilometers east of Rugbet el Hagina.

Thus, on 29 December it had not been possible for the pursuing troops to reach the enemy. The latter had evidently moved his forces up into the Giof el Matar area, and had also moved the forces which had been chased across the Wadi el Faregh to the same area. Therefore, a further advance to the east did not promise much success.

The *Afrika Korps*, therefore, ordered its divisions to discontinue the pursuit on 30 December and to go over to the defense along the El Haseiat–Agedabia track, fronting east.

Events on 30 December

During the night the *15th Panzer Division*, by means of wireless reconnaissance, located an enemy armored formation, probably an armored brigade, in the area 10 kilometers to the north of its location, i.e. approximately 15 kilometers east of Rugbet el Hagina. Although the *Afrika Korps* suspected the *Italian Motorized Corps* to be in this area, it approved of the suggestion by the

15th Panzer Division that the latter advance to the north at first light on 30 December to clarify its position. This advance encountered a large British tented camp with many vehicles and some 60 tanks 15 kilometers east of Rugbet el Hagina. At first the division thought that this was an Italian formation, as most of the vehicles were of Italian make. After a short while, however, the reconnaissance patrols of the division found out that this was a British armored formation. The enemy cleared out of his camp with great haste and retreated to the north, covered by his tanks. He was at once attacked and suffered heavy losses. In the course of the pursuit, the division, in spite of several British air attacks, advanced by way of Belaudah to the north-east, intending to continue to the north-east of Bir el Fenscia. However, it was ordered by the *Afrika Korps* to halt at Belaudah in consideration of the precarious fuel position. This short skirmish lost the British *7th Armored Division* another 35 tanks.

Depositions of prisoners of war showed that, in the fighting on 30 December, another armored brigade of the *7th Armored Division*, which had received new tanks on 29 December, had been smashed. These new tanks had been manned by crews of no more than two or three men owing to the heavy losses in men suffered in the previous fighting. This was a clear indication that the British *7th Armored Division*, so far the elite of the British *Eighth Army*, was now completely exhausted. During the afternoon of 30 December, the *Afrika Korps* moved the *21st Panzer Division* into the newly captured area around Belaudah. *Reconnaissance Battalion 3* was to continue the pursuit towards Bir el Fenscia, as wireless reconnaissance had shown that the enemy had been given orders to retreat towards Giof el Matar. However, the advance of *Reconnaissance Battalion 3* had to be discontinued half way because of lack of fuel. The assault group was concentrated 10 kilometers south of Belaudah, and the *15th Schützen Brigade* was deployed on a broad front in various strongpoints along the track. *Reconnaissance Battalion 33* was placed on the Gur el Nteilen height to watch the crossing at El Haseiat.

Local Skirmishes in the Agedabia Area

In spite of the success achieved in the counterattack against the British *7th Armored Division*, General Rommel stuck to his intention of giving up the Agedabia area and of withdrawing into the Marsa el Bregha position. As early as 26 December, he had started sending the headquarters of the infantry division of *X* and *XXI Corps* into the new position one after the other. The *90th Light Division* and the mobile forces of the *Panzergruppe* were to hold the Agedabia area as long as possible, so as to allow the Italian division time for settling down in their position. Moreover, there might be another opportunity to deal the enemy armored forces a new blow in a counterattack.

In accordance with this intention, *XXI* and *X Motorized Corps* were being taken back into the Marsa el Bregha position in night marches as from 25 December onward, where the newly established Italian *Infantry Division Sabratha* had prepared the positions for them. This division joined *XXI Corps*, which released *Infantry Division Bologna* to *X Corps* instead.

In the course of this operation, the *90th Light Division* took over the entire Agedabia position. It was not attacked by the enemy, but enemy reconnaissance patrols slowly moved nearer to its positions astride the Via Balbia. Enemy reconnaissance activity, however, was not lively. On the other hand, the enemy attacked the positions frequently from the air. In order to prepare a later evacuation of the position, strong engineer forces were used to mine the area around Agedabia thoroughly so as to delay the enemy advance to the Marsa el Bregha position.

The *Afrika Korps* and the Italian *Motorized Corps* were busy building a defensive line fronting east. Their formations were disposed in strongpoints. Artillery and antiaircraft guns dominated the outlying terrain. Reconnaissance patrols penetrated far to the east.

On 30 and 31 December, the enemy evidently had expected a further advance of the *Afrika Korps* to the east, and had retreated beyond Giof el Matar to the east. When, however, no German attack materialized, he slowly felt forward towards the German-Italian positions, first with reconnaissance patrols then with strong forces, but he always kept at a respectful distance. Fighting was limited to artillery duels. Around El Haseiat lively skirmishes between reconnaissance patrols developed. After 2 January enemy reconnaissance activity on the south wing became more lively. Enemy armored reconnaissance troops south of the Wadi el Faregh penetrated far to the west. The *Panzergruppe* feared that the enemy might once again outflank its position and advance to the Marsa el Bregha position. In contrast, the *Afrika Korps* was of the opinion that such an advance would be welcome as it would offer an opportunity to beat the enemy in a counterattack.

Nonetheless, on 3 January, the *Panzergruppe* issued a warning order for the *Afrika Korps* and the Italian *Motorized Corps* for a withdrawal to take place on one of the following days. On 5 January, the withdrawal was ordered to start during the night of 5/6 January. The *Afrika Korps* and the *Italian Motorized Corps* were to be taken back into an area on the Via Balbia 20 kilometers west of their present positions.

During the last days of 1941 the British attempt to cause the Agedabia position to collapse by enveloping it from the south and to cut off the troops occupying the area had ended in complete failure. The British advance into the area south of Agedabia ended in a heavy defeat. The British armored forces escaped destruction only by hastily withdrawing to the east and lost more than 110 tanks on the battlefield during 28 and 30 December, which constituted more than half of their total.

General Rommel had anticipated the enemy intention and taken the necessary defensive measures in good time. The counterattack on 28 December had been thoroughly prepared. It was not due to mistakes made in planning, but solely to unforeseen difficulties in the terrain, that the wing of the *Panzergruppe* which had to make the main effort did not advance rapidly enough, so that part of the enemy was able to escape annihilation. Pursuing the enemy to the east would probably have brought further success, but on account of the precarious fuel position of the *Panzergruppe* this was not possible.

The fighting south of Agedabia gave clear evidence that the enemy had also suffered heavily during the campaign. Indeed, he was able to replace the equipment lost from his rich reserves in Egypt, but he was unable to replace the battle-experienced tank crews which he had lost. The British *7th Armored Division* no longer constituted a danger for a long time to come. Thus, there is no doubt that it would have been possible to hold the Agedabia position for a long period. It is true that the possibility did exist that the enemy would move up new superior forces from Marmerica and Egypt in the near future. Then, the danger of an envelopment south of the Wadi el Faregh would again threaten. Such menace did not exist for the Marsa el Bregha position. There, moreover, the difficult sandy terrain west of El Haseiat and south-west of Gtafi was protecting the front; whereas, being in the rear of the Agedabia position, it would have constituted a danger to the formations of the *Panzergruppe*, should they be forced to carry out a rapid withdrawal to the west. Moreover, to abandon a stretch of desert of a depth of 40 kilometers did not mean much.

Thus, General Rommel's decision to withdraw to the Marsa el Bregha position, in spite of the successful operations at Agedabia, was undoubtedly justified.

The Withdrawal from Agedabia
into the Marsa el Bregha Position, 6–12 January

The nature of the terrain made the Marsa el Bregha position, which had been prepared to serve as a final defense line, very strong indeed. Its northern sector touched the coast to the left at Marsa el Bregha, then ran south-west as far as the Wadi el Faregh east of Bir Belchonfus, from there leaning to the Wadi el Faregh back to the south-west as far as Mn. Giofer. The southern sector of the position ran along the Mn. Giofer–Marada track as far as the oasis of Marada.

The northern sector was 70 kilometers long. Extensive salt swamps on both sides of the Via Balbia and sandy terrain difficult to negotiate further south before the front rendered an approach difficult for the enemy. High dunes inside the position offered excellent observation posts for the artillery. The Wadi el Faregh, with banks much steeper here than further to the east, constituted a strong obstacle on the front.

The southern sector of the position was 130 kilometers long. There was no need for strong protection as the very difficult terrain south of the Wadi el Faregh rendered an attack by stronger enemy forces unlikely on this sector.

As early as the end of December, the *Panzergruppe* had placed the Italian *XXI Corps* in the northern sector and the Italian *X Corps* in the southern sector so that they could improve the position before the arrival of the enemy, and in order to give the Italian troops time and the opportunity to reorganize their formations, and replace men and material which had been lost.

The construction of the line followed the principles successfully adopted in the Sollum–Sidi Omar position. A system of strongpoints was laid out. The length of the position, however, inevitably made intervals between the strongpoints too large for the decreased numbers of the Italian formations.

The Italian command took advantage of the rest period to reorganize its two infantry corps. The newly established *Infantry Division Sabratha* joined *XXI Corps*. It occupied the positions astride the Via Balbia on the left wing of the corps. To the south thereof followed *Division Trento*. The third division of the corps, *Infantry Division Pavia*, which had suffered heavily, was to take over the sector between Bir Belchonfus and Mn. Giofer, which was particularly well-protected by the Wadi el Faregh. *X Corps*, in the southern sector, had concentrated the bulk of its forces – *Infantry Division Brescia* and *Infantry Division Bologna* – in the northern part of its sector, and further to the south was satisfied with weaker covering forces. The Marada oasis was occupied by a mixed detachment.

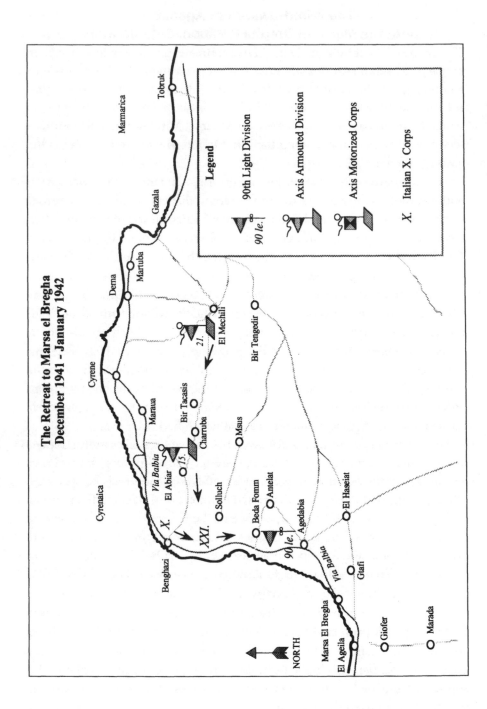

The Retreat to Marsa el Bregha
December 1941 - January 1942

Legend

90th Light Division

Axis Armoured Division

Axis Motorized Corps

X.   Italian X. Corps

Panzergruppe Afrika intended to have only these two Italian infantry corps in the positions, and to leave the mobile formations in the rear of the line. They were to stand by with the bulk of their formations behind the northern sector in a counterattack role. Elements of the *90th Light Division* were to strengthen the two cornerstones of the position, one on the Via Balbia and the other in Marada.

The Actual Withdrawal

The instructions of *Panzergruppe Afrika* provided for two stages of withdrawal. During the first night the Italian *Motorized Corps* on the right wing with the *Afrika Korps* on its left was to reach a line which ran to the north at the Via Balbia, 40 kilometers south-west of Agedabia. To the north, the *15th Schützen Brigade* was to maintain contact with the rearguards of the *90th Light Division* in the area 20 kilometers south of Agedabia; these rearguards were to hold Agedabia until the mining operation in progress had been completed. The protection of the southern flank had been entrusted to *Reconnaissance Battalions 3* and *33*. In a second night march, all the mobile forces were to be withdrawn behind the Marsa el Bregha position.

The withdrawal began during the night of 5/6 January. Evidently, the British had seen the movement and in several air attacks inflicted losses on the German-Italian formations. However, the enemy did not follow, and even during the ensuing days they only felt forward with reconnaissance patrols. The rearguard of the *90th Light Division* in Agedabia was able to complete its task without interference from the enemy. After having thoroughly mined every access to the town and also the Via Balbia, they abandoned their positions to the north and east of the town on 8 January.

During the night of 9/10 January, the Italian *Motorized Corps* and the *Afrika Korps* were taken behind the Marsa el Bregha position without the enemy interfering in the move. On 10 January, both corps stood behind the north wing of the position around El Agheila.

At first the enemy followed solely with reconnaissance units along the Via Balbia. Soon, however, reconnaissance formations of greater strength advanced north and south of the Wadi el Faregh towards the position of the *Panzergruppe*. Soon General Rommel became convinced that the main effort of the enemy was being directed against the center of the position. He moved the *Afrika Korps* behind the south wing of *XXI Corps* during 12 and 13 January. The *15th Panzer Division*, with its right wing at the Wadi el Faregh, had to drive away enemy reconnaissance forces on several occasions during the following days; these enemy pushes had been directed on to the gaps between the Italian strongpoints. As early as the middle of January, the enemy discontinued his reconnaissance operations. The *Panzergruppe* was now ready for defensive operations. Sea traffic to Tripoli having been restored, the fighting power of the German formations soon increased considerably, with reinforcements of personnel and equipment arriving and with fuel and ammunition being replenished. The Italian formations also increased their fighting power, and their self-confidence grew visibly during this operational pause.

The Situation in the Air

When, in the evening on 15 December, the order was given for the withdrawal from the Gazala position, *Fliegerführer Afrika* had not yet received new formations and had at his disposal only the old formations, weakened as they were by losses suffered. The tasks allotted to him in support of the withdrawal were manifold and difficult. On the one hand, he had to fight the mobile forces of the British and to delay their advance to Agedabia. On the other hand, it was also his task to facilitate the breaking away of *X* and *XXI Corps* from the Gazala position and to attack the British pursuing columns along the Via Balbia. Field Marshal Kesselring had pledged his word to the Italians that this latter task, less important though it was, would be carried out.

Simultaneously, the formations had to be moved up to their new airfields behind the Marsa el Bregha positions in stages and leapfrogging; the ground installations and supply dumps of the *Luftwaffe* had to be transferred from western Cyrenaica into the "Great Sierte" and to Tripolitania without interfering with the carrying out of the above-mentioned task.

It is a fact that the formations of *Fliegerführer Afrika* fought successfully during the withdrawal. On the south wing, their attacks undoubtedly contributed to the successful breaking away of the troops from the Gazala position, and to the delay imposed on the British pursuing columns, which were unable to arrive in the area north of Agedabia until 22 December. The self-sacrificing way in which the German *Luftwaffe* supported the two Italian corps on the north wing facilitated the operation considerably, and most likely was instrumental in preventing very heavy casualties from being inflicted on them. The airfields of Martuba and Derna were held to the very last moment. Antiaircraft artillery and ground personnel of the *Luftwaffe* took part in their defense against the enemy pursuing columns. Naturally, the losses in men, aircraft and antiaircraft artillery were considerable.

The formations of *X. Fliegerkorps* contributed indirectly to relieving the position of *Panzergruppe Afrika*. They attacked not only enemy sea traffic, but also railways and convoys through the desert in its full extent along the coast from western Egypt to Cyrenaica. Even though the losses inflicted on the enemy supplies were not too stunning, the enemy was compelled to have part of his air formations and of his antiaircraft artillery operating to protect his rearward communications, which meant that they were not available on the actual battle front.

This was one of the reasons that the activity of the RAF during the withdrawal was not so lively as the German command feared it would be. Nevertheless, their attacks on the troops involved in the withdrawal caused considerable damage, particularly in the narrows of the mountainous part of Cyrenaica where it was impossible to leave the roads, and noteworthy losses in men and material were suffered. As the withdrawal progressed, British air activity decreased considerably. During this fighting the problem of coordinating the operations of the flying formations of the *Luftwaffe* with those of the ground troops had not yet been solved satisfactorily. There were considerable difficulties, particularly during the fighting in the El Mechili area. However, the *Koluft* with *Panzergruppe Afrika*, Lieutenant-Colonel Heymer, contributed much in speeding up air reconnaissance. More than ever, the German command was supplied with air reconnaissance results regarding the progress of the enemy pursuit.

During the last third of December, after the Agedabia area had been reached, the air situation improved considerably. The formations of *Fliegerfügrer Afrika* were reinforced with two fighter groups.[1] Soon this showed a very favorable effect, as the enemy air force was now forced into a defensive role and was no longer able to attack the ground troops so frequently. The *Stuka* and destroyer formations were also reinforced and replenished. Their fighting against the British troops pressing on became more effective thanks to improved fighter protection. The fact that the staff of *Fliegerführer Afrika*, thus far under command of *X. Fliegerkorps*, had been placed under direct command of Commander-in-Chief South after the Gulf of Sirte had been reached also showed favorable results. The *Luftgaustab* [the administrative and supply organization of a theater of war, usually commanded by a full general] was transferred to Tripoli, where it could better supervise and organize supplies and replenishments for the German *Luftwaffe* formations.

---

[1] At this time a German fighter group (*Gruppe*) had about 36 fighter aircraft.

The improvement in the air situation made itself clearly felt towards the end of the year in the fighting south of Agedabia. Here, for the first time, the German *Luftwaffe* cooperated in close coordination with the formations of the army and played an important part in the tank battles, inflicting considerable losses on the enemy forces, particularly during the latter's withdrawal from the battlefield to the east. The liaison officers of the *Luftwaffe* attached to the German *Panzer* formations proved particularly useful; air liaison officers had been functioning on other war theaters much earlier. On the other side, the RAF only took part in the fighting on rare occasions, nor did it interfere very much with the withdrawal of the mobile forces of the *Panzergruppe* behind the Marsa el Bregha position from 5 to 10 January. The activity of the German-Italian air forces may have contributed to the fact that the British armored formations followed this withdrawal but hesitantly. After the Marsa el Bregha position had been reached on 10 January, comparative calm prevailed also in the air. The opposing forces were not equally strong. For the time being, air reconnaissance was the main task of *Fliegerführer Afrika*. He had to find out the whereabouts of all the enemy forces and whether they were preparing for a new attack.

A most difficult and thankless task given to the *Luftwaffe* was the supply by air of the Sollum front and the fortress of Bardia. As in other war theaters, it was shown in this one too that supplying larger cut-off formations by air was impossible for any prolonged period. Moreover, to supply the Halfaya Pass by air was particularly difficult, the reason being that there was no suitable landing ground in the vicinity of the Sollum front, so that the only way was to drop supply parcels; but even for that there was very little space. In addition, there were no formations of transport planes available in the beginning. The bomber formations which did the job were not trained for this task. Owing to the distance, the supplying aircraft had to do without fighter protection, which meant that it was a question of night flying. The season – late autumn and winter, with unfavorable weather conditions predominating (thunderstorms and sand storms) – rendered the execution of supply flying extraordinarily difficult.

British counteraction was considerable from the very beginning. The British placed numerous antiaircraft batteries around the invested strongpoint, and from the middle of December onward night fighters were employed to operate against the German supply aircraft. A number of deceptive devices were set up to lure the German supply aircraft into dropping their supply parcels on to British-occupied ground. The German supply and transportation formations suffered considerable losses, which increased as time progressed. In spite of all the sacrifices, it was not possible to provide the German-Italian troops with quantities of supplies sufficient for their needs. On the other hand, the Sollum front would not have been able to prolong resistance into the middle of January 1942 without the supplies dropped to them from the air.

While *X. Fliegerkorps* directly supported *Panzergruppe Afrika* in its struggle, *II. Fliegerkorps* had been entrusted with the battle for sea communications in the Mediterranean. As from the first half of December, Malta was being attacked by increasing forces and with increasing success. Thus, it was regarded as an extraordinary achievement when, during the middle of Decembe, two German convoys, escorted by Italian battleships, safely reached the harbors of Benghazi and of Tripoli for the first time. The onslaught on Malta, as the most important base for enemy torpedo-carrying aircraft and light naval forces, was increased in the period which followed. In this connection ship traffic increased, although many losses had still to be accepted.

The German-Italian air forces contributed a great deal to the success of the withdrawal and to the improvement of the situation of *Panzergruppe Afrika*. At the turn of the year, the ratio of forces in the air was once again equal on both sides on the African war theater.

The Supply Problem
during the Withdrawal, 5 December–12 January

The moving up of supplies during the withdrawal was rendered difficult from the very beginning by the fact that Rommel could not make up his mind from the outset whether to give up Cyrenaica. Thus, uniform planning in this connection for the purposes of the withdrawal was impossible; in particular, it had been impossible to make a timely start with the evacuation of the dumps built up in Cyrenaica.

On 4 December, when the withdrawal from the area east of Tobruk began, the supply position of the *Panzergruppe* was rather precarious. The sea route for supplies had not yet been reopened. The Quartermaster-General could count on no other supplies than those which had been accumulated during the summer. Although there was no acute supply crisis threatening as yet, supplies of fuel and ammunition had dwindled considerably. The equipment position was particularly unfavorable. The two German *Panzer* divisions had no more than 60 tanks altogether. The evacuation of supplies from the area east of Tobruk, which started on 5 December, was facilitated by the fact that German supply bases had been set up in the area west of Tobruk long before. The supply troops and the depots coming from the area east of Tobruk were disposed behind the Gazala position in the area around Derna and Martuba.

When, on 6 December, General Rommel decided to withdraw to the Gazala position, the only thing left to be done was to withdraw the supply basis west of Tobruk into western Cyrenaica. This withdrawal was, on the whole, a success, and so was the supplying of the German troops during the fighting south of Tobruk and during the withdrawal to the Gazala position. Unfortunately, the supply troops suffered considerable casualties and losses from attacks by the RAF during the withdrawal.

During the fighting around the Gazala position in mid-December 1941, the supply position of *Panzergruppe Afrika* had become very serious. The sea route had not yet been reopened for the transport of supplies. The fuel position caused the greatest anxiety. The German command was faced with the problem of whether to see through the battle round the Gazala position employing mobile tactics, using up the available fuel reserves, or to save up these fuel reserves for the withdrawal. There was not enough fuel for both purposes. The ammunition position also was deteriorating. There was already a serious shortage of some kinds of ammunition. On the other hand, the question of food and water offered no problem. Most serious of all had become the equipment position. Apart from the heavy fighting, wear and tear brought about many casualties in tanks. By the middle of December, the tank strength of the *Afrika Korps* had dwindled to 40, nor was a substantial increase of the number of tanks to be expected from repaired tanks returned from workshops. The guns of the motorized artillery, tank-destroyers and antiaircraft artillery became casualties in increasing numbers. The state the motor vehicles were in was deplorable, and not only limited the mobility of the motorized infantry but also the moving up of supplies, although the numerous captured vehicles which were pressed into service eased the situation to some degree. Thus it came about that the critical supply position was greatly responsible for Rommel's decision to withdraw from the Gazala position.

The decision to withdraw into the Marsa el Bregha position placed a particularly difficult task before the supply authorities of the *Panzergruppe*. On the one hand, the formations of the *Afrika Korps* had to be kept fully supplied during the withdrawal. This was most difficult, as the German *Panzer* divisions were withdrawing in the south of Cyrenaica, whereas all the supply depots were situated on the Via Balbia in the northern part of Cyrenaica. As the Iuartermaster-General did not learn of the intended withdrawal until the evening of 15 December, it was too late to organize this supply problem on uniform lines. Thus, it came about that parts of the *Afrika Korps* and the entire Italian *Motorized Corps* were immobilized for some considerable time south of Cyrenaica because of lack of fuel.

The main problem facing the Quartermaster-General was the evacuation of the supply installations in the western part of Cyrenaica, particularly around Benghazi, and the transport of the supply goods involved behind the Marsa el Bregha position in the very short time at his disposal. This was quite impossible with the little loading space, of which part had to be detached for transporting the Italian infantry divisions. The evacuation of the supply basis of Benghazi alone would have required more than three weeks, whereas there was only week to do it in. The Quartermaster-General decided to move the bulk of his depots into the area around Arco dei Fileni and En Nofilia, and some of the supplies to the area of Agedabia. In order to be able to make use of the important port of Benghazi for as long as possible, and so as to gain time to redirect supplies arriving by sea to land at Tripoli, Benghazi was to be held as long as possible. This was the more important as a convoy was expected in Benghazi, and actually arrived on 17 December, and also because the numerous wounded around Benghazi were to be evacuated in a hospital ship.

In the face of this situation, the Quartermaster-General drew up a priority list for the evacuation of this supply basis. The most valuable supplies – fuel and ammunition – were to be moved away. Rations and clothing were to be given to the German-Italian troops passing through. What remained was to be destroyed or made unusable. As it would have taken too much time and too much manpower to blow up the huge quantities of ammunition not in short supply, it was decided to unscrew the fuses, which served the same purpose.

The operation was rendered very difficult by the fact that German fighting troops were available for a very short period to cover it. As all the roads were completely jammed by Italian divisions passing through, it had become extremely difficult to move the goods by motor vehicles. The Arab population was not reliable. They began looting the depots. Shooting started in the streets. When the Quartermaster-General and his staff left early on 24 December, as the last German troops were leaving and the British were already entering the place, the most essential supply goods had been salvaged and nothing had been left behind which the enemy might have found useful. The supplying of the German troops during the long withdrawal into the Marsa el Bregha position was carried out according to plan. When the first two ship convoys arrived in Benghazi and Tripoli, the supply position became much easier. The fuel the convoys had brought restored to a certain extent the mobility of the *Panzergruppe*. The equipment for the two tank companies represented a considerable increase in the fighting power of the the *Afrika Korps*. At the beginning of January, another large convoy, again escorted by Italian battleships, arrived in Tripoli. The supply position then became quite normal. The fuel position was now such as to permit large-scale moves by the *Panzergruppe*. Ammunition and food were not plentiful owing to the losses suffered at Benghazi, but would be sufficient for the fighting that would follow. The equipment position was not yet uniformly satisfactory. Although the tank strength of the *Afrika Korps* had risen to 120, the vehicle position was still very unsatisfactory. The rifle formations of the *Panzergruppe* were of limited mobility, whilst the mobility of the artillery and antitank units was greatly reduced.

We have seen that Rommel's decision to withdraw from the Gazala position was chiefly brought about by the realization that the fighting power of the German-Italian troops was dwindling and by the seriousness of the supply position. It would have been fatal to engage in a decisive battle around the Gazala position with the superior enemy, unless the supply routes across the sea were reopened. It was Rommel's intention to gain time by means of this withdrawal and to avoid a decisive battle until the Commander-in-Chief South had succeeded in reopening the sea communications across the Mediterranean. The important thing to do was to accumulate enough supplies to restore the operational freedom of the *Panzergruppe*, and to make the German-Italian troops once more fighting fit by supplying them with fresh personnel and fighting units. At the same time, Rommel hoped that the British, when following and moving to Agedabia, would have to use strong forces to protect their lengthening lines of communications, which would leave them weaker on the front. Thus, he hoped to be able to balance his strength with that of the enemy by this withdrawal – at least to a certain extent.

As, in the middle of December, General Rommel was not yet able to foresee when supplies by sea would start coming in smoothly again, he fixed the Marsa el Bregha line as the final goal of the withdrawal. There, a rapid envelopment of his forces by the British pursuing forces seemed to be impossible. Before attacking this position, the British would first have to concentrate their forces.

The withdrawal would place the *Panzergruppe* in a serious position in any case. General Rommel had correctly foreseen that, mainly during the first days of the withdrawal, until the south-west of Cyrenaica was reached, there would be a great danger that the British pursuing columns might reach and occupy the area around Agedabia before the *Panzergruppe*. It was also possible that the British, by means of a frontal attack along the Via Balbia, would rapidly overrun the Italian formations. This might lead to grave losses – even to the complete disintegration of some of the Italian formations. Finally, it had to be accepted as inevitable that hardly any of the supplies accumulated in western Cyrenaica could be salvaged.

Thus, the speed of the *Panzergruppe* was of paramount importance: it was particularly important that the *Afrika Korps* arrive in time in the Agedabia area to be able to halt the enemy pursuit bent on overtaking the withdrawing formations. Rommel won the race of the mobile formations, and on 23 December inflicted a heavy defeat of the enemy pursuing forces. Thus, the German-Italian formation reached the Agedabia area without suffering serious damage to their fighting power.

In the Agedabia position, Rommel planned to do more than fight for time. This was to allow the Italian formations time to settle in the Marsa el Bregha position. This aim was attained in full; in addition, a tactical success of considerable importance was achieved. The British *7th Armored Division* was almost completely smashed. Moreover, this battle furnished proof that the fighting power of the British formations was also considerably impaired.

Nonetheless, General Rommel insisted on the continuity of the withdrawal to the Marsa el Bregha position, because he regarded it as possible that the British would move further forces from the Marmarica to the Agedabia area. He also deemed it necessary to gain more time until the supply route by sea could again function smoothly. In any case, the successful battles south of Agedabia brought it about that the further withdrawal behind the Marsa el Bregha position was almost undisturbed by the enemy. By 10 January, the *Panzergruppe* had arrive in the Marsa el Bregha positions with all its components. The bulk of the mobile forces stood ready for action behind the front, and an envelopment by the enemy seemed unlikely. The improvement of the supply position meant increased mobility for the *Panzergruppe*.

The improvement in the situation in the air meant a further easing off of the general situation. The decisive factor was the change brought about by the energetic handling of the situation by the Commander-in-Chief South in the battle for the sea communications as from the middle of December. The arrival of the first two ship convoys in the middle of December and the gradual reopening of the supply traffic were an extraordinary relief for the *Panzergruppe*. The fuel position, most critical until then, eased off visibly. As the nucleus of the formations of the *Afrika Korps* had been preserved, the arrival of a few *Panzer* companies meant a comparatively large increase in its fighting power.

That the morale of the Italian formations suffered so little during the withdrawal is due to the operations being carried through according to plan and under the skillful leadership of the *Panzergruppe*. The rest period they were granted and the arrival of reinforcements in the beginning of January had a favorable influence on the fighting spirit of the Italian formations.

In any case, the withdrawal of the *Panzergruppe* represented a completely successful operation. What General Rommel had aimed to achieve through withdrawal was achieved in full, and the ratio in strength had been corrected in his favor against a superior enemy. The brave resistance on the Sollum front had contributed a great deal to this success.

The leadership of the *Panzergruppe* and the German and Italian troops have every right to be proud of these successful withdrawal operations.

CHAPTER 7

The German Counteroffensive for the Reconquest of Cyrenaica, January–February 1942

On 11 January 1942, the formations of the *Panzergruppe* had arrived in the Marsa el Bregha position. The difficult withdrawal had been successful, without disproportionate losses being suffered. In the fighting around Agedabia at the end of December, the pursuing enemy had been shaken off, and a breathing space had been gained for the German-Italian formations. At long last the supply transport had begun to function smoothly, and the ammunition and fuel position was improving noticeably. The arrival of equipment for four *Panzer* companies meant a considerable improvement of the fighting power of the German *Panzer* formations. The formations of *Luftflotte 2* had also arrived.

Nonetheless, the command of the *Panzergruppe* still regarded its situation as serious. Even if it could be taken for granted that *Panzergruppe Afrika* could not possibly be outflanked in its present positions, its strength was hardly sufficient to main the position satisfactorily in its whole extension. It was mainly the Italian formations that had become very weak. But the strength in fighting men, and in particular the transport situation of the German formations, had also become very unsatisfactory.

This was brought home to General Rommel with absolute clarity when, on 12 January, accompanied by the Deputy Chief of the General Staff of *Panzergruppe Afrika* he flew over the front line of the Marsa el Bregha positions. Widely dispersed and with intervals too large to be properly kept under control, the strongpoints of the Italian divisions were distributed over the entire length of the position. There was nothing like a coherent manning of the position. Accordingly, it was hardly to be expected that a serious British attack would find any resistance worthy of the name.

Immediately after this flight over the front, a discussion on the situation took place at the *Panzergruppe* on 12 January. During this discussion, the Ic gave the following appreciation of the enemy situation:

The British Eighth Army was still far stretched out in depth. So far, it appeared that only the British *7th Armored Division* had approached the

German-Italian positions. The British *1st Armored Division* was supposed to be behind in the area north-east of Agedabia. The *4th Indian Division*, with strong elements, was evidently still around Benghazi, with elements advanced as far as the area of Agedabia. The *1st South African Division* was supposed to be in the area of Msus, the *2nd New Zealand Division* was evidently still in Cyrenaica, and the *70th Infantry Division* seemed to have remained in the Tobruk area.

This did not point to a strong British attack in the immediate future. The calculation of timing made by the Ic rather showed that, on the front, the German-Italian troops would enjoy a small superiority until 25 January; thereafter, until the end of the month, the forces would be more or less equal in strength. From that moment onwards the British superiority was bound to increase. But, on the other hand, the British even now had forces on the front strong enough to make powerful attacks. Considering the weakness of the garrison manning the positions, it had to be expected that in such a case parts of the position would be broken out. Such local attacks appeared to be threatening, chiefly in the area north of the Wadi el Faregh. In this section, the *15th Panzer Division* had to be moved immediately behind the front, and elements of the division had even to occupy some sectors of the front.

It seemed too dangerous to remain on the defensive and to wait for the enemy to attack. It was most likely that the enemy would attack in great strength and with vastly superior material. It was more than doubtful whether by that time the Italian divisions would be equal to the requirements of a heavy defensive battle.

For this reason Colonel (i.G.) Westphal proposed to take advantage of the present weakness of the British on the front, and of the fact that their forces were split up and widely dispersed all over Cyrenaica, and attack the enemy before he had completed the preparations for his attack, and to smash the enemy forces in the Agedabia area. At that juncture, he did not think of a further advance to the north-east or the north, or of a reconquest of Cyrenaica, as he regarded the forces available not strong enough, nor the supply position favorable enough, for such a far-flung operation.

At first, General Rommel was surprised at this suggestion and had grave doubts as to how it could be carried out, particularly with regard to the transport position. However, after a careful study of the overall position, he familiarized himself with the plan, and on 13 January he finally decided for the counterattack. Now he threw his wholehearted enthusiasm and all his energy into the plan, and his hopes rose far beyond what his Chief of Staff had dreamed of, for such was his nature. He did agree with him that the plan could only succeed if the attack came as a complete surprise to the enemy. He therefore regarded complete secrecy of the preparations for the attack as most important, not only with regard to the troops, but even to the German and Italian Supreme Commands. It was decided not to report the intention to attack to those above until immediately before the start of the attack. After the event, it is difficult to ascertain whether this decision was partly dictated by the fear that the *Comando Supremo* or the *OKW* might forbid the attack at the last moment.

Planning and Preparations for the Attack

General Rommel's first aim for the attack was the destruction of the enemy forces in front of the Marsa el Bregha position. For the time being, there was no need to deal with the enemy in front of the southern sector of the position, as only a few enemy reconnaissance units had been active south of the Wadi el Faregh and near Marada.

Rommel assumed that the bulk of the *7th Armored Division* and 2,000 vehicles would be near the front. How he came to this assumption is not clear. So far, air reconnaissance had sighted only a few hundred vehicles on the front, and ground reconnaissance up until 14 January had found nothing on the front sector bar reconnaissance troops reinforced by tanks and artillery.

Accordingly, Rommel wanted one assault group to advance to the north of the Wadi el Faregh and another one along the Via Balbia to the north-west, in order to surround the enemy in front of the northern sector or, if he were to escape the blow by rapid withdrawal, to inflict defeat on him by means of pursuit and battle. For this purpose, the *Afrika Korps* was to be concentrated as the southern assault group north of the Wadi el Faregh. The northern assault group was to consist of *Group Marx*, elements of the *90th Light Division* and the Italian *Motorized Corps*. There *Group Marx* – mobile elements of the *90th Light Division* reinforced by tanks of the *21st Panzer Division* – was to form the striking wedge. The Italian *XXI Corps* and the Italian *Motorized Corps* were to engage the enemy frontally and follow him frontally immediately behind.

Preparations for the attack were favored by the fact that, as from 14 January, the position on the front calmed down considerably. The enemy group which had advanced north of the Wadi el Faregh had bumped elements of the *15th Panzer Division* and withdrawn to the north-east as early as 14 January. Along the Via Balbia, the enemy limited his activity to occasional shelling. His most forward patrols were about 5 kilometers from the front.

The necessary regrouping was carried out in short night marches. The elements the *90th Light Division* in Marada were moved behind the north wing, whilst *Group Marx* was concentrated on the Via Balbia. Strict enforcement of camouflage was ordered, to make the enemy believe that nothing more than defensive actions were planned. All reconnaissance by German troops, particularly with tanks, was forbidden; the tanks behind the front were camouflaged as lorries. All traffic to the front with motor vehicles had to move by night.

Not until 16 January was the commanding general of the *Afrika Korps* informed in the strictest confidence. The commanders of the divisions were allotted their tasks verbally on 19 January. The attack was fixed for 0830 hours on 21 January. Misgivings aired on account of the state of the motor vehicles and on account of the shortage of artillery, which would not allow movements on a larger scale, were dispelled by remarks that, undoubtedly, during the attack so many enemy vehicles would be captured that full mobility would be restored. On 20 January the orders for the attack were issued, and simultaneously the Italian *Comando Supremo* and the *OKW* were informed of the intention to attack. Almost simultaneously with the beginning of the attack, the *Panzergruppe* was renamed *Panzerarmee Afrika*.

The Battle in the Area of Agedabia, 21–26 January

In order to deceive the enemy until the very last moment about the planned attack, and to create in him the impression of the beginning of a withdrawal, particularly elaborate measures to deceive him were taken during the night before the attack and in the morning of 21 January. The village of Marsa el Bregha and a freighter lying stranded outside the harbor were set on fire in order to create the impression that supply dumps were being destroyed. Simultaneously, at dawn all the vehicles which were not battleworthy were moved to the rear. Owing to bad visibility, however, the enemy seemed not to have noticed this maneuver.

The attack started at 0830 hours on 21 January along the entire front. The southern assault group – the *Afrika Korps* – advanced with the *15th Panzer Division* on the right along the Wadi el Faregh, with the *21st Panzer Division* echeloned to the left. To begin with, the attack advanced well to the east, with the going being good. The enemy covering patrols withdrew eastward, offering no resistance. But north-west of Bir Bettafal the leading troops arrived at sand dunes difficult to negotiate, and further east extensive sand fields were encountered. Tracked vehicles gained ground very slowly. All the wheeled vehicles got stuck in the sand and every single one had to be pulled out by tractors. An enemy reconnaissance detachment to the south of the Wadi el Faregh and withdrawing eastward caused considerable embarrassment by shelling, which did not stop until an energetic advance carried out with dash by *Antitank Battalion 33* across the Wadi el Faregh to the south silenced its guns. Towards 1000 hours the armored spearhead also encountered its first resistance, offered by several batteries and a few tanks. It was quickly done away with. The enemy left numerous motor vehicles and guns which had got stuck in the sand in our hands. Without waiting for the wheeled vehicles, the leading troops of the two *Panzer* divisions turned off to the north-east, and at 1430 hours reached the area of Mn. el Gefera. The bulk of the two divisions were still far behind, stuck in the sand, and there was no means of telling when they would be able to get across the sand dunes. The embarrassing fact was that the supply columns of both the *Panzer* regiments were also lagging far behind, so the fuel position soon became rather difficult.

Nonetheless, during the afternoon the *Afrika Korps* ordered the continuation of the advance northward towards Bir Bilal, to close the ring behind the enemy in front of the northern sector of the position. Bir Bilal was reached towards 1700 hours, but now the two *Panzer* regiments were immobilized without a drop of fuel in their tanks. Lesser elements of the *Schützen* regiments, which in the meantime had come up, were sent to the west to Bir el Ginn, but they had to report that the enemy had escaped from the pincer. On the other hand, there was still a weaker enemy group to the east of Bir Bilal which kept the two divisions under shell fire. Other enemy elements appeared to have withdrawn to the east along the Wadi el Faregh.

The *Northern Assault Group – Group Marx*, with tanks of the *Italian Motorized Corps*, and with the nonmotorized elements of the *90th Light Division* behind – had attacked at 0830 hours along the Via Balbia according to the plan. The weak enemy covering forces withdrew rapidly eastward, but delayed the attack with artillery fire. Swamps on both sides of the road, difficult to negotiate, allowed only slow progress in the attack. En Nogra was not reached until 1430 hours; there, the group adopted defensive tactics so as to allow the *Afrika Korps*, from which no information had been received, to close the eastern section of the ring around the enemy south of the Via Balbia. During the noon hours, however, *Group Marx* observed several enemy columns withdrawing from the Bir el Ginn area to the north and shelling the traffic on the Via Balbia. In several pushes to the south, the group was indeed able to capture a considerable number of enemy vehicles, but not prevent the enemy from withdrawing.

Appreciation of the Situation by the *Panzerarmee*

Until the evening of 21 January, General Rommel did not realize that the enemy on the front was considerably weaker than he had assumed before the attack. There had been no message from the *Afrika Korps* for a long time; thus, Rommel did not learn until the evening that the bulk of the corps had got stuck in the sand, and that it had not been possible to ring in the enemy before the front. From air reconnaissance and wireless intercepts, Rommel gained the impression that the enemy, who had withdrawn from the attack in a north-eastern direction, had joined up with the stronger enemy forces in the area east and south-east of Agedabia. Nothing more than weaker enemy groups seemed still to be around El Gdabia and B. el Tombia. To the east of Agedabia there appeared to be the bulk of the British *1st Armored Division* and perhaps elements of the *7th Armored Division*. Evidently, the attack had taken the enemy completely by surprise, and so far there was no reaction from him.

General Rommel realized that he could destroy this enemy only if strong forces moving by way of Agedabia reached the Antelat–Saunnu area at an early stage, and if they blocked the enemy's line of withdrawal to the north and north-east. He decided to place the *Schwerpunkt* on the left wing and to advance with all available forces along the Via Balbia via Agedabia to the north-east, where there seemed to be only weaker enemy forces and where the terrain was favorable for a rapid advance.

The necessary instructions were given during the night of 21/22 January. *Group Marx* was to advance before first light towards Agedabia; the *Afrika Korps* and the Italian *Motorized Corps* were to follow behind, moving to the north towards the Via Balbia, and, behind *Group Marx*, they were to move on 22 January over Agedabia to Saunnu. The *90th Light Division* was to reach the area north of Agedabia, there to take over the covering off to the north.

Events on 22 January

At 0530 hours on 22 January, *Group Marx* advanced along the Via Balbia to the attack. The enemy offered only slight resistance on the road. But bad going and mines laid by the Germans during December 1941 near the road, and only partially lifted by the enemy, delayed the attack.

Reconnaissance forces of *Group Marx* had found out early that the town of Agedabia was only weakly occupied. The British had lifted the mines on the Via Balbia south-west of Agedabia laid during the German withdrawal; but the minebelt around the town had remained unchanged.

In fact, the attack of *Group Marx* on Agedabia found but little resistance. The enemy tried to delay the attack by artillery fire from the area east of the Via Balbia. There were also a few casualties through mines. Towards 1100 hours the town had been recaptured.

General Rommel, who had traveled at the head, gave immediate orders to start the pursuit. He had the impression that the bulk of the enemy was still waiting in the area east of Agedabia. Now he began to visualize a plan to surround this enemy group of forces and destroy them. He brushed aside the objections of his chief of staff that it was doubtful whether the enemy would stay put long enough to allow the ring to be closed, and whether the weak German forces would be sufficient for this task.

Thus, at 1200 hours, *Group Marx* received the order to continue the advance forthwith, and to move to Antelat and from there to Saunnu. The enemy was taken completely by surprise when *Group Marx* suddenly appeared north-east of Agedabia. The supply columns of the enemy fled in all directions. A considerable number of motor vehicles were captured, and no resistance was encountered. Antelat was taken as early as 1530 hours. Without stopping, and disregarding the oncoming night, *Group Marx* moved on to Saunnu. The place fell into German hands after a short fight at 1930 hours. The enemy appeared to surround the whole area, but darkness made it impossible to clarify his position. Meanwhile, further German and Italian troops were approaching. As soon as the German and Italian troops coming up out of the desert arrived at and south of it, General Rommel sent them forward on the Via Balbia. This naturally resulted in a considerable mix-up of the formations, and during the evening of 22 January in traffic jams in the mined Agedabia. During the morning of 22 January the *Afrika Korps*, which represented the main hitting power of the *Panzerarmee*, delayed by heavy going and fuel shortages, had still be in the sandy area north-west and south-east of Bir Bilal. In obedience to the order of the *Panzerarmee*, the *Afrika Korps*, at 2 o'clock on 22 January, ordered its divisions to move to the north on to the Via Balbia forthwith, and to follow *Group Marx* on to Agedabia. But for both the divisions the execution of this order proved impossible for the time being, as most of their fuel supply vehicles were still stuck in the sandy area north of Bir Bettafal and to the west of Gefara. Nevertheless, the *15th Panzer Division* at 0730 hours ordered *Machine Gun Battalion 2*, as its most forward battle group, to move off, with all the fuel supplies of the entire division. At

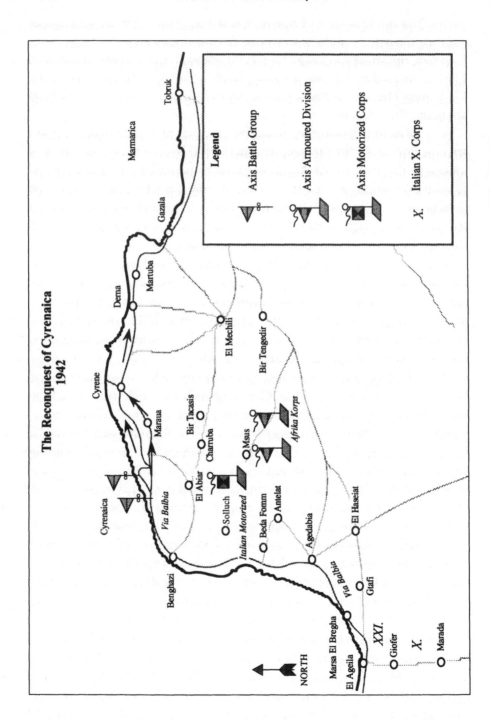

1200 hours, this battalion reached the Via Balbia at Ergh el Tereb and passed through Agedabia early in the afternoon. From there it was ordered on to Antelat by Rommel personally, with the instruction to cover the place on all sides against enemy attacks, but particularly against those coming from the north. At 2000 hours, the battalion reached its objective without meeting any resistance.

During the morning the *21st Panzer Division* was able to move up its supply columns from the Via Balbia. Towards 1100 hours, it moved off in a northerly direction, leaving behind strong elements of its artillery and rifle units. Passing through Agedabia during the evening, it was put on the track to Antelat by Rommel, with the instruction to close the ring around the enemy forces at Saunnu, with its left wing fronting south along the track running 15 kilometers south of Antelat to the east.

At 1430 hours, the *15th Panzer Division* dispatched the formations which had arrived in the meantime – *viz.* the reinforced *Panzer Regiment 8* less the bulk of the supply troops, the artillery regiment less one battalion, and lesser parts of *Schützen Regiment 115,* of the antitank troops and of the engineers – as *Group Cramer.* The remainder was to be collected under the command of the *15th Schützen Brigade* and to move up as soon as possible. Delayed by traffic jams, *Group Cramer* arrived at Agedabia at 2400 hours, and in the early morning hours reached the road fork 20 kilometers south-west of Antelat. Along the track to Saunnu, the division, with the left wing loosely joining *21st Panzer Division*, and with the right at the road fork, established two strongpoints for the defense to the south.

The *90th Light Division* had been moved by the evening with strong elements into the area north of Agedabia, making use of the little motor transport it had. The division took over the covering to the north on both sides of the Via Balbia. For the time being there was no contact with the enemy.

The Italian *Motorized Corps*, with its foremost elements, also reached Agedabia during the evening. It was placed by General Rommel 20 kilometers east of the town and along the track to Antelat, to close the ring to the west and to cover off to the north with some of its units.

The Tank Battles in the Area of Saunnu, 23–24 January

The troops of the *Panzerarmee* continued their moves during the whole of the night of 22/23 January. With weak forces, and making use of the element of surprise, they had pushed right into the middle of far superior enemy forces. Thus, in the morning 23 January the following situation had arisen:

Group Marx stood at Saunnu surrounded by a strong enemy. Nonetheless, during the night Rommel ordered it to advance before first light to the south-east towards El Grara, in order to close the ring in the east. The arrival of the leading elements of the *Afrika Korps (21st Panzer Division)* was not awaited, nor was the surrounding area of Saunnu cleared of the enemy, which was soon to have grave consequences.

The *Afrika Korps* was busy moving into a line of strongpoints 40 kilometers long running along the track to Saunnu. This line could only be manned with large gaps left open, as strong parts of the divisions had not yet arrived. At dawn, the *21st Panzer Division* was busy establishing two strongpoints. *Panzer Regiment 5*, with one battery and two antitank compa-nies, occupied Height Gseir el Amami; the remaining units of the division – *Machine Gun Battalion 8* and *II./Schützen Regiment 104*, with two batteries and one antitank company – stood 6 kilometers to the west thereof. During the morning, the *15th Panzer Division* to the west thereof settled down in several strongpoints, with the right wing on the track fork preparing for the defense to the south.

The covering lines of the Italian *Motorized Corps* and of the *90th Light Division* were also in the course of construction. *Reconnaissance Battalion 33* had been dispatched in the direction of Benghazi for reconnaissance. *Machine Gun Battalion 2* had enemy contact in Antelat and at dawn began to clarify the position in this area by pushes to the north and east.

During the morning, whilst only weak enemy forces were feeling forward from the south against the *15th Panzer Division*, the *21st Panzer Division* was involved in heavy fighting from dawn onwards. As early as 0730, superior enemy armor coming from the south-west attacked the two strongpoints of the division. Heavy fighting ensued, but the division succeeded in holding its positions, and by the afternoon had knocked out 45 enemy tanks. But the division was unable to prevent strong enemy forces from escaping past its positions to the north-east, particularly by way of Saunnu, which had been reoccupied by the enemy in the morning. Further strong enemy armor broke through between the two strongpoints of the division, as the weak artillery was kept busy in defensive action and was, therefore, unable to cover the gap.

Of these actions, and the course they took, Rommel had received no information for reasons unknown. He apparently assumed that, on 23 January, the enemy would stay put in the area east of Agedabia. He did not realize that the enemy was about to break out from the "bag" to the north-east. Soon after daybreak, he issued a wireless instruction for the *21st Panzer*

Division to continue its move to the east, to take over the sector so far held by *Group Marx* between Saunnu and Grara, and to close the ring around the enemy in the east.

Reconnaissance patrols of the *21st Panzer Division* had found out during the morning that in Saunnu there was no *Group Marx* but instead a strong enemy. The division had its hands full warding off the strong attacks by the enemy. There was no possibility of obeying the order of the *Panzerarmee*. By morning, the division had already requested that the *Afrika Korps* have the *15th Panzer Division* attacking to the east to ease the situation of the *21st Panzer Division*. But this attack did not come off. When, during the afternoon, the enemy attack seemed to ease, the division moved its *Panzer* regiment eastward towards Saunnu. At dusk, heavy fighting flared up again around Saunnu. When night fell the place was taken, 20 tanks were knocked out, two batteries were overrun and a large number of motor vehicles were captured in addition to an armor repair shop with 40 unserviceable tanks. During the night the division took up a hedgehog position to the south of Saunnu.

The commanding general of the *Afrika Korps* had established his battle headquarters on the extreme west wing of his corps. It appears that he did not appreciate the difficult position of the *21st Panzer Division*, and he may not have accorded its message the necessary weight. Thus, he allowed the *15th Panzer Division* to remain in its positions until the afternoon. This division, well informed about the position of the *21st Panzer Division* by its own reconnaissance patrols and by direct messages received from its neighbor, had, at noon, asked permission from the *Afrika Korps* for this attack to the east. The *Afrika Korps*, however, did not see its way clear to allow the attack, mainly because of a report from the air that a strong enemy force – evidently the *4th Indian Division* – was advancing from Beda Fomm to the south.

Not until 1500 hours did the *Afrika Korps* order the *15th Panzer Division* to take over the *21st Panzer Division's* sector, with the left wing at Saunnu. For this purpose, the *15th Panzer Division* left the weak elements of the *15th Schützen Brigade*, which had arrived in the meantime in its present position. It moved *Panzer Regiment 8* and the bulk of the artillery, together with two rifle companies in assault formation, in the sector so far held by the *21st Panzer Division*. Strong enemy columns were known to be advancing to the north. As early as 1500 hours, it got involved in fighting with enemy armor of like strength. The enemy was dispersed and withdrew to the north-east and the south-east. In order to intercept the enemy which had broken through, the division ordered *Machine Gun Battalion 2* to advance from Antelat to the south-east. This order was canceled by the *Afrika Korps; Machine Gun Battalion 2* was placed under direct command of the *Afrika Korps*. When night fell, direct contact had been established with the *21st Panzer Division*, which was still involved in fighting east of Saunnu. Thirty-seven tanks, 14 guns, 250 prisoners and numerous other items of booty were the result of the fighting. At nightfall the division, on instruction from the corps, reoccupied its strongpoints along the track leading from the west to Saunnu. *Group Marx*, not realizing in the dark how strong the enemy was around Saunnu, had marched right through the enemy supply columns to the south before dawn and had reached Uhr el Grara at 1430 hours on the same day. There, after a short fight with enemy columns, it took up defensive positions west and south of Grara.

In the sector of the Italian *Motorized Corps* on the west front of the "bag", there was no serious fighting during 23 January. Nor were the covering patrols of the *90th Light Division* north of Agedabia attacked. The enemy, which had been reported as advancing from Beda Fomm to the south, surprisingly discontinued his move during the afternoon. *Machine Gun Battalion 2* carried out several pushes to the west and the south from Antelat. It captured the British airfield at Antelat, destroying six enemy aircraft on the ground and shooting down three more. During the evening it succeeded in repulsing lesser enemy pushes from the west.

Events on 24 January

During 23 January General Rommel spent most of his time with the staff of the *Afrika Korps*. Until the evening he had the impression that, on the whole, the attempts of the enemy to break out of the "bag" had been successfully repulsed. He therefore assumed that the main forces of the enemy were still in the "bag" south-west of Saunnu, and he hoped to destroy them on 24 January in a concentrated attack. On 24 January, at 0000 hours, he gave orders to the *Afrika Korps* to have *Group Marx* at El Grara relieved as soon as possible by the *21st Panzer Division*, and to keep the group ready for a further advance towards the west. The *15th Panzer Division* was to attack from the north and the Italian *Motorized Corps* from the west in the direction of the "bag" and to destroy the forces assumed to be in it. During the night and in the early morning on 24 January, smaller groups of enemy armor and of supply vehicles attempted to break out in the sector of the *15th Panzer Division*, 20 kilometers west of Saunnu ,and in the sector of the *21st Panzer Division* south of Saunnu, but were repulsed.

The concentrated attack began at 0730 hours. However, only small-scale fighting with stragglers which had remained behind ensued. On the other hand, a large booty of motor vehicles and tanks which had become stuck in the sand fell into German hands. At 1400 hours, the foremost elements of the *15th Panzer Division* reached El Grara and linked up with *Group Marx* and the Italian *Motorized Corps*. Thereupon the division discontinued the attack, and in the evening returned to the area west of Saunnu. At 1300 hours, the *21st Panzer Division* relieved *Group Marx* at El Grara. The latter then moved to the west as far as El Haseit without meeting the enemy, and during the evening was recalled to Agedabia by *Panzerarmee*.

On 24 January, *Machine Gun Battalion 2* was attacked by considerable enemy forces, probably parts of the enemy which had broken out of the "bag", and was now trying to break through to the north-east by way of Antelat. However, *Machine Gun Battalion 2* was able to hold its positions, and during the evening to repulse the attacks made by Indian troops from the area of Beda Fomm.

The Advance of the *Afrika Korps* to Msus on 25 January

During 24 January, General Rommel had to acknowledge that the enemy had escaped the encirclement and that the "bag" so carefully laid out was empty. Ground and air reconnaissance, however, showed on 24 January that strong enemy forces – 150 tanks, about 2,000 vehicles and numerous supply dumps – still remained in the Antelat–Saunnu–Msus area. Apparently this was the enemy on which the *Afrika Korps* had inflicted heavy losses during 23 January.

General Rommel decided therefore in the evening of 24 January to move the *Afrika Korps* to Msus in pursuit during 25 January and to complete the defeat of the enemy. For this purpose, the *21st Panzer Division* was to advance from Saunnu to Bir el Melezz, the *15th Panzer Division* to the left from the area west of Saunnu to Msus and *Machine Gun Battalion 2* from Antelat to Msus. The Italian *Motorized Corps* and the *90th Light Division* were to cover off against the enemy still in the area south of Benghazi.

The *21st Panzer Division*, in its attack, met only weak enemy columns. Bir el Melezz was reached towards the evening, after light skirmishing with weak dispersed enemy forces which wanted to withdraw to the east before the attack of the *15th Panzer Division*.

On the other hand, the attack of the *15th Panzer Division* landed it in the very middle of a far superior enemy. At 0745 hours, 10 kilometers north-west of Saunnu, 30 enemy tanks, supported by artillery, opposed the attack by the division. Simultaneously, to the west and the east of the sector covered by the division's attack, numerous enemy columns with many hundreds of motor vehicles tried to escape the pursuit in rapid flight to the north-east. In a few minutes the enemy was bowled over by an attack by *Panzer Regiment 8*, supported by artillery. The armored units of the enemy seemed to have little battle experience and were evidently demoralized by the failure of the previous days. Soon the enemy withdrew to the north almost in panic.

At this juncture, the division continued the pursuit to the north on a broad front and at top speed, attaining at times a speed of 25 kilometers per hour on this desert terrain, which was as smooth as a board. Endless enemy columns – apparently the bulk of the British *1st Armored Division* and of the *1st South African Division* – traveled to the right and left of the division in the same direction, trying to overtake it. Other parts of the enemy coming, from the west, tried to break away to the east behind the division, which could not always be prevented due to the weakness of the rifle battalions following the attack. The booty of this pursuit increased rapidly. Wherever the enemy tried to make a stand, he was thrown back at once. During all this, the division hardly suffered any losses at all.

At 1100 hours, after a pursuit covering 80 kilometers, strong enemy supply columns at the Msus airfield were taken completely by surprise and mostly destroyed. The airfield was captured by *Panzer Regiment 8* and twelve aircraft ready to take off were captured. At this juncture, the pursuit unfortunately had to be interrupted for a while to allow the *Panzer* regiment the necessary time to refuel. Meanwhile, the *Afrika Korps* ordered the division to turn off to the east towards Bir el Melezz immediately in order to attack the enemy in front of the *21st Panzer Division* in his rear. For this purpose, the *15th Schützen Brigade* was diverted in that direction. In order to exploit the big success in full, *Panzer Regiment 8*, after refueling, continued the pursuit to the north. During this operation, the battle headquarters of the British *1st Armored Division* was captured 10 kilometers north of Msus. However, the bulk of the British forces had escaped to the north. During the evening, the division reassembled at Bir el Melezz.

Although the divisions of the *Afrika Korps* were numerically too weak to exploit the success of the day fully, the British *XXX Corps* had been utterly defeated, and, in the evening of 25 January, was hardly fit for any active operation. On this day, the *15th Panzer Division* collected a particularly rich booty: 85 tanks, most of them undamaged, 45 guns, 190 motor lorries and 200 prisoners were counted.

Machine Gun Battalion 2 was also very successful during the day's fighting. Throwing back superior enemy forces to the north-east, it reached Msus at 1500 hours, immediately after the arrival of the bulk of the *15th Panzer Division.*

January 25 passed without fighting in the sector of the troops which were to cover the north of Agedabia. The *4th Indian Division* did not attack to relieve the pressure on the British armored formations, but withdrew into the Solluch–Ghemines area. During the night of 25/26 January, the British air force carried out attacks against the formations of the *Afrika Korps* in the Msus–Bir el Melezz area. On 26 January the *Afrika Korps* did not continue the pursuit. The defeated enemy armored formations continued their withdrawal to the north and north-east. The *Afrika Korps* limited its activities to cleaning up the battlefield. An enormous booty of motor vehicles of all kinds was collected and used to fill the gaps in the *Panzer* formations and to render the *90th Light Division* mobile. In the Msus area, large dumps of fuel, rations and ammunition were found, in addition to several armor repair shops.

The successful counterstroke of *Panzerarmee Afrika* represents one of those surprising turning points in which the African campaign abounds. It is one of the very rare examples when an army on the defense breaks out of its position to resume the offensive in order to smash the troops of a superior enemy about to concentrate for the attack.

The decision to launch a counteroffensive, which at first appeared so daring, was indeed the only one that could be made. The measures taken by the British certainly contributed considerably to the success achieved. It is difficult to understand why, during January, the British command split up its forces to such an extent, and why it neglected to take necessary defensive steps. General Rommel skillfully took advantage of these mistakes. He hit the British *Eighth Army* at the moment of its greatest weakness. British supplies were not yet arriving in sufficient quantities, because the port of Benghazi was not usable. Transport of supplies by land was not yet functioning smoothly, as the coast road had only become available a few days beforehand, after the Sollum positions had fallen.

At the beginning of the counteroffensive, Rommel once again proved himself a past master at concealing his intentions and of deceiving the enemy. Thus, the surprise sprung on the British command was a complete success, not only operationally but also tactically. This does not do away with the fact that the attack on 21 and 22 January against the British formations on the front did not produce the expected results, and actually proved to be a thrust into empty space. The enemy was indeed considerably weaker than Rommel had assumed. The very unfavorable terrain encountered in the sector of the attack by the *Afrika Korps* came as a surprise to the German command and precluded a rapid advance of the main effort on which the plan of attack had been based. Forgoing detailed patrolling and ground reconnaissance in favor of surprise proved to be a grave mistake.

Despite the failure of the first few days, the battle nevertheless ended very successfully. This is chiefly due to Rommel speedily altering his initial plan and his determination, and also by his throwing the *Schwerpunkt* on to the left wing. Undoubtedly, it was daring to throw the leading troops of the attacking German formations into the area of Antelat and Saunnu, as was done on 22 January, and thus to place them across the rearward lines of communication of the enemy armor. This was undoubtedly the extreme limit to which the weak German armored formations could be pushed. In doing so, General Rommel ran grave risks, but, on the other hand, it gave him a sure chance of inflicting a crushing defeat on the enemy armored units.

In the execution of the plan, however, things were definitely stretched too far. It was certainly not a very happy decision to disperse the few available troops along an investing line 120 kilometers in length. On 23 January it was once again proved that it is simply impossible to prevent armored formations in the desert from breaking through an insufficiently manned encircling front. The German-Italian troops were far too weak to keep the far-flung front under close observation, let alone to defend it, particularly since some of their number were still stuck in the desert south of Agedabia, and were thus not available for the fighting during 23 January. Half of the German-Italian formations had been placed on the east and the west front of the encircling ring, where an enemy break-out was least likely. It was much more likely that the enemy would try to escape the pincer by a rapid withdrawal to the north or the north-east, along the lines of his rearward communications.

In order to frustrate such an attempt, the bulk of the German formations had to stand by in the Saunnu area. The assumption that the British armored formations would remain east of Agedabia during 23 January until the noose was finally drawn tight around them was an underestimation of the British command. Thus the breakout attempt on 23 January in the sector of the *21st Panzer Division* could not possibly be called surprising. Credit for the fact that the breakout of the enemy on 23 January did not develop into a regrettable setback goes to the division of the *Afrika Korps*, in particular to the *21st Panzer Division*. This division defended its strongpoints against a largely superior force, and inflicted heavy losses on the enemy. Thus, the British armored formations actually succeeded in breaking out on 23 January in the battle of Saunnu, but at the cost of great quantities of material, and, as became apparent on 25 January, with their fighting morale badly shaken.

It is surprising that General Rommel had not realized on 23 January that the bulk of the enemy formations had broken out of the "bag," and that he wasted 24 January in cleaning up an empty "bag." Only the failing of the reporting system of the troops and of the ground and air reconnaissance can explain this mistake. Thus, valuable time was wasted and much good petrol was burnt in useless traveling about in the desert.

Not until 25 January was the *Panzerarmee* able to reap the fruit of its daring operation. Now the *Panzerarmee* was bent on ruthlessly pursuing the enemy to the north-east, and to inflict on the defeated British armored formations as much damage as possible. The credit for the smashing defeat the enemy suffered in this operation goes mainly to the general commanding the *15th Panzer Division*, Major-General von Vaerst, who bowled over the superior forces of the enemy with unequaled energy and admirable versatility. The magnitude of the success, which was shown in the large quantities of captured material, came as a surprise even to the leadership of the *Panzerarmee*. Part of the great success in the battle of 25 January is due to the limited power of resistance of the British *1st Armored Division*, which had not arrived on the African war theater until a short time before. It was proved that armored formations needed a period of acclimatization during which to adapt themselves to the unusual terrain and the fighting conditions prevalent on the African war theater.

The Advance to Benghazi and Pursuit
to the Gazala Position, 26 January–6 February

With the successful conclusion of the armored battle of Msus, General Rommel had achieved the claim which he had staked out for his counteroffensive. The preparations for the offensive by the enemy had been broken up, and the Agedabia area was again firmly in his hands. In addition, the armored forces – the *1st* and *7th Armored Divisions* – at the disposal of the British leadership in Africa had been heavily defeated, and would not be available for operations of any considerable size in the foreseeable future.

To exploit his great success by an advance of the mobile German-Italian forces – the *Afrika Korps* and Italian *Motorized Corps* – towards Mechili was an alluring thought for Rommel. It would enable him to complete the defeat of the beaten enemy by pursuing him and cutting off and destroying the enemy forces which were still in Cyrenaica. The enemy armored forces, after their heavy defeat, hardly seemed to be in a position to prevent such an advance.

But there were grave reasons against mounting this enticing operation, which was expected not only by the British command, but also by the German troops. The fuel supplies of the *Panzerarmee* were hardly sufficient for all the armored formations to reach the south-east edge of Cyrenaica. In the east part of Cyrenaica and in the Marmarica, the enemy still had several undefeated divisions, which would enable him to collect a force in Cyrenaica considerably superior to the German. In no circumstances would the fuel supplies of the *Panzerarmee* be sufficient for operations of a longer duration in this area. Rommel did not regard the Italian *Motorized Corps* as sufficient to carry out such an advance alone, although it still had enough fuel. Moreover, he might well have feared that an operation of that kind might again lead to an overtaxing of his strength, as had repeatedly happened in the course of the campaign. An important part was also played by the resistance which the Italian *Comando Supremo* and also the Commander-in-Chief South, Field Marshal von Kesselring, lent to such plans. The Italian *Comando Supremo*, as well as the *OKW*, had been completely surprised by the German-Italian counteroffensive. Thereupon, on 21 January, Colonel-General Cavallero, accompanied by Field Marshal von Kesselring, proceeded at once by air to the Libyan war theater. On 23 or 24 January, they arrived at the battle headquarters of the *Panzerarmee* near Agedabia.

Cavallero pronounced himself emphatically against any further advance beyond Agedabia and he even made an attempt to forbid a renewed advance to Benghazi. He based his refusal to coutenance the reoccupation of Cyrenaica on the same arguments which Rommel had advanced in justification of the withdrawal from the Gazala position, *viz.* that the *Panzerarmee* would be exposed to the threat of encirclement by the enemy, and that for this very reason it would not be possible to hold Cyrenaica. In order to emphasize his viewpoint, he took away from Rommel the right to dispose *X* and *XXI Italian Corps*, which Rommel had instructed to concentrate around El Agheila with a view to having them move up to Agedabia. Colonel-General Cavallero in turn ordered them to remain in the Marsa el Brega position as support for the *Panzerarmee*. General Rommel refused to accept this limitation of his freedom of action and pointed out that he had to act according to the requirements of the situation.

All these reasons resulted in Rommel's decision to proceed step by step in the further course of the operations. The Benghazi area offered itself as the nearest operational objective. Apparently there were still strong elements of the *4th Indian Division*, perhaps reinforced by a brigade of the *1st South African Division*. According to reports from air and wireless reconnaissance, British forces were still holding Er Reghima, Solluch, and Ghemines. There was at least one British brigade around Benghazi, but movements observed on the road from Benghazi to Derna made it seem likely that the withdrawal of the enemy from the area of Benghazi was either imminent or had started already. In any case, General Rommel hoped to be able to come to grips with at least some of the enemy forces if he acted immediately. Moreover, he regarded a speedy occupation of Benghazi as important, as the harbor of this place was important for supply purposes. Its speedy recapture was bound to heighten German-Italian prestige.

Rommel regarded a frontal attack from the south towards Benghazi as not very effective. Only by an encirclement from the east would it be possible to cut off considerable parts of the enemy. However, particularly difficult mountainous and sandy terrain would make such maneuvers extremely hard to carry out. After the experience of the first day of the battle, he did not deem it advisable to take the *Afrika Korps* forward through this terrain. He therefore decided to use only small but highly mobile units for this operation; his choice fell on *Group Marx*, which had proved its mettle during the fighting of the previous days; for this operation the *Group* was allotted captured vehicles to make it fully mobile, and was reinforced by elements of the *21st Panzer Division* and by *Reconnaissance Units 3* and *33*.

Rommel intended to take the *Group* in a daring night march to Er Reghima east of Benghazi, to arrive there during the morning of 28 January and to fall on Benghazi from the east and take it in a *coup de main*. The *90th Light Division* and elements of the Italian *Motorized Corps* were to advance from the south towards Solluch and Ghemines, engaging the enemy and diverting his attention from the planned encircling move. The advance by strong elements of the *Afrika Korps* from Bir el Melezz to the east was to create the impression that an attack on El Mechili was about to be launched. For the rest, the *Afrika Korps* was to remain in the Msus area and to cover the area to the east and north-east. Nominally, the command of the operation was given to Colonel Marx; in reality, it was in the hands of General Rommel himself, who accompanied the advance in person.

The *Coup de Main* against Benghazi, 27–30 January

Group Marx – headquarters and *I./Rifle Regiment 155* and *II./Schützen Regiment 104* (less elements), *Reconnaissance Unit 3, Reconnaissance Unit 33,* one antitank company, and one battery of field artillery – was concentrated during the afternoon of 27 January in the area 20 kilometers west of Msus. After dark had fallen, it started its march to outflank the enemy under the personal command of General Rommel. In the beginning, navigation was made difficult by a violent sandstorm, then torrential rains poured down which changed the route into a morass, rendering the crossing of the deeply cut-in wadis almost impossible. Rommel's resourcefulness, however, always succeeded in finding crossings over the wadis. But, at 0300 hours on 28 January, the move had to be discontinued until dawn as the column was completely bogged down. Thus, it had become completely impossible to reach Er Reghima – the objective which had been set for the morning of 28 January. But General Rommel did not abandon his plan. On 28 January he led *Group Marx* towards Er Reghima over increasingly difficult terrain, and by 1100 hours he had reached a point 10 kilometers from the place. He was lucky in so far as strong British bomber formations flying over the column did not spot it. Er Reghima was not taken until 1600 hours, when it was attacked from the east. Then the advance continued westward to Benina. The enemy was completely taken by surprise when the German troops appeared from that direction, and offered only slight resistance. The British aircraft on the Benina airfield were able to get away safely in the nick of time only because the leading units opened fire too early.

General Rommel tried on the same evening to take Benghazi in a *coup de main* from the east. However, the attack broke down under the fire of strong antitank forces in position on the eastern edge of the place. Simultaneously, an advance by considerable enemy forces was reported from the south towards Benghazi. Thereupon General Rommel formed a line of strongpoints, Goefia–Benina–Er Reghima, to cut off Benghazi from the north and the east. The purpose of the gradual arrival of the Italian *Motorized Corps* and of the *90th Light Division* was to drive the enemy towards the strongpoint line and force him to surrender. During the night of 28/29 January, General Rommel received a wireless message from Mussolini giving permission to take Benghazi if the situation developed favorably. January 29 brought fall of the town.

During the early morning a motorized battalion of the *4th Indian Division* tried to break through the line of strongpoints near Goefia. After a short battle, the battalion was captured. More than 1,000 prisoners and 300 motor vehicles fell into German hands. The bulk of the British garrison in Benghazi – one brigade of the *4th Indian Division* – had succeeded under cover of night in escaping to the east through a gap in the line cutting off the town.

Towards noon the town was taken without any resistance being offered; the Italian and Arab population of the town welcomed General Rommel vociferously. Towards the evening, *Armored Division Ariete*, coming from the south, entered the town.

The advance of the *Afrika Korps* from Bir el Melezz towards Bir el Garrari did not lead to any contact with the enemy. During the evening of 28 January, the troops who had taken part in the thrust returned to El Melezz. At first, the enemy felt forward against the staging area of the *Afrika Korps* with small patrols, but as from 28 January he sent stronger reconnaissance detachments, supported by armor and artillery.

Although the *coup de main* on Benghazi did result in the destruction of the British garrison as was hoped, the capture of the town was nevertheless a very noteworthy success of German-Italian arms. In recognition of his achievement during this operation, Rommel was promoted to the rank of Colonel-General on 29 January.

The Pursuit into Cyrenaica, 30 January–6 February

After the recapture of Benghazi on 29 January, Colonel-General Rommel was quite sure that the British were about to abandon Cyrenaica. He expected that they would try to hold the area west of Tobruk, and for this purpose to concentrate the formations available in Marmarica in the Gazala position.

Colonel-General Rommel was now faced with the question whether to continue the pursuit through the Cyrenaica or to halt his forces in the Msus–Benghazi area. The most effective thing to do would have been to carry on the pursuit with the *Afrika Korps*, and the Italian *Motorized Corps* south of Cyrenaica. In the meantime, however, the fuel position had deteriorated considerably. The high fuel consumption of the tanks excluded an operation with armor. Therefore, Rommel did not consider an advance by the *Afrika Korps* south of Cyrenaica. But he decided to wrench Cyrenaica and its resources from the grasp of the enemy, and for this purpose to pursue the enemy to the east on the two branches of the Via Balbia, trying to inflict on him as much damage as possible by means of the strong pressure he would bring to bear on him. To achieve his aim, he employed forces of the strength of two motorized brigades. *Group Marx* was to advance on the northern branch via Barce–Cyrene–Berta to Derna, whilst *Group Geissler*– elements of the *15th Panzer Division* with the headquarters of *15th Schützen Brigade*, with *Machine Gun Battalion 2, I./Artillery Regiment 33*, two antitank companies, and one engineer company – was to advance from the Charruba area via Maraua to Martuba. The pursuit was to start early on 31 January.

Early on 31 January *Group Marx* started on its move from Benghazi to Barce. On receipt of a report from the air that enemy troops were being embarked in the small port of Tolemaide, one reinforced company was sent off along the coast, whilst the bulk of the fighting troops turned off from Barce to Tolemaide. It was learnt too late that the report from the air was a mistake. Much time was lost when, on its return, *Group Marx* got bogged down in the soaked roads and was unable to get going until the morning of 1 February. Then it advanced to D'Annuncio. However, in the east of this place, the Via Balbia was so thoroughly demolished that any thought of continuing had to be abandoned. For this reason, *Group Marx* was ordered to move to Maraua on the southern branch of the road.

Group Geissler had been concentrated around Charruba in the early hours on 31 January. There it came under the direct command of the *Panzerarmee*, and during the morning started its advance on Maraua. This place was defended by strong rearguards of the *4th Indian Division*. It proved impossible on 31 January to break the resistance of the British. *Group Geissler* did not penetrate into the place until early on 1 February.

On 1 February both groups advanced on the southern branch of the Via Balbia; towards evening they broke the stubborn resistance of Indian rearguards near De Martino. Parts of the enemy rearguards were captured. On 2 February, Rommel ordered *Group Geissler* to continue on the northern branch of the Via Balbia and *Group Marx* on the southern branch, both starting from the road fork east of De Martino. *Group Geissler* took Berta as early as noon on 2 February, but then was pinned down owing to the thorough demolition of the serpentine 20 kilometers west of Derna.

During 2 February, *Group Marx*, advancing on the southern deviation around Derna, proceeded eastward and was involved in continuous fighting. The rearguards of the enemy had repeatedly to be forced to withdraw by outflanking maneuvers, but in the area of the track-crossing near Gasr el Carmusa they suffered serious casualties. During the evening on 2 February, the group settled down to rest on the El Mechili–Derna track-crossing.

During the morning of 3 February *Group Marx* dispatched a battalion from Carmusa to Derna, which had been evacuated by the British. The bulk of the group continued via Martuba towards Tmimi. There, the enemy had occupied the easily defensible pass and seemed determined to defend it energetically. The group made an attempt to open the pass by an outflanking move; but, because of the difficult terrain, this proved a failure.

On 4 February, *Group Marx* bumped a new enemy east of Gasr el Ambar; it proved impossible to take this position. Reconnaissance determined that the enemy had established himself in the German-Italian positions of the Gazala line and had prepared them for defense. *Group Marx* therefore set itself up in defensive positions at Gasr el Ambar 20 kilometers north-west of the Gazala line; with one battalion it occupied a strongpoint south of the Tmimi pass, to serve as a support in the rear. During 4 February, the group prepared itself for the defense so as to be able to intercept a strong enemy force – approximately 1,000 vehicles – which had been reported by air to be moving from El Mechili to Tmimi. But this British column turned off to the south in time and reached the British main forces without having to fight. *Group Geissler* joined up with *Group Marx* during the evening.

On 5 February enemy reconnaissance activity grew more lively. The British air force also became more active, and in low-level attacks inflicted heavy losses in M/T on the two battle groups, particularly on their supply troops.

Reconnaissance Units 3 and *33*, were echeloned south-westward in the area north of Bir el Temrad, where they were to take over the protection of the south-west flank of the two battle groups.

When, during the following days, considerable British forces with superior artillery approached the foremost German positions, shelling them heavily from the Ghebel rim, and when British pressure from the south-west flank became noticeable, the two battle groups were withdrawn to the north-west into the area south of Tmimi in order to avoid a defeat by the superior enemy. But the enemy did not follow up.

The Situation on the Ground

When the German assault troops approached the Gazala position, the pursuit had achieved its object. The two weak battle groups had taken no more than five days to recapture Cyrenaica. The German pursuit groups arrived in front of the Gazala position, literally with the last drop of petrol.

It was apparent that the enemy had occupied the Gazala position in force. He had evidently concentrated several divisions in this area, and seemed to be determined to defend the area west of Tobruk. In spite of the heavy losses which the enemy had suffered during the withdrawal, his powers of resistance seemed in no way broken.

An attack on the Gazala position and a continuation of the advance towards Tobruk was not considered as it did not seem feasible with the limited forces available and the precarious fuel position. On the other hand, there was the danger that the enemy would advance from his positions and attack the weak German troops which had approached them, and that he would beat them in their isolation.

For this reason, Rommel decided to withdraw the pursuit troops to Tmimi and at the same time to move strong forces to the south flank. For this reason, the *Afrika Korps*, the *90th Light Division* and the Italian *Motorized Corps* were moved on 6 February to the Mechili area, and strong reconnaissance forces were dispatched into the area of Bir el Temrad. Efforts, too, were resumed to obtain the permission of the *Comando Supremo* to move *X* and *XXI Corps* into the forward areas. However, this permission was not granted until weeks later.

With the recapture of Cyrenaica, the Winter Campaign of 1941–1942 had come to a temporary conclusion. A great and most notable success had been achieved. The setbacks suffered during December 1941 had been squared off. Nonetheless, the question must be examined whether it would not have been possible to exploit the great initial success of the counteroffensive even more fully than was actually done.

Not only the British command, but also the German troops were surprised when, after the great success at Msus on 25 January, the two *Panzer* divisions of the *Panzerarmee* were halted instead of continuing the pursuit to El Mechili. After the smashing defeat of the British armor, they would certainly have met but little resistance. Even if the fuel position made pursuit by both of the *Panzer* divisions impossible, the booty of prisoners and equipment could have been considerably increased if only one of the German *Panzer* divisions had continued the pursuit to El Mechili.

On the other hand, Colonel-General Rommel may have deemed it too risky to penetrate into enemy territory with only part of his forces, particularly since he did not know how strong the British forces still were in Marmarica. Abandoning the pursuit meant, undoubtedly, a great measure of self-discipline, which cannot have been easy for Rommel with his tempestuous temperament, but which makes it more praiseworthy.

In connection with the *coup de main* on Benghazi, the skillful measures adopted to deceive the enemy deserve mention, as through them the surprise sprung on the enemy proved a complete success. Rommel was in his element when leading the *Group Marx* in person. That the group reached its objective so quickly, in spite of all the difficulties of bad weather and worse going, is due exclusively to Rommel's determination.

The booty captured at Benghazi was considerable, but it had not been possible to capture the garrison as had been planned. As happened so often before, the German-Italian forces taking part in the operation were too weak to bring about a complete investment without gaps remaining open, chiefly by night.

The pursuit through Cyrenaica was carried out energetically and vigorously by the weak forces which had been entrusted with the task. Operationally, it would have been more effective if *Group Geissler* had moved towards Mechili on the southern edge of Cyrenaica instead if advancing on the southern branch of the Via Balbia. General Rommel – quite correctly – may have regarded an operation of this kind as too risky, as strong British armored forces might still be expected to be in the El Mechili area.

The British command actually succeeded in avoiding the total destruction of its troops in Cyrenaica. This is nothing to be surprised about, as the pursuit was carried out with insufficient forces ,and as it was easy to hold the pursuing troops in the mountainous area of Cyrenaica by blocking the numerous passes and demolishing the roads. Nonetheless, owing to skillful leadership of the German battle groups, the enemy suffered considerable losses in some places.

The Situation in the Air

Side by side with the improvement of the ground situation, there was a marked turn to the better during January regarding the situation in the air. German air power was on the increase, whilst the British was decreasing owing to the splitting up of the formations over a vast area. The full effect of *Luftflotte 2* under Field Marshal von Kesselring was not felt until January. *Fliegerführer Afrika* had now at his disposal, amongst others, three *Gruppen* of *Stukas*, and three *Gruppen* of fighters – all in all more than 180 aircraft. The fighting strength of the Italian air force also increased to about 190 aircraft. This was chiefly due to the improvement in the supply position, which allowed a smoother replenishment of men and material. Cooperation of air reconnaissance and bomber formations with ground troops also improved noticeably. Everywhere it was noticeable that the entire air forces in the Mediterranean theater were now directed by Kesselring methodically and according to a preconceived plan.

The task of *Fliegerführer Afrika* inside this plan was to support the *Panzerarmee* directly by reconnaissance and bomber operations. *X. Fliegerkorps*, stationed on Crete, was assigned the task of operating against British supply routes across the sea and on land, and also against the British air force. *II. Fliegerkorps* was assigned the task of operating against Malta and the British sea traffic through the Mediterranean, and also of escorting own ships convoys. The corps carried out its task with increasing success. In the beginning, it was, however, not possible to prevent our ships convoys from suffering interference and losses. Actually serious setbacks occurred at the end of January.

For the preparation and the execution of the planned counteroffensive, the following tasks were assigned to the German-Italian air forces: to clarify the enemy situation on the front in the Agedabia area in Cyrenaica and around Tobruk; further to eliminate the headquarters of the British *Eighth Army*, of *XXX Armored Corps* and of the *1st Armored Division*, these tasks to be carried out on the first day of the offensive; and further to support the leading formations of the *Afrika Korps* and of *Group Marx*, and in particular to fight the British armored formations on the front. Air reconnaissance succeeded in obtaining an overall picture – on the whole correct – of the distribution of enemy forces before the start of the offensive. If Rommel assumed that the British *7th Armored Division* was at the front, it cannot be blamed on air reconnaissance, as it had reported nothing more than a few hundred vehicles in the area concerned.

Owing to unfavorable weather conditions, the planned elimination of the headquarters of the British at the start of the offensive was not effectively carried out. On the other hand, cooperation with the German assault groups during the attack was fully successful. Owing to navigation difficulties, it was inevitable that some German troops which had penetrated right into the midst of the enemy were dive-bombed by *Stukas*; such cases remained isolated, however. Strong German-Italian fighter formations, which almost completely paralyzed the British air force in its operations during the first days of the offensive, facilitated the operations of the attacking troops to a very considerable degree. Even during 25 January, when the situation was most critical for the British *Eighth Army*, the British air force operated almost exclusively by night, with accordingly little effect.

In the success of the armored battles at Saunnu and Msus, the *Luftwaffe* had a large share as it spotted the British armor at an early stage. By the concentrated attacks on these formations, in which *X. Fliegerkorps* also took part, the *Luftwaffe* contributed much to the attrition of the enemy fighting power. Unfortunately, the *Luftwaffe* was unable to spot in time the break-through of the British *1st Armored Division* at Saunnu on 23 January.

The German-Italian air forces played a lesser part in the further advance to Benghazi and in the pursuit through Cyrenaica, as they were moving to the east just like the British air force. This brought about a temporary great superiority of the British air force in the eastern part of Cyrenaica during the period 4–6 February. But a few days later, the airfields around Benghazi, Derna and Martuba were occupied by German air formations, which brought an early improvement in the air situation.

The Supply Situation

The supply situation of *Panzergruppe Afrika* took a surprising turn for the better during January. The armored formations did not carry out any large-scale moves. The supply dumps were still behind the Marsa el Brega position, and the supply routes were therefore short and fuel consumption was low.

This factor, and the arrival of a few convoys with German supply goods, brought about a considerable easing off of the fuel and ammunition situation as from the beginning of January, after it had been critical for some time. By the middle of January, large quantities of fuel were accumulated, so that the supply position could be regarded as favorable. Once more, all formations of the *Panzerarmee* were able to carry out large-scale moves. The supply position of the Italian formations had also improved considerably.

However, there was still a grave shortage in equipment, and supply was still unsatisfactory. The mechanical state and number of the available vehicles had reached an almost intolerably low level. Some rifle companies had no more than four vehicles, which had to tow each other and which had to be manhandled over spots where the going was bad. With regard to the motorized artillery, numerous guns had fallen out with axles broken. A permanent improvement of the equipment position was not to be expected unless the troops were granted some long period to overhaul their equipment.

On the whole, however, the supply position was more favorable than right through the fighting during December. This fact played a decisive part when the *Panzerarmee* decided to launch a counteroffensive.

During the first days of the counteroffensive there were no supply difficulties. Skillful measures adopted by those in command of supply during 22 January were instrumental in providing the *Panzer* divisions of the *Afrika Korps* with the necessary fuel, although the supply vehicles of the divisions had got stuck in the sand. On this occasion, and particularly during the battle near Msus on 25 January, the shortage of fuel cans was very noticeable; refueling had to be done from petrol barrels, which caused a great wastage of time, resulting in delays in moves and leading to tactical disadvantages.

The large booty which was taken during the fighting at Saunnu and Msus improved the supply position of the *Panzerarmee* considerably. This made it possible to increase the number of the vehicles of the armored formations, and even large parts of the *90th Light Division* were now motorized with British vehicles. The fuel found amongst the booty was not enough to influence the fuel situation of the *Panzerarmee* to any extent. But the huge quantities of rations found relieved those in charge of providing the troops with food of their worries for a long time.

During the second half of January, there occurred another delay of supply transport by sea which resulted again in a fuel crisis. Apart from other reasons, this was one which compelled Rommel to desist from sending his armor to Mechili in pursuit of the enemy. The fuel available was hardly enough to allow the small pursuit columns to move as far as the Gazala positions. The pursuit of the *Panzerarmee* was literally carried out to the last drop of fuel.

Now it was a matter of the greatest importance to get the harbor of Benghazi back into working condition as soon as ever possible. This had been achieved by the beginning of February, which led to a considerable shortening of the supply route. For the tactical command, it came as a pleasant surprise that, when Benghazi was recaptured, vast German dumps of ammunition were found intact. During the German-Italian withdrawal in December 1941, these dumps had not been destroyed owing to lack of time, but were made unusable by the removal of the fuses.

Rommel's counteroffensive during January and February 1942 was the dramatic last act of the entire winter campaign. With this counteroffensive the British autumn and winter offensive which had been started with such great hopes was definitely buried. Its aim, apart from the capture of Libya, had chiefly been the destruction of the German-Italian army and, with it, the final possession of Egypt. During the last days of December, Churchill had announced in the House of Commons that, in the course of the present offensive, the German troops had suffered such heavy losses that they could almost be regarded as destroyed. Their final liquidation would only be a question of time. And now, this very same army which had been looked upon as destroyed, rose once more, mustering enough power to launch an effective and dashing counteroffensive. Thus, the campaign ended with a grave disappointment and a serious setback for the British Eighth Army, which was able to book as the only achievement in its month-long fighting the relief of Tobruk and the possession of Marmarica.

In January 1942, Colonel-General Rommel reaped the fruit of his decision to withdraw from the Gazala position. Whilst up to the middle of December 1941 the situation regarding fighting power and supplies had become more and more unfavorable compared with the British, the withdrawal to the Marsa el Brega position had changed the picture completely. Now the rearward communications had grown much shorter and Rommel had gained time to get his supplies going and to replenish his divisions. Kesselring's measures to reopen the sea routes across the Mediterranean were now beginning to take effect also with regard to the battle by the *Panzerarmee*. The Italian formations also had gained from the breathing space they had enjoyed.

On the other hand, the British had become exhausted through the long pursuit and were becoming careless. Their supply routes had grown much longer; their supplies were less abundant accordingly. The occupation of Marmarica and of Cyrenaica swallowed large parts of their ground and air forces and induced them to split their forces over a vast area. On the other hand, it was no more than a question of time before the enemy would be able to reorganize his forces, and to get his supplies and his air force ready for the continuation of his offensive. Thus, the decision of the *Panzerarmee* to attack the British at the moment of their greatest weakness was a most appropriate one.

The first stage of the counteroffensive – the Battle of Agedabia – brought many a setback and many a crisis for the *Panzerarmee*. That, after all success was achieved is due to the exemplary secrecy and the surprise thus sprung on the enemy, to the skillful exploitation of the mistakes the enemy made, and, last but not least, to the versatility with which the *Panzerarmee* adapted its plans to the changing situation. On the whole, the first days of the battle furnished proof of the fact that first-class armored troops under first-class leaders can achieve great success in operations against a vastly superior enemy.

During the second part of the counteroffensive, Rommel showed that now he had learnt to adapt his aims and objectives to the forces at his disposal. In the previous year, he certainly would not have been able to resist the temptation to carry on to Tobruk regardless of the strength of the forces and regardless of supply difficulties. This time he chose the "small solution", which promised sure success, instead of the "big solution", which most probably would have been beyond the scope of the available forces. Again, Rommel, with his customary obstinacy, prevailed upon the Italian Supreme Command to have his intentions carried out. The fact that the counteroffensive was carried right to the Gazala position in spite of all the obstacles which had to be surmounted paid Rommel rich dividends when the summer offensive was started. This time, Rommel remained inside of what was possible, and achieved much with small means, suffering only small losses.

The achievements of the German *Panzer* formation during these operations deserve particular praise. It must be emphasized that, by the end of January 1942, these troops had been almost continuously operational since the middle of November 1941, without a break worth mentioning, and in full freshness and with the customary hitting power had bowled over an enemy which was very much superior. Whilst the *British Eighth Army* had been in a position to replenish its armored formation three times with new tanks since the start of the campaign, and, in January 1942, to bring forward a fresh formation – the British *1st Armored Division* – *Panzergruppe Afrika* did not receive any noteworthy replenishment either in men or in equipment, and received only 40 new tanks, during the entire campaign. For these reasons alone, Churchill's pronouncement made at the end of December regarding the losses in men and tanks suffered by the German troops evidently constitutes a manifold exaggeration, as the figures given by him are much higher that the actual number of tanks, including the 40 new ones, ever in action.

On the whole, Rommel's counteroffensive shows up as a well thought out and skillfully and energetically executed operation, which constitutes a page of glory in the history of the command and troops of *Panzergruppe Afrika*.

CHAPTER 8

Events on the British Side
18 November 1941–17 February 1942

During the night of 17/18 November, the British *Eighth Army* crossed the Libyan frontier south of Sidi Omar on a broad front. It advanced deep into the rear of the German-Italian forces and it did not meet any resistance until 19 November. *XXX Corps* had been given the main task, namely the destruction of the German-Italian armored forces. The operation of this Corps suffered from the very beginning under the ambiguity of the task allotted to it. Whilst General Auchinleck laid the main stress of the operation on the battle against the German-Italian forces, General Cunningham, the Commander-in-Chief of the *Eighth Army*, was first of all intent on bursting open the ring encircling Tobruk and on establishing a junction with the garrison of Tobruk.

This led to a splitting up of the forces. Whilst, during the first days of the offensive, parts of the corps tried to ward off the counterattacks of the *Afrika Korps* or were pinned down before Bir el Gubi, the leading elements of the assault troops advanced as far as Sidi Rezegh and to Belhamed south-east of the fortress. On 21 November, General Cunningham ordered the garrison of the fortress to break out to the south-east of the fortress. The attempt failed and brought heavy losses to the British. During the following days, the corps was defeated on several occasions during unlucky fighting with German armored forces, and by the evening of 23 November had lost 90% of its armor and the bulk of its artillery and heavy weapons.

General Cunningham did not yet give up the battle as lost, but ordered the *2nd New Zealand Division*, which until then had carried out the investment of the Sollum front under the Command of *XIII Corps*, to advance to the east.

Rommel's dash to the south-east on 24 November created a most difficult situation for the *Eighth Army*. The British supply troops and the headquarters in the frontier area were forced to retreat.

The *2nd New Zealand Division*, which was coming from the east and in the meantime had approached close to Tobruk, was now threatened in its rear. General Cunningham no longer saw an opportunity of bringing his offensive to a successful conclusion; and, therefore, he decided on 24 November to take his army back to Egypt in order to replace the heavy losses it had suffered before he would launch a new attack. General Auchinleck did not approve of the decision to withdraw and he replaced Cunningham – who had insisted on the withdrawal – with General Ritchie.

The new Commander-in-Chief was favored by luck; British stubbornness was victorious. By 27 November, the British had succeeded n replacing the heavy losses in equipment *XXX Corps* had suffered. On 25 November, the *2nd New Zealand Division* was able, together with the garrison of the fortress of Tobruk, to work a breach in the ring around Tobruk.

But the British troops were faced with a new and serious crisis when, on 27 November, the *Afrika Korps* returned from the Sollum front and attacked the *2nd New Zealand Division* in the rear. In desperate but unsuccessful battles, *XXX Corps* tried to cut the lines of withdrawal to Tobruk of Rommel's armored forces. On 30 November and on 1 December, the *2nd New Zealand Division* was smashed and the garrison of Tobruk was hurled back into the fortress. Even at that juncture, the British Commander-in-Chief stuck to his plan. By 4 December he had moved the *4th Indian Division*, which in the meantime had crushed the west part of the Sollum front, to Bir el Gubi, where he concentrated considerable forces, with which he wanted to advance to the north-east against Rommel's rearward communications. In Rommel's counterattack on Bir el Gubi, *XXX Corps* suffered considerable losses, but, on 7 December, the corps was able to halt the German-Italian counterattack at Bir el Gubi. The British advance beyond Bir el Gubi brought the first visible success of the offensive. Rommel was now compelled to abandon the investment of Tobruk. It also became noticeable that the German-Italian troops had suffered considerably during the weeks of heavy fighting and that their hitting power was dwindling, whereas General Ritchie was able to replenish his armored formations when needed.

When, on 7 December, the German-Italian forces started their withdrawal to the Gazala line, the *Eighth Army* at once and energetically advanced in pursuit. In doing so, it inflicted heavy losses on the Italian formations, and reached the Gazala line at the same time as they did.

During the battle for the Gazala line, the *Eighth Army* employed its armored forces to outflank the German south wing. In this they were, however, unsuccessful. On the other hand, the British center, in spite of some setbacks, succeeded in making a deep penetration at Bir el Temrad.

When, on 16 December, Rommel broke off the battle for the Gazlaa line, it was the *Eighth Army*'s main task to transform Rommel's withdrawal into defeat by pursuit. Whilst the British motorized divisions followed the Italian northern wing frontally, the British *7th Armored Division* tried to block Rommel's retreat in the area north of Agedabia, and for this purpose advanced through the desert in several pursuing columns traveling to the south-west. However, both groups were denied any noteworthy success. Whilst Rommel's north wing was able to shake off the pursuing troops in the mountainous area of Cyrenaica, the British armored forces were intercepted on 22 and 23 December north of Agedabia, before they reached the Via Balbia. A renewed attempt to advance into Rommel's south flank south of Agedabia ended in a costly setback during the last days of 1941. Rendered cautious by this setback, the British *Eighth Army* followed the withdrawing German-Italian forces during the beginning of January with only small advanced troops to the Marsa el Brega position.

During the seven weeks of fighting, the British *Eighth Army* had suffered so much that General Auchinleck regarded a continuation of the offensive against the Marsa el Brega position possible only after the arrival of further reinforcements, the reconstruction of supply bases in southern Cyrenaica and a well-planned deployment. On the other hand, he regarded Rommel as having been so badly beaten that he would not be able to manage a counterstroke on a larger scale. Thus, Auchinleck limited his efforts to pushing lesser covering troops towards the Marsa el Brega position, and concentrated the *7th Armored Division* and the newly arrived *1st Armored Division* in the area east of Agedabia. The remaining divisions of the army, some of which had been badly mauled during the previous fighting, remained distributed in the Benghazi area, in Cyrenaica and Marmarica. In the meantime, the German-Italian strongpoints in Bardia and on the Sollum front had been wiped out by *XIII Corps* by 17 January, so that at long last the coast road became available for the transport of supplies. The British started building up supply bases in the area of Agedabia and of Msus. On the other hand, it had not been possible to restore the harbor of Benghazi, which had been very thoroughly demolished, for the purpose of British supply.

The German-Italian counter-offensive on 21 January found the British *Eighth Army* completely unprepared. At first, the British thought it to be not more than a reconnaissance push with limited objectives. When they realized the scale of the counteroffensive, it was almost too late for the British armored forces in the area east of Agedabia to escape the German pincer.

During their breakout, the German *Panzer* divisions inflicted heavy losses on them. At first *XXX Corps* tried to hold the large supply center around Msus, but, on 25 January, the corps was completely bowled over and withdrew to the north-east in disorderly flight. The fact that the RAF, which during the entire campaign until then had maintained supremacy in the air over the battle area, had for the first time been chased out of the sky by day during January, contributed much to the defeats suffered by the British in these operations.

The necessary consequence of the defeat at Msus was the withdrawal of the forces around Benghazi and in Cyrenaica, which were threatened in the rear. The *4th Indian Division*, which was brilliantly led, succeeded in getting away from encirclement at Benghazi and in evacuating Cyrenaica in good order.

The German counteroffensive caused heavy losses to the British *Eighth Army*; in particular, huge quantities of supplies were lost. Now Auchinleck decided to try and hold the area west of Tobruk, and for this purpose to go over to the defense, concentrating all his available forces in the Gazala line 80 kilometers west of Tobruk.

As Rommel had followed the British withdrawal with only weak forces, the British succeeded in reorganizing their formations in the new area, and in building up a solid defensive line in a comparatively short time.

The overall result of the British autumn offensive was thus disappointing. After some brilliant successes, the offensive had ended in a grave setback. The aim – the destruction of the German-Italian forces in Libya – had not been achieved; the threat for Egypt from the west remained. But the fortress of Tobruk had been relieved after eight months of siege and the defensive front had been pushed 160 kilometers further to the west, to the very east edge of Cyrenaica.

The British offensive had started off in the most favorable circumstances imaginable. The British command had succeeded in achieving operational and tactical surprise, and in concentrating more than twice as many men and twice as much material as its enemy.

Many a mistake by the command, a certain slowness in arriving at decisions, an advance too methodical and an inclination to split up forces – all these things worked together in denying the British the expected results. On the other hand, there was the unfailing will for victory – a hardness and stubbornness which must be admired and which never flagged, even in situations which seemed to be hopeless. The courage of the British troops throughout the fighting has secured them the high esteem of their enemies.

On the whole, the achievements of the British troops, officers and men, are on a high level.

Conclusion

A comparative study of military history shows, once again, that in the initial stages of most wars the course of operations was most varying and that initiative and versatility of command played the main role, whereas during the later stages the part played by material became increasingly important and that the freedom of action of the command decreased. On a small scale, the first year in the Africa campaign was particularly dramatic and full of changes. At a later stage, this same air of expectation and the rapid change of the situation occurred on rare occasions, but was never exceeded.

In the year 1941, the African desert was a new world, not only for the German command and the German troops. Desert warfare as a form of fighting was something new for the entire modern science of war. It was found that the desert offered undreamed-of possibilities for the decisive weapons of modern war, *viz.* the armor and the air force. In the African war theater more than in other theaters of war, modern command methods found all the scope to show what could be done.

In other directions, too, the Africa campaign is of particular interest. For the first time, the Axis powers were faced with the problem of confederate war. For the student of military history, the African campaign offers fascinating themes, such as General Rommel's leadership and how he had been able to develop into a leading personality of the first order, a personality soaring to ever greater heights of achievement as the tasks grew more formidable and his experience − dearly bought − grew richer. For the German rank and file, it is particularly the first year of the Africa campaign which will be unforgettable. In no other war theater did the superb soldierly qualities of the German fighting troops show up so brilliantly as in Africa. Separated from home by thousands of kilometers, and cut off from any reinforcements and supplies for months by huge stretches of ocean ruled by the enemy, the German soldier has done his duty without fail and has adapted himself in a surprisingly short time to the unusual and difficult conditions of climate and terrain.

But justice demands that the achievements of the Italian armed forces do not go without recognition: they have done their very best in conditions much less favorable and equipped with inferior material; never have they fought more valiantly than under Rommel's leadership.

These qualities of the German and the Italian soldier had the opportunity to show themselves in a brilliant way because, in the North Africa campaign, they had found a brave and fair enemy in the British soldier. In this century of soulless mass warfare, the North Africa campaign stands out as an uplifting exception, where two chivalrous opponents borne by mutual respect fought decently and cleanly.

PART TWO

Artillery in the Desert

by the
US Army Intelligence Service

Artillery in the Desert

The tactical employment of artillery in the North African campaigns is influenced by two considerations:

(a) *The Task-Force Principle.* The development of the task-force principle underlines the importance of the coordinated tactical action of all arms. Therefore, while the main focus here is on artillery action, this will always be referred to the general operations in which artillery plays its part.

(b) *Special Conditions of Desert Warfare.* The terrain and climate of this theater have imposed certain limitations and set certain problems, some of which involve or affect the use of artillery.

Reconnaissance

Both large and small units operate over wide desert expanses. The lack of cover necessitates great dispersion, which in turn requires each unit to provide its own close-in defense – a situation emphasizing the need for reconnaissance.

Constant use is made of both ground and air reconnaissance units. Even the side which is weaker in air strength carries on air reconnaissance. Forward ground reconnaissance is usually executed by armored cars. Frequently German armored car patrols are supported by tanks, in a ratio of one tank to two armored cars, to provide sufficient fire power to overcome hostile patrols and outposts and thus extend the depth of observation. Once contact is gained by the Germans with an armored force, it is kept under observation, even though the German armored units may have withdrawn. As a result, German armored units have been able to avoid battle when conditions were not favorable, to make night attacks against bivouacs, and even to surround hostile bivouacs during the night with antitank weapons and destroy the armored vehicles from close range in the morning.

Methods of Observation

Although the desert is not completely flat, suitable vantage points for observation posts are never very high. This lack of height, together with the heat waves rising from the hot sand and rocks, sometimes reduces visibility in the desert. Mid-day is the least satisfactory period for observing fire.

Both sides endeavor to gain what high ground does exist in the desert. It has been noted that the German infantry in Libya, as elsewhere, have launched attacks for the purpose of obtaining observation posts for their artillery. In one instance, such an attack was made to gain ground only three feet higher than the surrounding terrain. Similarly, German artillery officers have been known to ride on top of tanks in order to gain height for observation.

In both German and British armored divisions, the artillery has its own armored vehicles for observation posts. However, even artillery with unarmored troops utilizes methods similar to those of the armored divisions. Forward observers are well out in front with those covering forces, armored cars, or carriers which are deployed for reconnaissance and outpost duty. Often these mobile observation posts must be with the armored car screen, and they are then in an armored car or scout car. Many British officers have spoken highly of the US M-3 Scout Car for this work. Its chief advantage is that it accommodates the entire *observation post* party, whereas the armored car has room for only three persons. Armored cars or scout cars are assigned to and maintained by artillery units. Enough cars must be provided so that all radio sets allotted to a battalion can be mounted in such vehicles; these can then be used by forward observers. The advisability of providing more than a few such cars has been quickly realized, because they wear out soon and have a high casualty rate. Unless the *observation post* is the same type of vehicle as that used by the supported troops, the enemy will concentrate its fire power on the *observation post* vehicle.

The British have found it to be impossible to assign tanks to artillery for *observation post* purposes. but they do have arrangements whereby each regiment of tanks modifies and, on occasion, reserves for artillery observers a certain number of tanks.

A problem of observation was revealed in one fast-moving situation which occurred during the winter of 1941–1942. The battery commander was traveling with the tank regimental commander. Two observers, one per troop, were directing fire while traveling with the forward elements of the regiment. When contact was actually made, the observers had their tanks stay on the flanks and drop back slightly from the front in order to avoid becoming directly engaged. All control was by radio, and the observer had his own radio operating in the artillery net, separate from the tank radio which operated in the tank net. Because of the limited number of frequencies available, it was necessary for all artillery units in a battery to be on the same frequency. The effect of this single frequency was unfortunate, for only one troop could be fired by one observer at a time, and a great deal of confusion occurred. When all control by observers breaks down, artillery support deteriorates into direct laying by individual pieces.

In addition to the armored observation posts, gun towers have been used to gain height for observing fire. These *observation post* ladders are used both as dummies to draw fire and for observation. They are mounted on trucks or may be removed quickly and set up at an observation post. The British observing towers are generally about 25 feet high. The Germans have a two-piece telescoping tube mounted on the side of their armored OP, which can be cranked up into observing position. To employ these gun towers effectively, there must be a number of them – at least one to each four guns. These, like the tanks and the slight rises in the ground, aid in overcoming the flatness of the desert.

Other difficulties arise in the desert which only keen eyes and training can surmount. There is the real problem which a forward artillery observer has in identifying his own bursts among the dust and heat waves when other units are also firing. Judging distance in the desert is as difficult as on the ocean. Lack of familiarity with the size and appearance of armored vehicles at various ranges is a frequent cause for misjudging distance. But it is even more important to remember that all tanks are not equipped with the same type of gun. German tanks armed with 75-mm guns can open effective firing at a range of 2,000 yards. Antitank guns with a smaller range waste ammunition by returning fire and, what is worse, give away their own positions.

Selection and Occupation of Positions

Suitability of position for accomplishing the mission assigned, and also cover and camouflage, are sought by the artillerymen in the desert as elsewhere. Since cover is practically impossible to obtain in most desert positions, the main concern in selecting a gun position is the suitability of the soil for digging pits and the possibility of arranging for mutual support with other units.

Terrain

Both sides make excellent use of those few accidents of the ground which occur in desert terrain. Maximum use is made of folds of the ground both to advance and to conceal tanks, artillery, and antitank weapons. Artillery and antitank guns have frequently been cleverly concealed in ground where the terrain was unfavorable for tank action.

Quick concealment from both the ground and air is obtained by digging gun pits and using light-colored camouflage nets. Gun pits which have no parapet, being flush with the surface of the ground, are more easily concealed than those which have. When possible, therefore, both Axis and United Nations troops distribute the soil and refrain from building a parapet. Gun pits are dug to permit all-around fire.

Often a diamond formation with sides of about 800 yards is employed for a regiment of four batteries. This enables the batteries to be mutually supporting. The guns within each battery are sited in semicircular fashion, 60 to 70 yards apart. On going into action, the British consider the priority of tasks to be:

(a) Concealment from ground and air;
(b) Digging of slit trenches;
(c) Digging of gun pits, command posts, etc.

Rapidly occupied positions may not be the best available. Therefore, reconnaissance for more satisfactory gun positions is always carried out in such circumstances, and a move is made as soon as possible. In the event of a severe shelling, batteries move to alternate positions if the new positions will still give the necessary mutual support.

Dispersion

Both dive-bombing and strafing aviation seek out artillery units for attack, as they are profitable targets. To define against such attacks, either cover or dispersion is necessary. Since sufficient cover is not usually available, the dispersion of vehicles has been great – 200 yards between vehicles being normal. Units spread out in this fashion offer no target for air attacks. When the enemy air force has been inactive, the distance between vehicles is sometimes reduced. This is done to insure better defense against tank attacks and to obtain more control over units. A New Zealand division, while in defense of the Sidi Rezegh–Belhamed area, reduced the distance between its vehicles because of the small amount of cover available, and vehicles at 50-

to 60-yard intervals did not suffer undue casualties during artillery bombard-ments. Undoubtedly casualties would have been severe if there had been an enemy air attack on that occasion.

Camouflage

In the desert every gun is dug into a pit if time permits, and covered with a net; every tent is set in a pit and camouflaged; and even each tank has a canvas top placed over it to make it look like a truck. All vehicles are painted with nonglare sand-color paint, and all glass is smeared with oil or a glycerin solution, and then dirt is thrown on these surfaces. Only a narrow unsmeared slit on the windshield is left to obtain vision. Wheel tracks are everywhere and cannot be disguised or obliterated.

A liberal application of dull yellow paint – the color of the sand – has been found to be the best method of rendering both artillery pieces and motor trucks less visible in the desert. The outlines of a piece are broken by the use of scrub and sand mats. The barrel and cradle are sometimes painted a dull sandy color, except for a 1-foot diagonal stripe of light brown or green to break up the pattern of the gun. Motor vehicles carry camouflage nets, which are stretched taut from a central position on the roof of the vehicle at an angle of nor more than 45 degrees, and then pegged to the ground and covered with threaded screen and bleached canvas, or with pieces of sandbags 50 to 70 percent of which are painted dull yellowish white. The vehicles them-selves are painted cream white, broken by irregular patches of light brown or green. The object is to neutralize dark shadows by an equivalent amount of dull white. Germans and British have adopted this sand color as camouflage. During recent operations German tanks were painted black, evidently to aid their antitank gunners in quick daytime identifications while also serving as night camouflage.

As a security measure and to prevent unauthorized persons gaining information regarding the identification of units and movement of troops, by observing motor transport movements, the practice of marking vehicles with unit designations has been discontinued. A code system, employing color and combinations of colors with numbers to indicate various tactical organizations, has been adopted.

Communications

Distance is the principal problem encountered in desert communications. Radio is used extensively, as wire is laid only when there is time – an element often lacking in desert operations. Radio presents a unique problem of security, because radio communication is like shouting from place to place – all who will can listen. This has necessitated the development of various codes and devices for the secret transmission of data by radio.

Visual Signals

Although visual signals are not used extensively for transmitting artillery data, flag signals are employed by both sides for short messages and for identification, especially in small tank units. Recently, the Germans had radio sets in a ratio of one set to three tanks. The three operated as a unit, flag signals being used to control the tanks which had no radio. Great use has also been made of pyrotechnic signals. Recently, two signals were used by the Germans to identify their tanks to German aircraft: a Very signal of three white stars, and an orange-colored smoke. Large flags have sometimes been used for the same purpose. Rockets have been used in profusion at night, apparently both to rally forces which were scattered when dark fell, and to confuse and harass the enemy. It is not known what method the Germans use to identify tanks to friendly antitank and artillery weapons. When the British used the method of approaching friendly troops with turret guns pointing to the rear, the Germans were quick to adopt the same method for purposes of deception, in order to approach close to hostile weapons.

Wire

Although the speed of operations in the desert may on occasion preclude the use of telephone lines, a greater degree of security and dependability is achieved by using wire. Almost all lines are laid on the ground. Motor vehicles traveling across the desert constantly are running over the wires. The results of bruising of wire are not so serious in the desert, since ordinary field wire operates better over the desert surface than it would over damp or moist ground. Also, laying and picking up wire are much less difficult in the desert than in swampy or wooded country. Of course, overhead wire circuits are more desirable when the situation becomes at all static. Communication over long field lines in most cases is good in the desert.

The wide dispersion of guns has made necessary the use of an enunciator system between the executive and the individual sections of the firing batteries. Such a system permits the executive to coordinate and command his guns in such a manner as to control rapidly the guns for effective concentrated fire.

Radio

Radio is the most important means of communication in the desert. During the summer of 1941, one British armored division conducted its entire communication network by radio. Every command vehicle had a receiving set. Each artillery troop has three No. 11 sets using one principal frequency, and, for emergency use, one switch in "frequency."

Each troop of this armored division was part of a mobile column, which furnished No. 9 command sets. Switch frequencies were in the overlap band of No. 10 and No. 11 sets, permitting use of No. 9 in displacement by a half-troop in case no extra infantry No. 11 set was available for the purpose. Artillery troops normally operated with two observation posts using No. 11 sets. A third *observation post* could be manned for emergency use by diverting a set from the infantry of the mobile columns.

Only one radio set could be provided to each gun position. This may have been caused by the fact that British radio sets are heavy and cannot be removed from the vehicle in which they are mounted. The range of the No. 11 set – voice, 15 miles – has been considered adequate for all troops used during the summer of 1941.

Codes

During active operations all messages below the division are usually sent in the clear. Christian names of tank and unit commanders and prearranged code names for places are used. Although there is little intentional enemy interference with artillery communications, there are active and efficient Axis radio-interception intelligence units.

The use of plain language, even when accompanied by code names and enciphered place names, enables radio interception to be employed effectively. By keeping a careful record of all names, key words, and numbers, both the Italians and the Germans have been able to bring their order-of-battle information up to date by a process of sifting and cross-indexing. Officers' names, either family name or given name, are the principal keys used in identifying intercepted messages. Captured German documents indicate that the careful compilation of names made by the Germans has enabled them to work out British code names. In addition to names, references to the personnel arm, such as "Gunner Smith," or "Rifleman Jones," have helped the Axis forces to identify said units.

One of the most interesting methods of enabling map references to be sent in the clear with security is the "thrust line" method used by the

Germans. (This method is similar to the code described in FM 18-5, "Organization and Tactics of Tank Destroyer Units," June 16, 1942, paragraph 231 b (2) (e).) It consists of a line drawn upon a map which theoretically may run in any direction but which actually usually extends in the proposed direction of advance or down the axis of a reconnaissance unit.

The line, which begins at a fixed point and continues indefinitely in the required direction, is usually divided into centimeters for convenience. To give a map reference, a perpendicular is dropped from the reference point to the thrust line. Measurements are then taken from the point of origin to the point where the perpendicular cuts the thrust line, then along the perpendicular to the reference point. Since the point may lie on either side of the thrust line, the second figure must be prefaced by either "right" or "left", as one looks toward the enemy.

A typical reference would be "6 right 3." The figures are always in centimeters; therefore, the actual distance on the ground will vary with the scale of the map used. The scale may start with an arbitrary figure, and have dummy figures interspersed, or it may start with the number of the thrust line when there are several in a given area. These devices make the code difficult to break rapidly.

Instruments have been found consisting of a transparent ruler graduated in millimeters, with a shorter ruler similarly graduated and fixed to slide up and down at right angles to the longer ruler. Practiced operators can give references very quickly.

German Tactics

No strict pattern is apparent in German operations. The Germans have in most instances employed a balanced and highly coordinated team of all arms and services, whatever the size of the force. Although their procedure has thus been elastic to suit the tactical situation, they have been found to proceed in general along the following lines.

Effect of Terrain

The Germans make full use of the freedom of maneuver which desert terrain affords and generally have not accepted battle under unfavorable conditions. Maximum use is made of the artillery and all auxiliary arms, both ground and air.

The lack of terrain obstacles and the supply difficulties have resulted in a modification of the German use of armored units in the desert as compared with their previous use in Poland and in Western Europe. In Libya, with the exception of isolated fortified localities such as Tobruk and Halfaya, no long defensive lines exist which can be probed to find a weak spot for penetration and exploitation. Nevertheless the cardinal principle of concentrating tank strength has been followed. On those occasions when the German forces advanced in several columns, the tanks were usually concentrated in one column. The object of the tank column is to destroy the enemy force, using maneuver to defeat him in detail whenever possible.

Formations

Various methods of advance have been used by German armored units. Usually the formation is in considerable depth. A battalion (65 to 80 tanks) frequently uses a "V" formation with two companies leading and one in reserve, or an inverted "V" with one company leading and two in reserve. Companies are usually in line, with tanks in column of threes at about 50-yard intervals, and three to five tank lengths in depth.

A German tank battalion in tactical formation moves in short rushes, taking advantage of the terrain. Frequently, the whole regiment advances in mass formation, with lines of tanks at regular intervals of about 50 yards, advancing in waves. The relatively close formation is more readily controlled than a widely dispersed one. Field artillery and antitank weapons are kept up close, although their location is not apparent until they go into action, usually on the flanks of the tank column. The Germans have in the past been able to bring effective artillery and antitank fire to bear on the British before the British could effectively fire upon them. In addition, RAF planes, because of the pilots' inability to distinguish between their own and German tanks, have not attacked German tank formations in the forward areas.

Offensive Tactics

In the desert, frontal attacks have not often been used, an effort being made more often to attack from one or both flanks. German tanks usually open fire at 1,500 to 2,000 yards, which is beyond the effective range of the hostile weapons that they have thus far encountered. When contact is made, the speed of advance is slowed down unless the movement is a quick thrust to force the withdrawal of weaker hostile forces. The 75-mm and 50-mm guns are used to keep hostile tanks out of range.

(1) *Usual German objectives.* The object of the Germans is to knock out quickly as many of the antitank guns and foremost field guns as may

be visible. When the German tank commander has decided to attack a position, his first objective has often been the British 25-pounders. By reconnaissance in tanks he first locates the British battery positions and makes his plans. This plan in principle always appears to be the same. He decides which battery to attack and he arranges to attack it from enfilade. His attack is made with 105-mm guns, the 88-mm dual-purpose guns, and both Mark III and IV tanks. The 105-mm guns fire from covered positions; their observation posts are in tanks. The 88-mm dual-purpose guns are towed. These guns use direct fire from their trailers after attaining defiladed positions at ranges varying from 2,000 to 2,500 yards. The Mark IV tanks assume positions in defilade and fire over open sights at ranges varying from 2,000 to 2,500 yards. The high-velocity 75-mm gun in the Mark IV tank and the 88-mm dual-purpose gun have far higher muzzle velocities than any artillery that the British have had in the desert.

(2) *German Mark III tanks.* The Mark III tank is used as the main striking force in attack. It has the dominant role in tank-versus-tank combat. Its heavy armor and powerful 50-mm gun give it a decided advantage over all types of tanks which it has thus far encountered in the desert. The 75-mm gun in the Mark IV tank is not an antitank gun but a close-support weapon. Its maximum range is 7,000 yards. Frequently these tanks use direct laying from a defiladed position in which, owing to the location of the gun in the turret, they offer a very small target. At other times the fire is massed, with indirect laying, and is adjusted by forward or flank observers in tanks. Tanks rarely fire while moving, although in at least one instance they were used to fire a rolling barrage at from 3,000 to 4,000 yards while advancing slowly. This forced the opposing tanks to close up doors and turrets.

The first wave of Mark III tanks overrun the gun positions. The second wave of Mark III tanks is closely followed by the motorized infantry, which detrucks only when forced to and cleans up the position with small-arms fire, assisted by tanks which accompany it. After the artillery has neutralized the tanks, the support infantry is attacked. Such attacks have nearly always neutralized the artillery, either by destroying it when the attack was driven home, or by forcing it to withdraw before the tank attack was launched. A successful defense against such attacks has been made only when a tank force was available to launch a counterattack from concealed positions against the flank of the German tank attack.

(3) *The German Mark IV tanks used as artillery.* In the attack the Germans maneuver to some position where their Mark IV tanks can take up a position in defilade. The Germans meanwhile make a reconnaissance, probing the enemy from all directions to test his strength, and to induce the defenders to disclose their positions by opening fire. During this period, observation posts keep close watch, and any guns which disclose their position are marked down for destruction when the main attack begins. Then, from their defiladed positions, the Mark IVs attack by fire all antitank guns or light artillery which are visible and within range. Light artillery, antitank guns, and machine guns with the same mission are pushed forward among and to the flanks of the tanks. Observers and occasionally infantry are pushed further forward.

Each German tank battalion has one company of 10 Mark IV tanks, which are employed in two principal roles: as highly mobile artillery, and as a component of a fast-moving column. Often field artillery cannot be immediately available in armored engagements; the Mark IV tank with its 75-mm gun, together with the artillery of the armored division, provides German armored formations with the necessary heavy fire power for a breakthrough.

The maximum range of the 75-mm gun is reported to be 9,000 yards. This relatively long range dictates to troops equipped with light antitank guns the time and place of a battle. In addition, the speed of the Mark IV tank is sufficient to enable it to take part in a rapid advance with the Mark III tanks. The Germans have used these tanks as sniper guns, as artillery against forward British columns, and as heavy concealed weapons in the ambushes into which German armored cars have tried to draw the British cars. In a defensive situation the Mark IV is able to engage British troops from outside the range of the antitank guns, avoiding at the same time, by their mobility, the British artillery fire.

(4) *Field artillery support.* The 105-mm mobile batteries and the 75-mm guns of the Mark IV tank furnish the principal artillery support for the German Mark III tank, which is the main attacking tank. Sometimes the 88-mm dual-purpose gun is used in conjunction with the Mark III tank.

Some reports indicate that the direction of this supporting fire is carried out by a system of air bursts, since air bursts have been immediately followed by HE concentrations. The fire of 75-mm and 105-mm guns using HE shells has not been reported to be extremely effective. Casualties caused to personnel and tanks by these weapons have been reported to be the result of a new flare – a 75-mm shell which envelops the tank in flames regardless of what portion of the tank is hit. One whole tank regiment was reported destroyed by this type of projectile. Although the casualties caused from these weapons may be slight, all reports agree that they have a high nuisance value to tanks because of the blinding effect of the smoke and dust. The 88-mm is effective; tanks hit squarely by this gun are destroyed.

The Germans stress the use of ricochet artillery fire against personnel as follows:

The much greater effect of ricocheting projectiles as compared with those bursting on impact has been confirmed by the testimony of numerous prisoners. Against all living targets not covered from above, more ricochet fire than hitherto will be employed therefore. Ricochet fire may also be employed against concealed targets if it can be observed from the burst, the noise of the explosion, or the flash of the exploding shell that a sufficient number (40 to 50 percent) of ricochets are occurring. Ricochets can be distinguished from projectiles which enter the ground by their sharper detonation sound, and by the brighter flash, visible even in daytime. This is particularly the case with shallow ricochets, which are easily mistaken for impact detonations. Projectiles which penetrate the ground make no, or very little, report and flash on exploding.

German Method of Forcing Gaps through Minefields

A heavy artillery concentration is placed on the point to be forced and upon the defending troops in the vicinity. After the defenders' resistance is lowered by the concentration, a comparatively small number of foot troops advance to the gap under cover of smoke or of dust raised by the concentration; they locate the mines by prodding the ground with bayonets or with mine detectors; the mines are then removed. Casualties are replaced from a reserve unit that is held immediately in rear. This method was used in forcing a gap through the minefield that was part of the defenses of Tobruk; the preliminary concentration lasted for two hours. After a gap is forced and marked, infantry followed by tanks or tanks followed by infantry attack through the gap. Infantry preceded the tanks in the battle of Tobruk.

Defensive Tactics

When an armored force is encountered, all tanks may take up a firing position in defilade, immediately reinforced by towed and self-propelled antitank guns and artillery. If the tanks are forced to retire, they withdraw under cover of antitank weapons and artillery. Usually the Mark III tanks withdraw first, the Mark IV assisting in covering the withdrawal with high explosive and smoke. When such withdrawals have been followed by the enemy, the well-concealed German antitank guns and artillery have caused such serious damage to the pursuing tanks that the pursuit has generally been stopped. Sometimes the tanks will withdraw through the antitank and artillery positions and then maneuver to strike the hostile armored force on its flank.

British Tactics

The Approach

The action of artillery with British armored forces during the approach has differed little from its action with infantry formations. The armored brigades move in open order in a formation usually like that shown below.

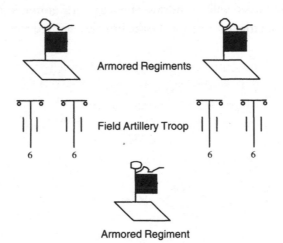

Armored Regiments

Field Artillery Troop

Armored Regiment

The artillery regimental commander rides in a vehicle near the tank brigade commander; the artillery battery commander rides near the tank regimental commander, usually in the same tank with the regimental second-in-command. Troop commanders are with their batteries; observers are in vehicles *on the flank* of the leading elements, or *in the rear*, so as to have observation in all directions. All communication is by radio.

Artillery regimental and battery commanders each have two radio sets, one for use in the tank net, the other for use in the artillery net. Each artillery observer has direct radio communication with his troop, but the battery commander can cut in on either of the troop frequencies if he desires. [This scheme presumes the pre-1942 organization of British field artillery regiments into two batteries of two troops of six guns each.—Ed.]

274

Some artillery observers accompany the leading armored cars, which are used by both sides for reconnaissance purposes. Only sufficient guns accompany these armored cars as are necessary to support them in the fighting required to secure the needed information. In addition, a certain proportion of antitank guns are used for protection.

The Attack

It has been found that an attack by tanks against an even hastily organized position in which there is a reasonable quantity of antitank and field guns succeeds only at disproportionate cost, unless the enemy guns are knocked out or neutralized first. When the British spot Axis guns, they engage them by direct fire from 25-pounders. As many as possible are knocked out.

Role of the artillery. Normally, at the beginning of combat the artillery regimental commander attaches his battalions to tank regiments, and does not try to control their fire.

Artillery battalion commanders usually keep one battery within 1,500 yards of the rear of the supported tank regiment, and the other several thousand yards in rear. As soon as the forward battery is committed to action, the rear battery is ordered forward to leapfrog the forward battery. This method provides for continuous support during an advance.

The artillery observers do not always use armored observation posts. It was discovered that isolated armored vehicles received concentrated fire as the enemy approached, whereas an isolated unarmored truck was often disregarded by the enemy during the initial stages of the action. Hence observers in tanks or other armored observation posts stay within the armored formation, and those in trucks get out on the flank, where they can see better and avoid the long-range fire which the Germans usually commence at 2,500 yards (or more) as the two opposing forces approach each other. The observer calls for two rounds, 100 yards apart, at a given range and at a measured compass direction. From these he shoots fire on to the target. He continues to observe and adjust the fire by this method until the Germans are so close that he has to withdraw; in these final stages the batteries usually employ direct fire.

The Defense

In the desert, mechanized attacks may come at any time and from any direction, as in a naval action. This has, of course, necessitated special formations for defense. Division "X" has been reported to have the best defense organization. This division, with a grand total of about 12,650 men, consists of –

3 infantry brigades of about 3,000 men each; total, 9,000 men.
3 artillery regiments of about 600 men each; total, 1,800 men.
2 antitank regiments of about 500 men each; total, 1,000 men.
1 tank battalion of 250 men.
Supply and repair echelons of about 500 men.
AA personnel of about 100 men.
Motor vehicles numbering about 3,000.

In moving this unit, three general methods were used: the brigades in column, two brigades in front and one in rear, and one brigade in front and two in line in rear.

In case of an attack, the division or brigade on the march halts and the defense is offered with the proper weapons. Antiaircraft defense is offered by three battalions of three batteries of four (Bofors 20-mm) guns each (a total of 36), distributed through the divisional area. Bren machine guns on the basis of five per artillery and infantry battalion are mounted ready for immediate use at any time. Artillery is used at the earliest possible time in an effort to break up the attacking enemy formations before they are within effective tank or infantry ranges.

The experience of one infantry brigade has illustrated well the possibilities of artillery in the defense. The commander of this infantry brigade pushes forward a "hard hitting packet" (four 2-pounder guns portee, four Vickers .303 MGs in carriers, two 3-inch mortars in carriers) to assist the armored car screen when it reports heavy armored forces to be approaching. He moves the brigade itself forward to a favorable position in which to receive an attack. The advance group usually meets the enemy and fights a rearguard action back to the perimeter, into which they move in their assigned positions. All the while this is going on, the brigade artillery, controlled by mobile observation posts, keeps the advancing tanks under fire. In this brigade, the commander has made six armored cars into mobile observation posts with radio sets which can contact the artillery headquarters and have artillery observers in each. With these mobile observation post, the enemy tanks cannot get away from effective artillery fire, for the mobile observation posts go where necessary to observe the fire. This brigade has never yet been without observed fire, even during the hardest engagements. These cars work around the flanks, and, as a result, the enemy cannot refuel or form up within range of the artillery without bringing down effective fire on himself. Armored cars are not afraid of tanks, as they can always outrun them.

In one instance, some time after the advance screen joined the perimeter, the Germans delivered a minor tank attack from the north-east. The brigade beat this off, burning out four tanks. One, however, came so close that it was captured by an officer who charged it in a ½-ton truck with a sticky-type bomb. The crew surrendered, and he brought it in to the brigade headquarters, crew and all. There were no more tank attacks that day, but the artillery continued its shelling.

During the night of 23/24 November, the brigade received orders to withdraw 7 or 8 miles to the south and establish a defended perimeter. Stragglers of another brigade commenced drifting back; so the commander waited until dawn and sent out armored car patrols to bring in as many as they could find. At 0730 the brigade commenced moving south, and at 0900 its leading unit arrived in the designated area. There was much miscellaneous transport in the area which had to be moved before the perimeter was established. This was a day (24 November) of a big breakthrough in the south, and there was considerable confusion.

The brigade remained in position all day and was engaged by the German *21st Armored Division*, and on the night of 24/25 November the Germans encircled the entire perimeter. The attack began in earnest at 0700 on the 25th with artillery fire from two medium batteries, one to the east and the other to the north-east.

7By 0730 the medium batteries were augmented by three field batteries firing from positions to the north, east, and south-east.

The first heavy attack, made up of approximately 60 tanks supported by motorized infantry and heavy mortars, came from the east. This force included a number of heavy tanks, German Mark IVs, which "fire everything they have as they move, making quite a show as they advance."

The attack was made in two waves on a front of about 1,000 yards, the light tanks forward and the heavier ones in the second wave. It lasted exactly 1 hour, and, after failing to penetrate the perimeter in a number of places and suffering heavy losses, the tanks withdrew and re-formed to the north. During the enemy attack, artillery fire was intensified and the brigade artillery answered them, firing primarily on armor; but some guns were spared for the soft column which usually functions close in the rear of the German armored column.

A second, and heavier, attack was launched from the north at 1000 hours. The violence of this attack was such that for about half an hour it was feared the Germans would penetrate the perimeter. The ground attack was intensified by air bombing. This brigade was attacked by dive bombers and fighters during the early morning from 19 November to 6 December, and by two or three large formation assaults during the day, but dispersion and slit trenches made air attack comparatively ineffective against personnel. However, the brigade did have 145 vehicles burned out during this period, the majority by the air. This brigade digs slit trenches whenever it halts, if even for an hour, and its vehicles are always dispersed by at least 200 yards. A slit trench for a temporary halt need be just deep enough so that the body of a man is below the surface of the ground.

The attack slowed down at 1030, when the remaining tanks moved widely around to the west, still constantly under the brigade's artillery fire. During this movement, smoke screens were laid by the tanks themselves, but the brigade's mobile observation posts moved around the screens and kept them under observed fire.

It appeared as if a third attack was imminent, but before this could be launched, an armored brigade arrived with 40 American light tanks. These were not sufficient in number or sufficiently armored or armed to counter-attack the numerically superior and heavier armored German tanks, and it was therefore decided that, should a third attack materialize, the armored brigade would counterattack into their flank. But this third attack did not materialize, probably as a result of the welcome reinforcement of the American tanks.

The artillery battle continued all the rest of the day. Towards sunset the enemy's soft column (motorized infantry and supply units), approximately 2,000 vehicles which were well within gun range, started withdrawing, with the infantry brigade's artillery continually shelling them until they moved out of range. During the withdrawal, the Germans interposed their tanks between their soft columns and this infantry brigade.

Withdrawal

If a withdrawal has to take place, it is conducted under cover of artillery fire. Orders are issued sufficiently early for a plan of withdrawal of the artillery to be made. If they are given too late, there is grave danger of batteries being unnecessarily overrun. Antitank guns are required to protect the flanks and the rearmost units of the force, especially those of the field artillery engaged in delaying the enemy advance. Antitank guns may have to be used from their portees, but this is avoided, if possible, in order to obtain better positions. In any withdrawal, a rallying point, beyond which no vehicle will pass, is established and announced to all ranks.

Counterbattery

(1) *General.* Organized counterbattery work has not occurred during the highly mobile stages of the fighting on the desert. Counterbattery operations have been used most effectively by the British during the more or less static situations which have been developed around such key points as the Omars, Sollum, Halfaya Pass, Bardia, and Tobruk. Special counterbattery officers are trained and employed by the British for this work, which often entails the aid of flash spotting. Whenever used, the effect of the heavy shell of the British 6-inch howitzer, both on the morale of the enemy artillery and as a destructive agent, has been most noticeable.

At Sollum the most effective counterbattery method used by the Germans was that of employing dive-bombardment aviation under divisional control for critical targets.

(2) *Flash and sound ranging.* The British flash spotters did some useful work by locating many isolated 105-mm, Italian 75/46, and antitank guns at the Battle of the Omars. They were hampered, however, by poor observation. On the whole, because of the fluid nature of the operations in the desert, small use has been made of flash and sounding ranging.

Naval Bombardment

Bardia, Tobruk, and Benghazi have been the scenes of considerable British naval bombardments. Observation has been conducted largely by airplanes. To enable such observation to be effective, there has to be complete air superiority or strong fighter protection.

The open country of the desert and the mobile nature of the fighting require considerable effort to be expended to maintain communication, so that the ships can fire where and when the troops require it. A naval liaison officer is stationed at army headquarters to direct calls for assistance. However, in highly mobile operations, the exact situation was seldom known, even at corps headquarters, in time for a naval bombardment to be arranged. Under such circumstances, it was found necessary for the naval liaison officer to be at division headquarters. But, even more satisfactory results were obtained when this officer was with the forward brigade commander.

A forward army artillery observer works with a naval assistant to observe the naval firing. This forward artillery observer (termed FOO – forward observation officer – by the British) is usually a field artillery captain trained in the observation of the fire of bombardment ships. He calls for fire on his own initiative or on order from his unit commander. He observes the ship's fire, and when the bombarding ship is at anchor and the ground is difficult, he himself may control the fire instead of only observing it. Similarly, an artillery officer is embarked in every bombarding ship. This officer's primary duty is to interpret calls for fire received from the forward artillery observer and to place at the disposal of the ship's officers his understanding of the military situation, his knowledge of procedure, and his training. Targets were on some occasions indicated to the ships by army artillery using some shells. An army liaison officer on board the ship provides a picture of the operation in progress to the naval commander.

When ships come close to shore, as they must for the purpose of bombarding land installations, an air attack on the ships can be expected from an alert enemy. This makes any naval bombardment a hazardous operation. To reduce the vulnerability of the ships to these dangerous air attacks, bombardments have in most cases occurred at night. Although strong fighter protection or complete local air superiority can make enemy airplanes less dangerous, a naval bombardment still remains a risky enterprise because of the havoc that can be wrought on the warships by enemy submarines, torpedo boats, and coastal batteries.

The main value of naval bombardments has been the demoralization caused in the enemy ranks. Bombardment with 15-inch naval shells has a paralyzing moral effect on the enemy. US observers have reported, after conversations with Italian prisoners, that the explosions of the big projectiles have a tremendous psychological effect on those being shelled. Used in conjunction with army artillery, the results can be devastating to the enemy's *esprit de corps* and heartening to friendly forces.

Antitank Operations

Since the number of guns in use in Cyrenaica has been inadequate, all available are used or emplaced before the close of each operation. The antitank weapons, which are considered artillery by the British, are under the command of the division artillery commander in the British forces, and he is responsible for so placing his artillery and antitank guns that they will be mutually supporting. For any action, the artillery commander issues the necessary orders allotting the antitank weapons to both artillery and infantry units.

Antitank artillery regiments of 2-pounders consist of three battalions of two batteries of eight guns each, totaling 48 guns. They are organized exactly in the same manner as the artillery units, except for the number of personnel assigned. A few 6-pounder and 18-pounder batteries are being used. The 6-pounder guns are mounted portee, and the 18-pounders are truck-drawn. These units are also organized in the same fashion as the artillery batteries. The trucks used for the 2-pounders and 6-pounders portee are in general of the 1½-ton type.

The minimum amount of antitank guns required with units necessarily depends on the type of country; the more open the country, the larger the number of guns needed. In the desert ,where there are no natural tank obstacles, an attack may come from any direction. Headquarters and rear echelons must be protected. The large frontages covered and the wide dispersion necessary to minimize the effects of air attack make this problem of protecting rear elements a difficult one.

In the Western Desert, there have been in use no antitank warning systems, but the British make use of armored car patrols to prevent any surprises, and, as a rule, when one weapon fires, all prepare for action. Observation posts to the front and flank warn by visual signals of the approach of enemy armor.

Positions

In some cases, one battery of twelve 2-pounder antitank guns is detailed to protect each infantry regiment. Each attached supporting battery of artillery is often given one troop of four antitank 2-pounder guns. Organic artillery has the support of one antitank troop per artillery battery. These 2-pounder antitank units are not usually grouped or held in reserve at any point, but are actually placed in positions from 100 to 300 yards from the unit protected.

British artillery regiments are armed with 25-pounders which, although not so designed, have formed the basis of the antitank defense. This has been necessary, because the 2-pounder antitank gun has not proved effective. The 25-pounders are sited to give protection in depth, and, where the terrain permits, to give all-around protection to the position.

Antitank guns are placed to cover the 25-pounders in front, in intervals, and on the flanks. A proportion of them may have to be kept on wheels, to counter a threat from an unexpected direction. The fewer the total number of antitank guns, the larger will be the proportion kept in mobile reserve. But positions which guns may have to occupy will, in most cases, be reconnoitered and prepared beforehand.

Despite the fact that the British have usually operated with one and sometimes two 48-gun antitank regiments to the division, they have still found the number to be too small, and consequently have had their choice of positions affected by the necessity of choosing terrain which could allow them the maximum use of their inadequate number of antitank guns. Unless otherwise dictated by the terrain, it is considered better to place the few antitank guns in comparatively small localities for all-around defense, rather than to attempt a complete defense in depth over a wide area. The batteries of 25-pounders are used to provide depth to the defense. Antitank weapons are often placed from 100 to 300 yards on the flank of a battalion in action. For all-around defense of an organization, they are placed from 500 to 1,000 yards in front or on the flank of a battalion, with instructions to move close to the battalion position when tanks approach to within 1,000 yards of their positions.

German Tank Tactics

Since the antitank gunners have a formidable and important job to perform, knowledge of the enemy's capabilities makes it easier to accomplish. German tank crews are trained to try to gain the opportunity to register hits at 90 degrees' impact (i.e., get the target head-on or broadside). They attempt to put their own tank in such a position that it presents both front and side at an angle to opposing guns. Stationary firing is preferred, although they have fired on the move to force opposing tanks to close down, or to intimidate outposts and hostile gun crews. Artillery and antitank weapon crews have suffered many casualties from German machine gun fire delivered from moving tanks. When antitank guns have held their fire until German tanks approached to within 600 yards, the crews have frequently been knocked out by machine gun fire which penetrated their shields. If the ground permits, the German tanks move rapidly by bounds, firing between bounds when halted in hull-down positions.

British Tactics

All British antitank guns, except 18-pounders, are mounted portee on vehicles and equipped with ramps for unloading. These weapons have on occasion been fired from their vehicles.

(1) *Guns mounted on vehicles.* In using these weapons mounted portee, the gun is usually dismounted during firing, and the vehicles are removed under cover. The firing of guns mounted portee is unpopular, but when it is on the reverse slope of a hill, the gun is pushed up sufficiently to clear the crest. The driver of the truck must manipulate his truck on orders from the gunner in order to point the gun or place it in the proper firing position.

Although firing guns mounted portee is frowned upon, reports indicate that some officers consider firing from portees to be necessary under the following conditions: (1) when on patrol with armored cars; (2) when on escort or convoy duty with supply echelons, headquarters, or brigade columns advancing across the desert to the attack. In such circumstances, the object is to keep the enemy as far as possible from his prey, and so enable the convoy to proceed without loss. Full use is made of the mobility of the portees, the opening range varying according to the thickness of the armor carried by the enemy raiding columns. Firing while the portee is in motion and opening fire on a moving target at over 1,500 yards or a standing target at over 2,000 yards are considered a waste of 2-pounder ammunition. Bren guns mounted on the portees are used to force the enemy to close down his hatches and so reduce his visibility.

Although the use of the antitank guns on portees is an improvisation, it has had some success. During the Italian retreat from Benghazi to Tripoli on 6–7 February 1941, the British sent three columns a distance of 150 miles in 30 hours to cut off the retreat. In the battle which resulted, the antitank guns on improvised mounts encountered the Italian tanks, and 100 out of a total of 130 brand new M 13 Italian tanks were destroyed. One 1½-ton truck carrying antitank gun pointed to the rear went up and down the Italian column and claimed to have destroyed 25 tanks.

(2) *Direct laying at short range.* Usually 2-pounder antitank batteries are directed not to use direct laying on tanks until the tanks are within 800 yards of their positions. For 25-pounders, direct fire is held until the enemy vehicles are within 1,000 yards. Opening fire at 600 yards has been found to be too short, because the enemy machine guns are then within effective range. At 800 yards the antitank gun is still comparatively as accurate as at 600 yards, whereas the machine gun has lost considerable accuracy and is likely to penetrate the gun shields. In one case near Sidi Omar in Libya, a battalion commander of 25-pounder guns, seeing a tank attack coming, issued instructions for withholding fire until he gave the order. When the Axis tanks

had approached to within 800 yards, commands for direct laying were given. The result was a bag of 10 tanks.

(3) *Guns placed well forward.* All artillery and antitank weapons are placed well forward in either defensive or offensive situations. This permits the guns not only to support the infantry but to break up the leading wave of German medium (Mark III tanks). In battle, 18-pounders go into action on the flanks of the battle position and well forward. These 18-pounder antitank guns are truck-drawn and are of course kept mobile during an advance. All are fully manned and placed in position ready to fire when a halt is made.

The antitank guns are employed more often in pairs or bunches than as battalions or batteries. They are scattered about – often in pairs, and staggered, an effort being made to prevent a single strong sortie of enemy tanks knocking out all the guns. Positions taken are usually those which command a field of fire covering known danger areas. Wadis, large and small, are usually avenues of approach for hostile troops and are therefore given particular attention when siting guns.

(4) *Emplacements.* Certain antitank guns have a very strong muzzle blast. In the desert terrain of the Middle East, the force of this blast throws up a cloud of dust and sand that quickly reveals the position to enemy observers and often completely obscures the field of fire. Consequently, it is necessary to provide such guns with a blast screen. To eliminate this difficulty, a simple device has been used. It consists of a net of fine wire mesh, supported on pegs extending about 1 inch above the surface of the ground. The wire mesh should be so painted as to blend into the surrounding terrain. Other provisions for eliminating the dust include covering the critical areas with concrete or cement, paving the areas with stone, or treating them with oil. These areas are camouflaged whenever the guns are not firing. Precautions are also taken to make the inside of the emplacements as dustproof as possible in order to prevent dust from being sucked up in the rush of air following the discharge. Alternate positions are provided, and all emplacements are constructed to permit easy removal of the guns. These provisions have been found indispensable, for the fire of the weapon will inevitably betray even a well-constructed position.

When the terrain permits, the gun is defiladed from the enemy by emplacement on a reverse slope, or, if the country is flat, behind a natural or artificial mound. If an artificial mound is constructed, it should be as low as possible. The area of fire is usually large; 180 degrees is normal. The guns are given overhead camouflage where possible, but the coverings are constructed so that they can be easily removed when there is need to close station rapidly. Basically, it is considered that the emplacement should be an open pit of minimum dimensions.

The Main Role: To Form a Secure Base

Every force, of whatever size, requires a secure base from which to attack if its intentions are offensive, or within which to maneuver for a counterstroke if its intentions are defensive. This problem is important in the desert, where attacks can come from any direction.

On a large scale, this secure base is called a "defensive position" by the British; on a small scale, they termed it a "pivot of maneuver." The terms are really similar, the only difference being that the "defensive position" is made up of a number of "pivots of maneuvers."

The framework of the pivot of maneuver consists of the antitank gun positions, and the formation of this framework is the chief role of the artillery, whether in attack or in defense. Every gun, field or antitank, is included in the framework. The framework also is strengthened temporarily by the inclusion of tanks in hull-down positions, particularly in the case of a pivot of maneuver formed by an armored brigade. The field artillery performs a secondary role as well – that of producing bombarding or harassing or covering fire. The more exposed sites are allotted to the antitank guns. Every gun section has nearby infantry protection, the two forming together a definite defense area. The escort is armed with machine guns whenever possible.

(1) *The Framework.* The actual form of framework, of course, varies with the ground. The main position is formed around the field artillery. Regiments are placed with their batteries in depth, so that attacks from any direction will meet with an equal reception. A diamond formation often is considered the best solution. The positions of the guns are laid out so that the zones of fire interlock, and at the same time so that the whole gun area can be covered with fire. Dead ground within the position is covered by antitank guns, normally drawn from those included in the composition of the field artillery regiments.

An outpost position in front of the main position toward the enemy is often required to prevent observation of the main positions. These outposts are formed of antitank guns, normally drawn from the infantry antitank companies, with the close escort of infantry, as mentioned above. The outpost dispositions are in depth, the front edge being placed on or just over the crest in front of the main position; and the antitank dispositions are coordinated with those of the main positions, so that the whole area forms one complete net. The field artillery may be unable to carry out its secondary role (covering fire) if this outpost position is not provided.

A reserve of mobile antitank guns is held within the position. From this reserve, guns can be sent to give close support to batteries attacking from the "pivot," to extend the flanks of the outpost position if an enemy threat develops from an unexpected direction, or to strengthen the outpost line or the main position if the force is thrown temporarily on the defensive.

(2) *In the attack.* The British consider that there are only two legitimate tasks for antitank guns in the attack: (a) to form the framework after a successful attack, and (b) to protect the flanks of attacking infantry tanks.

The antitank gun mounted on its portee is not a tank, and any attempt to use it as such by requiring it to accompany the leading waves of a tank or infantry attack inevitably results in severe losses. Every effort is made to place antitank guns in position at the objective as soon as it is captured.

The commander of the antitank guns detailed for consolidating the objective when captured is therefore given a free hand to move his guns as he thinks fit. Often, it proves best to move the guns in bounds as the attack progresses. The antitank commander himself accompanies the commander of the unit that he is supporting, and on arrival at the objective makes a plan of the framework of the consolidation defense. If an enemy tank counterattack is launched before the consolidation framework is made, the antitank commander places his guns on or near the objective as soon as possible, and then uses them from the portees, taking advantage of any cover that can be found. Speed is essential, and it is for that reason only that he uses his guns as if they were tanks. If the consolidation framework has time to get into position, its object is to destroy counterattacking tanks. In this case, therefore, the antitank guns are used on the ground, concealed to the utmost, and dug in as thoroughly as time will permit. They are taught not to reveal their positions prematurely by opening fire at long range. Their fire is held until the enemy tanks are within the range at which their armor will be pierced by the 2-pounder. Nearby infantry protection is provided with the guns, and snipers are placed to pick off enemy forward artillery observers who push in close with the object of spotting the antitank guns.

In protecting the flanks of attacking tanks or infantry, the object of the antitank artillery is to keep the enemy at a distance. Then, the gun is used from its portee and opens fire at longer ranges. But, since it is seldom possible to forecast the direction of an enemy attack, the guns are not normally committed to any positions at the outset. The antitank commander, therefore, keeps his guns mobile, and, together with representatives of his sub-units, carries out continuous reconnaissance of the area for which he is responsible, noting especially any ground in which hull-down positions are available. If an enemy flank attack develops, he moves his guns to meet it, either dropping into position on the ground to lie in wait when the enemy has to pass a defile, or fighting portee and using his mobility to prevent the enemy from closing the range.

(3) *In the defense.* In the defense, the antitank gun has one object – to kill tanks. The enemy will, of course, do all that he can to spot and knock out the guns of a defense before he launches his tanks. Every effort is made, therefore, to prevent the positions from being disclosed until the enemy tanks advance to the attack and are within range of the antitank guns. The range must be short enough to enable the shell to pierce the armor. Harassing and bombardment tasks are carried out by the 25-pounder guns that are situated in covered positions.

The efforts to avoid observation are directed toward concealment and protection. Scrub ground, or other rough ground, is chosen wherever possible, and digging is done with great care. Movement of all personnel is rigidly controlled.

Guns are placed so as to give effect to the principle of concentration of fire. This is necessary, as the German tanks usually attack in a mass, which cannot be engaged effectively by single guns.

Guns are, therefore, normally sited by troops. The four guns of the 2-pounder troop are spread over an area of about 400 yards square, and they must, of course, be mutually supporting. The four guns of the 25-pounder troops also adopt this formation if employed in a purely antitank role; but if the troop has a secondary role (covering fire) as well, it adopts a more concentrated formation in order to obtain fire control. For this purpose, an arrangement roughly the shape of a half-moon, with intervals of about 70 yards between guns, has been found satisfactory. Depth within the field artillery regiment is obtained by siting the troops in diamond formation, 800 yards between troops, all troops being mutually supporting.

Effect of Artillery on Tanks

The following is the German teaching on the effect of field artillery on the tanks which they have encountered in the desert:

Armor of 60-mm or less is penetrated at ranges up to 600 meters by the 105-mm gun-howitzer 18, with angle of impact from normal to 30 degrees using charge 5 or 6. The 105-mm gun, Model 18, penetrates all thicknesses of armor encountered at ranges up to 1,500 meters with medium-charge and armor-piercing shell. Direct hits from the 150-mm howitzer, Model 18, with IIE percussion-fuse (instantaneous) projectiles have set enemy tanks on fire, or put them out of action by destruction of the drive mechanism. Thus, when engaging tanks with the heavy field howitzer, the bursts should not be largely *over* as when firing armor-piercing shells, but should be evenly distributed, some *over,* some *short.* Concentrations of artillery fire have been very effective against tank assembly points.

Smoke

Smoke, although not used extensively, has been employed occasionally in Libyan operations, and in these smoke operations the artillery has been one method of releasing smoke.

Conditions naturally vary, but observers report that smoke can often be used effectively. Some difficulties with the use of smoke are caused by desert winds, which are sometimes quite variable. Different sizes of whirlwinds, which veer and change direction, constantly make it difficult to estimate the wind when laying a smoke screen. Smoke has, however, many possibilities in connection with operations by armored formations.

Characteristics

Three main factors affect the use of smoke in the desert, as elsewhere:

(1) The force and direction of the wind.

(2) Turbulence (which is the gustiness of the wind) and the effect of the bright sun or air currents.

(3) Humidity.

These factors do not remain constant, the force and direction of the wind being particularly liable to sudden change. Moreover, air eddies caused by the configuration of the ground may make the force and direction of the wind different at the spot where shells land and at the gun position. It is, therefore, impossible to specify particular weather conditions in which smoke will be effective. A decision on this point is reached usually by a method of trial and error, for which time must be allowed.

In desert areas, high-explosive shell produces a substantial cloud of dust, and it may therefore often be practical to mix HE with smoke and so produce a satisfactory screen when conditions are not entirely suitable for the use of smoke alone. This fact also makes it possible to economize in the use of smoke shell and bombs, only limited quantities of which are usually carried.

Tactical Employment

All antitank guns depend on direct observation to obtain fire effect. If they can be deprived of their observation, their fire is automatically neutralized. In this fact lies the greatest value of smoke, particularly to armored divisions.

In attacks, smoke has been used for the following purposes:

(1) To conceal local preparatory moves by supporting weapons such as antitank guns, machine guns, and mortars.

(2) To screen a forward movement preparatory to assault.

(3) To screen tanks from the observation of antitank guns and artillery observation posts on the flanks of the attack.

(4) To provide a smoke barrage on the front of the attack.

(5) To indicate the objectives to tanks.

Smoke screens required during the preparatory stages of the attack and during the advance to the objective are usually provided by the artillery. Assistance is sometimes given by infantry mortars when other tasks and the range permit. For a smoke barrage on the front of the attack, a crossing wind is necessary, and particular attention is paid to timing to insure that the attacking tanks are not placed in the dilemma of having either to wait for the barrage to lift, or to pass through it with the risk of being silhouetted against it on the far side.

In any attack, some guns are either not located or not destroyed. In such situations, some advantage has been obtained by smoke clouds laid down over the whole area, for the lack of visibility usually hampers the guns more than the tanks. This smoke is not used to form a screen, for it is considered more effective to form a pall of smoke over the enemy defensive area.

In defense situations, smoke is used to blind attacking enemy tanks. When used for this purpose, a smoke screen is put down beyond the effective antitank range. Otherwise it will merely assist the enemy by depriving the antitank guns of essential observation. The provision of a smoke screen of this kind usually is a task for the artillery.

German tanks in a hull-down position at over 2,000 yards' range are not only difficult targets, but also beyond the effective range of antitank guns. Much of the Axis fire is by direct laying. In many cases, therefore, the best method of dealing with Axis fire has been by a smoke screen. Care is then taken that this smoke screen is well clear of the British front lines, for if it is too close, it will merely serve as cover for the German advance.

While the smoke is in place, Axis unarmored troops are attacked by fire. Observation posts well out to a flank are found to be necessary, and every opportunity is taken to disorganize and cause casualties to the enemy while he is assembling for the attack.

Another use of smoke in the defense has been the blinding of the enemy's close-support tanks and other supporting weapons, by interposing a smoke screen between them and the enemy assault tanks. This task may be within the power of both the defenders' close-support tanks and artillery. When smoke was used for this purpose, care was taken to avoid assisting the enemy by providing him with cover, behind which he cold move forward infantry detachments in support of his assaulting tanks.

For covering a disengagement or a withdrawal, all types of smoke-producing weapons are used, smoke screens at the longer ranges being put down by the artillery, medium-range screens by close-support tanks, and short-range screens by the use of special dischargers and 2-inch bomb throwers. Tanks capable of producing tail smoke have also been used effectively for this purpose by both the Germans and the British.

Supply Methods

The outstanding characteristic of supply in the desert is the vulnerability of supply lines caused in large part by the fluidity of operations. The British have relied on supply dumps to a greater extent than the Germans, who use supply trains. The artillery plays an important role in the defense of both dumps and columns.

Supply trains are close up to maintain the momentum of the attack by supplying fuel and ammunition as required. Recovery crews go into battle with their units.

The Germans usually advance to the line of departure under cover of darkness in the early morning hours. They may give battle early in the morning, pause about midday for refueling and maintenance, and give battle again before dark. Return to bivouac is made after dark; hence the location of his bivouac area is difficult to discover. Whenever possible, tank attacks are made with the sun low behind the German tanks. Movement in the advance is fast – at least 20 miles per hour. The normal distance between halts, if no combat occurs, is about 40 miles. Refueling, replenishing of ammunition, and maintenance are carried out under the protection of artillery, antitank weapons, infantry, and overhead fighter protection. These operations are accomplished in full view of the enemy.

PART THREE

German Defensive Tactics, 7 May–15 June 1941

by the
US Army Intelligence Service

German Defensive Tactics,
7 May–15 June 1941

Original Doctrine

A sound defensive system existed in the German Army prior to the Libyan campaign, but it had to be expanded and altered to meet special conditions existing in the desert. The German doctrine of defense, which formed the basis of the system developed in Libya, may be summarized as follows:

(1) Effective fire is more important than cover.
(2) The object of the defense is to wear down an attack before launching a counterattack, generally with armored troops.
(3) Reconnaissance must be made to discover enemy intentions and to screen one's own positions, which are organized in depth.
(4) A linked fire plan must cover the entire front.
(5) Most of the fire should be concentrated to cover the *Stützpunkt* [strongpoint], which is the key to the position and the objective toward which the enemy is likely to put forth his main effort.
(6) A series of mutually supporting centers, each capable of all-around defense, must be organized in depth.

For the defense, troops are disposed in three main positions:

(1) *Vorgeschobene Stellungen,* or advanced positions.
(2) *Gefechtsvorposten,* or battle outposts.
(3) *Hauptkampflinie,* or chief battle line, corresponding to the US main line of resistance. This main defensive position is designed to be held until the counterattack.

In a paper written in early June 1941, a German major lamented the fact that "Our people know next to nothing about the construction of defenses. We have scarcely any exercise in this phase of warfare in our peacetime training. The junior commander does not realize that positional infantry warfare is 60 percent with the spade, 30 percent with the field glasses, and only 10 percent with the gun." In the same paper, the major indicates his belief in the superiority of British camouflage and deception.

This criticism was apparently well founded, for the plans for defenses in the spring of 1941 indicated the inadequacy of German defensive training at that time.

In the first German defenses in Libya there was a purely linear fire plan – that is, with units bivouacked within a thin ring of weapons, and weapons, if grouped at all, bunched without variety. This was natural; probably for the first time since they were formed as units, the Germans found themselves seriously on the defensive after their first failure at Tobruk. They regarded this defensive phase as purely temporary; units were to be covered by an artillery barrage of two batteries over the defiladed tanks of one regiment, part of one machine gun battalion, and two engineer companies.

A captured document dated May 15 shows a plan of defense for Fort Capuzzo. The antitank guns are strung out in a straight line on the road front. Defense is all-around, however, and there is an advanced position. The only specific roles in defense are assigned to artillery and antitank guns. Counterattack is the master thought in all these documents and infantry defense is a role left (in one paragraph) to an unpopular Italian battalion.

The Plan Unfolds

On 7 May, the commander of the *15th Panzer Division* reiterated previous defensive instructions which had been disregarded. Because of the width of the African front, he discarded the theoretical subdivision into advanced positions, battle outposts, and chief battle line, and divided defended areas into battle outposts, a main defense line, and reserves. The battle outposts, because of the huge front, were to be placed only where the enemy could approach unawares; their role was reduced to that of observation posts by day and listening posts at night. The main defense line (US main line of resistance) must be completely covered by fire. It is pointed out that this line must not be thin for two reasons: because in a thin line a penetration rapidly develops into a breakthrough, and because casualties are heavy when the artillery has registered on a line. During the day, only a part of the machine guns are moved up. This *15th Panzer Division* directive indicates that at least one-quarter of each company, battalion, and regiment must be kept in reserve for counterattack.

Following these principles, the commanding general of the *15th Panzer Division* gave his orders. The building of new defenses was to begin the next night. Half of the available force was to work in a zone 550 yards behind the front line; reserves and rear pickets were stationed farther back. Heavy weapons were to be sited the same night, the heavy machine guns on the flanks, the antitank guns echeloned in depth, with antitank rifles and some antitank guns in front of the positions. Sector reserves were to be formed – one or two sections to each company, one company to each battalion. Emphasis was placed on constructing dummy positions, removing and shuffling landmarks, and cutting radio masts to one or two yards in order to conceal headquarters.

Groups varying from 20 to 80 men, supported by antitank and antiaircraft guns, were pushed forward to operate as battle outposts. By 10 May, two nights after the order, some 560 positions were being planned, including rifle positions in depth 1,000 yards from the wire. Work started immediately on some of them.

In the pivotal Ras Meduaaur salient, positions were laid out in depth and heavy weapons were sited on the night of 8/9 May. There was a company front to every 550 yards and an antitank gun to every 200 yards. The salient was held by one battalion, with two companies in reserve.

The Meduaaur defenses were tested on 17 May, when the British attacked a *Stützpunkt* on the German left flank. The defense proved sound. Two German companies fought on in their antitank trenches after the position had been penetrated by tanks, finally repulsing the British. A second attack was driven off by a reserve of one tank company.

A separate group from the *15th Panzer Division* was located in the frontier area. On 14 May construction was ordered of a scarp sector and of two sectors of advanced positions at Point 191, just south of the Sollum coastal sector. Prior to this, advanced positions had been outlawed. On the coast, there were to be an antitank ditch, wired on either side and covered by fire; field positions for light and heavy weapons, connected by crawl trenches; and antitank emplacements with wire and mines in front of the positions and within them. Low sandbag fortifications had to be used on the scarp, where digging was impossible. Here nests were to be built around antitank weapons placed in groups, wire was to be laid around both nests and groups of nests, and the area between groups was to be strewn with mines and wire. The work was to be done at night and camouflaged by day against air observation.

Upon further orders from the corps to build positions on the frontier for "a long period of defense," the commanding officer of the Frontier Group appointed a reconnaissance headquarters of four officers to start work immediately at Fort Capuzzo. The principles laid down in the directive were: these *Stützpunkte* must be held by weak forces until the mobile reserve could counterattack; they must have all-around defense; they must be laid in areas where there is natural security against tanks, natural cover for infantry, obstacles, and observation posts; and there must be dummy positions.

The front (to be plotted on 19 May) was to be made up of four positions: Sidi Omar, Point 206, Point 191, and a coastal position in contact with Point 191. The rear (to be plotted on 20 May) was to contain another group of four positions – Point 208, Fort Capuzzo, Musaid, and Upper Sollum. About 500 men daily were needed for the work.

It can hardly be said that a free hand was given to the reconnaissance headquarters, for on 19 May there was an order to start construction of two *Stützpunkte* on 20 May, one at Point 206 and another at Point 196. The former is five miles south of Fort Capuzzo, while the latter includes Qalala. Each of these *Stützpunkte* was to have an advanced point. Work was to be done day and night in two shifts – 0200 to 0900 hours, and 1500 to 2000 hours. Two German engineer platoons and 160 men from the Italian battalion were to be used on each position, and they were to be heavily screened by tanks, armored cars, artillery, antiaircraft guns, and motorcycle troops. The garrisons considered necessary to hold the *Stützpunkte* were:

Point 206:
2 infantry companies.
1 heavy machine gun platoon.
1 heavy mortar section.
3 37-mm and 1 50-mm antitank guns.
3 20-mm and 1 88-mm antiaircraft guns.
1 artillery *observation post* and an alternative OP.

Point 196:
1 infantry company.
1 heavy machine gun platoon.
1 heavy mortar section.
1 light infantry gun battery.
13 37-mm and 1 50-mm antitank guns.
3 20-mm antiaircraft guns.
Several artillery observation posts.
Gun positions for 1 or 2 artillery batteries.

Advanced point:
1 reconnaissance section in foxholes.

Meanwhile, however, the main defense works of the German *Afrika Korps* were being constructed at Gazala (map No. 3) by a labor force of nearly 2,000 men. Great pains were taken; reconnaissance lasted from 9 to 13 May. Marking out began on 14 May, and the whole advanced position at Bir el Heial (Point 209), six miles to the east, was finished by 23 May. Work on the antitank defenses and at Alam Hamza began the next day.

The work was governed by three principles: all-around defense; the theory of the *Stützpunkt,* or main defensive position; and a model circular platoon position planned by Rommel himself, 270 by 270 yards and laid out in an interdependent series.

The view was that the Wadi Embarech was the key to the Gazala position, and it was therefore planned that it should be covered by a defensive area 2½ miles south of KM 110 on the Via Balbia, between Points 179 and 181. The position was divided into five sectors as follows:

(1) *Bir el Heial.* At this advanced position were 11 platoon defense areas between Point 209 and the escarpment. This fits into no known conception of advanced positions or battle outposts, but, as it was finished first, this position was probably meant simply to cover the rest of the work in case of an accident at Tobruk. The Germans felt that the situation on the frontier was "tense" at this period.

(2) *Coast.* Between the forward position on the escarpment at El Azragh and the sea at Point 22 (dune) were nine platoon areas.

(3) *Desert.* Between the main position, Points 179–181, and Alam Hamza were 15 to 20 platoon areas.

(4) *Rocks.* Between Points 179–181 and the Via Balbia were 11 platoon areas.

(5) *Block.* An antitank trench was placed at KM 107 on the Via Balbia, covered by antitank guns from caves in the scarp face.

Thus, at the main defensive position, including the outpost of Alam Hamza, there were to be 26 to 30 platoons out of a total of 46 to 51 platoons – that is, a total of about two regiments of infantry.

The alternative of defense on an arc was rejected because the front would then be too long. Positions were organized in depth with self-contained infantry squads as the basic units. Three of these squads formed a platoon area and three platoon areas made up a company defense area.

It was proposed that the Gazala position should be held either by two Italian divisions or by two Italian regiments, according to their strength, of which Rommel was ignorant. These were to be stiffened by German "corset-stays." It was noted in particular that, as visibility south of the scarp is five to seven miles, the advantage is with the position that has its back to heavily intersected country. The Wadi Embarech thus gives good battery positions, while the Wadi Balban and Wadi el Aasi give protection against tanks.

At last, a German theory of defense in the desert was emerging as a discontinuous line of big *Stützpunkte,* each crystallized out of model "triplices," three sections in the platoon, three platoons in the company, each of these small units capable of all-around defense. As yet, however, there had been no statement on the siting of the heavy weapons within the infantry group.

The frontier defenses then consisted of:

A Sollum group as the main "defense front," with one "positional battalion" – actually a battalion of *Schützen Regiment 104* had to support this position battalion; the *Reconnaissance Battalion 33* and a Bardia group on the right flank and in the rear; and a tank group and the divisional reserve ready for mobile intervention.

Sollum and Musaid were finally ordered built into independent *Stützpunkte* on the principles outlined on 18 and 19 May, and Qalala also was ordered built by the Italians into a *Stützpunkt* after the operation of 26 and 27 May. A fourth important position had been laid down on 18 May, but the order apparently had been countermanded the next day.

The tank group was to stand ready 4½ miles north of Capuzzo, with forward troops at Alam Abu Dihak and Qalala.

Although the main work was done at Gazala, the main proving ground was felt even now to be the frontier. On 23 May, the commander of *Panzergruppe Ost,* which now included most of the whole of the *15th Panzer Division,* warned that "the British may at any time try to relieve Tobruk, either by a thrust to the north against the *15th Panzer Division,* then encircling us from the west, or by a drive north-west from south of Sidi Omar while containing our positions at Sollum and Capuzzo." On the strength of this estimate, he ordered positions to be held at Point 208, Sollum, Point 206, and Qalala.

More heavy weapons were promised – 88-mm dual-purpose guns, Italian heavy artillery, and an antitank battalion. An entire antiaircraft battery was brought up. Artillery was to concentrate particularly on the area west of Capuzzo, and the tank patrol contact at Point 206 and Qalala, and was to move with *Panzer Regiment 8*, being prepared to lay a general barrage on the area west of the *Stützpunkt*.

In short, the development looks large on the map, but contains no new ideas on the details of defense.

On 26 and 27 May, the Germans captured Halfaya Pass from the British, and were able to make further plans. Musaid and Sollum ceased to be important positions; they became *Rückhalten* – in baseball terminology, backstops. The center of the defense became Halfaya, with Qalala only a second *Stützpunkt*, and Point 206 again an important position.

Forces were redistributed, and orders given for defense as follows:

(1) *Halfaya.* A Sollum–Halfaya Pass Group was formed, consisting of one infantry battalion, two antiaircraft batteries, and one Italian mobile artillery regiment. Both routes up the scarp to the plateau were to be held; the bulk of the antitank weapons were to be put on the right wing, above the scarp; an Italian company was to be located in the center; the left wing on the coast was to be weak, but well mined; an outpost was to be put at Bir el Siweiyat; Qalala was to be held by a reinforced company; and one or two Italian platoons were to be the backstop.

(2) *Capuzzo.* The defenses of Point 208 were to be started on 27 May; Point 206 was to be held by a reinforced company.

There had been work in this defensive period, not only at Gazala, Meduaaur, and on the frontier, but also at the fourth German point of contact with British forces, on the Tobruk–El Adem road. Here, by 23 May, two machine gun battalions had created a regimental *Stützpunkt* of enormous size. On a truncated ellipse of 9½ miles running out from the scarp, they had built 76 groups, each of three positions placed checkerwise. The depth of the defended belt averaged 550 yards. Over the five miles accorded to one machine gun battalion were 26 heavy machine guns, 13 light machine guns, and about 30 antitank guns – an average of just over 270 yards to every antitank gun. The principal development, however, is that here the trefoil principle of defense first finds its place on a German map in North Africa. Also the battle outpost recurs, well-mined but ill-armed.

(3) *Security and reconnaissance.* A reinforced tank company was to cover the guns at Qalala and a reinforced reconnaissance unit was to patrol the line Sidi Omar–Qaret Abu Faris–Sidi Suleiman–Bir el Siweiyat.

There were only slight modifications on 3 May, when the main *Stützpunkte* of the frontier finally crystallized into four – Halfaya, Qalala, Point 206, and Point 208.

At the same time new orders were given to the *15th Schützen Brigade*, which held the Meduaaur salient, to prepare all-around defenses to meet a possible attack from either the north or the south. Holtzendorff, who had made a defensive reconnaissance at Gazala, was appointed infantry commander. Both battalions of *Schützen Regiment 115*, one battalion of *Schützen Regiment 10*, and two oasis companies were placed under him. These were assigned to three sectors – one battalion of *Schützen Regiment 104* (left), one battalion of *Schützen Regiment 115* (center), and one battalion of *Schützen Regiment 115* (right). The other companies were held in reserve, as was one battalion of *Panzer Regiment 5*, which was south of brigade headquarters. The *Antitank Battalion 39*, one company of the *Antitank Battalion 33*, and one company of the *Antitank Battalion 605* – a total of 50 antitank guns –were allotted to the salient, in addition to an artillery regiment and an engineer battalion. The whole position was at once reconstructed on Holtzendorff's arrival. The south-eastern bulge, or nose, of the salient was given up after it had been thoroughly mined between 2 and 6 June, and booby traps were planted in the dead ground.

Under the new plan, each battalion had two rifle companies forward, the heavy weapons company halfway back to battalion headquarters, the heavy machine gun company somewhat farther forward, and the third rifle company in battalion reserve. Sketches of the layout show the great bulk of the light machine guns up against the wire in pairs, with intervals of 40 to 80 yards. Half of the antitank guns were in the front line. Company frontages were about 830 yards, and positions were between 445 to 500 yards deep. The average front of a light machine gun was 55 yards. There was a total of six antitank guns for each company front, or two to every 280 yards. The siting of these antitank guns conformed with the laws of depth.

As usual, defense plans involved the preparation of a counterattack, this time on the right flank with two rifle companies, tanks, antitank guns, and the usual reserve company. The Italians on either flank were always a problem, and when *Armored Division Ariete* on the right was relieved by *Infantry Division Pavia* on 4 June, their extreme left *Stützpunkt* was occupied and improved. This was done by *Oasis Company 10*, which turned it into three platoon positions, while the reserve company of *II./Schützen Regiment 115* turned its rest area into a well-organized defense area with platoon *Stützpunkte*.

Barrage schedules were prepared for heavy machine guns and mortars. Under the new plan, eight antitank guns, with infantry guns and heavy mortars, were concentrated on either side of the new minefield in the center. Much had been accomplished, but on 7 June still further improvement was made by bringing up the guns of one battery of *Flak Regiment 18.*

A few days later, there was a weakening of antitank forces, to be explained by the threat of action on the frontier (on 12 June, three days before the British offensive). Only nine of the antitank guns outside the battalions remained, and *Engineer Battalion 33* was also moved. Infantry reserves were reallotted.

Engineer Battalion 33 left a record of its work in the Meduaaur salient. Besides taking part in several attacks with its special storm sections, it had removed 3,000 British and 800 Italian mines under fire by early May. On 19 May it began to straighten the salient, and finished by 1 June. During this period it had built 33 *Stützpunkte* and 10 special positions, each for two antitank guns and one machine gun. It had used 5,185 sandbags, constructed a 3,170-yard double fence, and planted an S-mine ring and a T-mine field, with 674 S-mines and 1,674 T-mines. In the abandoned nose of the salient, it had left another large field of 2,300 T-mines, 159 booby traps, 1,560 pressure mines, and 139 trip-wire mines.

The improvement in German defensive practice is exemplified by the layout of the weapons in *II./Schützen Regiment 104,* which was in the left flank of the salient on 20 June. There were groups of weapons extending all the way back to battalion headquarters; the light machine guns were thinned out in the front line until there was only one each 110 yards; the antitank guns were placed at 330-yard intervals; company frontage was 990 yards; and company depth (to battalion headquarters) was 1,100 yards.

Major Halierstedt, a German officer who at this time wrote a report on positional infantry warfare in Africa, was not yet satisfied. He emphasized the difficulties of Africa, where the climate required that work be done at night and with limited control. It was difficult also to find sufficient fields of fire for the numerous light machine guns in mobile units. A battalion sector in the Meduaaur salient was about 1,780 yards, and, on the basis of a two-company front, each company with 18 light machine guns, there were only 50 yards for each weapon.

The answer was the old one: disposition in depth. Heavy weapons, too, must be withdrawn to positions where they could fire over the forward lines and be controlled by one officer, the *Führer schwerer Waffen* (heavy weapons commander). It was easy to cover every point with fire, for there were 80 heavy and light weapons in a motorized infantry battalion. Indirect machine gun barrages at 2,200 yards had failed, for the troops had forgotten accuracy and correction in France. Barrage fire from all weapons, he said, should be brief, only a quarter or a half minute; otherwise, it would cost too much ammunition. Antitank guns should be hidden and should fire only when tanks attacked. Battalion antitank guns should remain hidden, also firing only when tanks attacked. Battalion antitank guns (three) should support the front line; other antitank guns (generally two platoons, or six guns of an antitank company) should remain somewhere near battalion headquarters. Any part of the battalion system which they do not control must be mined.

An officer named Ballerstedt made the first statement in writing on the trefoil in defense, which was mapped by *Machine Gun Battalion 8*. All weapons must, he said, be placed in half-moon triplices, the heavy in the center and the two light machine guns on the sides. We shall see later how this developed under the instructions of Major-General von Ravenstein.

The time approached when German theory was to be put to the test. Orders warning of the approaching tanks came on 12 June. They indicated the attack, but not that it would be a general offensive.

The Theory Tested on the Frontier

The Germans (*15th Panzer Division*) had established four main *Stützpunkte*:

(1) Halfaya – one battalion (three companies of *I. / Schützen Regiment 104*, and one company from the Italian *Battalion de Francesco*).

(2) Qalala – one company (*6th Oasis Company*).

(3) Point 206 (5 miles south of Capuzzo) – one company (probably from *Motorcycle Battalion 15*).

(4) Point 208 (5 miles west of Capuzzo) – one company (machine gun company from *Motorcycle Battalion 15*).

Each of these *Stützpunkte* had its artillery. Halfaya had eight and Qalala four 105-mm gun-howitzers, but details of the other two *Stützpunkte* are not known. All posts had antiaircraft guns, as shown below, and all of them were used principally against tanks.

The second element in the German defensive system was a mobile infantry reserve, consisting of 45 companies of infantry, some antitank guns, and some antiaircraft guns. This reserve played an unimpressive part in the battle.

The third element was a tank striking force, which was divided into two parts:

(1) *Panzer Regiment 8.*

(2) *Panzer Regiment 5*, followed by the two motorized machine gun battalions, which "clinched" the Germany victory by its wide desert sweep of 55 miles.

"Clinched" is used advisedly, for this result was made possible only by the terrific antitank performance of the twelve 88-mm guns of *I./Flak Regiment 33*, attached to the *15th Panzer Division*. This battalion was distributed as follows:

Halfaya – Four 88-mm and eight 20-mm guns (also covering Qalala).

Point 206 – Four 20-mm guns.

Point 208 – Four 88-mm and two 20-mm guns.

Infantry reserve – Nine 20-mm guns.

Panzer Regiment 8 – Four 88-mm and eight 20-mm guns.

The 88-mm gun, *Panzer Regiment 5*, and the solid defenses of Halfaya and Point 208 won the battle for the Axis. Documents show that it was touch-and-go on the second day, when elements of the *15th Armored Division* very nearly let British tanks into Bardia, being saved only by their 88-mm guns with pickup crews.

The Germans, whose theory was that the defensive positions should effect a temporary check pending a powerful armored counterattack, had stocked them with food and water for only two days. They took a great deal of punishment, but played an important part by gravely damaging the British tank force before the final attack.

An observation post was formed at Sidi Suleiman by *Reconnaissance Battalion 33* and a motorcycle platoon, and there is mention of battle outposts, which appear to have been no more than listening posts.

Germany's side of the battle is best studied by reference to the reports of Major Bach and Lieutenant Paulewicz, who commanded, respectively, a battalion of *Schützen Regiment 104* and a machine gun company of *Motorcycle Battalion 15*, in the two main positions. Four captured documents tell of the futile movements of the mobile infantry reserve, whose commander, Colonel Knabe, was at one time hidden in a hole beneath the main road within the area occupied by the British. The difficulties of *Panzer Regiment 8* are also related in this document.

But the most illuminating picture is that of a battery of *Flak Regiment 33*, which chalked up 92 armored vehicles (including 82 tanks), which they claimed to have completely destroyed with 1,680 rounds of 88-mm shell and 13,500 rounds of 20-mm shell. As the 20-mm fire knocked out only three tanks, the 88-mm guns got a tank for every 20 shells fired in this action.

The Action at Halfaya Pass

The defending forces were as follows: one company on the coastal plain behind a minefield, one Italian company facing east on the edge of the plateau, and one company facing to the south and west of the Italian company. Four 88-mm antiaircraft guns were sited in the front line covering the open right flank. The eight Italian gun-howitzers were distributed between the front line and the interval between Halfaya and Qalala, and the battalion held a company in reserve.

The main attack by the British tanks on the open right flank was stopped by the 88-mm guns after fire had been taken up by the 20-mm guns and all other weapons at 440 yards. When the attack had been broken, a patrol was sent out to establish the position of the British infantry, which was then pinned down by Axis artillery. There was a counterattack by the battalion reserve, in which 67 prisoners and important codes and maps were captured. A second attack by the British followed, in which the Axis held fire until the infantry was within 440 yards, then opened with 20-mm antiaircraft guns. The British plan to attack by the coast was foreseen and one 88-mm gun was placed there.

Two more infantry attacks on the second day (16 June) were stopped short by an artillery barrage, accompanied by 20-mm and infantry fire. During the morning, German airplanes bombed their own artillery and antiaircraft positions, and in the afternoon the ammunition situation became critical – the artillery reporting that only 600 shells remained and that antiaircraft ammunition was running short. Bach was worried about food and water. A message from the German *Afrika Korps* was dropped by air at 2000 hours: "All depends on holding Halfaya." He answered: "All depends on your sending us ammunition and food." As time had not permitted him to reconnoiter positions, he did not obey Knabe's order to clear the shore and concentrate on the pass. The next day aircraft dropped ammunition for small arms and 20-mm guns. The British retreat began, harassed by artillery, antiaircraft, and heavy machine gun fire from Halfaya, and in the evening the position was relieved.

In the course of the action at Halfaya, 20 British tanks and eight armored cars were destroyed, and 98 prisoners were taken. Losses were small – eight killed and 32 wounded (excluding antiaircraft and antitank personnel). The Iron Cross, Class I, was awarded to Bach.

The report of *I./Flak Regiment 33* indicated that this unit played an important role in the victory. Its guns opened up on the tanks at 2,200 yards at 0500, knocking out one cruiser tank; then they held fire until the opposing tank force approached to within 330 yards, where dust did not obscure the targets, and bagged nine infantry tanks. After this the entire battalion fired high-explosive shell into the infantry, forcing it to take cover. The 88-mm guns on the coast knocked out three infantry tanks. On the second day, the 20-mm guns were pushed forward to eliminate machine gun nests and an *observation post* at 1,650 yards, while the coastal gun was used to scatter concentrations of motor transport and an infantry battalion. The antiaircraft guns thus eliminated 14 of the 20 attacking tanks, and doomed the British attack to failure.

The Action at Point 208

When the attack alarm was given, two patrols from Point 208 were sent two miles to the south because of mist which blanketed the area. Fire was held for some time after tanks were first observed, because they were in the barrage area of Point 206. The 37-mm antitank guns opened fire first, to drive off armored cars which were within 165 yards. Meanwhile, the barrage from Point 206 had ceased, but Paulewicz gave orders to hold all antitank fire until vehicles approached to within close range in order not to give away antitank positions prematurely. This policy proved effective, for subsequent British artillery fire on Point 208 was inaccurate.

At 1015 on 15 June, the British made a pincer attack on Point 208 with 45 tanks. The attacking force was soon reinforced to 70 tanks. Fire by all weapons was opened at close range. The left or easterly sector of the area was overrun, one 37-mm and one 20-mm antitank gun were knocked out, and one of the 88-mm guns was silenced. The commander of Point 208 immediately ordered the three 88-mm guns on the other flank to concentrate on the eastern sector, and this saved the situation for the Germans by enabling the silenced 88-mm to reopen fire. By 1130 hours 11 British tanks had been smashed and the rest driven away, and in the afternoon a new 14-tank attack was thrown back with eight tanks knocked out. After that, Point 208 was secure and was used as a base for re-forming *Panzer Regiment 8* and the mobile infantry reserve.

I./Flak Regiment 33 had knocked out 19 tanks with its 88-mm guns. The description of the battle given in the battalion report differs slightly from that of Paulewicz. The 88-mm guns opened up at 1,760 yards and drove back the first tank attack without inflicting any casualties. In the pincer attack, the gun on the left flank knocked out two cruiser tanks before it was overrun. The three other 88-mm guns on the right opened fire upon the other arm of the pincers at 1,550 yards without getting hits, but later knocked out seven cruiser tanks at close range. In the third attack, the 88-mm guns opened at 880 yards, knocking out eight cruiser and later two infantry tanks.

The Action at Point 206

Point 206 had no 88-mm guns, but five British tanks were knocked out by its antitank guns in the first attack. The 20-mm antiaircraft guns, however, proved useless. This *Stützpunkt,* the only one captured by the British, was finally overrun after the last 50-mm gun had been knocked out.

The Mobile Infantry Reserve

The 20-mm guns of the infantry reserve were ineffective against British tanks, even at close range. One battery engaged tanks at 110 yards in the area south of Capuzzo, but retired rapidly when its shells bounced harmlessly off the armor plates. Another 20-mm gun drove away an infantry tank without damaging it by firing 180 rounds in rapid succession at 110 yards. An 88-mm gun, detached from Halfaya and emplaced alone east of Capuzzo, opened fire at 2,200 yards and knocked out four infantry tanks.

The difficulties of the mobile reserve during this day have been recounted in the reports of its unit commanders. The commander of a company of *Motorcycle Battalion 15* described the fear among his troops when infantry tanks approached, and told how they unsuccessfully attempted to recapture Capuzzo. On one occasion, a platoon ran a mile while the German antitank guns were taking refuge under cover of a solitary 88-mm gun.

British tanks occupied Capuzzo after the mobile reserve advanced through it to relieve Point 206. After two ill-organized attempts to recapture Capuzzo, which had previously been held by Italian troops, the reserve found that their most powerful antitank guns could do nothing against the infantry tanks at 550 yards. In a fierce counterattack, these infantry tanks rolled over that part of the road where Colonel Knabe was hidden, and the mobile infantry reserve retreated.

This situation was admitted by the Germans to have been the most serious in the battle. There was danger of a breakthrough to Bardia, where their base installations were located, but they were saved by one 88-mm gun which had been lying derelict with a broken tractor north of Capuzzo. It was coupled to a truck, and a pickup crew was recruited from the transport column. The tanks of *Panzer Regiment 8* were being slowly driven back. For the moment, the 88-mm gun stopped firing and withdrew to avoid encirclement. In a new position, it knocked out two infantry tanks. The British tanks retired and formed for a new attack on the other flank. The 88-mm gun hurriedly took up a new position and knocked out two tanks. The rest retired, believing that they were opposed by a number of 88-mm guns. The gun then followed up to counterattack on the right flank of a German tank advance, and knocked out five more infantry tanks in front of Capuzzo. The situation was saved, and Knabe was released from his hiding place.

The Tank Striking Force

German defensive theory emphasizes the role of the armored striking force, stating that defense is simply a temporary expedient. *Panzer Regiment 8* meant it to be temporary indeed, for by 1030 on the first day of the action they were well up from their assembly area north of Capuzzo, and by 1130 one company was already engaged on the frontier. Reinforced by a second company, it nevertheless had to withdraw before superior numbers. In doing this, it ran out of ammunition, allowing the British to take Capuzzo.

By this time two Mark III tanks had been knocked out, and some others had fallen out with damage to their guns and engines. A third company was now called in to prevent the British from breaking through west of Capuzzo, but it also had to retire. Later in the day, the 1st and 2nd Battalions of *Panzer Regiment 8* attacked Capuzzo in succession, but failed to get through and withdrew before dark to a position near the Bardia road. *Panzer Regiment 8* had violated the rules of German tank doctrine by attacking in detail.

Next day, 16 June, the regiment was ordered to attack Capuzzo once more, this time with both battalions combined. The 1st Battalion had now only six, four, and nine of the 8 Mark IV, 18 Mark III, and 13 Mark II tanks, respectively, with which it started the battle. The British tanks struck out of the morning mist, and once more there were heavy casualties in the 3rd Company. The commander of the 1st Battalion had his tank shot through twice by fire from infantry tanks at 330 yards, and the 1st Battalion had to withdraw with only three operational Mark III tanks and one Mark II. It is clear that, if British tanks had been able to take Bardia, *Panzer Regiment 8* would have been finished.

By the evening of the second day, two Mark II, nine Mark III, and two Mark IV tanks had been repaired (the damage had been mostly to guns), and stood ready to defend Bardia.

The report by *I./Flak Regiment 33* explains some of these moves. The four 88-mm guns attached to the regiment had participated in the first frontier action. After opening up at 2,000 yards, they had knocked out 12 tanks, two of them infantry tanks struck at 1,320 yards. British artillery then forced the 88-mm guns to withdraw (it will be noted increasingly that the chief fear of the Germans is British artillery). During these engagements, a 20-mm gun knocked out an infantry tank with a lucky hit on the exhaust at 275 yards.

In the Capuzzo action of the second day, 88-mm guns, firing through a mist, knocked out eight infantry tanks, including one hit in the turret at 550 yards. British artillery, however, forced, the crews of the 88-mm guns to take cover, and British tanks meanwhile approached to within 330 yards and damaged three of the four guns. The one intact 88-mm and two 20-mm guns knocked out three more British tanks at ranges between 275 and 350 yards, but the German tanks were not in a condition to follow up this advantage.

II./Panzer Regiment 8 was now ordered to cross the frontier and join with *Panzer Regiment 5* of the 5th Division. An infantry officer who observed the resulting action attributed the regiment's success in breaking through a British tank force on the frontier to the artillery and antiaircraft support. The 88-mm guns appear here in a new role. The tank battalion had picked up those which had saved Point 208, and had repaired at least two others damaged at Capuzzo. Some of these ran on the flank of the advance, others went 220 yards ahead of the leading tanks. The first group knocked out two infantry tanks, and the second plunged straight ahead at the British formation of 20 infantry tanks, destroying seven of these before the German tanks had opened up. The way was clear to a rendezvous with *Panzer Regiment 5*, as well as to Halfaya. *I./Panzer Regiment 8* suffered heavy losses from two British air attacks while en route to join the 2nd Battalion. The first attack was by six strafing Hurricanes and the second by numerous bombers. Total losses were one Mark IV (knocked out), one Mark III (crew casualties), and one ammunition, one fuel, and one transport truck (rendered unserviceable). Five of the personnel were killed and 16 were wounded. The battalion turned back from this rendezvous.

The German defensive system had contributed heavily to a victory which might easily have been a defeat. Future historians may say that the battle was won by the 88-mm gun and the 50-mile drive of *Panzer Regiment 5* through the desert to Sidi Suleiman, but it was the stubborn defense of *Stützpunkte* that gave an opportunity for the employment of offensive tactics. The organization of these defensive positions in depth had allowed them to hold out until a typical German limited counteroffensive could be put in motion.

Without the 88-mm gun, however, none of the positions could have repulsed the British drive. It opened fire either at 2,200 to 1,760 yards or at 880 to 550 yards, but its most effective ranges were certainly in the lower bracket. British sources state that artillery is the most effective means of combating this gun, which is said to have destroyed 79 tanks as compared with the 64 claimed by the tanks of *Panzer Regiment 8*.

New Theory From Experience on the Frontier

The frontier warfare resulted in a flood of theory on defense, much of which originated with Rommel and his three major-generals, Neumann-Silkow, Summermann, and Ravenstein.

Neumann-Silkow

Neumann-Silkow emphasized the value of antitank trenches, as at Point 208, which remain tenable even when an enemy has penetrated a defense area. He ordered them to be dug at all positions. He declared the personality of the *Stützpunkt* commander (undoubtedly thinking of the fine showmanship of Bach) to be one of the most important elements in *Stützpunkt* defense.

For special emphasis, he singled out the camouflage of Point 208, where the British had not seen the position, even after penetrating the defended area. He directed that stone walls be removed and used in future only on dummy positions, and that 88-mm guns should open fire before the 37- and 50-mm weapons, which should remain hidden and fire armor-piercing ammunition at short ranges.

The artillery in defense, he said, has three principal missions: to attack concentrations of tanks and motor transport; to disperse columns pushing past *Stützpunkte*; and to lay a barrage on infantry attacks. It was not to fire upon individual tanks except at close range, when the position had been penetrated. All artillery (including antiaircraft) must be prepared to move rapidly out of the *Stützpunkt* in an offensive role.

In the counterattack, artillery was to fire upon tank concentrations, infantry in trucks, enemy batteries, and retreating forces of all kinds. The 88-mm guns were to be used for opening a tank battle. German tanks were not to halt while under enemy fire, but were either to make a sudden dash in one direction or to disperse.

Summermann

Summermann worked out an elaborate timetable for individual weapons in the defense of a *Stützpunkt*. By the time he wrote his report, the individual positions on the frontier had been vastly improved in the light of the recent battle, and he believed them to be impregnable (in the German sense, that is, tenable until the counterattack by tanks). The governing principle was all-around antitank defense with every weapon, including rifles, that can damage any part of a tank. Summarized, the system was this:

First phase. Antiaircraft and antitank guns open fire on attacking tanks, the heaviest fire being directed on masses of tanks and tanks attacking gaps in the minefields. The artillery fires on enemy artillery accompanying the tanks and on all active batteries; if there is no artillery accompanying the tanks, the artillery fires on tank masses. The infantry defends with heavy machine guns, light machine guns, and rifles against low-altitude air attack, there being no other weapon then available against enemy aircraft.

Second phase. Antiaircraft and antitank guns, then guns and antitank rifles, fire on the tanks, aiming now at the nearest, often firing very low over the heads of their own troops. The artillery fires on the enemy artillery covering the attack of the motorized infantry, and fires also on any masses concentrating behind the tanks. The infantry divides its attention between enemy aircraft and the tracks of tanks.

Third phase. Antitank guns continue to fire on tanks, concentrating on those that have penetrated the positions. This fire naturally endangers the defending infantry, but is less dangerous to them than the enemy tanks. The artillery continues to fire counterbattery and on targets of opportunity. The infantry now finds its position eased by the arrival of friendly aviation over the *Stützpunkt*, and turns to fighting tanks with hand-to-hand weapons – bottles of gasoline, grenades, explosives – at the same time engaging the enemy infantry.

Enemy penetrations into subsectors are driven out by counterattacks of strong forces in pincer formation. Penetrations between subsectors are blocked by antitank guns supported by artillery and infantry.

Ravenstein

Ravenstein's report was more specific than the other two. He felt that he still had to combat the idea of linear defense. He expanded Ballerstedt's principle

– one heavy weapon, two light machine guns connected by crawl trenches 33 yards away – by applying it to isolated platoons. Varying with the width of front allotted, the minimum depth for a platoon was to be between 110 and 220 yards. In *Stützpunkte,* the command posts of the infantry, field artillery, and 88-mm guns should be close together. Dummy positions should be built when time permits and camouflage techniques should be improved. There should be no long communication trenches, as these tend to weaken a position's power of resistance by thinning out the defending troops and giving the enemy cover for penetration. Minefields, carefully marked, should be laid inside and outside of positions.

Orders were given to build a new defensive line in accordance with the above principles. The 200th Regiment was the first in the field. The *2nd* and *8th Machine Gun Battalions, Oasis Company 2,* and the regimental reserve were assigned to build and occupy a series of southern defense areas extending to Sidi Omar. These positions were Bir Girba and Point 202 (headquarters of *Machine Gun Battalion 2*); Points 205, 206, and 204 (on the frontier, headquarters of *Machine Gun Battalion 8*); and two *Stützpunkte* at Sollum. As usual, all-around and subsector defenses were ordered, and each position was to have at least one heavy antitank gun and several 37-mm guns, antitank rifles, heavy machine guns, and light machine guns.

On 10 June, however, *Panzer Regiment 5* referred to the armament of each *Stützpunkte* as "one machine gun battalion, one battery of artillery, one antitank company, and two or three 88-mm guns." This seems nearer to their eventual strength after the Italian battalions and the oasis companies had been added.

Antitank guns were to be fixed in their firing positions and well dug in against British artillery fire. Engineers were to do this for the 88-mm guns. Artillery was to be emplaced so as to fire over open sights, but protected against tank attack by being located well within the system. Every antitank gun was to be able to fire in all directions. Another document, dated 2 June 1941, shows that the *3rd Reconnaissance Unit* was covering this work, based on Sidi Suleiman, and that the *15th Panzer Division* was working from Capuzzo to the sea. Further protection was given by I./*Field Artillery Regiment 75* and II./*Field Artillery Regiment 33.* Counterattack roles were assigned to *Panzer Regiment 5* and *Antitank Battalion 605.* Antitank weapons were to vary between two (both 88-mm) and 17 in the separate *Stützpunkte.* The strongest positions were to be Point 206, with three 88-mm guns, and Bir Girba, with two 88-mm guns. Artillery orders show that there was to be concentration of direct fire against tanks, and that guns would be able to swing rapidly to other targets. One section of each battery was to be prepared for mobile work.

Halfaya, in spite of its already formidable defenses, was to be strengthened. One thousand mines were to be added to the minefield on the coast, and company positions were to be rebuilt. The frontages of two of these were 720 and 770 yards, and 1,980 yards of wire were laid in front of them. Two thousand more mines were needed to cover the gap between Qalala and the artillery position on the right flank, through which the British tanks would have broken on 15 June had it not been for the 88-mm guns. Qalala, it was reported, could be completed in 10 days. Two 88-mm guns each were proposed for Qalala and Halfaya.

Rommel

On 27 July, possibly dissatisfied with the standard of work done by the *5th Light Division*, Rommel ordered the *15th Panzer Division* to take over the fortification of the frontier. A completely new plan was mapped, which included reestablishing the frontier defenses as they existed when broken by the British offensive of November–December 1941. To help man the line, *Oasis Companies 10* and *13* were brought forward on 22 June (*Oasis Companies 2* and *3* were already there. These were placed for a few days at Capuzzo, and then, together with *Machine Gun Battalion 8*, *Motorcycle Battalion 15*, and I./ *Schützen Regiment 104*, over the whole system.

The line ordered was: from Sidi Omar to Halfaya, inclusive, four *Stützpunkte* of battalion strength and three intermediate *Stützpunkte* of company strength, the whole divided into two building sectors, the West Sector in charge of *Schützen Regiment 104* (commanded by the experienced Colonel von Holtzendorff), and the East Sector in charge of the *15th Schützen Brigade*. The East Sector was divided into subsectors, Halfaya (battalion *Stützpunkt 4* at Halfaya and company *Stützpunkt 4a* at Point 187, to the south-west) and Qabr el Qaha (battalion *Stützpunkt 3* at Point 207 and company *Stützpunkt 3a*, two miles north-west of Alam Abu Dihak). The West Sector was divided into two subsectors, Got Adhidiba (battalion *Stützpunkt 2*) and Sidi Omar (battalion *Stützpunkt 1a* at Omar Nuovo). Great speed was enjoined; reconnaissance of all these positions was to be completed on 26 June, and building was to begin the following day.

Libyan Omar and Omar Nuovo were allotted *Machine Gun Battalion 8*, *Oasis Company 10*, a battery of artillery, three 88-mm and eight 20-mm antiaircraft guns, and some antitank guns of unspecified caliber.

Got Adhidiba was allotted an Italian battalion, *Oasis Company 13*, two 88-mm and four 20-mm antiaircraft guns, and a battalion of artillery, in addition to two engineer companies for constructing the position.

Point 207 and the nearby company position were allotted *Motorcycle Battalion 15, 2./Schützen Regiment 104, Oasis Company 2*, two 88-mm and four 20-mm antiaircraft guns, ten antitank guns, and a battalion of artillery, as well as two engineer companies for the construction of the position.

Point 187 and Halfaya were allotted three companies of *I./Schützen Regiment 104, Oasis Company 6*, four 88-mm and five 20-mm antiaircraft guns, six antitank guns, and a battalion of artillery.

One earlier weakness in the *Stützpunkt* system was mitigated by an order to stock each position with two full echelons of ammunition, 2,000 gallons of water, and rations for six days. Emergency concealment was stressed in orders which required all motor transport to be kept more than a mile from the positions, or, in the case of gun tractors, to be dug in at the gun emplacements. Holtzendorff ordered that Libyan Omar be built in a form more linear than the trefoil, "because we have no mines for the position." He admitted that the plan differed from Rommel's idea of the advanced position at Gazala (Bir el Heial), as the reinforced squad areas (antitank gun with two machine guns) lay 220 yards apart. At Got Adhidiba, where there were mines, he had carried out the trefoil in companies and platoons.

There were 22 antitank guns, mostly Italian 47-mm guns, with the infantry units at Libyan Omar and 16 at Got Adhidiba.

The Omar Nuovo area was laid out as a battalion *Stützpunkt* after an Italian battalion of three companies joined the defenses. The position was laid out in German trefoil and held by about 720 men with four 65/17 guns and eighteen 45-mm mortars. Initially there was no antiaircraft or antitank defense.

Security was systematically organized. Each subsector was to send forward once or twice at different times each day a motorized antitank patrol, and also to send another patrol to make contact with the adjoining positions on the left. During the daytime subsectors were to maintain observation posts, and at night double listening posts were to be established. These posts would be 5/8 mile forward and would have the special job of reporting any sound heard. Each was allotted a motorcycle messenger. They were to be withdrawn only at daybreak, or during mists or sandstorms. All patrols were to warn the *Stützpunkte* of a surprise attack by long bursts of fire, and were to return to their *Stützpunkt* from the rear. Platoons were organized to support each other with fire, and field artillery developed defensive barrage plans. A map of *Oasis Company 13* at Got Adhidiba shows its three platoons dispersed at 1,000-yard intervals.

Holtzendorff gave ranges for opening fire as follows: 88-mm guns, 1,650 yards; antitank guns, 440 yards; 20-mm antiaircraft guns (concentrated on infantry and heavy machine guns), 440 yards; all infantry weapons, 440 yards.

Rommel was displeased by the linear positions at Libyan Omar, where *Machine Gun Battalion 8* had laid out trefoils of one heavy weapon and two light machine guns along the three sides of an empty triangle. Holtzendorff and Major Teetz, who commanded the new oasis battalions, went there to modify the defenses by new section sectors according to the principle of defense in depth. Defense groups were shifted so that machine guns were more than 40 yards from supported antitank weapons. An interesting note by Holtzendorff shows that German defense theory was becoming standardized in detail: *Machine Gun Battalion 8* has the sketches for the laying of section *Stützpunkte* at Ras el Meduaaur, but not the second sketches for the laying of platoon and company *Stützpunkte* at Gazala. This is apparently because these positions took a rather different form in the Meduaaur sector, owing to their combination with fixed fortifications. The Gazala sketches are being issued to all units.

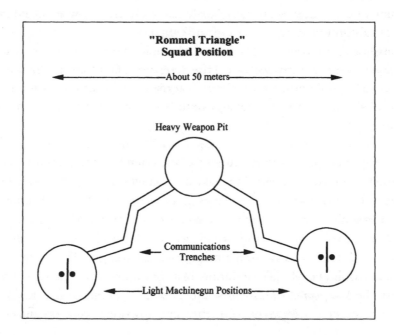

"Rommel Triangle"
Squad Position

About 50 meters

Heavy Weapon Pit

Communications Trenches

Light Machinegun Positions

Finally, on 1 July, the *15th Panzer Division* started building a large minefield in front of the *Stützpunkte*. Gaps were marked in various ways: some with red and yellow paint on stones, others by lines of gasoline cans.

Shortly after 12 July, an order signed by Rommel shows that *Machine Gun Battalion 8* and *Motorcycle Battalion 15* were to be replaced by Italian units, the *Savona Division* taking over the entire front except for Halfaya and Point 187. The only German troops to remain in the Italian sector were *Oasis Companies 2, 10,* and *13,* and antiaircraft units. These were to stiffen the defenses of Alam Abu Dihak, Libyan Omar, and Got Adhidiba, respectively. German antitank guns were replaced by Italian, and the artillery in each *Stützpunkt* was increased by one or two batteries.

Even so, Rommel was not satisfied with the all-around defense of Point 187, and strengthened it with another oasis company, presumably to hold the breach extending north to Sollum. The antitank defense was augmented by the addition of some 75-mm antitank guns. Halfaya had become a company *Stützpunkt,* and a string of immobilized tanks used as pillboxes was placed to strengthen the line Qabr El Gaha–Halfaya–Point 187. (This idea seems to have been Rommel's own.) Halfaya was to get one 88-mm gun and three 75-mm antiaircraft guns, while Point 187 was allotted one 75-mm antiaircraft gun.

The system was completed by the construction of battalion-strength positions at Point 187, Halfaya, Alam Abu Dihak, Qabr el Qaha, Got Adhidiba, Omar Nuovo, and Libyan Omar, with a line of *vorgeschobene Stützpunkte* (advance posts) about two miles in front of them. Until November, the only contact with British forces was by the German reconnaissance unit, whose job it was to discover changes in the British armored car outpost line and to defeat British reconnaissance. During this period an almost continuous minefield was laid along the defense line.

The Action at Tobruk

On the night of 2/3 August the Meduaaur salient of Tobruk, from which *Schützen Regiment 115* and *II./Schützen Regiment 104* had not yet moved, was attacked by the British. German documents give a fairly complete story of this assault.

The right and left flanks of the salient were attacked by three companies drawn from two Australian battalions. The extreme position on the left flank was taken, but was recaptured by the Germans on the following day, 3 August. German losses were 30, British much higher.

The first defensive measure, at least of *II./Schützen Regiment 115*, was barrage fire. Just after the report that the enemy had broken in behind the position on the right flank, all telephone communication was destroyed. The battalion at once sent out two patrols to see if the next position was held, and heavy machine guns concentrated their fire around the flank position. It was found that the British had used one company and an engineer platoon in attempting to make routes through the minefield protecting the right flank, but had been stopped with many casualties by heavy machine gun and mortar fire and then had been driven back by small-arms fire. German casualties were four dead and six wounded.

The commander of *Schützen Regiment 115* reported that he observed 18 British field artillery batteries in action, delivering extremely heavy fire for two hours. He said that if the attack on the right had concentrated on silencing heavy machine guns in the supporting positions, the British thrust might have succeeded. The British company in the center was halted when it stumbled into the German minefield. On the left, which was defended by *II./Schützen Regiment 104*, the British bypassed the minefield and crossed the gap between *II./Schützen Regiment 104* and *Infantry Division Brescia* without being observed. The report of *II./Schützen Regiment 104* notes that they were wearing rubber-soled shoes and were heard neither by the forward listening posts nor by the sentinel to the west of the position.

Meanwhile, British field artillery had scored five direct hits on another position, and it was taken from the rear. The six wounded survivors of the garrison leaped into the antitank trench and tried to recapture the central position with grenades, but found that they were not strong enough. An immediate counterattack by part of the battalion reserve also failed because of British artillery and Italian machine gun fire from the left. When British tanks were reported, the Germans brought up their mobile antitank reserves, but the next day the position was recaptured. German losses were 18 killed and 32 wounded. This encounter added little to German defensive doctrine – the value of intersecting antitank trenches had again been shown, and once more British field artillery had proved to be effective against defensive positions. On the basis of its experience, the German command issued elementary instructions in defense to *III./Infantry Regiment 268*, which arrived in Africa on 16 August. Stress was laid on the early preparation of positions in an advance, and the newcomers were instructed to build positions for the covering party and observation posts before establishing positions and headquarters for the main fighting force. They were next to build obstacles, then crawl trenches and shelters, and finally dummy positions. Antitank trenches were to be dug at 55-yard intervals across areas where enemy tanks were likely to penetrate. Alternate positions were to be constructed 55 to 65 yards from the original positions. Very vaguely, an ideal company position was suggested with light machine guns and antitank guns disposed along the front line. The directive also gave camouflage instructions.

An equally elementary document, coming from Tobruk on 30 September, ordered rations to be stored for two days (prompted by the experience of Halfaya) against the danger of encirclement. A company order, this document shows that the total width of the left platoon sector was 330 yards, and that it had only one antitank gun (these new units were notoriously weak in antitank defense by German standards). The left platoon was ordered to lay down a light machine gun barrage if attacked in darkness, sandstorm, smoke or fog. Each forward section had a night listening post 500 yards from the enemy position. For an unexplained reason, the antitank gun crew was given rations for eight days. Dummy positions behind platoon headquarters were being shot up by the British artillery. There is no data on the width of the right platoon sector, but there was an interval of 165 yards between headquarters and sections, 40 yards from sections to the wire, and 75 and 100 yards on the right and left flanks. Antitank rifles were distributed to the left and right sectors and to headquarters. There was a light machine gun barrage, and snipers were ordered to concentrate on enemy commanders and forward machine guns. The minefield in front of the platoon was laid in four rows, checkerwise, with intervals of four yards between rows and five yards between the mines in each row. Behind it was a fence mined with concentric charges which could be exploded by pulling a wire in the position. (The British position was between 275 and 330 yards away.) In the center platoon area (the company had three platoons up), as in the right platoon area, there were three squads forward and two back, and each forward squad was equipped with two antitank rifles. Heavy mortars had firing positions 550 yards to the rear, near company headquarters. The antitank gun with the left platoon was to destroy British tanks at ranges of about 220 yards. Antitank guns were to stop the enemy attack before it reached the main line of resistance, and were to use high-explosive shells against infantry who broke the line. Fire was not to be opened against light tanks at ranges of over 330 yards; antitank guns were to hold their fire until the tanks approached to within 220 yards.

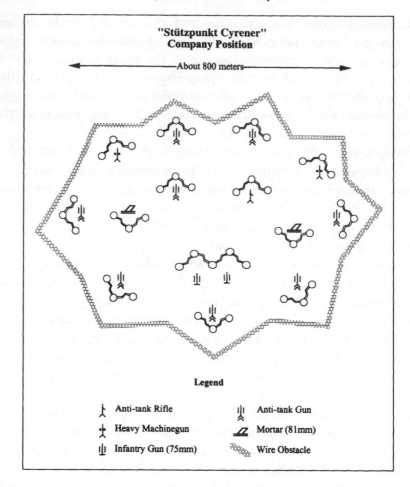

"Stützpunkt Cyrener"
Company Position

←——————About 800 meters——————→

Legend

Anti-tank Rifle		Anti-tank Gun	
Heavy Machinegun		Mortar (81mm)	
Infantry Gun (75mm)		Wire Obstacle	

The November Offensive

By the beginning of November, as the long lull was drawing to a close, proposals about the ideal *Stützpunkte* were advanced by both *I./Schützen Regiment 115* and *II./Schützen Regiment 104* . Their dimensions were 1,760 yards front by 2,200 yards depth for *I./Schützen Regiment 115*, and 1,760 yards front by 1,320 yards depth for *II./Schützen Regiment 104* . The difference was due to much stronger lateral protection provided in the second plan. It is interesting to compare these plans with those of Point 207 on the frontier, where 770 by 600 yards was given as the dimensions of a company position, and 400 by 175 yards as those of a platoon position.

All these systems met the requirements of the trefoil, both in organization and in weapons. *I./Schützen Regiment 115* had a two-company front, each company being 880 yards wide. The heavy weapons in the rifle companies were well forward, with the heavy machine guns on the flanks, the light antitank guns in the center of the front line, and two heavier antitank guns immediately behind them. The bulk of the antitank guns, however, were in pairs in the front line of the rear company, in front of pairs of heavy mortars interspersed with pairs of heavy machine guns, and all controlled by the *Führer schwerer Waffen* (the officer commanding the battalion heavy weapons).

II./Schützen Regiment 104 had more support: it was reinforced by an antiaircraft battery of four heavy and two light guns, a light antiaircraft platoon of four guns, and an antitank company of six heavy and four light guns. Two rifle companies were placed on the flanks and strengthened by dividing the antitank weapons of the antitank company equally between them. Each forward position (four on each flank) had an antitank gun, and the remaining light guns were stationed well to the rear. As usual, light machine guns in pairs protected heavy weapons. The heavy weapons company of the battalion (less its two infantry guns, which protected the front of battalion headquarters) protected the rear. Once more, antitank guns were in the front line. The heavy machine gun company was divided between the center of the front, the rear, and the flanks; and a group of six heavy machine guns protected the rear of the heavy antiaircraft battery, which formed a concentrated mass 440 yards broad in the center of the front (where it seems that it would present an excellent target for artillery). The exposure of the heavy antitank guns both contrasted with the methods of *I./Schützen Regiment 115* and marked a change from the practice of *II./Schützen Regiment 104* in May and June 1941.

The defensive line on the frontier had been completed, or at least was as near completion as it would ever be. The principal features of this line were:

(1)   The main *Stützpunkte* were Libyan Omar, Omar Nuovo, Got Adhidiba, Qabr el Qaha, Alam Abu Dihak, Halfaya, and Point 187.
(2)   These *Stützpunkte* were held by mixed troops.
(3)   They were held in either company or battalion strength, and in the latter case they were to be subdivided into company positions, each with all-around defense down to include platoons.
(4)   The distances between the main *Stützpunkte* were 1¼, 2½, 3-1/8, 2½, 1½, and 3-1/8 miles – thus each could support its neighbors or cover the intervals with artillery.

(5)   Distances between the company positions within the main *Stützpunkte* varied between ¼ and 5/8 mile in general.

(6)   A deep minefield with only nine openings covered the whole front between Halfaya and Sidi Omar.

(7)   In front of the minefield were eight *vorgeschobene Stützpunkte* (advance posts). Each depended on the main position in front of which it lay. Their distance from the minefield varied from 1½ to 2½ miles, and from the main positions, 1½ to 3 miles.

(8)   Immediately in front of these positions, for a depth of 3½ miles, was the artillery barrage zone of the main positions.

(9)   In this there were three bands, each 1¼,miles wide, to allow patrols to maneuver.

(10)   These patrols lay at three points (Qaret Abu Faris, Sidi Suleiman, and Bir Nun), respectively 4, 4, and 4¼ miles from the main *Stützpunkte,* and were the most advanced observation points.

It should be noted that, in a very strong battalion and company position like Alam Abu Dihad, there were six or seven 88-mm guns.

There is only one complete report of how such a position resisted the offensive of November 18 – the remarkable record of Lieutenant Schon, whose *12th Oasis Company* held out at Libyan Omar until 30November, then retired to Got Adhidiba with 80 survivors from his original 150 men. His company and attached antiaircraft destroyed 17 infantry tanks and five armored cars. He had to withdraw because the food supply had run out and because all his antiaircraft and antitank guns had been knocked out by British artillery and tanks. From Schon's account, the following principles can be deduced:

(1)   The *vorgeschobener Stützpunkte* (advance post) was commanded by a noncommissioned officer with 11 men, one antitank gun, one light mortar, two light machine guns, rations for five days, and emergency rations. Its mission was to observe, not to draw fire. There were three telephone wires running to *Oasis Company 12*, the Italian battalion, and the Italian artillery (attached to the oasis company for the defense of Libyan Omar). In fact, the post remained unspotted from 18 to 23 November, and only withdrew on the main position a day after the main battle started. The post was able to observe behind British lines.

(2)   The main *Stützpunkte* was manned by *Oasis Company 12*, consisting of four officers, 24 noncommissioned officers and 112 enlisted men,

disposed in 10 positions – one for each section and one for headquarters. The supporting arms, some of which may have been placed with the neighboring Italian battalion, were very strong: six 75-mm field guns; two or three 88-mm guns and two 75-mm antiaircraft guns; three 37-mm antitank guns; and four heavy machine guns and ten light machine guns. There was ammunition for three days and food and water for eight days. Radio communication also was established with *Battalion 300* and *Reconnaissance Battalion 3*.

Schon's record shows that the reconnaissance unit was forced to withdraw in the first two days, and that the envelopment of Libyan Omar began on 20 November. On that day, the 88-mm gun destroyed a British observation post at a range of 3½ miles, south of Libyan Omar; later it fired at vehicles at a distance of half a mile.

On 22 November, the main attack began. Omar Nuovo had fallen very easily in the morning, and the British tanks then came over to Libyan Omar, where three of the four Italian companies surrendered with little resistance. The assault on the German positions began late in the afternoon, and the 88-mm guns knocked out 17 infantry tanks before dark. As usual, the 88-mm guns were vulnerable to British artillery, and a combination of artillery and tanks silenced them just before nightfall. At this range, the smaller antitank shells (presumably including 37-mm) were bouncing off the infantry tanks. Then night fell and the attack was called off.

During the night, one 88-mm and two 75-mm guns were repaired, and the next morning the position was ready for battle again, with 100 German infantrymen, 38 antiaircraft crews, and 130 Italians.

These troops were continually cheered up by propaganda. The Army News *(Wehrmachtbericht)* was taken regularly on the radio and the news given to the troops. The German successes in other areas were rapidly communicated to the Italians as well, and this tended to relieve the feeling of helplessness before British tanks which Schon noticed among Germans as well as Italians.

Nevertheless, the troops were always expecting to be relieved; there was no idea of holding out indefinitely. A counterattack by German tanks would settle the battle. It was therefore a great day on 26 November when German tanks appeared over the horizon, and the men were puzzled when the tanks did not relieve the position.

Libyan Omar was now plastered by British artillery, and on 25 and 27 November the last antiaircraft positions were knocked out. Schon then requested orders from the 300th Battalion to evacuate the position. He was told to hold out, and promised either speedy relief or supply by air, but neither of these was forthcoming. Between 27 and 30 November he repulsed an attack by Indian infantry.

Conditions were very unpleasant, as nobody could move outside of the position in the daytime because of the snipers, and the command had to be on guard all night, growing stiff with cold. Rations and water were very short. After the infantry attack, the positions were attacked by a pair of infantry tanks, which eventually smashed every heavy weapon but were unable to hold their gains because (to the surprise of the Germans) they were not followed by infantry. Schon now asked for permission to retire, as further resistance would involve only an "unnecessary sacrifice of blood." He got the permission, and reached Got Adhidiba (where there was another German company) after a forced night march.

Sollum, the supply base of *Oasis Company 12*, had been cut off from the Omars since 19 November, when the Italian supply transport broke down. Since that time, the position had received no food. Twelve days, therefore, was probably the limit of any of the frontier positions without supply from base.

Here again, the total reliance of the enemy on 88-mm and 75-mm antiaircraft guns, and the vulnerability of these guns to artillery fire, are apparent. There was an unusually long-range opening in this battle, but the concealed observational role of the advanced *Stützpunkte* was probably characteristic of the seven positions along the frontier.

Unfortunately, there are no records of the enemy's defensive methods at Tobruk and Gazala, and only a few sketches of units in the retreat, when they had lost much material and personnel. The *155th Schützen Regiment* had a *vorgeschobene Beobachtungstellung,* or advanced OP, and boldly stuck its four 88-mm guns on high ground in the main body. A more detailed plan shows that, in the hurry of retreat, the unit forgot its doctrine on all-around defense. Antitank weapons were used well forward, with the exception of the four 88-mm guns. Nineteen were in the front and on the flanks, and only three in the rear.

Comments and Lessons

Conditions existing in the North African Desert are very different from those in the training areas of Germany; therefore, German defensive practices have developed largely from actual combat experience in the desert. Commanders have kept in close touch with the situation and constantly striven to improve their tactical methods. They have never appeared to be satisfied with their defensive positions, and have continually put forth every effort to make them more impregnable.

German defensive theory emphasizes that *Stützpunkte* are not simply positions from which an attack can be checked, but localities from which to launch a powerful armored counterattack. All supporting units are instructed to be prepared to move forward on short notice.

Dummy positions and other ruses are habitually used by the Germans to deceive the opposing army as to the location of their main line of resistance. Keeping the enemy guessing is an important part of their doctrine, both on the offensive and on the defensive.

Antimechanized Obstacles

Minefields were extensively employed in front of defended localities. They were placed from a quarter to a half mile in front of these minefields.

Tank obstacles of all kinds were used liberally where possible. In the desert, this form of defense is handicapped to some extent by the hard, rocky nature of the soil.

Artillery

Barrages were laid immediately in front of the most advanced defensive positions, thus furnishing them with a screen of fire that would protect them from attacking infantry and tanks. Lanes were left in these barrages to allow German patrols to operate during an attack.

All platoons were supplied as liberally as possible with supporting weapons, and these weapons were always employed in close coordination with the defending infantry.

Perhaps the most outstanding single element in German defenses was the 88-mm gun. It sometimes opened fire at ranges up to 2,000 yards, but was most effective at about 800 yards. The 50-mm and 37-mm antitank guns opened fire at between 400 and 800 yards.

Reconnaissance

All new defensive positions were thoroughly examined before building began. This reconnaissance took into consideration enemy dispositions and capabilities. Thus the main centers of resistance were located at points of maximum effectiveness.

Morale

The captured German documents used in the preparation of this bulletin again emphasized the great care that the enemy takes to keep morale at a high level in critical situations. One officer recognized the personality of the *Stützpunkte* commander as the most important single factor in defense. All enemy officers agree that the will to resist is vital to success.

Bibliography

Balin, George. *Afrika Korps Tanks Illustrated.* London: Arms and Armour Press, 1985.

Bidwell, Shelford and Graham, Dominick. *Fire-Power: British Army Weapons and Theories of War, 1904–1945.* 1982.

Blanco, Richard L. *Rommel, the Desert Warrior: The Afrika Korps in World War II.* 1982.

Caesar, Kurt. *Rommel's Year of Victory: The Wartime Illustrations of the Afrika Korps.* London: Greenhill Books, 1998.

Chamberlain, Peter and Ellis, Chris. *Afrika Korps: German Military Operations in the Western Desert, 1941–42.* Edgware: Almark, 1971.

Culver, Bruce. *Afrika Korps in Action.* Carrollton: Squadron/Signal, 1979.

English, John, and Gudmundsson, Bruce. *On Infantry.* New York: Praeger, 1995.

Forty, George. *Afrika Korps at War* (2 vols). Hersham: Ian Allan; and New York: Scribner's, 1978.

Fraser, David. *Knight's Cross: The Life of Field Marshal Erwin Rommel.* London: HarperCollins, 1993.

Gudmundsson, Bruce. *On Artillery.* New York: Praeger, 1993.

Irving, David. *The Trail of the Fox: The Life of Field-Marshal Erwin Rommel.* London: Weidenfeld and Nicolson; and New York: Dutton, 1977.

Lewin, Ronald. *The Life and Death of the Afrika Korps: A Biography.* London: Batsford, 1977.

Luck, Hans von. *Panzer Commander.* New York: Praeger, 1987.

Macksey, Kenneth J. *Afrika Korps.* New York: Ballantine, 1968.

———. *For Want of a Nail: The Impact on War of Logistics and Communications.* 1989.

Mitcham Jr., Samuel W. *Triumphant Fox: Erwin Rommel and the Rise of the Afrika Korps.* New York: Stein and Day, 1984.

Rommel, Erwin (trans. Koob, Cyril). *Problems for Platoon and Company.* 1995.

Rommel, Erwin. *Infantry Attacks.* (Trans. from *Infanterie Greift an: Erlebnisse und Erfahrungen,* pub. 1937 by Voggenreiter, Potsdam.) London: Greenhill Books, 1995.

Rutherford, Ward. *The Biography of Field Marshal Erwin Rommel.* 1981.

Van Creveld, Martin. *Supplying War: Logistics from Wallenstein and Patton.* Cambridge: Cambridge University Press, 1977.

Index

acclimatization, 239
air filters, on German tanks, 54
air force troops in ground combat, 147, 214
air forces, supply of, 214
air liaison officers, to Panzer divisions, 216
air superiority, British, 147
airfields, capture of, 191
Alexandria, 21
ammunition shortages, 149, 217–18
antiaircraft guns, 88mm, 34–5, 45, 170
antitank battalions, of Panzer divisions, 46, 170
Archives, US (US National Archives and Record Administration, NARA), 12
Ark Royal (British aircraft carrier), 24
armored signals vehicles, 47
artillery: fortress and siege, 40–2; of Panzer divisions, 45–6
Auchinleck, Sir Claude, 57, 151

Bach, Major Wilhelm, 36
Barham (British battleship), 24
Bastico, General Ettore, 20
battleships, as convoy escorts, 24–6
Benghazi, 21, 27
Bizerte, 25

Cavallero, General Ugo, 20, 27, 177
civilian population, 219
climate, effect on operations, 28
Comando Supremo, 20–3, 27, 32, 98, 177
command and control, within Panzer division, 47
communications, within Panzer division, 47

cooperation, between German and Italian airmen, 51
courier aircraft, German, 147
Crete, 19
Crüwell, General Ludwig, 68–75, 82
Cunningham, Sir Alan, 57

deception (British measures to mislead German supply aircraft), 216
destroyer aircraft, 49, 99

East Africa, 20, 24
engineer troops, of Panzer divisions, 46

Fayum Road, 49
Flächenmarsch (tactical formation), 45
Fliegerführer Afrika, 146, 215
flying column, British use of, 60
Foreign Military Studies (US Army Program), 12
Frongia, battle for strongpoint at, 95
fuel cans, shortage of, 250
fuel supplies, for ground forces, 217–18; for ships, 24
Führer Directive of 30 June 1941, 19

Gambara, General Gastone, 26
Gariboldi, General Italo, 27
Gause, Colonel Alfred, 32
Generalkommando (German echelon of command), 21
German Navy High Command (*Seekriegsleitung*), 19
Göring, Hermann, 27

Halfaya Pass, 34

Italian Air Force, *see Regia Aeronautica*

Kesselring, Field Marshal Albert, 23, 27, 98, 146, 179, 247
Koluft Libya (German 'Air Commander Libya'), 147, 215
Kriebel, Colonel Rainer, 11–13
Kriegsakademie (German Staff College), 13

lines of communication, interior, 188
logistics, 21, 52–3, 58, 103, 148–50, 183–7; within Panzer division, 48
Luftgaustab (administrative organization), 215

Malta, 21, 183–6
Me 110 (German destroyer aircraft), 49
Mediterranean Sea, 21
'Midsummer Night's Dream' (*Sommernachtstraum*, 13/14 September 1941), 39
motor transport, capture of British, 150; loss to British air action, 150, 165; maintenance and repair, 54, 218, 249; shortages, 218, 220, 249
Mussolini, Benito, 27

National Archives and Record Service (NARA), 12
Nehring, General Walther, 12

Oberkommando (German echelon of command), 21
Oberquartiermeister (German Quartermaster-General), 103
Ordonnanz officers, 89
organization (of military units), 15

Panzergruppe (echelon of command), 16
Paulus, General Friedrich, 27
port capacity, 21

Qu 1 (German staff officer), 103
Queen Elizabeth (British battleship), 24

railway, from Alexandria to Libyan frontier, 58

rain, effect of on air and ground operations, 52
rations, 53
reconnaissance, air, 50–2, 122, 141, 215, 247, 190
reconnaissance battalions, tactics of, 47–8
Red Sea, 24
Regia Aeronautica (Italian Air Force), 51, 146–8, 183–6, 215
Ricardi, Admiral Arturo, 23
Rintalen, General Enno von, 21
Royal Air Force, 51, 96–97, 146–8, 183–6, 215

Schützen (German motorized infantry), 15, 46
Seekriegsleitung, see German Navy High Command
Sidi Barani, 28
Sidi Omar, 29
signals intelligence, German exploitation of, 48
Sollum, 29
Sommernachtstraum, see 'Midsummer Night's Dream'
strongpoints (as frontier defenses in 1941), 29, 34–7, 211
Stuka (German and Italian dive-bomber), 49–50, 99, 157, 181, 247
submarines, 21; in transporting supplies, 150
Suez Canal, 20
'Sunday of the Dead' (*Totensonntag*), 90–4
supplies lost at sea, 21
supply depots: evacuation of, 218–20; looting of, 219
supply, of ground troops by air, 148, 216

tactics, of Panzer divisions, 45–6, 94
tank engines, loss of by wear, 149
Tank Mark II (Matilda), 95
Tedder, Sir Arthur, 57
Tobruk, 19–20, 29, 40–4, 51–6
torpedo-carrying aircraft, 21, 217
Totensonntag, see 'Sunday of the Dead'
Tripoli, 21

Tunis, 25

units (Allied):
  1st Armoured Division, 236–9, 249
  1st South African Division, 58, 66, 77,
    84, 94, 100, 102, 236
  2nd New Zealand Division, 59, 84, 91–2,
    105, 111–21, 126, 134–6, 152, 253–5
  2nd South African Division, 58
  4th Armoured Brigade, 83, 196
  4th Indian Division, 37, 59–60, 65, 84,
    95, 106, 123, 144, 166, 191, 243, 253–4
  7th Armoured Division, 58, 60, 65–6, 78,
    84–5, 92–6, 100, 102, 119, 124,
    144,152–3, 195, 239
  9th Australian Division, 40
  XIII Corps, 58, 253
  XXX Corps, 58–9, 80, 160–6, 253
  70th Infantry Division, 40
  Carpathian Rifle Brigade, 40
units (Axis):
  II. Fliegerkorps, 23, 146, 215
  2nd Panzer Division, 13
  5th Light Division, 19, 30
  X. Fliegerkorps, 21, 76, 97–9, 146, 215,
    247
  15th Panzer Division, 13, 28, 30, 44, 60–
    96, 103–46, 170, 188
  15th Schützen Brigade, 30, 77, 86, 190, 213
  21st Panzer Division, 30, 34, 38, 43, 60–96,
    103–46, 170, 188
  90th Light Division, 20, 165, 188–9, 213
  Afrika Regiment, 31, 81, 90, 92
  Antiaircraft Machine Gun Battalion 606, 83,
    91, 137
  Antitank Battalion 33, 78, 134–6, 202, 227
  Armored Division Ariete, 30, 31, 41,77, 83,
    89, 93, 102, 105–7, 111, 117, 123, 126,
    131, 134, 138, 172–3, 193, 243
  Artillery Command 104, 44
  Division z.b.V. Afrika, 20, 41, 44, 53, 126,
    131, 138
  Engineer Battalion 33, 78, 90, 114, 116, 144
  Fernaufklärungsgruppe 121, 50
  Group Ballerstedt, 201
  Group Bötcher, 114–18, 128, 132–3

Group Briel, 137
Group Crämer, 231
Group Geissler, 144, 204–7, 244
Group Giarabub, 109
Group Knabe, 70, 104, 109, 144
Group Marx, 225–34, 241–8
Group Mickl, 132–6, 141, 144, 160
Group Ravenstein, 109
Group Schuette, 172–4
Group Stephan, 68–70
Group Wechmar (with Panzer Regiment 5),
  113
Infantry Division Bologna, 41, 44, 66, 144,
  170–1, 209
Infantry Division Brescia, 197
Infantry Division Pavia, 41, 44, 83, 170–1,
  174
Infantry Division Sabratha, 209
Infantry Division Savona, 30, 35, 65, 107,
  123, 170–1
Infantry Regiment 155, 79–80
Italian Motorized Corps (XX Motorized
  Corps), 26, 32–3, 42, 68, 84, 101, 144,
  125, 138, 170–3, 188
Italian X Corps, 32, 189
Italian XXI Corps, 32, 76, 125, 138, 164,
  170–1, 189
Jagdgeschwader 27, 49, 50
Luftflotte 2, 23, 247
Machine Gun Battalion 2, 31, 90, 129, 134–
  6, 172, 175–6, 229, 235
Machine Gun Battalion 8, 31, 144
Motorcycle Battalion 15, 31, 78, 90, 134–6,
  164, 192, 201
Motorized Artillery Regiment 33, 31, 159
Motorized Infantry Division Trento, 41
Motorized Infantry Division Trieste, 20, 30,
  41, 105, 138, 170–1, 193
Muncheberg Squadron, 49
Northern Assault Group, 227
Panzer Regiment 5, 69, 77–8, 81, 86–90,
  104–6, 109–10, 113, 195
Panzer Regiment 8, 69, 77–8, 81, 86–90,
  92, 114, 131, 134, 144, 155, 160, 176,
  195
Panzer Signal Battalion 33, 31

Panzergruppe Afrika, 21, 32, 50–55, 60–96, 101

Reconnaissance Battalion 3, 37, 39, 62, 65–6, 68–75, 110, 116, 130, 152, 155–8, 170, 190, 208, 232

Reconnaissance Battalion 33, 37, 39, 62, 65, 68–75, 105–15, 122–3, 152, 155–9, 190, 202, 208, 232

Reconnaissance Group Wechmar, 62

Regiment z.b.V. 200, 31, 77–8, 90, 92, 106, 114, 125, 132

Schützen Regiment 104, 31, 36, 77–8, 81, 89, 104–6, 109, 232

Schützen Regiment 115, 32, 41, 88–90, 92, 106, 114, 117, 131, 134, 175, 231

Stuka Geschwader 3, 50

Zerstörergeschwader 26, 50

Valiant (British battleship), 24

water: for drinking, 53; supply of, 149

Wavell, Sir Archibald, 57

Westphal, Lieutenant-Colonel Siegfried, 102, 111

withdrawal, loss of equipment due to, 182